Virginia Woolf

Virginia Woolf

A Feminist Slant

Edited by

Jane Marcus

**University of
Nebraska Press**

Lincoln and
London

Susan Squier's "A Track of Our Own:
Typescript Drafts of *The Years*" has
previously been published in *Modernist
Studies: Literature and Culture, 1920–1940* 4
(1982):218–31.

Carolyn Heilbrun's "Virginia Woolf in Her
Fifties" has previously been published in
Twentieth Century Literature 27, no. 1
(Spring 1981):16–33

The paper in this book meets the guidelines
for permanence and durability of the
Committee on Production Guidelines for
Book Longevity of the Council on Library
Resources.

**Library of Congress Cataloging in
Publication Data**
Main entry under title:

Virginia Woolf: a feminist slant.

   Includes index.
   1. Woolf, Virginia,
1882–1941—Criticism and
interpretation—Addresses, essays, lectures.
   2. Feminism and literature—Addresses,
essays, lectures.
I. Marcus, Jane.
PR6045.072Z892   1984   823'.912
82-24787
ISBN 0-8032-3081-8

For Tillie Olsen

Contents

Preface

As we celebrate the centennial of Woolf's birth in 1982, we identify with the Society of Outsiders proposed by Virginia Woolf in *Three Guineas* and with her notion of a "conspiracy" of feminists bent on creating a "woman's republic" in letters and in life. It is our contention that feminist critical theory develops from the practice represented in this book. We have no masters (though you may hear echoes of Marx and Freud and their descendants) whose theories might be imposed on the body of Woolf's work. The material conditions of Woolf scholarship have determined that we learn other arts than deconstruction; the arts of biography, textual scholarship, history. In Woolf's case, as in that of other women writers, the published texts are less likely to yield their secrets to the deconstructor than are the texts of a male writer. It is in the drafts of her novels, her notebooks, her diaries and letters, and the history of her family that we find an even more radical and feminist Woolf and can see her suppressing and repressing thoughts dangerous for publication.

It is no accident, given Virginia Woolf's wide appeal to women readers right now, that the contributors to this volume include a novelist, a political scientist, a mystery writer, a graduate student, an iconographer of Egyptian mythology, a specialist in reading education, and an Elizabethan scholar, as well as those trained specifically in the field of modern British fiction. It is also of historical interest that I edited this volume while unemployed. This exile from the profession was unsought, but it did provide the energy to proceed in transatlantic and transcontinental communication. The Newberry Library Feminist Criticism Seminar (organized several years ago by Judith Kegan Gardiner, Bonnie Zimmerman, and me) has proved an unfailing source of support, as has Portia, my Evanston women's network. Brenda Silver has provided many of us with material from her forthcoming study of Woolf's reading notebooks. Both Lola Szladits, curator of the Berg Collection, the New York Public Library (Astor, Lenox and Tilden Foundations), and the curators of the Monks House Papers, University of Sussex, have provided the contributors with manuscript materials. We are also grateful to Quentin Bell and Angelica Bell Garnett of the Virginia Woolf estate for permission to quote from published and unpublished materials. In the course of our work, Joanne Trautmann, Nigel Nicholson, and Anne Olivier Bell, editors of Woolf's letters and diaries, and Quentin Bell have answered many questions and courteously shared their knowledge with the contributors. We thank William McBrien, editor of *Twentieth Century Literature,* for permission to reprint Carolyn Heilbrun's "Virginia Woolf in Her Fifties."

My thanks to the University of Texas Research Institute for a grant for final preparation of the manuscript and to my student Susanne Fawcett for her help in proofreading.

The Contributors

Naomi Black teaches in the Department of Political Science, York University, Toronto. Her essay "The Life of Natural Happiness," in *Feminist Theorists*, edited by Dale Spender (1982), treats Woolf's feminism at length.

Louise DeSalvo teaches at Hunter College, City University of New York. She is the author of *Virginia Woolf's First Voyage*, editor of *Melymbrosia*, and author of several essays on *The Voyage Out*, an essay in *New Feminist Essays on Virginia Woolf* (1981), and one in the special Woolf issue of *Twentieth Century Literature*. She is currently editing, with Mitchell Leaska, Woolf's early journals and Vita Sackville-West's letters to Virginia Woolf.

Alice Fox is an Elizabethan scholar at Miami University in Oxford, Ohio, and has published essays on Shakespeare and Spenser. She is at work on a book-length study of Woolf and the Elizabethans. Her essay "Virginia Woolf at Work: The Elizabethan *Voyage Out*," appeared in 1981, and she presented a paper titled "Literary Allusion as Feminist Criticism in *A Room of One's Own*" at the 1981 Modern Language Association meeting.

Diane Filby Gillespie, associate professor of English at Washington State University, Pullman, has written articles on Virginia Woolf, Dorothy Richardson, and May Sinclair as well as on Christopher Fry and August Strindberg. She is currently completing a book entitled *The Sisters' Arts: Virginia Woolf and Vanessa Bell*.

Evelyn Haller, professor of English at Doane College in Crete, Nebraska, has written on Woolf and Willa Cather and is working on a book-length study of Woolf and Egyptian materials.

Carolyn Heilbrun, professor of English at Columbia University, former president of the Virginia Woolf Society, is the author of *Reinventing Womanhood* and many scholarly articles and, as Amanda Cross, of novels, the most recent of which is *Death in a Tenured Position.*

Emily Jensen heads the English Department at Lycoming College in Williamsport, Pennsylvania, and is at work on a study of women writers and suicide.

Ann McLaughlin's Ph.D. dissertation was on Woolf and Mansfield, and she has published several articles and reviews. She has taught in the Washington, D.C., area and has written two novels.

Jane Marcus is an associate professor at the University of Texas, Austin. She edited *New Feminist Essays on Virginia Woolf* (1981) and *The Young Rebecca West, 1911–1917* (1982), has published several essays on Virginia Woolf, and is editing Dame Ethel Smyth's letters to Virginia Woolf.

Beverly Schlack teaches at Marymount College, New York City, and is the author of *Continuing Presences: Virginia Woolf's Use of Literary Allusion* (1979) and several essays. "Fathers in General" was given at the 1981 Modern Language Association Virginia Woolf Society meeting.

Sallie Sears, professor of English at the State University of New York, Stony Brook, is the author of a book on Henry James and is currently working on Sylvia Plath. Her essay on sexuality in *The Years* appears in the 1977 Woolf issue of *Bulletin of the New York Public Library.*

Brenda Silver teaches English and women's studies at Dartmouth College. Her edition of Woolf's reading notebooks was published in 1983.

Susan Squier teaches at the State University of New York, Stony Brook. Her work appears in *New Feminist Essays on Virginia Woolf* (1981), in *Twentieth Century Literature Modernist Studies,* and *Anima.* She has edited *Women Writers and the City: Essays in Feminist Criticism* (1984). Her book *Virginia Woolf and London: The Politics of City Space* is expected to appear shortly.

Abbreviations

BA *Between the Acts.* New York: Harcourt Brace Jovanovich, 1970 (first published 1941).

B&P *Books and Portraits.* New York: Harcourt Brace Jovanovich, 1977.

CDB *Captain's Death Bed and Other Essays.* New York: Harcourt Brace Jovanovich, 1973 (first published 1950).

CE *Collected Essays.* Edited by Leonard Woolf. 4 vols. New York: Harcourt Brace and World, 1967.

CR *Common Reader: First Series.* New York: Harcourt Brace Jovanovich, 1955 (first published 1925).

CW *Contemporary Writers.* New York: Harcourt Brace Jovanovich, 1976 (first published 1965).

DM *Death of the Moth and Other Essays.* New York: Harcourt Brace Jovanovich, 1974 (first published 1942).

DVW *Diary of Virginia Woolf.* Edited by Anne Olivier Bell. New York: Harcourt Brace Jovanovich. Vol. 1, *1915–19* (1974); vol. 2, *1920–24* (1978); vol. 3, *1925–30* (1980); vol. 4, *1931–35* (1982).

F *Flush: A Biography.* New York: Harcourt Brace Jovanovich, 1976 (first published 1933).

FW *Freshwater.* New York: Harcourt Brace Jovanovich, 1976.

G&R *Granite and Rainbow.* New York: Harcourt Brace Jovanovich, 1975 (first published 1958).

HH *A Haunted House and Other Stories.* New York: Harcourt Brace Jovanovich, 1966 (first published 1944).

JR *Jacob's Room.* New York: Harcourt Brace Jovanovich, 1978 (first published 1922).

KG *Kew Gardens.* London: Hogarth Press, 1919.

L *Letters of Virginia Woolf.* Edited by Nigel Nicolson and Joanne Trautmann. New York: Harcourt Brace Jovanovich. Vol. 1, *1888–1912* (1977); vol. 2, *1912–1922* (1978); vol. 3, *1923–1928* (1980); vol. 4, *1929–1931* (1979); vol. 5, *1932–1935* (1979); vol. 6, *1936–1941* (1980).

M *Melymbrosia.* Edited by Louise DeSalvo. New York Public Library, 1981.

MB *Moments of Being: Unpublished Autobiographical Writings.* Edited by Jeanne Schulkind. New York: Harcourt Brace Jovanovich, 1978.

MD *Mrs. Dalloway.* New York: Harcourt Brace Jovanovich, 1964 (first published 1925).

MDP *Mrs. Dalloway's Party: A Short Story Sequence.* New York: Harcourt Brace Jovanovich, 1973.

MOE *The Moment and Other Essays.* New York: Harcourt Brace Jovanovich, 1974 (first published 1947).

MOT *Monday or Tuesday.* New York: Harcourt Brace, 1921.

N&D *Night and Day.* New York: Harcourt Brace Jovanovich, 1973 (first published 1919).

O *Orlando: A Biography.* New York: Harcourt Brace Jovanovich, 1973 (first published 1928).

P *The Pargiters: The Novel-Essay Portion of "The Years."* Edited by Mitchell A. Leaska. New York: New York Public Library, 1977.

RFB *Roger Fry: A Biography.* New York: Harcourt Brace Jovanovich, 1976 (first published 1940).

ROOM *A Room of One's Own.* New York: Harcourt Brace Jovanovich, 1963 (first published 1929).

SCR *Second Common Reader.* New York: Harcourt Brace Jovanovich, 1956 (first published 1932).

TG *Three Guineas.* New York: Harcourt Brace Jovanovich, 1963 (first published 1938).

TTL *To the Lighthouse.* New York: Harcourt Brace Jovanovich, 1964 (first published 1927).

VO *The Voyage Out.* New York: Harcourt Brace Jovanovich, 1968 (first published 1915).

W *The Waves.* New York: Harcourt Brace Jovanovich, 1978 (first published 1931).

WD *A Writer's Diary.* Edited by Leonard Woolf. New York: Harcourt Brace Jovanovich, 1973 (first published 1954).

W&W *Women and Writing.* New York: Harcourt Brace Jovanovich, 1980.

Y *The Years.* New York: Harcourt Brace Jovanovich, 1969 (first published 1937).

Frequently cited books about Virginia Woolf

CH *Virginia Woolf: The Critical Heritage.* Edited by Robin Majumdar and Allen McLaurin. London and Boston: Routledge and Kegan Paul.

NFE *New Feminist Essays on Virginia Woolf.* Edited by Jane Marcus. London: Macmillan; Lincoln: University of Nebraska Press, 1981.

QB *Virginia Woolf: A Biography,* by Quentin Bell. 2 vols. New York: Harcourt Brace Jovanovich, 1977.

Introduction:
Virginia Woolf
Aslant   *Jane Marcus*

> *Tell all the Truth but tell it slant —*
> *Success in Circuit lies*
> *Too bright for our inform Delight*
> *The Truth's superb surprise*
> *As Lightening to the Children eased*
> *With explanation kind*
> *The Truth must dazzle gradually*
> *Or every man be blind —*
>> Emily Dickinson, 1129 (ca.
> 1868)

Emily Dickinson's lines are luminous with purity and violence, the wisdom of sage, worldly advice from a recluse. They describe accurately the "appropriate form" for feminist critics of Virginia Woolf. North American feminists in particular have found that telling it "like it is" too often alienates the readers we wish to convince, and hostility greets our new readings of the novels, the essays, and the life. It sometimes seems as difficult to revise the literary canon as the theological. Centuries of struggle were necessary to achieve the canonization of Joan of Arc. The triple threat of chastity, mysticism, and revolutionary violence in one woman met as much resistance as it aroused fear in men. The clearinghouse for literary canonization is manned by as timid and reluctant a clerisy. They have approved a quiet niche in an imaginary Sussex church in the country where we may contemplate Virginia Woolf as Ophelia. But the move to Westminster Abbey in the city of London, which is constantly besieged by her novels, with Woolf enshrined as a Sappho, say, or Lysistrata, is viewed with alarm.

The image of the virgin mystic out for vengeance touches some archetypal spring of cultural dread, and the doors to the house of fiction swing shut. "We'll give her a room of her own at the back," they say. "All she wanted was a room of her own." There they hope she will stay quiet with all the other women writers labeled "minor" and "mandarin." But before they can turn the key she has scooted across the corridor and incited her fellows to rebellion, the working-class writers, the exiles, the Jews, the Africans, the eccentrics. Samuel Butler is at her side writing down her comments in his notebook. Sydney Smith takes off his donkey's head and leads with a laugh. "Trespass," she whispers, and before you can say "Jane Harrison" they have taken over the dining room and the library without a shot's being fired. Out of the closets come Colette and Mrs. Radcliffe. Carefully they cover the statues of great men with sheets and carry up to the attic all the relics of their reign—the slippers and locks of hair, the quill pens and writing desks. Ethel Smyth is in the music room helping her student with a serenade for eight harps and two dozen explosive bombs, and Janet Case is reading Greek with working-class boys.

In a corner some working women from the Cooperative Guild are reading and editing the letters of literary ladies. And Joseph Wright and his collaborators are working on a dictionary of cockney rhyming slang—perhaps they will translate the song of the working-class children at the end of *The Years*.

Perhaps fantasy is not the right method for the revision of history. And it is possible that Emily Dickinson did not imagine that some men prefer blindness to sight. If *Orlando* is any example, the "dazzle" is very gradual indeed, and more than "kind explanation" is needed to see in it a modern myth of historical development, what Rebecca West called the "high fountain" of its genius. How infirm our modern delights are was attested by Virginia Woolf herself, and how aslant our vision—when she compared us with the Greeks. They could look largely and directly, while we look "minutely and aslant." After the catastrophe of war the only poets who could speak to the purpose spoke "in the sidelong, satiric manner." The safety of the Greek view of life allowed them "to step into the thick of emotions which blind and bewilder an age like our own." We now need to have our emotions "broken up for us, and put at an angle from us." Constructing these angles with ingenuity was all her narrative technique. Squinting sideways she constructed labyrinths, finding success in circuitous routes to her own truth. If we would follow, the critical squint, the sidelong gait, are necessary to our stance.

Crossing the thresholds of her fictional mazes, we must not lose the Ariadne's thread that gets us out again. This thread is a braided narrative with three separate strands of thought, the mystical, the "Marxist," and the mythical. The work of Jane Harrison and Caroline Stephen as well as her own socialist politics are the keys to Woolf's work. Unless we acknowledge these influences, we as readers are children hiding under the bed to avoid the flashes of her lightning. We cannot make common cause with her concerns—like Forster's contemptuous dismissal of her writing from the temple of greatness as having "no great cause at heart." The critics in this collection claim the opposite, that Virginia Woolf's cause was then and is now a great one. We who share it would further claim that as an artist and a thinker Virginia Woolf was revolutionary in both form and content, that her achievement was not limited to aesthetics alone, for she left us a feminist ethic, a morality that entreats our present movement to remember our working-class brothers, that their oppression is ours.

In a Victorian house of sex, violence, incest, and guilt, Virginia Woolf forged an ethic of purity, pacifism, and privacy. From an intellectual bastion of antifeminist thought, ruthless individualism, respectable misogyny, aggressive godlessness, and the hero worship of great men, she emerged to define her own freedom in art that celebrates collective vision, feminist and socialist action. She began organizing early. She perceived power and recognized and named her oppressors. Her first "conspiracy" was to organize her brother and sister in the nursery. Later she longed to belong to the conspiracy of socialist feminists who surrounded Margaret Llewelyn Davies and the members of the Women's Co-operative Guild. This conspiracy sustained her for a lifetime and kept her constantly in touch with working-class women.

The 1917 Club was another home for her radical homelessness, a place where she sought the company of other intellectual revolutionaries. With Janet Case she struggled to master Greek, to overthrow in her intellect the foundations of British culture; with her women friends she played out her utopian deadly serious game, imagining a "republic of women." Avidly she read Jane Harrison to find a prehistoric world of female power. From these anthropological texts she not only formed an identity in female history but found a set of symbols, a matriarchal mythology with which to forge the collective conscience of her sex. We as feminist critics are just beginning to see how these myths and symbols inform her whole *oeuvre* as surely as the Odyssey informs *Ulysses*. Mated to a misogynist and wedded to misogyny on principle, Virginia Woolf's mother was the principal obstacle to this development. The haunting of Woolf's heart ceased only when she examined in *To the Lighthouse* the woman artist's need to think back through her mothers, even when those mothers desire bondage, not freedom, for their daughters. This was the most daring and difficult act. Most women can claim kinship with their mothers only by becoming mothers themselves, an experience that allows us to forgive our mothers their sins against us. *To the Lighthouse* is Julia Stephen's grandchild, a daughter's reliving of her mother's experience, a final forgiving.

Woolf would not tolerate the "separate spheres" her father and uncle dictated for men and women, and she sought in her fiction to attack the double standard and to penetrate with wit and mockery the "sphere" of the enemy. With her fellow conspirators all around her, she was fairly safe. But the death of her friends, the lack of an audience against whom her words would echo, the loss of reader-collaborators who would understand her analysis of fascism's patriarchal origins, made a conspiracy of one impossible. She heard voices.

There had been a large socialist-feminist audience for *A Room of One's Own,* and a hundred other books with the same ideas that it superseded in style. But *Three Guineas* fell on deaf or hostile ears. Leonard, often her last resort as a fellow conspirator with whom to feel "in league together against the world," was strongly opposed to her position in the essay, and he had disapproved of her great historical novel *The Years.* She was increasingly alone with her voices, the memories through which she plumbed her own experience. As muse, memory was a stern taskmistress, and, as one can see in *Moments of Being,* she was getting closer and closer to dealing with the origin of her fears of sexual violence. Leonard's horror at Nazi sexual atrocities against Jews must have exacerbated her fear of rape and murder. Her voices were of two kinds, those that raced ahead as she wrote her novels—the creative impulses—and those that cursed her and threatened punishment for opposing the patriarchs. The birds, messengers of Jane Harrison's mother goddess, warned in Greek of the revenge of fathers and kings. Joan of Arc heard voices too, and doubtless they were of two kinds—the voices that urged her to action and the others (in diplomatic French perhaps, or church Latin) warning and threatening patriarchal revenge. Retaining her savagery and purity, one can say, Virginia Woolf chose death by water, not by fire. It was as much a moral and political choice made in sanity, a response surely to deep inner stress about outward reality, as it was the act of a madwoman. She made a dignified descent into the arms of mother water. Feminist critics are out not to canonize the suicide or sanctify such actions, but to see their social and political origins as she would have done. Our readings, we hope, will give the reader, in Emily Dickinson's words, some "superb surprises."

This is our second book of new feminist essays on Virginia Woolf. As in the first, the approaches to her life and work cover a wide range within the discipline of feminist scholarship. I discuss her aunt, Caroline Emelia Stephen. Louise DeSalvo, author of *Virginia Woolf's First Voyage* and editor of *Melymbrosia,* combines her expertise as a textual scholar with a rational feminist psychology that allows us to see Virginia Stephen at fifteen, struggl-

ing with selfhood and sexual identity and succeeding in both, despite great
obstacles, by keeping a diary.

Comparative aesthetic approaches to the work of contemporary women
writers inspire Diane Gillespie and Ann McLaughlin to study the stylistic
growth of Virginia Woolf and of Dorothy Richardson and Katherine
Mansfield. Both studies are rewarding in their insights into what literary
sisterhood means. Beverly Schlack, whose book *Continuing Presences* (1979)
studies Woolf's extraordinary range of literary allusion, contributes a witty
and erudite commentary on the mockery of male institutions in Woolf's
novels. Like Woolf's speech/essay ''Professions for Women,'' it reveals a
deep suspicion of the evils of patriarchy, using ''strategies of scorn'' but cau-
tioning against bitterness. The essay might have been entitled ''Professions
for Men.'' Political scientist Naomi Black fills in the historical picture so that
we may see the exact context of Woolf's feminism, and she describes for the
first time Woolf's connections to the women's suffrage movement in
Britain.

Alice Fox writes of Woolf's fascination with Queen Elizabeth and the
Elizabethans, using Woolf's unpublished reading notes and the wealth of the
Berg Collection to document her study. She discusses Woolf's lunch with
Lytton Strachey as he wrote *Elizabeth and Essex* and her own need to find the
facts uncolored by the ''masculine point of view.'' Her delight in Strachey's
quotation from Queen Elizabeth's retort to an ambassador, ''Had I been
crested and not cloven you would not have dared to write to me thus,'' was
in the queen's style, she says. But one might imagine that Woolf agreed with
the sentiment and often found herself in the same position, seeming to some
to be ''Queen of Bloomsbury'' but treated by others as a mere cloven
creature.

Another exciting contribution to contemporary Woolf scholarship is
Evelyn Haller's unveiling of the references to Egyptian mythology in
Woolf's fiction. She has unraveled a system of symbol and metaphor that informs her work. It centers on the figures of Isis and Horus, the antimadonna
and child whose figures recur throughout Virginia Woolf's writing:
''Mysterious figures! Mother and son. . . . Wherever I go . . . I see
you. . . . If I fall on my knees, if I go through the ritual, the ancient antics,
it's you, unknown figures, you I adore.'' For some readers the truth of
Evelyn Haller's insights will ''Dazzle gradually,'' as Emily Dickinson explains, but her essay is provocative, new, and exciting.

Emily Jensen disagrees with most recent critical work on *Mrs. Dalloway*.
As a close reader of the text, she asks us to consider at what cost to herself

Clarissa maintains her respectable life. She has committed a very common form of female suicide, destroying herself to maintain the social norms. This is an unusual and stimulating approach to the novel, one of the first to analyze its lesbian content.

Susan Squier, who discussed Woolf and the city in our first book and is editing a volume called *Women Writers and the City,* continues her research into the genesis of *The Pargiters* and *The Years* with an edition and commentary on some draft pages from Sussex. Sallie Sears uses the technique of close reading to analyze the language of *Between the Acts,* discussing the novel as a meditation on language, "words the defilers . . . words the impure." She studies the novel as theater and analyzes its feminist politics in an essay that will aid students in their reading.

In "Virginia Woolf in Her Fifties" Carolyn Heilbrun argues that in writing *The Years* Woolf began a new life and a profound and liberating struggle that allowed her to write *Three Guineas,* fully expressing her feminist anger. This point of view is not a common one, though Carolyn Heilbrun has expressed opinions on Woolf's suicide, on Leonard Woolf's behavior, and on the genius of *Three Guineas* that most feminist critics share.

Brenda Silver analyzes the letters Woolf received and kept in response to *Three Guineas* as a "valuable exercise in psychology." Woolf herself called the notebooks she kept throughout the thirties, documenting the misogyny of her age, as "enough powder to blow up St. Paul's." Brenda Silver's passionate political essay on her readers' responses is a demonstration of the way feminist Woolf scholarship continues the politically engaged work of Woolf herself in a nuclear age even more threatening to feminist values than her own. We hope that our several circuitous approaches to Virginia Woolf's life and work, our feminist critical slant, will be revealing of the type of "explanation kind" Emily Dickinson imagined.

The Niece of a Nun:
Virginia Woolf, Caroline
Stephen, and the
Cloistered Imagination   *Jane Marcus*

*Often down here I have entered into a
sanctuary; a nunnery; had a religious
retreat; of great agony once; and
always some terror: so afraid one is of
loneliness: of seeing to the bottom of
the vessel.*
DVW 3:196

The Erotics of Chastity

Virginia Woolf's model for female power derived from chastity had two
sources: the life of Queen Elizabeth (an early and lifelong interest of the
woman named "Virginia")[1] and the example and history of nuns, including
her aunt, Caroline Emelia Stephen, a great Quaker theologian. Woolf's
work, like her aunt's, based religious and political stances on a celebration of
celibacy and remade male repressive ideology into a feminist ideology of
power.

Caroline Stephen's major work before her conversion to the Quaker
religion was *The Service of the Poor* (1871),[2] a history of sisterhoods. There is
no more heartrending example of the plight of Victorian womanhood than
the tortured ambivalence of this book. The young woman's passion to escape
the patriarchal family into a sisterhood was harnessed into many years of
study, firsthand research, and writing what became powerful propaganda
against sisterhoods, a book used to convince "daughters of educated men"
that such salvation was selfish. Celibate women living separately in convents,
she says, are a dire threat to the patriarchal family, which needs for survival
the unpaid cheerful labor of its unmarried daughters. With what personal
pain and almost erotic longing for escape into a self-governing world of
women does Caroline Stephen argue against the desire for freedom from
family constraints. Chafing at these bonds herself, she was an extremely effective spokeswoman for patriarchal protestantism. Her harshest criticism
was for the bonding of women in groups. It was many years before she found
a personal solution that would not dishonor the memory of her father—the
mixed religious meetings of the Society of Friends, where class and sex boun-

daries could be transcended without threatening the structure of the family, where she could experience community and also establish a private life in a nunnery of one. These breeding grounds for a female collective haunt the imagination of her niece, Virginia Woolf, in her dream of "a woman's republic," her idealization of girls' schools and women's colleges because she had never experienced this bonding, her work in women's suffrage, the Women's Co-operative Guild, and the Women's Service League and Library. In "A Society" she created a sisterhood of intellectual inquiry that foreshadowed her lifelong friendships with women. In *A Room of One's Own* she outlined a strategy of the collective voice of women artists united over history, and in *Three Guineas* she sketched the utopian woman's college of the future, where the possibilities of sisterhood might be explored and tested, and called for an "Outsiders' Society" where female marginality could be exploited for collective political purposes.

In *Three Guineas* Virginia Woolf eroticizes the idea of chastity as the romantics eroticized the idea of liberty. What an idea—the erotics of chastity—but it can be traced in the writings of nuns like Saint Teresa and the image of the chaste virgin warrior in the life of Joan of Arc and in the adoption of that Amazonian image by Christabel Pankhurst and the British suffragettes. The sexualization of politics and the valorization of chastity at the end of the suffrage campaign have been dismissed by historians as hysteria, but there is no question that they infused the suffragettes with an enormous feeling of power and intimidated men far more than the espousal of free love by other feminists.[3]

The chosen state of celibacy has been elevated by some women to the status of freedom, since it represents escape from the bonds of family. The inviolate body suggests youth and life when compared with the body of Victorian motherhood, battered by childbirth. Both Annie Thackeray (before her marriage to a man much younger than herself) and Caroline Stephen, lecturing to university students on the joys of spinsterhood, suggest that the chaste life with female friends allows a woman her own work and her choice of emotional ties. It was a form of rebellion against the patriarchal family, and the idea of that rebellion was itself erotic. Virginia Woolf's choice of a Jewish "outsider" husband in a companionate marriage with no children and her attacks on the patriarchal family in her novels, especially *The Years,* make her own inheritance of this female tradition clear.

In "Toilers and Spinsters" (1873) Anne Thackeray wrote, "May not spinsters climb up craters, publish their experiences, tame horses, wear porkpie hats, write articles in the *Saturday Review*? They have gone to battle in

Top-boots, danced on the tight-rope, taken up the Italian cause, and harangued the multitudes. They have gone to prison for distributing tracts; they have ascended Mont Blanc, and come down again.'' Money, Annie argued, was more important than virginity. In ''Living Alone,'' a lecture given at Newnham College in 1906 and published in *The Light Arising: Thoughts on the Central Radiance* (1908), Caroline Stephen described the ''austere charm'' of the single life. ''We cannot be finally freed from loneliness except by encountering it. It will be subdued only by those who dare to meet it with a hearty embrace,'' she wrote. The imaginative power to outline your own life is not a misfortune, she told the students. The family protests at first when a daughter begins to break ties, but ''An admonition or two, a gently affixed label of eccentricity, and the thing is done.'' ''The hermit,'' she wrote, ''is impervious to many an arrow which scatters dismay among the flock.'' Like Virginia Woolf in *A Room of One's Own,* Caroline demands a feminist territorial imperative. The single woman has ''an open space in the labyrinth of life,'' and she encourages the young women to claim it: ''That there is in the human mind a power of making the 'iron bars' of our cage into a hermitage, and the empty spaces around us into a sanctuary, we all instinctively feel; but it needs some reflection to understand what is the spell by which such transformations are to be wrought.'' In *A Room of One's Own* Virginia Woolf also uses this image of the cage and bars to describe the space in which the feminist historian can investigate men's opposition to women's freedom.

Woolf's erotics of chastity is deeply feminist and is even, perhaps, a screen for her lesbian imagination. What she has done is to take the Victorian ideal of female chastity, which was patriarchal culture's enforced imprisonment of women's bodies and minds, and created in *Three Guineas* a modern ideal of ''intellectual chastity.''[4] Intellectual purity is then equated with intellectual liberty. This concept, once stated, leaps backward onto that Victorian beast, men's obsession with female chastity, and transfers the concept to the mind. This new chastity of choice suggests power, both mental and physical, and has an ascetic beauty and fierce attraction. The single women in Woolf's novels represent aspects of the powerful privileging of purity in her imagination, as the deaths of Rachel Vinrace and Judith Shakespeare represent women's loss of freedom in heterosexual relations, marriage or rape. Lily Briscoe's artistic integrity seems to derive from her refusal to marry, and Mary Datchet, Eleanor Pargiter, and Lucy Swithin are almost high priestesses of virtue rather than heroines. Perhaps the most interesting case is that of Clarissa Dalloway, whose honor seems to have derived from her

failure to be Richard's sexual partner.[5] As virgin mother, Clarissa lives the
life of a nun in her attic room, her narrow white bed. Her "virginity preserved through childbirth" and the memory of her blissful love for Sally
make Clarissa a very attractive figure. She may lack "something central
which permeated" in her relations with her husband, but she is erotically in-
flamed by memories of Sally, by Miss Kilman's threat to steal her daughter,
and by listening to the confidences of other women. She is the lesbian who
marries for safety and appearances, produces a child, cannot relate sexually to
her husband, and chooses celibacy within marriage, no sex rather than the
kind she wants. Denial of desire is easier than living Miss Kilman's life, she
feels.

It is interesting regarding Clarissa's celibate marriage that, in Caroline
Stephen's history of sisterhoods, one of the groups studied is the *Clarissan*
nuns, an order of women who were married but signed vows of celibacy
with their husbands, lived at home, and were secret nuns. They performed
good works without threatening the family by living in groups.

On the Clarissans, the Third Order of Saint Francis, Caroline Stephen
quotes her father's *Essays in Ecclesiastical Biography.* (Virginia Woolf read her
grandfather's essays when she was fifteen.) As lay nuns, the Clarissans were
allowed to hide the scapulary and cord; they needed only the "tacit consent"
of their husbands to their vows of celibacy. As "poor ladies" the Clarissans
cared for the insane and "fallen women." Woolf also felt the appeal of the
secret life of a nun under the protection of marriage, and her Clarissa is like
"a nun withdrawing." Clarissa's call is even clearer in her relationship with
the "insane" Septimus Smith. There is really only a difference of degree between Septimus's voices and Clarissa's, between her desire for celibacy in
marriage and his. The historical relationship of nuns to the mad, the ill, and
prostitutes is an interesting one, outsiders caring for outsiders.

The erotics of chastity has parallels in politics, in religion, and in speech. In
Woolf's thought pacifism is privileged as morally superior to war and imperialism, unassailably correct by any standards. Mysticism has the same aura
in religion. Mysticism is nonhierarchical and private, a harmless creed with
no hatred.

Caroline Stephen's mystical writing—*The Light Arising: Thoughts on the
Central Radiance, Quaker Strongholds,* and *The Vision of Faith,*—constitutes a
subversive female discourse, and it strongly influenced Virginia Woolf.[6] If
pacifism is the purest political stance, mysticism is the purest religious concept. It allows access to the community of saints without the dogmas and
disciplines of organized religion. Objecting to the *language* of piety as spoken

and written by patriarchal priests, Caroline Stephen advocated communal silence and the direct utterance of spiritual experience, unfettered by form, of Quaker testimony. Though she claimed she was not a feminist, her effort is godmother to Woolf's search for a feminine sentence. Caroline's weariness with the language of men is symptomatic of her century, her class, and her family.

Caroline wanted to revive a religious image of her father, the author of ecclesiastical biographies, in direct opposition to the portraits of power painted by her brothers, Fitzjames and Leslie, in their studies of him as colonial administrator and professor of modern history. The men created an image of the master of the language of imperialism in their portraits of James Stephen. When Fitzjames and Leslie were safely dead, she collected her father's letters to show him as master of the language of piety.[7] Instincts of filial piety and filial rebellion were at war within her until her old age. She could not blot out her brothers' pronouncements, but she could suggest revision. It is clear from Virginia Woolf's letters that Caroline was concerned with truth-telling in biography, and she struggled with Maitland (and the young Virginia) to no avail over the prettified portrait of Leslie Stephen that neglected to sketch in his temper and his emotional bullying of women.[8]

Caroline's brother Fitzjames literally "laid down the law" in his legal digests, his political essays, and his reactionary response to John Stuart Mill, *Liberty, Equality, Fraternity*. His legal language of controversy, argument, aggressive denunciation, and judgment, with its Old Testament thundering about punishment, damnation, and law and order, was male discourse of immense and ferocious authority.[9] Even Leslie Stephen's essays were authoritative male discourse, argumentative and assertive. The *Dictionary of National Biography* is a patriarchal masterpiece in its exclusion of women and of men who did not fit the pattern of power. Sitting on the library shelves, the volumes of the DNB are a horizontal monument to phallocentric culture.

The spinsterhood of silence in Caroline Stephen's work is a rejection of male discourse. She was weary of words as weapons, though she was obviously powerfully convincing enough to turn the Society of Friends away from evangelical preaching and back to simplicity, silent worship, and "inner light." Fitzjames and Leslie not only were argumentative, they were highly emotional. What Virginia may have found at The Porch to heal her sorrow and self-destructive desires was a calm and very rational peace. Listening, that highly developed female art, was offered by Caroline to her niece as a method of spiritual survival, the first step in learning to trust oneself that the artist needs. "We talked for some nine hours; and she poured

forth all her spiritual experiences. . . . All her life she has been listening to inner voices, and talking with spirits'' (L 1:229).

Ex cathedra: Caroline, Cathedral, and Cloister

> Stop shaking.
> Imagine her. She was a cathedral.[10]

These are the words the poet Denise Levertov addressed to herself at the end
of her elegy for Muriel Rukeyser. The form of feminist elegy is itself
transformative. The political poet does not mourn; she organizes herself and
the reader to move beyond the despair of ''We've made / our cathedrals, /
had our chance, / blown it.'' to respect for Rukeyser's work, its commitment to social change, the clarity of her imagination. The traditional elegaic
tone of lugubrious mourning is rejected. The poet wears white, not black;
seeks light, not darkness. So the poem celebrates the life of the poet and imagines the political and poetic work as a permanent monument, a cathedral.

Levertov succeeds in imagining her sister poet by leaving off lamentation
and forcing the ancient elegaic form to give over its grieving for a celebration
of spiritual liberation. Much of Virginia Woolf's work began as elegies for
her own dead. The ghosts of her loved ones haunted her imagination, and she
played god, the writer, resurrecting them into fictional life.

The extraordinary revival of interest in the life and work of Virginia
Woolf has, I believe, a single source—the political themes of her novels and
the ethical and moral power of her writing, both essays and fiction.

Despite their distaste for idolatry in all its literary forms, and because of
their own struggles against the canon and canonization itself in our
cathedrals of learning, feminist critics have been reluctant to build a female
church or to erect statues to our sainted literary mothers. Saint Virginia
herself would have been appalled at shrines or pilgrims on bended knee. But
now that we have examined the social and political themes of her novels, the
attacks on capitalism, patriarchy, and imperialism that are the backbone of
her work and the reason our generation calls her blessed, let us return to
those other ''isms'' that so infuriated the radicals of her own day—her
pacifism and her mysticism. Why does she insist on equating feminism with
pacifism in *Three Guineas*? How can she be a mystic and as materialist as a
Marxist at the same time? Did the same hand that wrote *The Years* write *The
Waves*?

We may see this conjunction of revolutionary materialism, a tremblingly violent pacifism, and a simultaneously erotic and sublimely chaste mysticism in the intellectual response to modern fascism of two other important figures, Simone Weil and Walter Benjamin.[11] The saintly trinity of self-defined outsiders rejected their bourgeois origins—the German Jewish intellectual was torn between the Kabbalah and *Das Kapital*; the French Jewish pacifist was torn between physical labor for the working class and Catholic mysticism, and the English daughter of middle-class evangelical professional reformers called herself a Jew and yet attacked patriarchy in all its forms. Their studies of power and violence are invaluable to us; their ethical purity is unassailable. Their suicides—seemingly so socially determined as political acts—fill us with humility and rage. Did they mean to be scapegoats in self-slaughter or martyrs to fear of fascism? Walter Benjamin predicted their predicament in "Ministry of the Interior": "the more antagonistic a person is toward the traditional order, the more inexorably he will subject his private life to the norms that he wishes to elevate as legislators of a future society. It is as if these laws, nowhere yet realized, placed him under obligation to enact them in advance at least in the confines of his own existence" (*Reflections*, 69). Having given up family, class, country, they could administer the interior of their own minds under an ethical imperative too pure, severe, and ascetic in its mysticism and pacifism for the real world.

This place, this space, was for each a refuge of silence, an inner cathedral. Woolf described herself as retreating to a nunnery when she wrote, and she extolled as high virtue for professional women the ideal of "intellectual chastity." Simone Weil was equally enamored of silence, and her concept of the inner void that must be experienced to achieve spiritual purity is remarkably like Woolf's room of one's own in the soul and Walter Benjamin's "ministry of the interior." Unlike existentialists, these three mystical "Marxists" came to reject action and choice for "waiting," "attention," meditation, and mystical moments of illumination.

Their intense austerity and emphasis on personal purity and the search for truth seems self-destructive to us now, though it has a rare ascetic authority. As the whole of Europe seemed to immerse itself in the destructive element, their vows of silence, poverty, and intellectual chastity bear personal witness to the idea of goodness. Pacifism in the face of fascism may seem to us, as Christopher Caudwell said, a bourgeois luxury, and perhaps only an alternative for the middle-class intellectual, but it was an honorable alternative. Yet pacifism was also part of the politics of the weak, the spiritually oppressed. Its first premise is untenable for the revolutionary—that is, that the powerful will stop destruction and violence once they see the error of their ways, that one can make a rational appeal to warriors and politicians in the midst of battle. (Trotsky said the powerful would ignore all rational appeals for peace unless they came from a united working class.)

Even their mysticism was nonviolent. No frenzied ecstasies or joyful dancing unto the Lord, it was a "rational mysticism" the three outsiders shared—a mysticism based on ethics and morality, a vision of history and socialist community.

For Virginia Woolf this rational mysticism had a specific and real origin. *The Waves* is haunted by the vision, mystical and mysterious, of a "lady at a table writing." This "mystical eye-less book" is also a mystical I-less book, the one in which ego is most diminished by the writer as minister of the interior. Here she celebrates that memory makes us moral and that community is collective memory.

The lady at a table writing was a real person, Virginia Woolf's aunt, Caroline Emelia Stephen, as she appears in a photograph in her last book of essays, in her plain gray Quaker dress and cap, writing at a window overlooking the garden in her Cambridge cottage called "The Porch" after George Herbert, her antechamber to heaven.[12] The young Cambridge Quakers to whom she was mother-mentor (in fact she wrote to one student of her "inward motherhood") called Caroline Stephen "Nun." It was an appellation she earned through years of struggle, torn between duty to the patriarchal family and the desire to join a sisterhood. Much as the young Virginia Stephen mocked her aunt's celibate mysticism, it was an attitude she herself adopted more and more as she grew older, even to the equation of writing with the notion of retreat into a nunnery.

Virginia Woolf succeeded in imagining her aunt Caroline Emelia Stephen (1834–1909) not only in the obituary she wrote at her death[13] but in the figures of Eleanor Pargiter in *The Years,* Lucy Swithin in *Between the Acts,* and "that odd little priestess of humanity," Sally Seale in *Night and Day,* fifty-five and carrying on her father's work with her crossed crucifixes and her dedication to the cause. Even the maiden aunts in *The Voyage Out* and Hirst's Aunt Lucy who works in the slums of Lambeth—an anti-intellectual who celebrates the inner life of feeling and faith—owe something to Caroline Stephen.

Woolf's comic life of her aunt does not survive, but we may imagine that its genre was a feminist utopia, like her portrait of Violet Dickinson, another Quaker spinster, composed at the same time. These "antibiographies" were a relief from the real work of helping Maitland with his biography of Leslie Stephen and were anticipatory of *Orlando* and *Flush.* Woolf later envisioned her aunt as "the lady at a table writing," the self-cloistered nun she compared herself to as she equated celibacy with creativity and withdrew into her room of her own for mystical visions, moments of being that are remarkably like Caroline Stephen's experiences of "inner light" as she describes them in *Quaker Strongholds* and *The Light Arising: Thoughts on the Central Radiance.* In bad times Woolf could tell herself to stop shaking, to imagine her aunt's life as a Quaker "nun," a spiritual cathedral of mystical vision and rational peace.

After nursing her father until he died in 1904, Virginia Stephen had a breakdown and attempted suicide. Her cure was effected by Violet Dickinson and Caroline Stephen. She wrote to Violet from The Porch: "This is an ideal retreat for me. I feel as though I were living in a Cathedral Close, with the big bell of the Quaker's voice tolling at intervals."[14] Between them, the two Quakers set Virginia to work as a writer and got her reviews published in the *Guardian* (church weekly). Her first lesson in becoming the historian Caroline wanted her to be was to help with Leslie Stephen's biography. What is interesting is that her letters at the time show her as her father's champion against Caroline's negative view of her brother, whereas in Woolf's later memoir she criticizes her father for the same faults Caroline had seen.

At first glance the life of Caroline Emelia Stephen seems to be one of those "lives of the obscure" Woolf wanted to write. There were, she pointed out, "no lives of maids in the *DNB*." There were, however, some lives of Quakers, and they were written by Caroline. What is amazing to the student of history is Leslie Stephen's portrait of his sister in *The Mausoleum Book*[15] as an utter failure. He invented a reason for the failure of her life—unrequited love—a mythical Percival who dies in India. Leslie's motives were not malicious, one feels, but simply an example of a rather good male Victorian mind utterly unable to comprehend the value of a woman's life if it did not revolve around marriage and motherhood. Like her niece Virginia, Caroline produced books instead of babies. They were "little," said Leslie. In their diminution he perhaps found some satisfaction, since his own works were so big.

Of her single-handed revival of the almost extinct English Society of Friends he says nothing. In a querulous tone he blames her loss of health on travel for the Quaker cause. But Caroline's health was lost, alas, not as a Quaker martyr but as a dutiful Victorian daughter and sister, nursing at the sickbeds and deathbeds of her family. She collapsed after three weeks of caring for Leslie and Laura after Minny's death, and Leslie complained that her nurse and doctor carried her off to her own house in Chelsea—as if she had no right to a house of her own and work of her own, after so many years as nurse to her parents.

Quaker historians have recorded that Caroline Emelia Stephen was their foremost religious thinker in the Victorian period.[16] *Quaker Strongholds* and *The Light Arising*, as well as her talks and travels, her essays, and her personal influence in Quaker meetings in London, Cambridge, and Malvern, saved the Society of Friends. The Quakers had been deeply affected by evangelical trends and had lost contact with the purity of their origins. She wrote as a convert and revived the spirit of the early Quakers. She was in her own way a great Victorian theologian, insisting that an agnostic could have faith and live a good life, explicating "rational mysticism," and achieving such a reputation that she was elected to the ministry, only to start a movement to abolish ministers.

Leslie was not proud of his sister's achievements. He blamed religion for her ill health and was contemptuous of her "taking up with the Quakers." He misnamed her book "Strongholds of Quakerism," the -ism of which makes it sound like quackery, irrational and eccentric, and called it "another little book of hers." Yet some historians claim it had a "very great" influence both within and beyond the Society of Friends, and it still does.

Leslie's sketch continues, "But even in 1877 she seemed to be broken in spirit. She had no power of reaction. She was hardly even 'a reed shaken by the wind,' she was more like a reed of which every joint has been crushed and which can only float down the stream." (Leslie's reed image suggests the Syrinx/Pan myth and its sexual connotations, clues to his characterization of Caroline as frustrated.) For Caroline Stephen the break with the Clapham sect evangelicalism of her father and brother Fitzjames, then being, as Rufus Jones says, "more or less forced intellectually to take an agnostic position by her brother Leslie," was exhausting. Silent worship with the Quakers gave her "indescribable relief." "What I felt I wanted in a place of worship was a refuge, or at least the opening of a doorway toward the refuge, from doubt and controversies; not a fresh encounter with them. Yet it seemed to me impossible that anyone harassed by conflicting views of truth, with which just now the air is thick, should be able to forget controversy while listening to such language as that of the Book of Common Prayer. It seems to me that nothing but silence can heal the wounds made by disputations in the region of religion."[17]

Hardly the words of a helpless, spineless reed. Caroline's conversion was an out and out rejection of the disputatious patriarchal religious controversies of her two quarrelsome brothers. But to Leslie she was Silly Milly, criticized by Julia as too fond of her brother. He admitted that she still makes "a few pathetic little attempts to turn her really great abilities to some account." Perhaps Leslie's most perverse judgment was made on a working life that began with a monumental history of sisterhoods, *The Service of the Poor* (1871) (Leslie did confess that this was one work of hers he could call "able.") Caroline's study was an exact counterpart to her brother Fitzjames's codification and professionalization of the law and to Leslie's professionalization of the higher journalism and biography. She argues for the professionalization of nursing and social work and against private philanthropy. Torn by the desire to join a convent herself after her first reading of Florence Nightingale's study of Kaiserswerth, she uses the writing of the book to convince herself and her readers that all female desire to live in sisterhoods is spiritual vanity and a very serious threat to the power of the patriarchal family.

The second important phase of Caroline Stephen's life was her philanthropic work with Octavia Hill, her work with an organization to help servant girls, and the building of Hereford Houses in Chelsea in 1877 as artisans' dwellings. The architect was Elijah Hoole, who later built Toynbee Hall. In the archway over the twenty-eight-flat building she placed a stone with words from Psalm 112, "Unto the upright there ariseth light in darkness." The interesting point about Hereford Houses, aside from their design for light, air, and privacy, was the installation of a shower bath and washhouse on the roof.[18] Obviously Eleanor Pargiter in *The Years,* surrounded as she is by the imagery of light, with her charity work and the building of houses with the stamp of the sunflower, and her excitement over her shower bath, has a source in Caroline Emelia's life and work. One of her strongest concerns was with the relations of mistress and servant, which we may interpret as matriarchal and antidemocratic, but she won the devotion of her own maid, Leah Gwillam, who wept in Virginia's arms at Caroline's cremation and confessed that her mistress had called her "bearkin." The servant question hounded Virginia all her life—simple matriarchal benevolence was out of the question, and the extraordinary portraits of charwomen and servants in her novels are a continuation of a theme about which both her mother and her aunt were concerned.[19] After her Quaker conversion in 1879, Caroline Stephen gave up social work for spiritual labor and began her second career as a writer and speaker for the return to silence and the experience of inner light in the Friends' worship.

There were other political questions on which Caroline remained as conservative as the stance of her book on sisterhoods. With her cousin Albert Dicey, she opposed Irish home rule, and through him she spoke for the Anti-Suffrage League. Her last essays on "Women and Politics" in the *Nineteenth Century* in 1907 and 1908 must have occasioned some interesting debates with her niece Virginia. She argued that the vote would be too burdensome a responsibility for women and then outlined a plan for a national consultative chamber for women acting as another second chamber, modeled on the Women's Yearly Meeting of the Society of Friends.[20]

Caroline Stephen's work, thought, and life, in their combination of the radical and the conservative, constitute a perfect study of the plight of Victorian womanhood. She became an invalid after long years of nursing her parents as a dutiful daughter. The rest of her life, from late middle age to old age, freed her for work of her own, for fame and friendship, and for the role of mother-mentor to a generation of Cambridge Quakers. Alternating between debilitating illness and intense periods of writing and speaking, she left to her niece a legacy of the value of silence, inner light, and the absolute authority of one's own mystical experience. One cannot dismiss her economic legacy, for Woolf tells us in *A Room of One's Own* that it "unveiled the sky" to her.

The achievements of the invalid Quaker visionary were noted by Virginia Woolf in her obituary, which seems to be a private rebuttal of her father's portrait of a mystical old maid in *The Mausoleum Book*. Caroline Stephen taught a simple method of spiritual exercises, of clearing an inner chamber (a room of one's own in the soul) to prepare the way for visionary experiences in which daily life was lit up to incandescence. It was a method of spiritual self-reliance in which no exterior aids were invoked except the need to wait receptively in silence.

Caroline Emelia Stephen was a woman of ample girth. She was not beautiful, high-strung, or fussy about food like her brother Leslie and her fastidious father, who had strong ideas about the duty to be beautiful and to dress well. What she may have suffered in a family that so prized physical beauty goes unmentioned. Her father was described as a "wild duck," distinguished but erratic. But Caroline was an ugly duckling. If Leslie could criticize Julia Stephen's classic nose, what did he say of his sister's, which was large and prominent? Virginia's youthful candor described her aunt's tear-stained "pendulous cheeks" as she visited her dying brother. In her book on sisterhoods Caroline had written, "I cannot wonder at the longing to join a religious sisterhood which is secretly cherished by many young women." But she warned that the romantic attraction of a nun's habit was only "the outward livery of religion." One of her first essays was "Thoughtfulness in

Dress," published in the *Cornhill* in 1868. With what joy did she finally embrace the plain gray dress and cap of the Quakers, a nonthreatening nun's habit; she did not object when nicknamed "Nun" and even signed her letters so. While Virginia Woolf was initially embarrassed at being the niece of a "nun," the relationship was an enabling one, and she gained a good deal from it. She herself was troubled by clothing, and women like Ethel Smyth, who had adopted a protective and eccentric uniform of baggy tweeds and three-cornered hats, were annoyed at Woolf's anxieties. The nun's habit or Quaker dress is a form of transvestism even more protective than wearing men's garb; it signals celibacy and demands respect.

Virginia Woolf wrote of her aunt:

> One could not be with her without feeling that after suffering and thought she had come to dwell apart, among the "things which are unseen and eternal" and that it was her perpetual wish to make others share her peace. But she was no solitary mystic. She was one of the few to whom the gift of expression is given together with the need of it, and in addition to a wonderful command of language she had a scrupulous wish to use it accurately. Thus her effect on people is scarcely to be decided, and must have reached many to whom her books are unknown. Together with her profound belief she had a robust common sense and a practical ability which seemed to show with health and opportunity she might have ruled and organized. (*Guardian* [church weekly] 21 April 1909)

Woolf's biographical portrait of her aunt is a complete revision of her father's dismissal of his sister in *The Mausoleum Book*. While Leslie describes an old maid destroyed by the loss of a mythical lover, Virginia describes the "maternal" qualities of the creative spinster, an echo of the quality of "inward motherhood" that young Quakers found in Caroline Stephen. What Leslie saw as a wasted life of a will-less crushed reed, Virginia saw as having "the harmony of a large design."

Rufus Jones, the Quaker historian, treated her as one who *had* actually ruled and organized: "One of the most important events in the history of English Quakerism . . . was the convincement of Caroline E. Stephen to its faith. The influence of her exposition of its central ideals and practices was very great both within and beyond the Society." He described her conversion when "the old faiths and forms did not meet her personal spiritual needs, nor speak to her condition":

> Caroline Stephen, with her fresh experiences, soon became the foremost interpreter in the Society in England of Friends' way of worship and of

the type of religion they were endeavouring to maintain and express. She fortunately cared little for the traditions of Quakerism; she held many of the accumulated forms lightly, and yet she was gifted to penetrate to the heart and living secret of the faith which she had accepted. She belonged by bent and experience to the order of the mystics. She had seen truth at first hand, had received a direct revelation, and, according to her own testimony, she had been able to "sink into the innermost depth of her being" and "become aware of things which are unseen and eternal." She was, furthermore, a woman of broad culture, of rare insight, of beautiful personality, possessed of a graceful literary style, and thus she was able to do the work of interpretation which so few Friends of the time could hope to accomplish. [21]

"What she did," the Quaker historian wrote, "more clearly and emphatically than anyone else at that time was to call the attention of Friends to the richness of their own inheritance, and to help them to see and realize the immense inner possibilities of their faith." She calls her readers to experience "the central glow of Light and Love," to find the "spiritual radiance" within themselves, a radiance she described as like the sunshine shed upon shadowed family life by her mother and by her aunt Emelia. She had struggled for years to find this light among the Clapham Saints and evangelicals, to no avail. Though her father felt he was one of the "saints in the light," he was a deeply unhappy and dissatisfied man, with a puritanical sense of outward election that masked his inner turmoil. Caroline rejected the outward forms of piety. As Rufus Jones says, "She interpreted worship better than any other modern Quaker writer had done, she raised silence to a new significance and she gave 'spiritual radiance' a new and living meaning." He found her too inward looking, too individualistic, for his own Quaker emphasis on democracy and cooperation, but he had to admit that her mystic visions were a great inspiration to many Victorians lost in the maze of materialism and religious controversy.

In *Three Guineas*, when Woolf demands vows of intellectual chastity and poverty for new women professionals, she significantly leaves out a vow of obedience. The Quakers have used "civil disobedience" as a way of remaining true to their pacifist principles and confronting the conscience of leaders of the state. Caroline Stephen's own rebellion began with an articulation of the idea of "filial disobedience" (though she would have been shocked at these words). In *The Service of the Poor* one finds both the suppressed passion to become a nun and the suppressed violence of the daughter at home chafing at the bonds of family. She argues there against convents because of the irreversible authoritarian nature of a vow of obedience, which offers a girl protection but no individual freedom. "I wholly disbelieve," she cries passionately, "in the competence of one human being to discipline the soul of another."[22] It is a statement perfectly consistent with Woolf's views. But, one wonders, did Caroline Stephen include in her creed the competence of fathers to discipline the souls of daughters? Is it consistent with her views on mistresses and servants?

The Service of the Poor contains several such slips that suggest Caroline's rebellion had already started before she finished the book: "Who is there who would not escape from a multitude of care, anxieties and sorrows, as well as lose much happiness, if it were possible altogether to obliterate family life?" she asked.

The very mention of the *obliteration* of family life as a possibility suggests a violent response to her own life of self-sacrifice and an appeal to other women who have felt the same annihilating urge. It is here that she appeals to the martyr in women, urging them to stay at home precisely because it is more painful. Sentiment then swallows all: "For what booklearning is to be compared with the intellectual exercise of association with educated men? What training in the world can be so valuable to a woman as the daily intimacy of family life with her father and brothers?"[23] Thus speaks the classic "daughter of an educated man" to her sisters. There were many kinds of training more valuable to women, as she herself was to find. Caroline Emelia Stephen is undermined by her own rhetoric. The problem of woman's relation to paternalism is posed as a rhetorical question. But it can be read as a straightforward query once you dispose of the notion that to answer it is unthinkable effrontery on the part of the daughter of an educated man. If in her philosophy no one has the right to discipline the soul of another, it is a short step to questioning paternal and fraternal intimacy as the alternative to professional training.

The Service of the Poor makes an effort to define charity as social work and to remove religion from the debate. Works of charity should not be used by women as acts of worship, for this encourages pauperism in the poor and spiritual pride in the ladies. "You do not pay a daughter to wait upon a mother, nor a father to bring up his children," she writes in defense of the "natural" claims of the family. But "to find the right way of employing single women is a problem of some difficulty." It would be wrong, she suggests, to use sisterhoods "as a remedy for the preponderance of women, as if women ceased to exist when they retired into them, and as if the one object to be aimed at with regard to single women was to get rid of them.'' This was a social question of some importance, but she was not to be distracted: ''If good single women are really the salt of the earth, society can ill afford to spare them.'' On vows of poverty, chastity, and obedience, Miss Stephen is equally logical: ''If poverty, celibacy, and dependence are good things in themselves, so that women ought to be encouraged to choose them, then riches, marriage, and independence are comparatively bad things, and women ought to be encouraged to renounce them.''

In ''taking up with the Quakers'' Caroline Stephen got to have her cake and eat it too. She had a nun's life without a vow of obedience. Caroline Stephen paid her dues with a patriarchal history of sisterhoods. Like Miranda in *The Tempest,* she was her father's best student. Her reward was not a mainland marriage but an island of her own. She ''migrated,'' she said, like a bird, and her niece Katherine reports she often said that if one did not have ''a family of one's own,'' one should live like a bird of the air.[24] With the Foxes at Falmouth she attended her first Quaker meeting. She described in a letter the peace she found: ''It is as if my painted roof had been smashed and, instead of the darkness I had dreaded, I had found the stars shining.''[25] The image is a beautiful one, but as violent as her earlier imagination of the ''obliteration'' of family life. To smash the painted roof is obviously an image of destruction of that ''cathedral'' of her childhood with her father. The painted roof was the prison of the patriarchal home. Her escape to freedom left one less Victorian ''madwoman in the attic.'' That Virginia Stephen had shared this knowledge with her aunt is revealed in her similar metaphor, that her aunt's legacy had ''unveiled the sky'' to her.

When Caroline Stephen wrote ''to have been my father's child was like having been brought up in a cathedral. In his presence the very atmosphere seemed full of awe and reverence,''[26] the daughter's voice is dutiful but edged with pain. It was dark and gloomy in that cathedral, and she went to her mother for ''sunlight.'' She nursed her father in his bouts of madness and acted as his amanuensis. Her brother Leslie remembers his father's Miltonic tread as he dictated to his daughter.

It was Milton's God, ferocious male patriarch, whom Caroline rejected when she smashed the painted roof of evangelical cathedrals that literary and religious fathers offered their daughters as places for worship. Virginia Woolf was obviously moved by this image, and in *A Room of One's Own* she explicates it: ''Indeed my aunt's legacy unveiled the sky to me, and substituted for the large and imposing figure of a gentleman, which Milton recommended for my perpetual admiration, a view of the open sky.'' The ghost of "Milton's bogey," the patriarchal God and the patriarchal father, is laid for Woolf by the visionary example of a maiden aunt and her very practical legacy.[27] Caroline's father had behaved like a bishop and made his home into a cathedral. She had escaped—smashed the painted roof—and from her chair at the window of The Porch she dispensed peace and blessing. It was only a nunnery of one, but its purity and freedom were the models on which Woolf imagined a *society* of outsiders, the collective version of her aunt's vision—not a convent but a union, of the daughters and nieces of those Victorian women who dared to smash those painted roofs. If one could "unveil the sky" above the home and above the church, it was possible to imagine unveiling the sky above the roofs of courts, universities, parliaments, and war offices.

The Language of the Light

From Caroline Stephen, Virginia Woolf learned to speak the language of the light. Her mysticism, "agnosticism with mystery at the heart of it" was a particularly suitable philosophy—one could hardly call it a religion—for the daughter of a Cambridge-educated man with such an emotional attachment to the rational as Leslie Stephen and the wife of a Cambridge-educated man with such an edgy and psychological attachment to the rational as Leonard Woolf. Those mystical meditations on life and death, the Jungian suggestions of a collective unconscious in Woolf's novels—one thinks of the "Time Passes" section of *To the Lighthouse,* what Suzette Henke calls "the communion of saints" in *Mrs. Dalloway,* and the whole of *The Waves*—are essentially rational. The author and her characters are always tapping on the door of personal and collective memory, and ghosts from the past answer them. In *Between the Acts* Lucy Swithin (like Caroline Emelia Stephen) is absorbed by the prehistoric, and Miss La Trobe plans to set her next play at the dawn of human life. The author was experiencing "inward motherhood," like Caroline Stephen with the young Quakers, and wanted to give birth to the *first* characters.

Since her own mother was so "central" to her memories, as she says in "A Sketch of the Past," it is not surprising that in her memoir Woolf should revise her aunt's metaphor to fit her own case: "Certainly there she was, in the very centre of that great cathedral space which was childhood; there she was from the very first" (MB 81). Virginia Woolf describes her mother as "one of those invisible presences who after all play so important a part in every life . . . well, if we cannot analyze these invisible presences, we know very little of the subject of the memoir; and again how futile life-writing becomes'' (MB 80). In her revision of Caroline's confessions (where one can see the connections between the cathedral, ''Milton's bogey,'' the patriarchal God, and her father, and her dream of smashing the painted roof and unveiling the sky) Woolf is equally revealing. For Julia is called a madonna, an ''obsession'' worked out only by writing *To the Lighthouse*. Women very seldom smash the painted roofs of their mothers' houses, but they can abjure idolatry, as Martine Stemerick says, by recognizing that their idol has clay feet, as Woolf effectively does in *To the Lighthouse*. Caroline Stephen was one of those ''invisible presences'' that unveiled the sky to Woolf. Milton's bogey may have been blocking her vision, but it took another woman to help her up from her knees before the statue of the virgin mother that dominated the ''great cathedral space'' of her childhood.

I believe that Virginia Woolf took the central figure of the lighthouse in her novel exorcising her mother's ghost from an eloquent passage in Caroline Stephen's essay ''Divine Guidance,'' in *The Vision of Faith* (49):

> Have you ever seen a revolving lighthouse at night from across the sea, with its steadfast light alternately hidden and displayed? Have you watched the faint spark as it glows into splendour for a few seconds and then fades away again into darkness? And have you considered how the very fact of its intermittency is the means by which it is recognized and its message is conveyed? It is a light given not to read by, but to steer our course by. Its appearances and disappearances are a *language* by which the human care that devised it can speak to the watchers and strugglers at sea. That care does not wax and wane with the light; but in its unchanging vigilance it provides a means of communication which no unaltering beam could afford...speaking to us in a language understood by the trusting heart alone.

The language of the light and the language of the lighthouse are clearly the language of hope, an agnostic's faith that ''human care'' will help us understand the mysteries of life and death. Mrs. Ramsay's identification with the pulsing of the lighthouse beam is both erotic and domestic as she merges with the forces of life and death in *To the Lighthouse*. The lighthouse itself is a well-worn symbol of philanthropic and religious groups. The language is a common one, but Woolf transforms it without reference to a specific god into a mystical language of her own. The intermittence is like Morse code, alternating rhythms of light and dark, life and death, but signifying safety in the end.

There is much in Caroline Stephen's mystical writing that appealed to Virginia Woolf—her concept of "faithfulness to the light," her argument that grief should be "confirming, cleansing, raising, making free," and above all her devotion to silence. Her description of her own "illuminations" resembles Woolf's "moments of being": "There is something in the unsought, undreamed of harmonies, which from time to time shine through the ordinary course of struggling life, which seems to tell of a melody continually accompanying that course, though mostly hidden by its clamour" (*Vision of Faith,* 41–42). Caroline's "inward revelations" did not make her feel elite or elect, and she cautions against those dangers, for she had her visions but passed them on. Late in life (1907) she wrote that "to give up the hope of radiating is very much like giving up life. . . . If words are failing us, it is surely because Light is spreading, and prayer is no longer to be confined within the banks of language but is suffusing all life." The language of the light was both female and democratic; one might even say it was a spiritual demotic.

Caroline Stephen was not without humor. "It is the *artificial* element in religion that I want to get rid of," she said; "perhaps the starch without which it would collapse into a limp heap." Her natural and untutored (or perhaps detutored) approach to religion was like Woolf's approach to scholarship in "On Not Knowing Greek." In "The Faith of the Unlearned," Caroline advocated thinking, not reading, and said that one should look at life steadily from the standpoint of the inexperienced human spirit. There was no point in gathering crumbs from the table of philosophy: "The trouble is that other people's thoughts are apt to act the part of the scriptural patch of new cloth on an old garment, whereby 'the rent is made worse' " (*Vision of Faith,* 137). This philosophy fell on willing ears, for an autodidact like Woolf, deprived of formal education, needed the defense of the power of one's own inner voices. Caroline's figure was a useful one for a novelist—she points out that Scheherazade stopped her ears with wool to block out other voices so she could tell her own stories.[28] Catherine Smith reports that 82 women were among 650 authors granted imprimatur by the Quakers between 1650 and 1700. There was a respected place for women in the Society of Friends. Caroline Stephen's search for female predecessors in religion with her history of sisterhoods and her biography of Caroline Fox and for the roots of radical Quaker thought in its origins is a precursor to Woolf's concept of "thinking back through our mothers" for women authors.

In *The Light Arising: Thoughts on the Central Radiance,* Stephen wrote of "intimations," of "apparitions and visions and dreams and voices," and wondered how to interpret these signs. She cited William James (he was one of her admiring readers), speaking of "touches of the very 'finger of God' [Woolf found God's finger threatening]—whispers of the inspeaking 'still small voice'—gleams of the innermost radiance" (176). Quaker practice preserved sanity, for after a vision one was to wait and then consult other Friends. Caroline quotes Sir William Gull (often consulted as a psychiatrist by the Stephen family) in connection with the idea of conferring with others: "the human mind needs ventilation." Her perception of visions and voices (a notion that must have appealed to Woolf) was not that they defined the visionary as a superior authority: "But mystery, like music, in itself neither proves nor authorises, but appeals—and for the moment at least exalts—as with the pledge of a beauty not belonging to earth" (179).

"Rational Mysticism" is a brilliant essay. By excluding from her subject history, theology and psychology, Caroline Stephen grounds her work in experience and "inner light," and an "Inward Monitor" of experience that is the self. By this definition it is clear that both the daughters of educated men and the sons of uneducated men can be mystics. Intermittence, as in her figure of the lighthouse, is an important element, but so are language and the value of certain words, though she is opposed to theorizing. She believes that mysticism is accompanied by "practical efficiency and shrewdness." But, like other women mystics, she insists that reason must be combined with illumination to reach wisdom. The power to sink into the depths of one's own mind she compares to "the power to flee to a City of Refuge" (20). She is very English and Victorian in declaring that ethics, not ecstasy, is her aim, and she wants no association with the occult.

On silence Caroline Stephen is equally eloquent, for intellectual controversy in the Stephen family had upset her: "Words can always be opposed. You cannot oppose silence" (64). Silence is a woman's weapon against patriarchal arguments and a form of passive resistance, but it is also a form of stern self-discipline in Quaker worship; it is the *gathering* of the silent that is important. "War and Superfluities" is an eloquent pacifist piece, in Victorian religious language a precursor to the socialist pacifism of *Three Guineas*. Her footnotes attack the stockpiling of weapons, deliberate panics, and the keeping of too many servants and remind one of the power of Woolf's footnotes. "Living Alone" and "The Fear of Death" are descriptions of the joys of spinsterhood and an argument against mourning. She explicates George Fox's idea of inner light, rejects paid ministry, affirms the pacifist position, and insists on a return to silent worship. "A true mystic believes that all men have, as he himself is conscious of having, an inward life, into which, as into a secret chamber, he can retreat at will" (32). Inner light was, then, a room of one's own in the soul.

"In this inner chamber he finds a refuge from the ever-changing aspects of outward existence. . . . He finds there, first repose, then an awful guidance; a light which burns and purifies; a voice which subdues," Caroline explained. Mystics are "indisposed to discipleship. . . . They sit at no man's feet, and do not . . . greatly care to have anyone sit at theirs." "Faithfulness to the light" is not the same as obedience to conscience, for conscience can be morbid and is never an absolute guide. "God created the animals but left it to each one to develop its own fur or feathers" (47).

Although public worship among Friends is pledged to silence, everyone can speak. "It is sometimes as part-singing compared with unison. The free admission of the ministry of women, of course, greatly enriches this harmony. I have often wondered whether some of the motherly counsels I have listened to in our meetings would not reach some hearts that might be closed to the masculine preacher." With heartfelt eloquence she tells of her own spiritual struggles. Before she became a Quaker, Caroline Stephen felt like "a moth dashing itself against an iceberg." In the midst of Babel she praised the "thrice-blessed power of silence," and in a day of extravagance in dress she spoke of the "mute eloquence" of plain dress as a language that expressed quiet, gentleness, and purity.

I have quoted Caroline Stephen at length here because of the difficulty of getting her books. Clearly her work belongs to the great tradition of English women mystics. And I think we need search no further for the origins of Virginia Woolf's pacifism and mysticism, for we have caught a glimpse of one of the "invisible presences" in her life. In "A Sketch of the Past" Woolf wrote that the influence of Bloomsbury on her was minor compared with the influence of her mother. It was also minor compared with the influence of her aunt.

As a feminist critic I had avoided the subject of Woolf's mysticism, and of *The Waves*, feeling that acknowledging her as a visionary was a trap that would allow her to be dismissed as another female crank, irrational and eccentric. I was drawn to her most anticapitalist, anti-imperialist novels, to Woolf the socialist and feminist, logical, witty, and devastating in argument. But Catherine Smith has raised an important issue in her study of Jane Lead, the seventeenth-century mystic.[29] Smith asks us to study mysticism and feminism together "to learn more about the links between envisioning power and pursuing it." She argues that "idealist analogues of transcendence may shape political notions of sexual equality as much as materialist or ra-

tionalist arguments do." To study both traditions together—and certainly
Woolf's writing embodies both—would teach us about "the structure of vision in feminist politics." Smith concentrates on the figure of Sophia, or
"the woman clothed with the sun," in women's mystical writing. If there is
a feminist collective unconscious, this figure was passed down to Woolf from
her aunt Caroline and lives in Eleanor Pargiter and Lucy Swithin. With the
vision comes a female language of the light, a language of silence—acts of
light and acts of silence.

Caroline Stephen laid out very carefully a structure of vision that included
a pacifism and a mysticism that could be embraced by the socialist-feminist.
Virginia Woolf did learn from her aunt how to speak the language of the
light—it was a "little language," unknown to most men, perhaps best
achieved in that combination of soliloquy and colloquy in *The Waves*. Is it
possible to see the structure of *The Waves* as a Quaker meeting, as interior
monologues in which each character comes to terms with death and grief?
Was the most successful Bernard, that rational mystic? Caroline Stephen had
one enemy she struggled against all her life as the daughter of an educated
man: the power of religious words—the Bible and the Book of Common
Prayer—to oppress and suppress individual religious feeling. Sermons, the
set pieces of preachers, and the traditional forms of protestant worship
seemed to imprison her. Silence set her free.

What Woolf learned from her aunt was that that crippling and debilitating
label—"daughter of an educated man"—stamped on the foreheads of
women of their class was not indelible. It could be erased and a new identity
established. Caroline repressed her desire to join a convent, served her parents
until they died, then braved her brothers' wrath and led the British Quaker
renaissance. Woolf learned to harness her grief for her art and to forge an
identity as the niece of a nun, one who had forgone sisterhood at the command of a patriarch but managed an old age in a nunnery of one. Woolf
learned to turn her lack of education to advantage; she trained herself to trust
memory and inner voices. Her journey to a nunnery was shorter than her
aunt's, but the example of her achievement was crucial to her own development as an artist. Virginia Woolf found that cloistering her imagination
promised a secret and profound creative life. Her inner room of her own was
a clean, well-lighted nun's cell like the "cathedral close" of Caroline's house
in Cambridge.

When Woolf left The Porch in 1904 for a new life in Bloomsbury, she
was, in a sense, "born again," but not in the sense of her evangelical
Clapham sect forebears—nor did she join the Quakers. She remained an

agnostic, a rational mystic. She came to terms with her father's death and discarded the identity of "daughter of an educated man" for a new identity as "niece of a nun." While we can see her pacifism and mysticism in the context of other European leftists like Simone Weil and Walter Benjamin, we can also see their derivation in the life and work of her aunt, which was part of the British female mystical tradition. A nunnery was not a negative space for Virginia Woolf, and quite clearly she felt that mental chastity (the lack of attachment to patriarchal or imperialist institutions) would make her free. Let us imagine her not as a cathedral, not even as a plain Quaker meetinghouse, but as a room of her own. Like Walter Benjamin, she was engaged in a "ministry of the interior," establishing in her own mind a model for a future state where socialism, feminism, and pacifism would be possible in the collective.

> What is the meaning of life? That was all—a simple question; one that tended to close in on one with years. The great revelation had never come. Instead there were little daily miracles, illuminations, matches struck unexpectedly in the dark.
>
> *To the Lighthouse*

As readers we are continually struck by the archetypal imagery of Woolf's novels, the light/darkness contrasts, the sea, the sounds of birds, the voice/speech/silence images. In his study of early Quaker sermons, Phillip Graves analyzes these images as a rhetorical strategy of the Quakers.[30] Unlike other religious writing or sermons, the Quakers did not explicate biblical texts or logically explain doctrine. The speaker poured forth an abundance of archetypal images in plain language to a point where "metaphor has transcended its normal function, and instead of merely indicating a point of resemblances between two differentiable entities, it has totally merged them."[31] Jackson I. Cope describes the technique of "an incredible repetition" with a result that was "not ungrammatical but agrammatical." The effect of this literature is a great affirmation of life and faith. Woolf's prose style has all these characteristics in common with the early Quakers and her Aunt Caroline's writing. There is an authenticity and sincerity combined with verbal simplicity and purity of speech or writing that comes from "hearing voices" and experiencing the "inner light" of visions. Woolf often described the difficulty of writing when her voices were racing ahead of her. The Quakers esteemed the role of listening in silence, and it is here that the writer is like the Friend who then relates her inner experiences to the meeting. The relation of the writer and the reader (the common writer and the common reader speaking a common language) I have described elsewhere as an experience of "the Collective Sublime," a political act on the part of Woolf as a socialist writer. But clearly there is a mystical analogue for her acts as well. The experience of waiting in silence for the word in a collective "gathering," then the extraordinary importance of the spoken word, is one Woolf wants to imitate in her relationship to her audience. The power of her writing is in the reader's response to archetypal imagery—the pulse of the lighthouse, Ralph Denham's vision of the birds besieging the lighthouse, the match in the crocus in *Mrs. Dalloway,* the vision of ancient women beating carpets in *Jacob's Room,* Eleanor's sunflower in *The Years.*

From a feminist perspective it is clear that women mystics drew authority from the Spirit, rather than from the Father or the Son. The pen was so clearly like the penis, as Gilbert and Gubar have demonstrated, that one is tempted to see the Quakers' spatial concepts of the "Inward Light" and the Word, received passively by the silent self in an "inner chamber" as the equivalent of the authority of the pen/penis in female physical terms. The inner chamber receives the light as Mary received Christ from the Holy Spirit.[32] Virgin motherhood or "inward motherhood," or the writer as nun, is then a strategy of power for the woman mystic or artist. It is a chaste vagina, the room of one's own in the soul, to be sure, but then creativity is much like an immaculate conception. One could, by embracing these concepts, subvert the patriarchy without having to take up male aggressive attitudes, words, or arms. These concepts naturally appealed to women and working people, in a world where language was an aggressive weapon for argument and controversy and for the wielding of power. Chastity then becomes erotic in these mystical terms because in union with the light and the word the soul experiences enormous power. This English concept is very different from the sexuality expressed in the writings of Saint Teresa, but it resembles Joan of Arc's experiences.

Very interesting work has been done on the ethnography of speaking and on Quaker speech that sheds light on Virginia Woolf's fiction. Maurice A. Creasey studies the spatial terms of contrast by which the Quakers expressed belief, inward and outward, spiritual and carnal, as well as mystery and history.[33] If the origin of the peculiar language of the Quakers was in a revolt against rhetoric that matched the Puritans' revolt against royalty, two kinds of "authority" were being challenged. Plain speech and plain dress (which was also a language) challenged the hegemony of the priesthood and of the rich and learned. The marginal, working people and women, were claiming that God speaks directly to all people. One must wait in silence to hear this voice—it is an inner light that claims only the authority of one's own experience. In a logocentric society the Quakers esteemed silence. They were tired of Latin obfuscations and valued only the heartfelt utterance of spiritual experience in one's own words, not the words of a religious text. After their initial building of the society, they did not attempt to make converts, but strove to live simply and give good example by their lives.[34]

If we look at *Three Guineas* in these terms rather than as another 1930s antifascist pamphlet, the political anger and utopian idealism it exhibits seem to come from the female mystical/political tradition. Like the Quaker philosophy of Caroline Stephen, *Three Guineas* attacks war, the pompous dress of men in power, the university, the established church, and the professions. Its radical break with the pamphleteering tradition is the identification of fascism with the patriarchal family. Otherwise the Outsiders' Society could be the Society of Friends. Louise Bogan, reviewing *Three Guineas* (*New Republic*, September 1938) claimed that Woolf demanded "a moral pattern so severe that it has never been adhered to by anyone who was not by nature an artist or a saint." Virginia Woolf was both an artist and a saint. The moral vision she gives in her novels is that of a rational mystic who calls for human community from her cloistered imagination.

Acknowledgments

My thanks to Miss Carpenter and her staff at Northwestern University Library Interlibrary Loan for their help over several years in securing for me the books and essays needed for research for this paper. I am also indebted to many colleagues for discussion of the issues raised here, including Catherine Smith, Louise DeSalvo, Betty Sue Flowers, Joanna Lipking, Martine Stemerick, John Bicknell, Martha Vicinus, and Evelyn Haller. I have also discussed Caroline Emelia Stephen in "Thinking Back through Our Mothers" in *New Feminist Essays on Virginia Woolf,* ed. Jane Marcus (London: Macmillan; Lincoln: Nebraska University Press, 1981) and in "Virginia Woolf and Her Violin: Mothering, Madness and Music," a paper read at the Woolf Centennial Conference at West Virginia University, March 1982 and in "Liberty, Sorority, Misogyny," in *The Representation of Women in Fiction,* edited by Carolyn Heilbrun and Margaret Higonnet (Baltimore: Johns Hopkins University Press, 1983).

Notes

1. See Alice Fox's essay in this volume, "Virginia Liked Elizabeth."

2. Caroline Emelia Stephen, *The Service of the Poor: Being an Inquiry into the Reasons for and against the Establishment of Religious Sisterhoods for Charitable Purposes* (London and New York: Macmillan, 1871). The main argument of the book is against private philanthropy and for the professionalization of nursing and social work, a parallel to her brother Fitzjames's professionalization of law and Leslie Stephen's professionalization of the higher journalism. All three Stephens as middle-class intellectuals played the role of what J. K. Stephen called "the intellectual aristocracy" in solidifying the interests of their class and securing important positions as ministers of English culture. Virginia Woolf's attacks on professional men are described by Beverly Schlack in "Fathers in General" in this volume, and her fears for women are expressed in "Professions for Women" and in *Three Guineas.*

3. For a recent attack on the Pankhursts, see David Mitchell, *Queen Christabel* (London: Macdonald and Jones, 1977). Marina Warner's *Joan of Arc: The Image of Female Heroism* (New York: Knopf, 1981) discusses the power of the image of female chastity.

4. "It should not be difficult to transmute the old ideal of bodily chastity into the new ideal of mental chastity" (TG 82). Nor is it difficult to revive physical celibacy as an ideal once it has been associated with mental power.

5. See Emily Jensen's essay in this volume, Suzette Henke's "*Mrs. Dalloway:* The Communion of Saints" in *New Feminist Essays on Virginia Woolf,* and Elizabeth Abel's forthcoming essay on *Mrs. Dalloway* in her book on mothers and daughters in literature, coedited by Elizabeth Abel and Marianne Hirsch.

6. *The Light Arising* was published by Heffer in Cambridge in 1908; *Quaker Strongholds* was published by Headley Brothers in 1890; *The Vision of Faith,* a collection of essays, was published by Heffer and Sons, Cambridge, in 1911, with a memoir by Katherine Stephen. There is an excellent monograph on Caroline Stephen by Robert Tod, which will be part of a new series of Quaker biographies. Tod's monograph also contains a bibliography and chronology of Caroline Stephen's life.

7. Caroline Stephen, *The First Sir James Stephen* (Gloucester: John Bellows, 1906, privately printed). James Fitzjames Stephen's memoir of his father appears in the fourth edition of James Stephen's *Essays in Ecclesiastical Biography* (London: Longmans, Green, 1860). Leslie Stephen described his father in *The Life of Sir James Fitzjames Stephen* (London: Smith Elder, 1895). In letters printed by Katherine Stephen in *The Vision of Faith,* Caroline wrote of her bafflement at editing her father's letters: "It seemed so impossible to *combine* satisfactorily with what my brothers had said, or to fill up the gap left by them, without the appearance of opposition." Sally Seale in *Night and Day* seems to be a partial portrait of Caroline. A suffragist, she is an enthusiast because her father was before her, "and on his tombstone

I had that verse from the Psalms put, about the sowers and the seed'' (N&D 91). ''Dressed in plum-colored velveteen, with short, gray hair, and a face that seemed permanently flushed with philanthropic enthusiasm'' (N&D 81), Sally Seale represents women philanthropists of Woolf's Aunt Caroline's age, who combined religion and social causes and were eventually replaced by the efficient Mr. Clactons.

8. See Woolf's letters, 1904, and her reversal, siding with Caroline's view of Leslie Stephen in *Moments of Being*. Robert Tod quotes a letter of Caroline's to Maitland from Cambridge University Library about his biography of Leslie Stephen: ''Julia's death laid bare the chasm between Leslie and me,'' and he suggests that Caroline was hurt that Leslie turned to Stella Duckworth for comfort. Caroline, for her part, was always trying to leap over the chasm to include agnostics like her brother in her religious philosophy. In October 1902 she wrote, ''Agnosticism with mystery at the heart of it seems another description of the 'rational mysticism' which is my favorite expression of my own ground'' (*Vision of Faith*, cxi). This seems to me to be an exact description of Virginia Woolf's mystical philosophy. On truth-telling in biography, see also Caroline Stephen's *Caroline Fox and Her Family* (Philadelphia: Longstreth, 1883). Caroline Stephen accepted the Quaker practice of not mourning the dead. I suspect this is what alienated her from Leslie Stephen in his lugubrious guilty raving over the deaths of his wives, though the same principle probably soothed Virginia considerably on the death of her father. Woolf's experience with both Quakers, Violet Dickinson and Caroline Stephen, provided a sympathetic background for her description of Roger Fry in her biography. But, unlike her aunt, she could not tell the truth about his domestic life, hence the cramped quality of the book. (While Bell calls Dickinson a Quaker, Robert Tod has been unable to find evidence of actual membership.)

9. James Fitzjames Stephen, *Liberty, Equality, Fraternity* (1873), new edition by R. J. White (Cambridge University Press, 1967). Fitzjames was an extraordinarily aggressive person even for his age and was called ''the Giant Grim.'' He ferociously attacked his enemies in print and thundered as a judge in the High Court. He defended punishment as a natural desire of men against their fellowmen and justified war and imperialism. In *Quaker Strongholds*, Caroline Stephen takes a brave stand against men like her brother and anticipates the pacifism of her niece Virginia. But the most important point in her discussion of Quaker pacifism (*Quaker Strongholds*, 134–43) constitutes a complete rebellion against her colonial administrator father and her brother Fitzjames, who codified the laws of India and England and justified war, violence, and punishment: ''we regard the opposing of violence by violence as a suicidal and hopeless method of proceeding; we feel, as Christians, that the weapons of our warfare are not carnal. . . . Would any one say that at the time of the Indian Mutiny the Governor-General of India ought not to have permitted the use of arms for the protection of the women and children? I doubt whether any Friend would be

found to maintain this. But it is equally to be remembered that no true Friend could well have occupied the position of Governor-General. No nation which had from the beginning of its history been thoroughly Christian could, I suppose, have found itself in the position which we occupied in India in 1857. . . . Had we been from the first a thoroughly Christian nation, our whole history must have been different, and would (as we Friends believe) have been infinitely nobler'' (*Quaker Strongholds,* 135, 136). Caroline Stephen goes on to argue that the roots of war and oppression are in material greed. It is a short step from this position to her niece's argument in *Three Guineas* that war and imperialism are derived from capitalism and patriarchy. John Bicknell points out that Leslie Stephen wrote some lives of women in the *DNB,* including Harriet Martineau, Mary Wollstonecraft, Elizabeth Elstab, and Eliza Craven. Caroline also agreed with Leslie's ''What Is Materialism?'' (*An Agnostic's Apology,* 1903 ed., 127–67, which also is the source of ''Think of a kitchen table then when you're not there,'' from *To the Lighthouse.*)

10. Denise Levertov, ''In Memory of Muriel Rukeyser,'' *In These Times* 26 March–1 April 1980.

11. See *The Simone Weil Reader,* ed. George A. Panichas (New York: David McKay, 1977), and Walter Benjamin, *Reflections,* ed. Peter Demetz (New York: Harcourt Brace Jovanovich, 1978).

12. ''I don't quite know how to convey to the perverse public that it is the house itself, not the entrance, which is the true Porch. What I like about the name is that it sounds plausible to the multitude and may be called 'academic,' while a smaller inner circle know what it means to me as shelter under which to sit beside the closed door, the opening of which, I trust, is to let me in to Home, a shelter I am so thankful to have reached'' (*Vision of Faith*). Aside from the fact that she would have been a fascinating novelist, Caroline makes reference to George Herbert's poem—though, given her more persistent imagery of light, she reminds one of Vaughan. The Porch as a woman's nunnery, with its glass doors opening onto an enclosed garden with a pear tree, and her fierce guarding of her privacy suggest Woolf's concept of ''a room of one's own.'' Katherine Stephen, principal of Newnham, boasted that she converted her conservative aunt to the cause of women's education once she had seen the girls' rooms at Newnham. This enclosed space surrounded by nature has an erotic charm for the woman who has had to live in the family or ''public'' space of a household. The place where one works, if work is a forbidden pleasure, is both erotic and chaste. This ''room of one's own'' recurs as a figure in women's novels.

13. The obituary is reprinted in the notes to my ''Thinking Back through Our Mothers,'' in *New Feminist Essays on Virginia Woolf.*

14. Virginia Woolf, L 1:144. Virginia was also irritated with her aunt, ''perpetually flowing with rather trivial talk, which nevertheless she takes great, and painful, care to express well and pronounce exquisitely. Also I disagree entirely with

her whole system of tolerance and resignation.''

15. Leslie Stephen, *The Mausoleum Book,* ed. Alan Bell (London: Oxford, 1977), 55. John Bicknell points out Leslie's loving concern for Milly in his letters to Julia.

16. See Rufus M. Jones, *The Later Periods of Quakerism,* vol. 2 (London: Macmillan, 1921), and Dr. T. Hodgkin's memoir in *The Vision of Faith.* Caroline Stephen's influence, while important, was not the dominant force among Victorian Quakers. Her mysticism was less influential than Rowntree's social philosophy.

17. Quoted in Jones, *Later Periods of Quakerism,* 968.

18. See Robert Tod's monograph.

19. For a discussion of Caroline Stephen's views on servants, see Martine Stemerick's dissertation, University of Texas, 1982.

20. ''Women and Politics,'' *Nineteenth Century* 61, no. 360 (February 1907); rejoinder in April, 61, no. 362; ''A Consultative Chamber for Women,'' *Nineteenth Century* 64, no. 382 (December 1908).

21. Jones, *Later Periods of Quakerism,* 969.

22. *Service of the Poor,* 249.

23. Ibid., 255.

24. Introduction to *Vision of Faith.*

25. Ibid.

26. *First Sir James Stephen,* 291.

27. See Sandra Gilbert's essay on ''Milton's Bogey'' in Sandra Gilbert and Susan Gubar, *The Madwoman in the Attic* (New Haven: Yale University Press, 1979).

28. For a fascinating aside on Scheherazade see Susan Gubar's '' 'The Blank Page' and the Issue of Female Creativity,'' *Critical Inquiry* (Writing and Sexual Difference, ed. Elizabeth Abel, 8, no. 2 (winter 1981): 243–63.

29. Catherine F. Smith, ''Jane Lead: The Feminist Mind and Art of a Seventeenth Century Protestant Mystic,'' in *Women of Spirit: Female Leadership,* in *The Jewish and Christian Traditions,* ed. Rosemary Ruether and Eleanor McLaughlin (New York: Simon and Schuster, 1979). See also Ruth Perry's ''The Veil of Chastity: Mary Astell's Feminism,'' *Studies in Eighteenth Century Culture,* vol. 9 (Madison: University of Wisconsin Press, 1979).

30. ''The Rhetoric of the Inward Light: An Examination of Extant Sermons Delivered by Early Quakers, 1671–1700,'' Ph.D. diss., University of Southern California, 1972.

31. ''Seventeenth Century Quaker Style,'' *PMLA* 71 (September 1956): 725–54.

32. Simone Weil's concept of the void is much the same. See Gilbert and Gubar, *Madwoman in the Attic.*

33. '' 'Inward' and 'Outward': A Study in Early Quaker Language,'' Friends Historical Society Pamphlet (London, 1962).

34. It may be argued that late-nineteenth-century rhetoric (in religious controver-

sy and legal discourse, which most affected Caroline Stephen) was as convoluted and elaborate as that of the seventeenth century, and women were under great restraint. Early Quaker doctrine, "Let your words be few," was "an indescribable relief." Richard Bauman, in several essays, in *For the Reputation of Truth: Politics, Religion and Conflict among the Pennsylvania Quakers, 1750–1800* (Baltimore: Johns Hopkins Press, 1971), and in his forthcoming *Let Your Words Be Few: The Symbolism of Speaking and Silence among the Seventeenth Century Quakers,* has analyzed the tension between speaking and silence among the early Quakers. A similar tension appears in Caroline Stephen's writing and in Woolf's novels, from the novel about silence of *A Voyage Out* to the gaps and "scraps, orts and fragments" of speech that make up *Between the Acts* and the unfinished sentences of the conversations in *The Years*. Bauman identifies the Quaker distinction between charismatic authority and traditional authority. Excluded from the ranks of educated men, Virginia Woolf, I believe, used these concepts of her aunt's religion as an artist. She listened to her own inner voices. Many feminists, including Adrienne Rich and Tillie Olsen, have remarked on women's connection and concern with silence and with being silenced and the feelings women writers have about breaking silence.

In "Speaking in the Light: The Role of the Quaker Minister" Bauman raises some interesting questions about the tension between speech and silence among the Quakers that seem to me to be applicable to women writers and especially to Virginia Woolf. The minister is on the edge of difficulty at all times under these conditions, for he must speak only from inspiration and a real experience of inner light; otherwise he is like any other preacher. The writer is also constrained to be original and plain—the only reason to break silence is to reveal truth. Paradoxically, then, speech is all the more valuable because it is limited—words and the Word are taken very seriously.

Virginia Liked
Elizabeth   *Alice Fox*

When Helen McAfee of the *Yale Review* suggested to Virginia Woolf that she write an essay on Queen Elizabeth, Woolf summarily rejected the idea: "The suggestion you make about an article on Queen Elizabeth is of course attractive; but I fear that I could not undertake it. My knowledge of English history is rudimentary in the extreme, and to write anything of interest about Elizabeth one would have to make a far more serious study of the time than I have leisure for" (L 5:20). That her time was taken up is certainly true; but we need not give much credence to statements made to American editors. Since at the time Woolf was in fact compiling the *Second Common Reader,* a volume that included her greatest concentration of essays alluding in one way or another to the queen, an article for the *Yale Review* would have taken little or no additional reading.

Woolf could easily have dashed off an essay on, for example, the nature of Elizabeth's personal contacts with her subjects, given her frequent notes on that topic up to 1932. She knew about Elizabeth's relationships with Sidney and with Raleigh: after giving the latter a commission to the West Indies, the queen recognized that conditions were so altered as to be unfavorable and sent him "letters of revocation, with commandement to relinquish (for his owne part) the intended attempt, and to leave the charge and conduct of all things" to others.[1] The queen knew these men personally, and she smiled on them if she guessed it would benefit the country or frowned if that seemed wise, given their personalities. Over the years Woolf noted cases of each—as, for example, the queen's allowing the feckless Thomas Stukely to amuse her at court but flatly denying his absurd request that she "sign over Ireland to himself & a friend." Similarly, she allowed Drake to outfit some ships to "go down to the coast of Spain and see what was going on," then like a good diplomat turned on him and apologized to the Spanish "for the burning of the transports at Cadiz as done against her orders."[2] Even with so politically insignificant a creature as the Cambridge scholar Gabriel Harvey, Elizabeth took the time to chat for a moment on her progress at Audley End, as Woolf mentions in an essay she was then writing for the *Second Common Reader* (CE 3:39). Elizabeth was a hardworking monarch whose contacts with her subjects Woolf could easily have documented.

In 1909 Woolf reviewed Frank Mumby's *The Girlhood of Queen Elizabeth,* a book that gave a full account and printed original documents to tell the story. Woolf also used for background material on the reign of Elizabeth Froude's *History of England.*[3] She approached Mumby in a spirit that differed somewhat from that of the Oxford man who wrote the introduction. He saw in the documents "illustrations of the environment of the Princess Elizabeth up to her accession to the Crown."[4] Woolf considered this environment a means to an end, the end being "the temperament of the woman who ruled England from the time she was twenty-five, and whose whims and qualities lay at the centre of the vast expansion of the Elizabethan age. If we can arrive at some knowledge of her nature and of the circumstances that formed it, we shall read our history with a greater understanding."[5]

The documents in Mumby included material missing from both Froude and the *Dictionary of National Biography* life of Elizabeth written during Leslie Stephen's editorship. In the DNB account, which is generally workmanlike enough, the headmaster and antiquarian Augustus Jessopp, using the evidence then available, said categorically that "there is nothing, absolutely nothing, to show that Elizabeth had a heart, nothing to indicate that she ever for a moment knew the thrill of sentiment, the storms of passion, or the throbs of tenderness." Such prose, and the underlying attitudes it betrays, would have been less than helpful to anyone trying to understand the temperament of a queen "whose whims and qualities lay at the centre of . . . the Elizabethan age." Woolf preferred Mumby's factual approach, especially his concentration on the imprisonment of Princess Elizabeth at Woodstock, where she was moved after a couple of months in the Tower in 1554. "Some of the most interesting letters in the collection," she said, "are the Bedingfield papers concerning her imprisonment at Woodstock" (176); and she devoted a long paragraph to Elizabeth's behavior at that time. Her conclusion was that the "cold and harsh feelings" universally ascribed to the queen were a necessary armor given the violence of the political machinations in which she was involved during her imprisonment, and indeed for the first twenty-five years of her life.

Elsewhere in the review Woolf continues to see Elizabeth from her own angle. Two points that emerge strongly from Mumby's treatment of the princess are her learnedness and her deliberate "policy, if not her inclination, to cultivate a taste and reputation for piety and sedateness" (63). Although Woolf does not utterly fail to mention Elizabeth's "piety" (she accurately alludes to her embroidering the covers of a Bible and requesting an English Bible, [176]), she soft-pedals it. She mentions that in Ascham's account of the sixteen-year-old Elizabeth there is evidence of the princess's enormous range of foreign languages (174–75), but she fails to mention that Ascham also praised Elizabeth's achievements in "religious instruction" (71). And in reporting Elizabeth's letter to Catherine Parr: "Not only knowing the effectuous will and fervent zeal, the which your highness hath towards all godly learning" (24), Woolf changes the word "godly" to "goodly" (174). The small error, and it may have been just that, makes of Elizabeth a person with whom Woolf could feel more natural sympathy.

The tone of the review is indeed entirely sympathetic. Woolf skillfully draws on Froude to see in Elizabeth's months in the Tower during her sister Mary's reign a warmer Elizabeth: "the memory of her unhappiness was bitter enough also to rouse in her the one 'sustained and generous feeling' of her life; she showed, Mr Froude thinks, true pity for the Queen of Scots when, years afterwards, she too lay in prison" (Froude, 586; Woolf, 175). And so it goes throughout the review: Woolf is fair to Elizabeth, in spite of the princess's overbearing and argumentive qualities, and yet she does not in any major way distort Mumby's book. It was a source of information such as Woolf always valued, letters by and about a woman, and she read it, as nearly as I can tell, in its entirety. The letters are often long-winded, yet she extracted from them the kernels of fact that made for an informed view of a lesser-known part of Elizabeth's life. At the same time she had an eye for beauty: in Il Schifanoya's letter to the Castellan of Mantua is this description of the coronation: "On the morning of Saturday the 14th, as in the afternoon Her Majesty was to make her state entry into London, the whole court so sparkled with jewels and gold collars, that they cleared the air, though it snowed a little" (Mumby, 299). This Woolf transmuted into an ending for her essay that places Elizabeth in just the right light: "a fine snow kept falling over her, but the gems and the golden collars shone clearly through the whiteness" (177).

Material from that book and from other works Woolf had read about

Elizabeth during the early days of reviewing was to remain with her throughout her life. And issues raised in Mumby were to be called to the forefront again some twenty years later.

But her crowning virtuosity was her command over the resources of words. When she wished, she could drive in her meaning up to the hilt with hammer blows of speech. . . . In private talk she could win a heart by some quick felicitous *brusquerie*; but her greatest moments came when, in public . . . the splendid sentences, following one another in a steady volubility, proclaimed the curious workings of her intellect with enthralling force. . . .

The tall and bony frame was subject to strange weaknesses . . . intolerable headaches laid her prone in agony. . . . Though her serious illnesses were few, a long succession of minor maladies, a host of morbid symptoms, held her contemporaries in alarmed suspense and have led some modern searchers to suspect that she received from her father an hereditary taint. Our knowledge, both of the laws of medicine and of the actual details of her disorders, is too limited to allow a definite conclusion, but at least it seems certain that, in spite of her prolonged and varied sufferings, [she] was fundamentally strong. . . . she took a particular pleasure in standing up. . . . Probably . . . most of her ailments were of an hysterical origin. That iron structure was prey to nerves. The hazards and anxieties in which she passed her life would have been enough in themselves to shake the health of the most vigorous; but it so happened that . . . there was a special cause for a neurotic condition: her sexual organisation was seriously warped.

From its very beginning her emotional life had been subjected to extraordinary strains. The intensely impressionable years of her early childhood had been for her a period of excitement, terror, and tragedy.

She was not yet fifteen [when a member by marriage of the family, twice her age, amused himself with her]. Bounding into her room in the early morning, he would fall upon her, while she was in her bed or just out of it, with peals of laughter, would seize her in his arms and tickle her, and slap her buttocks, and crack a ribald joke.

A deeply seated repugnance to the crucial act of intercourse may produce, when the possibility of it approaches, a condition of hysterical convulsion. . . . Everything points to the conclusion that such—the result of the profound psychological disturbances of her childhood—was the state.

Is this an analysis, oversimplified and indeed crude, of Virginia Stephen Woolf? Although it might be so viewed, it is in fact Lytton Strachey's account of Elizabeth in the second chapter of his *Elizabeth and Essex*.[6] Strachey's attitude toward the fourteen-year-old Elizabeth, whose stepfather, a man in his early thirties, seized her, tickled her, and (in Strachey's version) slapped her on the buttocks, can be gathered from his decision that "the looks and the ways of Thomas Seymour had delighted her" (21).

There are other ways to handle the presumed facts of the case, one that of the DNB:

> there came rumours that Seymour had availed himself of his position to indulge in familiarities with the princess which would have been unseemly towards a child of six, and were wholly inexcusable towards a young lady whom he had actually offered to make his wife a few weeks before.

After Catherine Parr's death, and the continued advances of "her worthless husband" Seymour toward Elizabeth, Seymour was imprisoned. But Elizabeth

> had been in some way implicated in the doings of her suitor, the principal persons of her household were arrested also, and she herself was kept under surveillance. . . . Then followed examinations and confessions on the part of her servants in the Tower—hearsay stories, backstairs gossip, and all the vulgar tattle of waiting-maids and lackeys. Then the princess herself was questioned. There was nothing to be got from her that did not tend to weaken confidence in the so-called evidence that had been carefully compiled. . . . Seymour was brought to the block on 20 March 1549. When they told Elizabeth she did not betray emotion. "This day died a man with much wit and very little judgment," she said, and passed on.

Woolf would have seen in the DNB's attenuation of the matter a pargeter busily at work. In Mumby's *The Girlhood of Queen Elizabeth* she found a rather different account: Mumby felt that Elizabeth's morals, and the marriage of Catherine Parr and Thomas Seymour, suffered from her remaining in their home. A governess testified that Seymour went into Elizabeth's room "and if she were up he would bid her good morrow, and ax how she did, and strike her on the back familiarly." Once he even tried—unsuccessfully—to kiss Elizabeth; and twice the queen and Seymour together tickled her in bed. The queen "realized her folly when she surprised her husband and Elizabeth alone one day—Elizabeth in his arms'' (34–35). Mumby felt there was probably ''nothing worse than unseemly romping in the conduct of Seymour''; but that he ''seems to have kindled a spark of real affection'' in Elizabeth because of her ''parentage and precociousness'' (37–38).

Although one might accuse Mumby of other things, he was no pargeter. Nor was Woolf. In her review of his book she mentions Elizabeth's ''serious flirtation'' with Seymour. But, far from belaboring what she calls Elizabeth's ''precocious love-making,'' Woolf finds matter for sympathy in an area on which Mumby had not thought to comment: ''Yet, though Elizabeth was forward enough according to her governess, it seems pitiable that a girl of that age should have her feelings made the subject of inquisition by a council of noblemen'' (174). Years later, when Strachey elaborated on the bedroom scenes with details of his own invention and decided that Elizabeth had been ''delighted,'' it must surely have struck Woolf as another sitting of that council.

Strachey's dwelling on parts of Elizabeth's life that bear some similarity to Woolf's, coupled with his facile psychologizing, could well have alienated her. Their meetings while he was researching and writing the biography probably alerted Woolf to the annoyance she would feel on reading it. It would certainly have been clear to her that the book promised to be antifeminist, as it turned out to be.[7] She wrote Quentin Bell, apparently in anticipation of the immense popularity the book would enjoy, that she would not read it, and thus ''wear a glory round my head'' (letter 1964, 22 November 1928).

Of course she did read *Elizabeth and Essex,* and six days later noted in her diary that it was a ''lively superficial meretricious book'' (DVW 3:208). She could not say anything to Strachey about it when they met a few months later: ''the spectre of Queen Eth stands between us. With the sensibility of an author he knows what I dont deny; and wont ask me; so we keep to trifles'' (letter 2002, 15 February 1929). But she had just written Hugh Walpole that she did not in fact ''much care for Elizabeth and Essex—thats not the sort of imagination he has—he becomes all purple and gold, like the cheaper effects at the Pantomime: style to match; dum-dum-dum. Its odd how bad it is compared with the others (but no doubt I'm up a tree of my own and see this wrong)'' (letter 1997, 10 February 1929).

If she was ''up a tree'' of her own, and she could have been because of the similarities in experience and psychological orientation revealed in Strachey's crude analysis of the queen, she nonetheless had firm critical bases for her rejection of the book. Strachey's imagination does indeed tend to ''purple and gold,'' and his style is often annoying. But, most important, he fails to bring alive a remarkable woman, and one is neither edified nor entertained, except sporadically, in reading the book today.

Within approximately two weeks of reading *Elizabeth and Essex,* Woolf decided to have her own say about the queen. At first—if one can glean so much from an offhand remark to a friend—she genuinely contemplated ''a little article on Queen Elizabeth's nose for *Eve*'' (letter 1868, 6 March 1928). I believe the genesis of this idea was her reading, in *Ben Jonson's Talks with Drummond,* that ''Queen Elizabeth never saw her self after she became old in a true Glass. they painted her & sometymes would vermilion her nose.''[8] But an essay stressing Elizabeth's unwillingness to see herself accurately would have been, on the heels of Strachey's book, adding insult to injury. Woolf wrote instead about the wax effigy of the queen at Westminster Abbey, dominating the Islip Chapel ''as she once dominated England.''

> Leaning a little forward so that she seems to beckon you to come to her, she stands, holding her sceptre in one hand, her orb in the other. It is a drawn, anguished figure, with the pursed look of someone who goes in perpetual dread of poison or of trap; yet forever braces herself to meet the terror unflinchingly. Her eyes are wide and vigilant; her nose thin as the beak of a hawk; her lips shut tight; her eyebrows arched; only the jowl gives the fine-drawn face its massiveness. The orb and sceptre are held in the long thin hands of an artist, as if the fingers thrilled at the touch of them. She is immensely intellectual, suffering, and tyrannical. She will not allow one to look elsewhere.[9]

It is a brilliant evocation of the queen, and a needed antidote to Strachey's own waxwork figure. Although the essay is brief, in it Woolf raises even a wax effigy to the status of art. One thinks of the aesthetic effect of Wallace Stevens's jar in Tennessee, for the waxwork of the queen is a ''presence'' that seems to control the abbey's ''incoherence'' (206). The power of the figure of Queen Elizabeth in the essay derives from Woolf's imaginative grasp of the queen's life.

Orlando, written with the same jeu d'esprit as ''The Waxworks at the Abbey,'' draws on the same vision of the queen. Orlando sees the ''memorable hand'' of Queen Elizabeth,

> a thin hand with long fingers always curling as if round orb or sceptre; a nervous, crabbed, sickly hand; a commanding hand; a hand that had only to raise itself for a head to fall; a hand, he guessed, attached to an old body

that smelt like a cupboard in which furs are kept in camphor; which body was yet caparisoned in all sorts of brocades and gems; and held itself very upright though perhaps in pain from sciatica; and never flinched though strung together by a thousand fears; and the Queen's eyes were light yellow. (O 23)

This queen looks down at Orlando with eyes that "were always, if the waxworks at the Abbey are to be trusted, wide open" (23). The waxwork of the queen, then, had for Woolf when she wrote both essay and novel the significance of a work of art: it embodied a symbolic truth. Strachey's overwrought, often inaccurate, superficial portrait had met its match.

In "The Art of Biography," which she wrote seven years after Lytton Strachey's death, Woolf was still working out the problem of his failure in *Elizabeth and Essex*. Now she attributed it to the nature of biography rather than, as in her earlier thinking about the book, to the nature of the biographer. She felt that too little was known about Elizabeth for a "straight" biography, while at the same time too much was known for an imaginative one. The result was neither one thing nor another. With characteristic generosity, then, Woolf bolstered the memory of Lytton Strachey, agreeing with him that Elizabethans were "strange spirits." "The whole of Elizabeth's life," she said, "was lived behind a veil" (CE 4:224–25). Friendship, combined with her unique difficulties in writing *Roger Fry*, probably prompted Woolf to venture so sweeping a statement. For no veil covered one aspect of Elizabeth's life, at any rate, and that was her active role in the voyages of discovery. Woolf had been reading about it since she was a child and, with reviews in mind, taking notes from as early as the first decade of the century. She gathered a great deal of material on the voyagers of the sixteenth century, and on Elizabeth as the monarch whose men went down to the sea in ships, some to be captured, some to die, some to return home laden with stories and treasure.

In 1906, for example, Woolf jotted down in her reading notes, "Condition of discovery: must go as Pirates: Queen cd. not acknowledge it."[10] The passage on which she made this comment indicated that, if the pirates won their battles, "The Crown would gladly accept a share in the spoil; if they lost, they knew what doom to expect. It is surely a high tribute to Elizabeth, and to the trust and love she inspired in her subjects, that they accepted these conditions without a murmur." This sort of positive association of Elizabeth with the voyagers sounds in Woolf's essay on Sir Walter Raleigh, where she quotes that Elizabethan's tribute to his queen: "For I thought it to belong unto the honour of our Prince & Nation, that a few Ilanders should not think any advantage great enough, against a fleet set forth by Q. Elizabeth'' (CE 3:28).

Such links between Elizabeth and the voyagers were thus firm from the start. But one, forged very possibly as early as Woolf's first reading of Hakluyt's *Voyages,* in 1897, but demonstrably no later than the rereading of 1918, remained in Woolf's mind with a peculiar tenacity thereafter, to the end of her days. It reminds one of Woolf's memory of Vita Sackville-West in the fishmonger's shop, and like it is clearly a moment of vision. The vision grew out of two separate elements. The first of these is a passage describing mariners, "all apparelled in Watchet or skie coloured cloth," rowing to Greenwich

> (where the Court then lay) presently upon the newes thereof, the Courtiers came running out, and the common people flockt together, standing very thick upon the shoare: the privie Counsel, they lookt out at the windowes of the Court, and the rest ranne up to the toppes of the towers: the shippes hereupon discharge their Ordinance . . . and the Mariners, they shouted.[11]

In her essay "Trafficks and Discoveries," in the *Times Literary Supplement* of 12 December 1918, Woolf quotes from this passage, including the lines about the Privy Council—all as it should be. But in a curious transformation she moved the entire scene from its proper date, 1553, to the reign of Elizabeth—at least five years later. It was an imaginative purloining, for Woolf shifted these facts to tally with her own conception of what was in the final analysis truer, and that was not Edward's, but rather Elizabeth's, central role in the voyages of discovery. Other material from the same reading of Hakluyt provided the support for that conception: the queen's granting of patents for monopolies; her magnificent perfumed letters to foreign rulers; her shrewd handling of the privateers; and so on. More important, however, that reading of Hakluyt supplied a second passage that, coupled with the one I have just cited, formed the completed vision. Frobisher's first voyage to the Northwest, in 1576, began thus:

> The 8. day being Friday, about 12 of the clocke we wayed at Detford, and set saile all three of us, and bare downe by the Court, where we shotte off our ordinance and made the best shew we could: Her Majestie beholding the same, commended it, and bade us farewell, with shaking her hand at us out of the window.[12]

The scene would recur in Woolf's imagination over the years. In the essay "Reading" (1919), she remarks that

> Elizabeth, of all our kings and queens, seems most fit for that gesture which bids the great sailors farewell, or welcomes them home to her presence again, her imagination still lusting for the strange tales they bring her. (CE 2:17)

The description leads naturally to that other scene of the courtiers at the palace windows at Greenwich, watching the voyagers set out (18). The two scenes were becoming a single entity in Woolf's mind. Her essay on the voyagers for the *First Common Reader,* "The Elizabethan Lumber Room," flatly states that the scene of the Privy Council looking out of the windows at Greenwich in fact transpired "in the reign of Queen Elizabeth" (CE 1:46).

In a holograph draft of this essay written on 18 January 1925, the vision asserts itself in the opening paragraph:

> To read in these magnificent books* is to set out in one of those little ships which were no bigger than a nobleman's yacht. . . . That is the charm of them—vastness & strangeness, & the sea booming & swinging; &, for us, too, the curiosity of being afloat with Elizabethans—men who might have seen Shakespeare, who had seen Elizabeth waving her hand when they raised anchor at Greenwich.[13]

A monarch, as Woolf well knew, is under the necessity of "conforming to an unnatural standard, so that it is only at rare moments that one can see how he behaves as an individual."[14] And if we are prevented from knowing monarchs by the peculiarity of their position, we are further frustrated by their failure to write about their personal lives. Thus it is, said Woolf, that "there is practically no evidence available by which we can guess at the feelings of the highest in the land. What does a King feel? What does a Duke think? We cannot say" (CE 1:219). Quite true; but one might ask a slightly different question: What does a queen feel? Woolf was able to venture one guess on this subject, based on her apparent assumption that women, regardless of rank, must share certain ways of looking at themselves and at the world. Thus she was able to exhibit sympathy for the young Elizabeth when her most private feelings and actions were scrutinized by a body of men. As mentioned above, she found "pitiable" the council's examination of the princess's "precocious love-making." Woolf attributed another feeling to the queen, this one based on a shared interest in narrative and adventure: she assumed that Elizabeth eagerly anticipated hearing stories brought back to her by the voyagers.

But beyond these presumably shared feelings, Woolf recognized the difficulty of knowing what a queen felt. Yet the difficulty need not be viewed negatively. Were Woolf to have known, or even to have believed that she knew, precisely what Elizabeth felt, the gain in knowledge would probably have occasioned a loss as well. In her satiric essay "Royalty," Woolf noted the public's chagrin in discovering, as a result of the crown crisis of the thirties, that members of the royal family had feelings "like ours" (CE 4:213). The discovery was for a time fatal to veneration of royalty, since the public needs to feel that the beautiful people surrounded by pomp and circumstance are "immune from human weakness" (215). Thus separated from ordinary people, the monarch "gives us a Paradise to inhabit" (212). It follows that the humanization of any monarch would precipitate another paradise lost. The achievements of an extraordinary monarch, on the other hand, would in a sense legitimize both the "love of spectacle" and the "need for a vicarious existence" that Woolf noted were the components of the public's delight in royalty. Such was the case, I believe, in her own lifelong adulation of Queen Elizabeth. If she knew too little about the queen's feelings to write an essay for the *Yale Review*, she knew all she needed to know of Elizabeth's achievements to admire her.

Woolf tested that admiration several times by reducing Elizabeth to the least common denominator. She was, after all, an Elizabethan, presumably with the same negligence toward personal hygiene, the same bad table manners as her subjects. We all know stories of meats spiced to cover their decay, of streets running with excrement, of clothes heavily perfumed to hide body odor, of bones thrown at table to waiting dogs. Why should Elizabeth not be part of such a scene? "After all," Woolf commented in the midst of a review of an American novel, "though Queen Elizabeth was a model of vigour she was also a dirty old woman, dabbling her fingers in the gravy, and amenable, one supposes, to pains and pleasures only of the most direct kind."[15] So offensive was this test-case queen that Woolf speculated on the necessity of our absenting ourselves had we been invited to one of her dinners. Her crudeness of both behavior and feeling might simply have been too much for us.[16] In the essay "Reading," which I mentioned above, it is a crude woman indeed who

raps out her favourite oath as Lord Herbert of Cherbury heard it . . . she shows a masculine and rather repulsive vigour. Perhaps, under all that stiff brocade, she has not washed her shrivelled old body? She breakfasts off beer and meat and handles the bones with fingers rough with rubies. It may be so, yet. . . .(CE 2:17)

There is always the "yet." Elizabeth failed the test, "yet . . ." Woolf's admiration was undiminished. It was in the reign of Elizabeth that both exploration and literature flourished in England as they had not done before and, arguably, were not to do again. They flourished in part because there was on the throne a woman of great learning, shrewdness, intelligence, and independence. As we saw earlier, Woolf envisaged Elizabeth "at the centre of the vast expansion of the Elizabethan age." Elizabeth worked at uniting a country torn by religious conflict; she worked at establishing an advantageous position for her country, politically and financially, among the nations of Europe. As Froude acknowledged in the *History,* in a passage from which Woolf had extracted another quotation years earlier, Elizabeth "had a proper contempt . . . for idle luxury and indulgence. She lived simply, worked hard" (583). In *Three Guineas* Woolf reflects this proper emphasis on work: she speaks of a young woman's aspirations to attend Queen's College, "where the daughters of educated men enjoy the happiness not of ladies 'but of Queens—Work and independence!' " (TG 204). Woolf saw Queen Elizabeth as the great exemplar of work and independence.

In the pageant in *Between the Acts* it is a working woman who portrays Queen Elizabeth—Eliza Clark, "licensed to sell tobacco"—a commodity, by the way, introduced into England during Elizabeth's reign. Mrs. Clark "could reach a flitch of bacon or haul a tub of oil with one sweep of her arm in the shop" (BA 83). Here is the Elizabeth of unaristocratic associations and "masculine vigour"; and "yet. . . ." In "Reading" Woolf followed that "yet" with a statement I have already quoted, but that bears repeating: "yet Elizabeth, of all our kings and queens, seems most fit for that gesture which bids the great sailors farewell, or welcomes them home to her presence again, her imagination still lusting for the strange tales they bring her" (CE 2:17). In *Between the Acts* Eliza(beth) calls herself

> Mistress of ships and bearded men
> Hawkins, Frobisher, Drake,
> Tumbling their oranges, ingots of silver,
> Cargoes of diamonds, ducats of gold,
> Down on the jetty, there in the west land—

The ashen haired babe
(she stretched out her swarthy, muscular arm)
Stretched his arm in contentment
As home from the Isles came
The sea-faring men.

                                                              (84–85)

These two passages, from the beginning and the end of the speech, physically enclose the military, architectural, and literary achievements of Elizabeth's reign. They symbolize what can be done by a hardworking, independent woman; and they are a tribute from another hardworking, independent woman.

This tribute in the last novel Woolf was to write is echoed on a holograph sheet among the papers written during her last year of life. At the top of the page Woolf wrote, "People one wd have liked to have met." There is under that heading only one entry, which I shall quote in its entirety:

Queen Elizabeth. Not face to face; but with a pane of glass between us. [Not in her palace; but] At Greenwich: [pacing up & d] The first word wd be awkward About the Tower perhaps. The 2nd. . . .[17]

It is not difficult to complete the thought. Woolf wanted to see Elizabeth not in her palace, attractive though that waxwork figure had always been, but as "mistress of ships and bearded men." For the location, at Greenwich, brings to mind Woolf's moment of vision: the great queen bidding farewell to men setting out, in ships no larger than a modern yacht, on their voyages of discovery.[18]

Notes

1. Woolf noted the page in *Hakluyt's Collection of the Early Voyages, Travels, and Discoveries of the English Nation,* 3 vols. (London: R. H. Evans, 1809–10), 3:9, with the comment, "E. withdraws her consent to R's going: he misunderstands." Sussex MHP/B2d, fol. 28. For Sidney, see Virginia Woolf, CE 1:19.

I am grateful to Quentin Bell and Angelica Garnett for permission to quote from unpublished Woolf materials, as well as to the University of Sussex Library (here, and hereafter, Sussex) and the Henry W. and Albert A. Berg Collection, the New York Public Library, Astor, Lenox and Tilden Foundations (hereafter Berg) for permission to cite passages from their Woolf holographs and typescripts.

2. Woolf's notes on James Anthony Froude, *English Seamen in the Sixteenth Century* (London: Longmans, Green, 1901), 46, 224, 241; Sussex MHP/B2d, fols. 30–31.

3. James Anthony Froude, *History of England from the Fall of Wolsey to the Defeat of the Spanish Armada,* 12 vols. (New York: Charles Scribner's Sons, 1890), vol. 12, especially 581–87.

4. R. S. Rait, introduction to *The Girlhood of Queen Elizabeth: A Narrative in Contemporary Letters,* by Frank Mumby (London: Constable, 1909), xix.

5. "The Girlhood of Queen Elizabeth," *TLS,* 30 December 1909, 516; reprinted in B&P 174.

6. *Elizabeth and Essex: A Tragic History* (New York: Harcourt Brace, 1928), 18, 19–20, 21, 24.

7. For example, Strachey says in praise of Elizabeth (13): "Only a woman could have shuffled so shamelessly, only a woman could have abandoned with such unscrupulous completeness the last shreds not only of consistency, but of dignity, honour, and common decency, in order to escape the appalling necessity of having, really and truly, to make up her mind. Yet it is true that a woman's evasiveness was not enough; male courage, male energy were needed."

8. Berg, Holograph Reading Notes, vol. 25, fol. 52.

9. "Waxworks at the Abbey," *New Republic,* 11 April 1928; *Eve,* 23 May 1928; reprinted in CE 4:205.

10. Sussex MHP/Bla, fol. 146, dated 23 March 1906. The source is Walter Raleigh, *The English Voyages of the Sixteenth Century* (Glasgow: James MacLehose, 1906), 66.

11. *Hakluyt's Collection,* 1:272; Woolf's note on the passage, Sussex MHP/B2d, fol. 23.

12. *Hakluyt's Collection,* 3:52–53; Woolf's note on the passage ("The Queen waving her hand to Frobisher"), Sussex MHP/B2d, fol. 28.

13. Berg; Mrs. Dalloway (corrections). Holograph, in notebook dated 52 Tavistock Sq., 22 November 1924, fol. 107. Woolf's asterisk indicates a footnote to Hakluyt.

14. "The Girlhood of Queen Elizabeth," B&P 173. "To see the pageant [of royalty] is strange enough, but it is far stranger to look into the mind of one of the great actors themselves and to watch the normal human being struggling, an ant laden with a pebble, beneath the super-human burden laid upon it by its fellows."

15. "The Pursuit of Beauty," review of *Linda Condon,* by Joseph Hergesheimer, *TLS,* 8 July 1920; reprinted in *Contemporary Writers,* ed. Jean Guiguet (New York: Harcourt Brace Jovanovich, 1965), 113.

16. "Rambling round Evelyn," reprinted in CE 3:46. We might also "have

found it necessary to leave the room because of Shakespeare's habits.'' One thinks of Shakespeare as he appears in *Orlando,* "a rather fat, rather shabby man, whose ruff was a thought dirty'' (21).

17. Berg; typescript fragment of "Anon,'' unsigned, [late 1940], holograph fragment, 8ᵛ. Square brackets in text indicate Woolf's deletions.

18. I elaborate on many of the points made in this essay in my forthcoming book on Woolf and the Elizabethans.

Fathers in General:
The Patriarchy in
Virginia Woolf's Fiction *Beverly Ann Schlack*

> *The struggle with her own father was
> over. But the struggle with fathers in
> general, with the patriarchy itself, was
> deferred to another place and another
> time.*
>
> Three Guineas[1]

A Room of One's Own and *Three Guineas* express directly, polemically, and
with footnotes Woolf's feminist metaphysics of society as patriarchy. Yet the
ways this conviction was reshaped aesthetically by the urges and demands
of writing strictly imaginative fiction have not been thoroughly examined.
Feminism was undoubtedly a perspective that expanded Woolf's consciousness of life and her imaginative works with both psychological and
political metaphors unavailable to nonfeminist writers. Transformed by vision and imagination, feminism is solidly present in all her works. Not to see
that is to fall victim to *narrow* interpretive approaches (the very charge leveled
by antifeminists against feminist criticism of Woolf!) that make Woolf's
politics and art mutually exclusive, fracturing the symbiotic, simultaneous
connections she wanted from life and literature, private and public worlds.
At the age of twenty-four, Woolf was arguing against the very separation to
which subsequent critics sometimes subjected her work: "if you must put
books on one side and life on 't other, each is a poor and bloodless thing. But
my theory is that they mix indistinguishably" (L 1:272).[2] This is, therefore,
a writer who will try to walk the art/politics tightrope in her works of vision
and of fact. To have Woolf whole, we must have *both* fiction and feminism,
interacting subtly and reinforcing one another.

   In the novels written before and after *A Room of One's Own* and *Three
Guineas,* wherein Woolf offers what has been called "an anatomy of the sins
of the fathers,"[3] there is a veritable portrait gallery of male characters who
abuse their positions of authority. Since the traditional psychological pattern
of dominance/submission is at its most fundamental in family life, the
primary villains are fathers, brothers, and husbands. But since the family is

the state, society, culture in miniature, there are surrogate villains as well. These Woolf saw as "the fathers in public, massed together in societies, in professions" (TG 138).[4] The private and public spheres "are inseparably connected; the tyrannies and servilities of the one are the tyrannies and ser- vilities of the other" (TG 142). Good Christians, intellectuals and critics, scholars and professors, politicians, devoted fathers—all the privileged haves of society—are very busy in Woolf's fictional world, keeping the have-not women in their deprived places. It is astonishing, once looked at in detail, how many of the nominally *nice* characters who are supposed to know better than chauvinism are not (nice) and do not (know better).

The Family

Fathers in Woolf's fiction are oppressive or ineffectual. In either case they manage to burden, demean, or disappoint their women. The father of the heroine in Woolf's first novel—a novel begun after the death of her own father freed her to write fiction[5]—is reported to have bullied his late wife Theresa and inflicted upon his daughter Rachel "nameless atrocities" (VO 24). The use of a word like *atrocities* makes this father-daughter relationship a battlefield, and Willoughby Vinrace, though scarcely present in the action of *The Voyage Out,* is the first in a long line of portraits of the father as oppressor.

In *Night and Day* Katharine Hilbery struggles under the yoke of *two* fathers (one regular/alive, one grand/dead) who dictate the shape of her life. The book about poet Richard Alardyce is "a duty that they [Katharine and her mother] owed the world."[6] Woolf's own editorial chores were strikingly similar to Katharine's task of keeping the manuscripts in order: "I am get- ting through my copy—and now I have to go through 2 vols. of extracts from Father's and Mother's letters to each other" (L 1:148). "I must toil at the letters," Woolf says of Sir Leslie's correspondence (L 1:155); or she com- plains, "My life here is practically spent with old letters" (152). Very like her creator, Katharine puts together "a string of names and dates" (37) and sits "with faded papers before her" (40), accomplishing the female task of presenting male excellence to the world.

There is also Sir Francis, alias "that old Turk" (221), who broods over his less than star-spangled career in the foreign service at the expense of the females around him. Since he has inflicted upon his daughter the comically dreadful name of Euphemia, the pointed irony of the Greek etymology simp- ly adds insult to injury, for Euphemia functions as her father's secretary-drudge: "the prime of her life was being rapidly consumed by her father. To her he dictated the memoirs which were to avenge his memory, and she had to assure him constantly that his treatment had been a disgrace" (217).

Much later in her career, Woolf would still be chronicling the fate of daughters assisting their fathers' writing chores. In *The Years,* Kitty recalls how "an awkward brush with her arm" spilled ink over her father's historical manuscript. After that "accident," she can still remember "him say with his usual courteous irony, 'Nature did not intend you to be a scholar, my dear,' as he applied the blotting paper" (81).[7]

Mr. Hilbery, another of those tyrant-fathers who *expect* blood sacrifice from the females in the family,[8] is an important source of his daughter's suppressed but surprisingly strong rage. When her angry impotence does break through to the surface, Katharine acknowledges a desire to beat people down, then softens it presentably to " 'I only mean,' she corrected herself, 'that I want to assert myself and it's difficult, if one hasn't a profession' " (54).[9] However, financial support as justification for male dominance is a "justification" dismissed by Woolf in the opening of chapter 33:

> Considering that Mr. Hilbery lived in a house which was accurately numbered in order with its fellows, and that he filled up forms, paid rent, and had seven more years of tenancy to run, he had an excuse for laying down laws for the conduct of those who lived in his house, and this excuse, though profoundly inadequate, he found useful. (506)

Mr. Hilbery is, oxymoronically enough, a mild tyrant,[10] distanced from mundane reality and "inclined to take the easiest view of his responsibilities" (494). When others come to him with their tangled skeins of romance, love, and marriage, Hilbery examines his fingernails and "imperturbably" remarks, "It's a little too complicated for me to take in all at once, I confess" (491). He sees "no way out until Katharine herself came to his help" (492), and his many anxieties merely tempt him "to ask Katharine to solve [them] for him" (495). He reacts to Katharine's engagement announcement with faintly Freudian distaste,[11] delivers himself of a curt response ("I hope you'll deserve her"), and leaves the room. This behavior leaves "in the minds of the women, a sense, half of awe, half of amusement, at the extravagant, inconsiderate male, outraged somehow and gone bellowing to his lair with a roar" (530). The general condition beyond this particular novelistic incident is documented by the narration, which insists that the father's outraged roar "still sometimes reverberates in the most polished of drawing rooms" (530).

Indeed, "the great Victorian fight between the victims of the patriarchal system and the patriarchs [is the fight] of the daughters against the fathers" (TG 64).

In *To the Lighthouse* the father-daughter struggle is rendered within the context of childhood. The word Cam and James use for Mr. Ramsay's authority is *tyranny*,[12] which they resist with all the hostility of the coerced ("They hoped he would be thwarted. They hoped the whole expedition would fail," 243).[13] Cam's feeling of admiring pride for her father's brave and adventurous spirit is constantly mitigated by the omnipresence of his autocratic tyranny: "Their [hers and James's] grievance weighed them down. They had been forced; they had been bidden. He had borne them down once more with his gloom and his authority, making them do his bidding" (246). Cam's perpetual problem as daughter is "to resist his entreaty" (251) by remembering, always, the iron-handed oppression. Woolf herself never forgot the way her own father presumed upon his daughters; she wrote a pre-*Lighthouse* reminiscence that echoes Cam's feelings:

> he [Leslie Stephen] was quite prepared to take Vanessa for his next victim. . . . We made him the type of all that we hated in our lives; he was the tyrant of inconceivable selfishness. . . . We were bitter, harsh, and to a great extent, unjust; but even now it seems to me that there was some truth in our complaint. (MB 56)

The oedipal dimension of Cam's feelings for Mr. Ramsay is given by Woolf when Cam looks at her brother and thinks "you're not exposed to it, to this pressure and division of feeling, this extraordinary temptation" (252–53). Against his immense attraction, described as both physical and psychological, there is still "that crass blindness and tyranny of his which had poisoned her childhood and raised bitter storms." She cannot forget his "insolence" and "his dominance: his 'Submit to me' " (253). Moreover, the dramatic moment at which James's oedipal conflicts are put to rest by Mr. Ramsay's proud praise is a triumph Cam cannot share: "There! Cam thought. . . . You've got it at last. . . . you've got it now" (306).

Flush: A Biography is fantasy feminism in which Elizabeth Barrett's escape equals a victory over onerous patriarchy. Both Flush and his mistress have been kept on a very short leash; both breathe with difficulty "in the pale greenish gloom" (14) of Victorian bedroom-prisons; both are, ultimately, liberated. "Were they about to escape together from this awful world of dog-stealers and tyrants?" (69) the narration asks rhetorically, neatly coupling dognappers and fathers. Elsewhere Woolf wrote of Elizabeth Barrett that "she had been immured by the tyranny of her father";[14] in *Flush* she actualizes Mr. Barrett through the dog's brute senses: a knock at the door is "no tap of enquiry but a demand for admittance"; "the blackest, the most formidable of elderly men" enters the room and observes whether "his commands [had] been obeyed." Woolf likens Flush's terror to that of a savage shuddering "when the thunder growls and he hears the voice of God" (29). It is original; it is full of humor; it is an oblique portrait of the rule by fear of a tyrant-father.[15]

In *To the Lighthouse* Cam felt the simultaneous pull of being both daughter and sister: "Her brother was most god-like, her father most suppliant. And to which did she yield, she thought, sitting between them" (251). According to Woolf, the brother-sister relationship simply repeats the sacrificial essence of the daughter's relation to her father.[16] Society has replaced "the private brother" with "a monstrous male, . . . [who] enjoys the dubious pleasures of power and dominion" (TG 105). Brothers, inheriting the patriarchal world, perpetuate the sins of the fathers; the brother-sister relation becomes a tainted one of "You shall not learn; you shall not earn;[17] you shall not—" (TG 105).

Long before Arthur's Education Fund in *Three Guineas,*[18] Terence Hewet was telling Rachel Vinrace: "And then, of course, the daughters have to give way to the sons; the sons have to be educated" (VO 212). On the subject of the "sacred career" of the sons-brothers, Hewet observes: "Can't you imagine the family conclaves, and the sister told to run out and feed the rabbits. . . . No one takes her seriously, poor dear. She feeds the rabbits" (213). From feeding the rabbits to Arthur's Education Fund there is little progress.

When the oppressed daughter-sister moves on to the role of wife, she finds marriage saddled with the patriarchal evils of the first, primary family. Woolf's lover-husband figures exhibit dual potentials for positive unity (through love and companionship) and negative tyranny. If the lover or husband resembles the father, he is the familiar tyrant; if he offers liberation from the primal tyrant he is a species of savior—as the separate cases of Mr. Barrett and Robert Borwning in *Flush* indicate. At first the imposed shadow of the father hangs over Elizabeth and Browning,[19] until the latter becomes the saving husband who frees the daughter from the paternal prison. Several of Woolf's earlier works approximate the same dilemma: Will marital union *per se* prove antithetical to a woman's personal independence and development? This is Katharine Hilbery's worry, as it was Rachel's before her. If the husband becomes a second father, the major forms of despotism (overtly or mildly tyrannical) will be reinstituted all over again, and the oppressed daughter merely graduates into the oppressed wife.[20]

In *Mrs. Dalloway*, Richard Dalloway echoes the mild-mannered tyranny that readers encountered earlier in Mr. Hilbery. "Simple by nature, and undebauched" (185), even Dalloway can invoke the inherent authority of the exacting husband, and he does not hesitate to do so: "No decent man *ought to let* his wife visit a deceased wife's sister" (11, italics mine). Mr. Ramsay of *To the Lighthouse* is the despotic husband full-blown. One wonders if the encoded message of his surname (the *ram says*) was meant by Woolf to conjure subliminal visions of the supreme male bull decreeing commands to his lesser females. Lily Briscoe experiences Ramsay as "petty, selfish, vain, egotistical; he is spoilt; he is a tyrant; he wears Mrs. Ramsay to death" (40). From his wife's point of view, it is the universal condition of "the subjection of all wives . . . to their husband's labours" (20). However noble as philosopher, Mr. Ramsay "pursues truth with such astonishing lack of consideration for other people's feelings, . . . so wantonly, so brutally, [it] was to her so horrible an outrage of human decency" (51). For Mrs. Ramsay "the beak of brass, barren and bare" (58) is Ramsay's essence, a harsh metaphor of domination leaving little doubt of how he is experienced by the opposite sex, whatever his admirable qualities as a scholar and intellectual.

Ramsay is given to exaggerating his wife's "ignorance, her simplicity, for he *liked to think* that she was not clever" (182, italics mine), very much as his disciple Tansley *chooses to believe* that women cannot be artists. Ramsay the Terrible is a tyrant variously described as one who *forces* (225) women to give him attention, who *demands* (228) sympathy, who *commands* (250) pity or praise. In his coercive emotional blackmail of females, he is not above absurdly petty acting: "he had assumed a pose of extreme decrepitude; he even tottered a little as he stood there . . . all the time he was feeling, think of me, think of me" (227).

Ramsay is also an intellectual sexist whose premises move too easily from particular to general, damning all women on the basis of one example. In a single sentence, he contemplates his wife's inadequacy ("the extraordinary irrationality of her remark"), then enlarges this "fact," one mere comma beyond, to generalizations about the essence of the entire sex: "the folly of women's minds enraged him." He stamps and swears "Damn you!" (50)—not, of course, "extraordinary irrationality" of behavior when *he* does it—and goes right on to conclude, "women are always like that; the vagueness of their minds is hopeless" (249). His tyranny is ultimately indiscriminate, directed toward "any woman" (225). It is no wonder poor frightened Lily sees him as "a lion seeking whom he could devour" (233).

The images of entrapment that visited Woolf's first heroine, Rachel Vinrace, in waking meditations and unquiet dreams as she considered marriage plague Woolf's last heroine in *Between the Acts*. Isabella Oliver, "entangled by her husband" (note: *by*, not *with*), feels "pegged down on a chair arm, like a captive balloon, by a myriad of hair-thin ties into domesticity."[21] With Giles, Isa feels "prisoned. Through the bars of the prison, . . . blunt arrows bruised her; of love, then of hate" (66). She writes poetry secretly, in an account book, "lest Giles might suspect," for she is "afraid of her husband" (50). She sees her frowning husband as resenting his role of breadwinner, of "making money for her to spend" (111). Indeed, Giles redirects his impotent anger over the state of the world toward and against women: "he hung his grievances" on women "as one hangs a coat on a hook, instinctively" (46). He resents what he imagines to be their "foolish, free" lives, even as he covets the subjugating power his financial support gives him.

Society

For Woolf the authoritarian state is the patriarchal family expanded. In the larger public world, the tyrants simply mass together into business and professions. Be they professors, clerics, doctors, men of commerce, lawyers, politicians, or policemen, they are instruments of the patriarchy—hence tyrants in different forms: "Society it seems was a father" (TG 135). In her first novel, Woolf has Hewet paint a picture of "the ordinary hard-working, rather ambitious solicitor or man of business," with the reminder to Rachel: "Consider what a bully the ordinary man is" (212).

There was little doubt in Woolf's mind that the progressively worsening world situation was a result of the strident masculinity of society's approach to its problems. From the perspective of the private house where women are kept from participation in public life, "your world, then, the world of the professional, of public life . . . looks queer," though perhaps at first sight "enormously impressive" (TG 18). Hewet had commented on "what an amazing concoction," what "a miracle the masculine conception of life is—judges, civil servants, army, navy, Houses of Parliament, lord mayors—what a world we've made of it!" (213). It is indeed very close to a Dickensian comment upon the various denizens of Oxford and Parliament that Woolf made to Roger Fry: "But what humbugs they all are!" (L 1:283). "Watch in the spring sunshine the stockbroker and the great barrister," Woolf commanded in her first feminist work, "going indoors to make money and more money and more money when it is a fact that five hundred pounds a year will keep one alive in the sunshine'' (ROOM 29). Earlier, she had given to Terence Hewet, whose sympathies are significantly female (he ''instinctively adopted the feminine point of view'' [213]), a vision of ''the drudgery of a profession if a man's taken very seriously by every one—if he gets appointments, and has offices and a title, and lots of letters after his name, and bits of ribbon and degrees'' (213).

Woolf's conception of the likes of lawyers and judges is most clearly revealed in her fact-fiction brace of works, *The Years* and *Three Guineas*. The latter is itself addressed to a middle-aged male lawyer with a practical nature, ''a busy man, an honorary treasurer, like yourself, Sir'' (TG 31). In that angry work a pompous, sexist judge pontificates on woman's innate love of dress and finery even as *he* sports ''a scarlet robe, an ermine cape, and a vast wig of artificial curls'' (TG 150n). In *The Years*, Celia observes her husband in his yellow wig and thinks him ''odd''; she finds his costume gives him ''a framed look, like a picture.'' Indeed, they all look suitably distanced and impressive, ''emphatic, cut out, like eighteenth century portraits'' (109). When his lordship the judge enters, Eleanor feels ''a little thrill of awe,'' for the trappings of his profession make the judge seem ''awful, magisterial, in his robes'' (109).[22] Yet, as Woolf had noted, a second look tends to diminish awe. When another barrister rises, Eleanor sees ''a chicken-breasted little man, wearing gold pince-nez'' (109). She hardly recognizes her brother and the formal gestures that belong ''to his public life, his life in the Courts. And his voice was unfamiliar'' (110). Once ''the solemn sallow atmosphere'' (109) is subjected to scrutiny, she finds ''the glamour had worn off'' (111), and she leaves ''the dark little Court and its cut-out faces'' wondering only ''How could Morris stand it?'' (112).

On the less glamorous side of the law stands the policeman. An early one at Ludgate Circus is ''smoothly sculptured'' and ''impassive,'' yet ''his face is stiff from force of will, and lean from the efforts of keeping it so. When his right arm rises, . . . not an ounce is diverted into sudden impulses, sentimental regrets, wire-drawn distinctions'' (JR 156). No wonder that, given such rigid maintenance of authority, ''the buses punctually stop'' (156). Buses, and undoubtedly *women* in patriarchal society.

In Woolf's last novel, the policeman representing Victorianism appears during the nineteenth-century portion of the pageant, announced by ''a pompous march.'' He is ''a huge symbolical figure'' (160) wearing a helmet and with medals on his chest.[23] Budge the constable is director of ''the traffic of 'Er Majesty's Empire''; he flourishes his nightstick and recites such lines as "all of 'em Obey the Rule of my truncheon" (162). It is Woolf's ultimate father figure: authority and tyranny, rules and regulations, domination and repression, the superego rampant (to say nothing of the phallic implications)—all combine in this extraordinary figure. He oversees "the purity and security of all Her Majesty's minions" and exacts obedience for "the laws of God and man." His duties are "protection and correction; we give 'em what's due. . . . Over thought and religion; drink; dress; manners; marriage too, I wield my truncheon. Prosperity and respectability always go, as we know, 'and in 'and'" (162). In the syntax of those contemptuous singsong rhythms and rhymes, Woolf bludgeons to death the smug, repressive Victorian era she so despised. The "eminent, dominant" figure, "glaring from his pedestal. . . . his truncheon extended; his waterproof pendant" is the "very spit and image of a Victorian constable" (163) as he prates of "purity our watchword; prosperity and respectability" (163). It is social criticism of the truncheon at its most trenchant.

The professional system interlocks, of course, with the educational and political realms. Of science per se, Woolf says little,[24] unless medical doctors are included in that category. In *Mrs. Dalloway*, Sir William Bradshaw's profession is described as "this exacting science which has to do with what, after all, we know nothing about—the nervous system, the human brain" (149). Not surprisingly, considering the circumstances of her personal experiences with medical men, Woolf was convinced that they were frauds. Her letters from first to last, for example, stress her total disbelief in their accuracy or knowledge. She had "learnt their utter helplessness when Father was ill. They can guess at what's the matter, but they cant put it right" (L 1:148). "I cant conceive how anybody can be fool enough to believe in a doctor," she says in another letter (1:159) to Violet Dickinson. And, again to Violet, she characterizes doctors as "a profoundly untrustworthy race; either they lie, or they mistake" (1:306). Nearly thirty years later, she complained to Ethel Smyth: "the truth is doctors know absolutely nothing, but as theyre paid to advise, have to oblige" (5:307). An early (1904) analogy is especially revealing: "Really a doctor is worse than a husband! Oh how thankful I shall be to be my own mistress and throw their silly medicines down the slop pail! I never shall believe, or have believed, in anything any doctor says" (1:148).

Woolf's fictional portraits hardly contradict such expressed opinions. Dr. Lesage (named with bitter irony for the wisdom he does not have) and Dr. Rodriguez are her first brace of incompetents, anticipating their apogee in the hated Drs. Holmes and Bradshaw of *Mrs. Dalloway*. Dr. Lesage of *The Voyage Out* has the "curt speech and the sulky masterful manner" that impress others; Rodriguez manages to be "obsequious as well as malicious" (342). In *Orlando* doctors are also demolished—but with wit:

> But the doctors were hardly wiser then than they are now, and after prescribing rest and exercise, starvation and nourishment, society and solitude, that he [i.e., Orlando] should lie in bed all day and ride forty miles between lunch and dinner, together with the usual sedatives and irritants, diversified, as the fancy took them, with possets of newt's slobber on rising, and draughts of peacock's gall on going to bed, they left him to himself, and gave it as their opinion that he had been asleep for a week.[25]

In *Mrs. Dalloway* the powerful, respected doctor, a pillar of the community, becomes a sinister force. Holmes and Bradshaw, seemingly all neatness and efficiency, proportion and order, actually embody ignorance, repression, and rigidity. As the alleged spokesman of proportion (and "health is proportion" [149]), all Bradshaw can do with a patient who has a Christ delusion and suicidal tendencies is invoke the absurdly impotent prescription "drink milk in bed" (151). Bradshaw's "infallible instinct" (151) for declaring one thing madness and another sense is respected by colleagues and feared by subordinates. With "divine proportion" as his guide, he acquires wide powers, prospering personally and serving England at the same time: he "secluded her lunatics, forbade childbirth, penalised despair, made it impossible for the unfit to propagate their views" (150). If power corrupts, proportion shades into conversion. Lady Bradshaw, the usual female victim of male dominance, must minister "to the craving which lit her husband's eye so oilily for dominion, for power" (152), while Sir William "swooped; he devoured. He shut people up" (154).

If she despised doctors for their despotic use of power, Woolf sensed and opposed the very same tendency in the religious profession. Clerics too had and used more authority less responsibly than Woolf liked. "What I can't abide is the man who wishes to convert other men's minds; that tampering with beliefs seems to me impertinent, insolent, corrupt beyond measure," she observed in a letter (L 4:333). She could have been describing Dr. Bradshaw, but she was in fact simply discovering the same spector of conversion rearing its *religious* head that she had condemned in the medical establishment: "I never pass through Hyde Park," she continued, "without cursing separately every God inventor there" (333). Science is an infected father, and God too is "of patriarchal origin" (TG 184n); Saint Paul is a protofascist "of the virile or dominant type, so familiar at present in Germany, for whose gratification a subject race or sex is essential'' (167n). And since so many contemporary clerics ''base their educational theories upon the teaching of St. Paul'' (152n), we should not be surprised to find that the religious establishment gives men advantageous powers even as it oppresses women. In *Three Guineas* Woolf makes plain her conviction that the inferiority of the female sex was a concept used by religion not to serve God but to enhance the position of his mundane male ambassadors.[26] She notified Hugh Walpole, whom she acknowledged as ''the son of a Bishop'' that ''I hate the arrogance and monopoly of Christianity'' (L 4:83). And after reading a work by the eighteenth-century evangelical divine Henry Venn, she wrote to Ethel Smyth: ''Oh how I loathe religion. . . . How can you belong to such a canting creed?'' (L 5:320).

Reverend Bax in *The Voyage Out* is agreeable, simple, and kind, ''though by no means clever''; Rachel finds him ''an epitome of all the vices of his service'' (229). When he surreptitiously sneaks political remarks into his sermon, he seems ''to speak with a certain innocent craftiness'' (231). Note that Woolf designates his *craftiness* as the point at which Bax is ''more definitely clerical'' (231). In Woolf's conjunction of religion and chauvinism, Reverend Bax addresses condescending remarks to women, assuring them that ''the humblest could help; the least important things had an influence.'' Somewhat redundantly, Woolf adds: ''he was used to assigning them their duties in his innocent clerical campaigns'' (231). Many years later, in *Three Guineas,* Woolf would link ''both priests and dictators'' for insisting on a theory of woman's natural inferiority that is ''essential to their domination'' (181n).

In *The Years,* Sara and Martin meet in front of Saint Paul's (recall what Woolf thought of Saint Paul and his misogyny) to discuss religion over lunch. When asked what sense she makes of it, Sara opens her prayer book ''at random and begins to read: 'The father incomprehensible; the son incomprehensible—' '' (229). It is subtle but pointed criticism of the intimidating unknowability of male theological structures. Woolf tweaked her own friends rather mercilessly on the same point: ''I thought, Really now, Ethel [Smyth] believes in God, does she? How very very queer!'' Or, ''God—no—God we say, God is merely a—a what?'' (L 4:321).

The roles of religion and of the clerical profession are explored in some detail in Woolf's last novel, which offers interesting matches of fact and fiction; that is, passages in the novel corroborate Woolf's stated opinions. In her letters Woolf comments on ''this bell-ringing religion'' (5:319); in *Between the Acts* ''the church bells always stopped, leaving you to ask: Won't there be another note?'' (207). Bart Oliver observes of Lucy that religion has made her ''imperceptive. . . . The fumes of that incense obscured the human heart'' (203); in a letter, Woolf lectured Ethel Smyth on ''the prime human virtues'': ''But what warrant have you for assuming that they are more commonly found among those who believe in God. . . . None, I should say'' (L 5:322).[27]

In the 1860 Picnic Party section of the pageant, Woolf uses Eleanor Hardcastle and Edgar Thorold to mock overzealous religious service and missionary zeal.[28] Learning that Eleanor has secretly ''longed to convert the heathen'' (BA 166), Edgar proposes that they marry and spend ''a lifetime in the African desert among the heathens!'' (166). A subsequent sermon by Mr. Hardcastle is Woolf's opportunity to puncture religion's uneasy alliance with nature in general and science in particular: he thanks God for ''*the beauties of Nature; for the understanding with which Thou hast enlightened us* (he fumbled with his fossil).'' After stumbling briefly on Darwinism, Hardcastle intones ''*grant us to spread the light of thy*'' at exactly the moment that Albert, the village idiot in his pageant costume as ''the hindquarters of the donkey,'' becomes ''active'' (171). The narrative asks if this action was ''intentional'' or ''accidental?''—disingenuously enough, *after* the blasphemous connection between *belief* and *manure* has been suggested.[29]

In this novel Reverend G. W. Streatfield is indecorously referred to as God's ''mouthpiece'' (25) or ''that skunk the Reverend Whatshisname'' (36). He is ''an intolerable constriction, contradiction, and reduction to simplified absurdity. . . . Of all incongruous sights a clergyman in the livery of his servitude to the summing up was the most grotesque and entire'' (190). Streatfield is, in short, a relic, ''a piece of traditional church furniture; . . . fashioned by generations of village carpenters after some lost-in-the-mists-of-antiquity model'' (190).

In sharp contrast to Woolf's first minister in *The Voyage Out,* her last reverend is a symbol of the very uneasy (perhaps expedient?) adaptations Christianity has had to make to modern times. Streatfield speaks to the assembled audience in his capacity as ''Treasurer of the Fund,'' which has as its highly ironic purpose ''the *illumination* of our dear old church'' (193, italics mine). When religion solicits money in *Between the Acts,* the coins rattle unpleasantly in the collection boxes: ''how creepy it made one feel! Here came Albert, the idiot, jingling his collecting box—an aluminium saucepan without a lid. . . . He rattled and sniggered; chattered and jabbered'' (193–94). As if a literal idiot soliciting alms for religion were not pointed enough, Streatfield, ''a butt, a clod, . . . an irrelevant forked stake in the flow of the summer silent world" (90–91) confesses his puzzlement as to the meaning of the play. That is to say, addressing itself to art, culture, and history, religion has no answers: "If he didn't know, calling himself Reverend, also M.A., who after all could?" (191).[30]

Woolf showed very little more mercy for the other educated tyrants of society; her fictional professors fare as badly as do the clergy. They belong to the same clamoring class of "fathers in general," the "bishops and the deans, the doctors and the professors, the patriarchs and the pedagogues all" (ROOM 97). In the spirit of the gadfly and the questioning philosopher—"No, no, nothing is proved, nothing is known," she sings in "The Mark on the Wall" (HH 43)—Woolf insults unworthy representatives of the thinking mind. She was, for instance, contemptuous of academicians who lectured on literature. Her "Walter Raleigh" essay granted that he "was one of the best Professors of Literature of our time; he did brilliantly whatever it is that Professors are supposed to do" (CE 1:315).

In *A Room of One's Own,* her satirical sallies at pedantry include a reference to the "seventieth study of Keats and his use of Miltonic inversion which old Professor Z and his like are now inditing" (94). "The dominance of the professor" (33) is to be seen in his roles of power and influence, even in his financial holdings.[31] She refers to "the patriarchs, the professors, . . . [who] had money and power, . . . the instinct for possession, the rage for acquisition which drives them to desire other people's fields and goods perpetually" (38). Professor von X writes his *Mental, Moral, and Physical Inferiority of the Female Sex,* while Oscar Browning of Oxford is of the opinion "that irrespective of the marks he might give, the best woman was intellectually the inferior of the worst man" (ROOM 55). For their formidable resistance to educational equality Woolf does not forgive the males in power, particularly those males whose "job" it is to dispense knowledge and behave wisely. She dissects the "masculine complex which has had so much influence upon the woman's movement; that deep-seated desire, not so much that *she* shall be inferior as that *he* shall be superior" (ROOM 57). She was to say in *Three Guineas* that the eminence of the platform "encourages vanity and the desire to impose authority" (155n). A decade earlier in *A Room of One's Own,* she observed "Professor X rush for his measuring rods to prove himself 'superior' " (92). With just enough Freudian awareness, Woolf captures both the phallic and the rational hubris involved. When in *Three Guineas* she equates academic ceremony ("the sartorial splendours of the educated man") with "the rites of savages" (20–21), she is merely recasting a blistering passage from "The Mark on the Wall":

What are our learned men save the descendants of witches and hermits who crouched in caves and in woods brewing herbs, interrogating shrew-mice and writing down the language of the stars? And the less we honour them as our superstitions dwindle and our respect for beauty and health of mind increases. (HH 43)

"I detest pale scholars with their questioning about life, and the message of the classics, and the bearing of Greek thought upon modern problems" (L 1:386), she asserted in a letter. In "The Mark on the Wall," she mused about "a very pleasant world. . . . A world without professors or specialists" (HH 43).

But neither the world nor Woolf's works is free of them. Some species of professor, intellectual, scholar, or critic haunts every one of the novels. Hughling Elliot and William Pepper, the dons of *The Voyage Out*, embody the petrified pedantry, the parade of useless learning, that Woolf enjoyed ridiculing. True to her feminist theory of patriarchal tyrants, both of these gentlemen scholars are smugly chauvinistic. Hughling Elliot the Oxford don discourages women from intellectual endeavors, brushing aside Miss Allan and her book on literature with "Be persuaded you will benefit the world much more by dancing than by writing" (164). William Pepper, himself a singularly unattractive man, nevertheless ignores his own inadequacies of form and temperament as he outlines his exacting requirements for the very special woman fit for consorting with very special him.[32] He possesses that comforting male chauvinist superiority that allows him to sit at the dinner table in "his neat ugly suit" (42) and condescend to those ultimate defec-tives, women. When another (female) guest observes that "one talks of the equality of the sexes," he retorts, "Does one?" (43). In the final paragraphs of the novel, after the storm that follows Rachel's death, Woolf cannot resist mentioning that Pepper has been beaten at chess.

In *Night and Day* we find the scholarly literary editor Mr. Hilbery, whose occupation is "placing together documents by means of which it could be proved that Shelley had written 'of' instead of 'and,' or that the inn in which Byron had slept was called the 'Nag's Head' and not the 'Turkish Knight,' or that the Christian name of Keats's uncle had been John rather than Richard" (108). Woolf grants Hilbery enough awareness and simple com-mon sense to realize "the humour of these researches, but [she adds] that did not prevent him from carrying them out with the utmost scrupulosity" (109). As for his human adequacy when a family crisis interrupts his high labors, Mr. Hilbery's absurdly insufficient response is "Meanwhile, let us try to behave like civilized beings. Let us read Sir Walter Scott'' (505).

The assorted agents of learning in *Jacob's Room*—professors, scholars, researchers in the reading room of the British Museum—fare little better. The narrator after all has warned us that "it is not simple, or pure, or wholly splendid, the lamp of learning" (39) and asks us to take a closer look, "there under its light" at its practitioners. We find that they look "priestly" (40), and that the university is "like a suburb where you go to see a view and eat a special cake! 'We are the sole purveyors of this cake' '' (40).

Old Professor Huxtable, despite having what Pope has immortalized as "loads of learned lumber in his head,"[33] is a creature of vague anxieties and penury, "grudging . . . secretive and suspicious as an old peasant woman with all her lies" (40). Professor Sopwith—the *sop* who *literally* cuts and purveys the special (chocolate) cake of learning to undergraduates—is always "talking, talking, talking, as if everything could be talked" (40). Chubby Professor Erasmus Cowan is an absurdly diminished representative of literary genius, "holding up in his snug little mirror the image of Virgil" (41). His once noble task of purveying Virgil's special cake has dwindled to "ruling lines between names, hanging lists above doors" (42). Woolf's assessment of this academic world is grim: "Such is the fabric through which the light must shine, if shine it can" (42).

The effect of the patriarchal fabric upon female figures in the academic carpet is revealed in Miss Umphelby, a lecturer on Virgil. Her lectures "are not half so well attended as those of Cowan" (42), and in her isolation she is given to melancholy meditations upon woman's massive exclusion from historical consideration. Apart from wondering what would happen if she actually met Virgil, "she lets her fancy play upon other details of men's meetings with women which have never got into print" (42). In the academic weave, as in other professional tapestries, anonymous is indeed a woman.

Professor Brierly in *Mrs. Dalloway* is a lecturer on Milton and "a very queer fish" (267): arrogant yet insecure to the point of mild paranoia, "with all those degrees, honours, lectureships between him and the scribblers he suspected instantly an atmosphere not favorable to his queer compound" (267–68). That "queer compound" is defined as "his prodigious learning and timidity; his wintry charm without cordiality; his innocence blent with snobbery" (268). Confronted with rebels, geniuses, anything ardent or otherwise threatening, Professor Brierly quivers, then recovers and intimates "with a little toss of the head, with a sniff—Humph!—the value of moderation; of some slight training in the classics in order to appreciate Milton" (268). Mr. Hilbery had Walter Scott to heal family crises; Brierly (difficult,

barking, and thorny?) serves up Milton as antidote to the poison of un-
conventionality. Values like proportion and moderation are espoused by the
oppressive, villainous doctors of this novel; Brierly is one of their ilk: "the
Professor on Milton; the Professor on moderation" (269). That fatal coupling suggests the love of power, use of authority, and belief in superiority
that Woolf found common to her tyrannical doctors—of medicine or
philosophy.

In *To the Lighthouse* Charles Tansley, that "miserable specimen, . . . all
humps and hollows. . . . [who] poked and shuffled" (15), likes best to be
discussing with Mr. Ramsay "who had won this, who had won that, who
was a 'first-rate man' at Latin verses, . . . who was undoubtedly the 'ablest
fellow in Balliol, . . . [and] bound to be heard of later" (15). Tansley is a
purveyor of "ugly academic jargon, that rattled itself off so glibly, . . . an
awful prig—oh yes, an insufferable bore" (22). His dissertation subject is
"the influence of something upon somebody" (22) *or* "the influence of
somebody upon something" (101–2, 156). The very interchangeability of
the concepts underscores Woolf's clear disgust with the whole futile
business.

Tansley is an unusually harsh portrait of the scholar as neurotically competitive, perpetually hostile (especially to women), absurdly insecure—and
simperingly sycophantic. Tansley the toady follows his mentor at a respectful distance, undermining the reputations of his peers: "brilliant but I think
fundamentally unsound" (15). Woolf gives readers, as advertised, "an X-ray
photograph, the ribs and thigh bones of the young man's desire to impress
himself" (137). His festering drive for recognition causes him to vow that
"one of these days every single person" would know "that he was Charles
Tansley"; they would, predicts our gentle, attenuated scholar, "be blown
sky high, . . . one of these days by the gunpowder that was in him" (138).

This quivering Jello mountain of insecure hostility is a nasty sexist who has
decided, "It was the women's fault. Women made civilisation impossible
with all their 'charm,' their silliness" (129). A year later, in *A Room of One's
Own*, Woolf pondered the strange phenomenon of the powerful males, "the
professors, or patriarchs," who are nonetheless as angry as they are privileged: "Or is anger, I wondered, somehow, the familiar, the attendant sprite
on power?" (34). Anticipating her fictional treatment of Tansley, with his
spiteful litany of women can't paint and women can't write, Woolf suggests
that "when the professor insisted a little too emphatically upon the inferiority of women" (ROOM 34) he was actually "protecting rather hot-headedly
and with too much emphasis" (35) his own need to retain a myth of
superiority. The spinster painter Lily Briscoe contemplates the Tansley taunt

and understands that he is "making it his business to tell her women can't write, women can't paint, not so much that he believed it, as that for some odd reason he wished it" (292). She realizes "clearly it was not true to him but for some reason helpful to him, and that was why he said it" (130).✳

In *Orlando* Woolf offers exacting portraits of the scholar (the biographer-narrator) and the man of letters (Nick Greene, writer-critic). The former is a perfect illustration of Mary Datchet's contention that "Men are such pedants—they don't know what things matter, and what things don't" (N&D 88) as he plods—in the interest of exhaustive scholarship—through naming all twelve months of the year of Orlando's life that passed from one November to another: "After November, comes December. Then January, February, March, and April. After April comes May. June, July, August follow. Next is September. Then October, and so, behold, here we are back at November again" (174). In addition to such masterpieces of redundance, our narrator quotes approvingly Byron's chauvinistic pronouncement that love is "woman's whole existence" and exhorts them to "give over this pretence of writing and thinking" (175). It is a milder, funny Tansley; Hughling Elliot *redux*.

Authoritarian Nick Greene ultimately becomes a professor of literature, vain of his titles, awards, and degrees. Orlando turned female is frustrated and annoyed by her contemplation of the male critical establishment, which seems to her to be only day-long talk and "little anecdotes . . . about what Tupper said about Smiles" (187). Near tears at her inability to mimic their professional behavior, she finds "they're all so manly; . . . and though I'm spiteful enough, I could never learn to be as spiteful as all that, so how can I be a critic" (187).

The Waves is a work singularly unconcerned with the real, public world of power and patriarchy, yet even *it* contains glancing blows at the headmaster Dr. Crane. Neville cannot abide "the Doctor's pompous mummery" (216); Bernard sees Crane as "convinced, it seems, of his immense superiority" (208). Recalling the doctor as imperious issuer of commands, he makes Woolf's generalization: "People in authority always become melodramatic" (344).

Kitty in *The Years* thinks undergraduate males look "silly," and the "portentous old men" seem "carved, mediaeval, unreal," somehow "like gargoyles" (Y 74). Edward the scholar appears to North as "sealed up, stated," "vain" and "touchy," and above all "established" (407); he is "glazed over with the smooth glossy varnish that *those in authority* wear" (407, italics mine). North feels unable to communicate—an important concept whose lack is bemoaned throughout *The Years*—with Edward because he is "too formed and idiosyncratic; too black and white and linear" (408). The closed, privileged world of the intellectual he sees reflected in Edward's meticulous, limited, abstract life makes North want to pry open Edward's fine head and share forcibly "the past and poetry" (408). "Why can't he flow?" North wonders in dismay. "Why's it all locked up, refrigerated?" and answers his own question: "because he's a priest, a mystery monger, . . . this guardian of beautiful words" (408–9).

There is a new dimension to Woolf's portrayal of the scholar as sexist in *The Years,* however. Where Miss Craddock, Kitty's teacher, is awed by "the greatest historian of his age!" (66), Kitty merely sees "Old Chuffy" (65) with irreverence. And with good reason: "Well, he doesn't talk history to me," she says, "remembering the damp feel of a heavy hand on her knee" (66). In the distinguished historian as feeler of young women's knees resides the ultimate feminist disillusion with scholar-patriarchs: the great scholar as dirty old man.[34]

Dictatorship is a word Woolf felt could apply to "Oxford or Cambridge, in Whitehall or Downing Street" (TG 103). Thus connections between the scholarly and political worlds in her novels need not be forced, given her patriarchal thesis. That she did not think highly of politicians can be documented through twenty-seven years of correspondence. In 1908 she was writing, "I think politicians and journalists must be the lowest of Gods creatures, creeping perpetually in the mud, and biting with one end and stinging with the other" (L 1:332). To Janet Case she wrote of "the inhuman side" of politics, "how all the best feelings are shrivelled" (1:441). Another letter finds her complaining, "What watery and wobbly minds these politicians have—and always afraid to say what they mean, and such an air of being behind the scenes" (2:348). Elsewhere she characterizes politics as "all phantasies and moonshine, only mudcoloured moonshine" (2:582). To Margaret Llewelyn Davies she complained, "I cant conceive how you politicians can go on being political. . . . I finally felt it so completely silly, futile, petty, personal and unreal" (4:392). And as late as 1935 she was muttering, "All politics be damned" (5:436).

In her fiction the male political establishment is at worst malevolent, at best incompetent.[35] In *Jacob's Room* it is unknowable, impossible to fathom, as well: "the men in clubs and Cabinets" (155) move like shadows, at once very real, capable of affecting the destiny of nations, yet remote and insubstantial. Political actions

together with the incessant commerce of banks, laboratories, chancellories, and houses of business, are the strokes which oar the world forward, they say. And they are dealt by men as smoothly sculptured as the impassive policeman at Ludgate Circus. . . . It is thus that we live, they say, driven by an unseizable force. (156)

The poetry of this passage should not obscure Woolf's vision of male-run society as darkly significant, yet quite *out of female hands*. The female narrator of this novel has twice resorted to that famous phrase of the uninformed and powerless everywhere, *they say*, and concluded by defining that structure in which she has no active part as *an unseizable force*. When "the wires of the Admiralty shivered with some far-away communication" (171), the result is diplomatic meetings in the Reichstag, riots in Milan, or the fleet at Gibraltar.[36] Gentlemen in comfortable chairs sign papers and "decreed that the course of history should shape itself this way or that way, *being manfully determined*, as their faces showed" (172, italics mine). We need not wait for the explicitly bitter anger of *Three Guineas* to see that Woolf had always had a dark vision of the connection between manhood and patriotism, politics, and war. The statesmen who have taken upon themselves the hubristic responsibilities of governing are all too fallible: "some were troubled with dyspepsia; one had at that very moment cracked the glass of his spectacles: [i.e., unseeing, blind politicians] . . . altogether they looked too red, fat, pale or lean, to be dealing . . . with the course of history" (172).

In *The Voyage Out* Richard Dalloway appears as a pompous self-appointed benefactor of mankind, yet hopes "to be in my grave before a woman has the right to vote in England!" (43). In *Mrs. Dalloway*, Richard and Hugh Whitbread are the types of patriarchal tyrants who in their roles as minor government officials direct the affairs of the great world. To Peter Walsh, Dalloway and his political colleagues are "the conservative duffers" (244). He wants solid answers from these people who pretend to know how to govern: "What did the Government mean—Richard Dalloway would know—to do about India?" (244). But Dalloway does not know, and neither does Hugh Whitbread, who "kept guard at Buckingham Palace, dressed in silk stockings and knee-breeches, over what nobody knew. But he did it extremely efficiently" (155). Sally Seton holds Whitbread directly "responsible for the state of 'those poor girls in Piccadilly' " (110). She deems him comparable to "a first-rate valet . . . somebody who walked behind carrying suit cases; [or] could be trusted to send telegrams" (111). In his "little post at Court," Hugh the snob *looks* important ("a magnificent figure he cut too, . . . as if he beheld the world from a certain eminence, and dressed to match," [156], but he is a lackey nonetheless, who bows and scrapes and "polished the Imperial shoe-buckles" (111) and hoards unimportant secrets. The judgment on such a masculine life of pomp is merciless: "Such were his rattles, his baubles, in playing with which he had grown white" (262).

Whitbread has "one or two humble reforms to his credit" (156), and Dalloway too is part of "the public-spirited, British Empire, tariff-reform, governing class spirit" (116); but, as far as Walsh is concerned, "the rascals who get hanged for battering the brains of a girl out in a train do less harm on the whole than Hugh Whitbread and his kindness" (263). Woolf's own view of the efficacy of social reform may be inferred from her portrait of the goddess Conversion, who "shrouds herself in white and walks penitentially disguised as brotherly love . . . offers help but desires power" (151). It might also be inferred from her earlier portrait, in *Night and Day*, of Mr. Clacton, who works for the cause of women's suffrage. Woolf the feminist surgeon exploring the philanthropic male finds chauvinist tumors among the do-gooders. Clacton, for example, "loved to issue from his inner chamber [office] with documents in his hands, visibly important" (171). He has a "magisterial way to check the unbalanced enthusiasm of the women" (278) working with him. Ostensibly on the side of the feminist angels, Clacton is really waiting for the proper moment to unleash that dominance that is the natural inheritance of the male: "He envisaged a time when it would become necessary to tell her [Mary Datchet] that there could not be two masters in one office" (280). Woolf's private remarks are in much the same vein.[37]

If Mr. Clacton of *Night and Day* loved looking "visibly important, with a preoccupied expression on his face that might have suited a Prime Minister" (171), the actual prime minister at Clarissa Dalloway's party has an ordinariness that is laughable: "You might have stood him behind a counter and bought biscuits—poor chap, all rigged up in gold lace" (261). Although the man is "doing his best, and good luck to him, to look important" (265), he is very far from dazzling Woolf's sardonic eye.

Significantly, the reader's last vision of the sexist scholar Charles Tansley is that of a power-seeking man turned social reformer and public speaker: "He was denouncing something: he was condemning somebody" (TTL 292). The same confusion that had been reflected in the interchangeability of Tansley's dissertation topic (*somebody* and *something*) has been transposed to the political realm. The moral seems to be that all tyrants speak the same language. On a platform preaching, or as a scholar lecturing the inferior sex, the more Patriarchal Charles changes, the more he remains the same, and the more he resembles all other worldly careerists like Bradshaw, Whitbread, Dalloway, Clacton, and the marginally realized statesmen, the "Rajahs and Kaisers" (172) of *Jacob's Room*.

In the Yeatsean world of *The Years*, where things fall apart and the center cannot hold, the politician shades into the fascist. Eleanor's indignant reaction to the newspaper picture of "a fat man gesticulating" is "damned bully!" (330), and the narrative equates men talking politics to dangerous children: "It was like hearing small boys at a private school, hearing these young men talk politics. 'I'm right . . . you're wrong' " (404). Martin and Sara walk through Hyde Park observing various activists—one speaker on a platform holding a slate in his hand and talking of Jews; another talking with a cockney accent of justice and liberty; an old lady with a book (presumably the Bible) whose thin voice cannot be heard "above the catcalls and whistles" (241). Martin decides "there was a mixture of comedy and tragedy in the scene" (241).

In *Three Guineas* Woolf declared that politics was the profession "most closely connected with war" (13). Certainly the presence of world war in six of her nine novels (excepting *The Voyage Out, Night and Day,* and *The Waves*) can be seen as "perhaps her most pointed and damning condemnation of the 'masculine' world."[38] Because "the tyranny of the patriarchal state" is analogous to "the tyranny of the Fascist state" (TG 102), "all the other professions, according to the testimony of biography, seem to be as bloodthirsty as the profession of arms itself" (TG 63). "The quintessence of virility," the "perfect type" of manliness, is the soldier in uniform, medals on chest, sword in hand. In full dress, he is "a ridiculous, a barbarous, a displeasing spectacle" (TG 21),[39] his love of impressive costume revealing his shallow vanity and his desire to inspire submissive awe. Nor should we forget that as a participant in the 1910 Dreadnought Hoax, Virginia Woolf had literally acted out her ridicule and contempt for the mentality and the costumes of the military establishment. It is a poignant fact that Woolf was familiar from early childhood with Thomas Hughes's *Tom Brown's School Days*—a novel read aloud by her father, a classic text in the very values of manliness that Woolf came to equate with and despise in the patriarchy. One example from Hughes should suffice:

> After all, what would life be without fighting, I should like to know? From the cradle to the grave, fighting, rightly understood, is the business, the real, highest, honestest business of every son of man. (part 2, chap. 5)

Woolf's fictional vision of war combines power, machinery, inhumanity, and lethal game playing, all somehow as unreal as they are insanely destructive:

Like blocks of tin soldiers the army covers the cornfield, moves up the hillside, stops, reels slightly this way and that, and falls flat, save that, through fieldglasses, it can be seen that one or two pieces still agitate up and down like fragments of broken match-stick. (JR 155–56)

In *Mrs. Dalloway* "the fingers of the European War" were said to smash "a plaster cast of Ceres" (129); it was a magnificently appropriate image for Woolf's notion of war as masculine, phallic, death dealing; of Ceres as female, life giving, creative.[40] Just as "having served his country" (JR 25) left Captain Barfoot lame and minus two fingers, so in *The Years* Colonel Pargiter's lost two fingers suggest the same castration: the end of manliness in violence, force, and injury; the mutilated spirit of the Victorian tyrant in both private family and public world. In *The Years* Sara can sneer at North in "his mud-coloured uniform, with a switch between his legs, and his ears sticking out on either side of his pink, foolish face" (285) and contemptuously dub him a lieutenant in "His Majesty's Royal Regiment of Rat-catchers" (314).

The last novel confronts rape—the ultimate act of tyrannical force, masculine aggression, and violent oppression of women. Woolf makes the connections among tyrant-hunter-killer-sexual oppressor absolute by having the rape committed by a soldier: troopers have dragged a woman "up to the barrack room where she was thrown upon a bed" (20). The rape, sexual evil in its most extreme form, symbolizes not only malevolent relations between the sexes, but historical and political meanings (Europe raped by masculinist dictators) as well. At their most evil, fathers in general become the soldier-rapists of the world.

Woolf declared in "Thoughts on Peace in an Air Raid," written in August of 1940, that women can fight for freedom and peace not with arms and brute strength, but "with the mind" (CE 4:173). She quotes Lady Astor's remark that women "are held down because of a subconscious Hitlerism in the hearts of men" and defines this Hitlerism as "the desire for aggression; the desire to dominate and enslave" (174). We must, Woolf concludes, substitute some better, life-affirming activity for the male quest for victory and power. We must reeducate men and women against the prevailing, limited notions of their roles: "If we could free ourselves from slavery we should free men from tyranny" (174). Put differently, Woolf's prescription for the fathers in general would be—no more dutiful daughters.

Notes

1. Virginia Woolf, *Three Guineas,* 65. Subsequent quotations from this work will be cited in the body of the paper, using the abbreviation TG.

2. Much later on in life (1930), Woolf would slyly reprimand Margaret Davies: "perhaps I include a good deal more in literature than you would" (L 4:191).

3. Herbert Marder, *Feminism and Art: A Study of Virginia Woolf* (Chicago: University of Chicago Press, 1963), 69.

4. Sonya Rudikoff has observed that "the explicit challenging mockery of patriarchal society was certainly to be seen in Woolf's letters and writing as early as 1910 [and] in letters to her friends long before." "How Many Lovers Had Virginia Woolf?" *Hudson Review* 32, no. 4 (winter 1979–80): 549. Jane Marcus has also noted Woolf's attack on patriarchal institutions "in both pamphlet and fiction." "Art and Anger," *Feminist Studies* 4, no. 1 (February 1978): 77.

5. The entry Woolf wrote on the anniversary of Sir Leslie Stephen's birthday is: "His life would have entirely ended mine. . . . No writing, no books; inconceivable" (WD 135).

6. *Night and Day,* 35. (Further page citations will be given in parentheses within the text.) Cf. Woolf's observation that the woman's "sacred duty [is] to sacrifice herself to the father" (TG 134).

7. In the brief but chilling story "The Introduction" (*Mrs. Dalloway's Party: A Short Story Sequence*), Woolf makes clear the crushing inferiority felt by the female as student-scholar. Lily Everitt has written an "essay on the character of Dean Swift" (37), deemed "first rate" by her professor, yet she feels uneasy with the burden of being merely female in "this massive masculine achievement" (40) of civilized society: "churches and parliaments, flats, even the telegraph wires—all, she told herself, made by men" (42). One Bob Brinsley demolishes her achievements, making her feel like a pitiful fly whose wings have been torn off by his male superiority. The fatalistic moral of these enactments of sex-role stereotyping is, "Why not, since he is the greatest of all worldly objects? And to worship, to adorn, to embellish was her task, her wings were for that" (42).

8. Woolf commented that for her own father "the woman was his slave" (MB 125).

9. Cf. "To depend upon a profession is a less odious form of slavery than to depend upon a father" (TG 16).

10. Jane Marcus describes Mr. Hilbery as a "formidable and rational benevolent despot." "Enchanted Organs, Magic Bells: *Night and Day* as Comic Opera," in *Virginia Woolf: Revaluations and Continuity,* ed. Ralph Freedman (Berkeley: University of California Press, 1980), 111.

11. Compare the reaction of another father in the "complementary" novel, *The Years*. There Colonel Pargiter thinks that Eleanor "has her own life to live. A spasm of jealousy passed through him. She's got her own affairs to think about" (104).

12. Section 4 of part 2 repeats some variation on resisting or fighting tyranny six times; section 12 reiterates it; in section 13 James adds the synonym *despotism* (*To the Lighthouse*). Further page citations will be given within the text and abbreviated TTL.

13. Woolf confessed her own "passionate affection for my father alternating with passionate hatred of him" (MB 161).

14. "Aurora Leigh," in *Collected Essays* (New York: Harcourt Brace and World, 1967), 2:212. The passage by Elizabeth Barrett that Woolf quotes makes an interesting contrast in attitudes. Elizabeth Barrett uses the much gentler noun *seclusion* to describe her interment by her father; Woolf comments more dramatically, "at last she broke the *prison bars*" (213, italics mine).

15. In *Three Guineas,* Woolf discusses the sums of money Mr. Barrett allowed his daughter, remarking that "though belonging to Elizabeth [the money was] under Mr. Barrett's control" (156). She also notes the case of Sophia Jex-Blake and her father as a paradigm of the daughter forbidden to earn her own living: "He wished to keep his daughter in his own power. If she took money from him she remained in his power" (132); allowed to earn money, "she will be independent" (133).

16. The clearest sense of patriarchal victimization of woman as sister occurs in *A Room of One's Own,* where Woolf projects Shakespeare's sister Judith. Although gifted, she does not have the advantage of an education; she is betrothed to a stranger; beaten by her father; unsuccessful because untrained in her chosen craft; seduced by a worldly male. She ends as a pregnant suicide. (See ROOM 48–50.)

17. Rudikoff observes of Woolf's own family structure: "How important it was that that seductive half brother had £1,000 a year, and she had only £50!" (564).

18. See my article "Virginia Woolf's Strategy of Scorn in *The Years* and *Three Guineas*," *Bulletin of the New York Public Library* 80, no. 2 (winter 1977), on Arthur's Education Fund and its repetitious insistence.

19. In "Aurora Leigh" Woolf described the lovers as "oppressed, [yet] defiant" (CE 1:209).

20. In *A Room of One's Own* Woolf cites a passage from Trevelyan's *History of England* that illustrates the movement from daughter to wife as just more of the same oppression; that is, the daughter who refuses to marry as her father dictates is "locked up, beaten and flung about." Once married, she is subject to "wife-beating, . . . a recognized right of man" (44).

21. *Between the Acts* (New York: Harcourt Brace and World, 1941), 5 and 18–19 respectively.

22. Lawyers share with professors this absurd preoccupation with appearance: "in courts and universities, we find the same love of dress. There, too, are velvet and silk, fur and ermine" (TG 21).

23. Woolf saw the nineteenth century as "that purely patriarchal society" (ROOM 77), and in *Three Guineas* she equated Victorian patriarchy with the fascist state.

24. "Science, it would seem, is not sexless; she [*sic*] is a man, a father, and infected too," Woolf declared (TG 139). To Violet Dickinson she characterized H. T. Norton, the Cambridge mathematician, as "crude" for drawing "diagrams of the Ovaries on the table cloth, taking it for granted that a woman is the same shape as a kind of monkey" (L 1:465).

25. *Orlando: A Biography* (New York: New American Library, Signet Classics, 1960), 43. Further page citations will be given in parentheses within the text.

26. "A biography of the Deity," Woolf noted acidly in *Three Guineas*, "would resolve itself into a Dictionary of Clerical Biography" (153n).

27. Woolf continued to tweak Ethel Smyth about "the God in whom you trust" (L 5:270), or to inquire "Why is Christianity so insistent and so sad?" (L 5:319).

28. Woolf's opinion of the missionary mentality ("impertinent, insolent, corrupt") has been documented above. To it may be added this sly pun from her letters: "they were both perverts—I mean converts—I mean lately born into the Roman Catholic Church" (L 4:254).

29. Compare Jane Marcus on Woolf's description in *Jacob's Room* of patriarchal culture as "that whole bag of ordure." Marcus links this to Woolf's experience of her father's cancer of the bowel and his tirades at her mother over "inadequate toilet facilities." "Tintinnabulations," *Marxist Perspectives*, spring 1979, 161.

30. Cf. the epistemological issue implied in *The Years*, when Sara read in her prayer book of Father and Son both "incomprehensible." If religion dares to speak with authority, says Woolf, it must *know*. Thus, in *Three Guineas*, she criticized the Church of England for its "worldly confusion" and "divided counsel" (10) on the war issue.

31. Woolf censured the educational establishment for not keeping literature "out of the hands of middlemen and free from all association with competition and money making" (TG 155n).

32. The lucky woman would have to be beautiful, read Greek and Persian, and be "able to understand the small things he let fall while undressing" (25)—which may be more of a feminist joke than Woolf consciously intended.

33. Alexander Pope, *An Essay on Criticism*, part 3, line 613. The preceding line, "The bookful blockhead, ignorantly read," also captures that sense of debased or misused scholarship that Woolf, like Pope, could not abide.

34. While working on *The Years* in 1933, Woolf records in her *Writer's Diary*: "It is an utterly corrupt society, I have just remarked, speaking in the person of Elvira Pargiter. . . . Now, as Virginia Woolf, I have to write—oh dear me what a bore—to the Vice Chancellor of Manchester University and say that I refuse to be made a Doctor of Letters. . . . Nothing would induce me to connive at all that humbug" (184–85).

35. Several actual political figures are briefly invoked in the novels; for example, Garibaldi in *The Voyage Out,* Marbot in *Mrs. Dalloway,* Parnell in *The Years.*

36. "Walk through the Admiralty Arch . . . and reflect upon the kind of glory celebrated there," Woolf commanded (ROOM 39).

37. Cf. Woolf on "social reformers and philanthropists . . . [who] get so out of hand and harbour so many discreditable desires under the disguise of loving their kind" (WD 28).

38. Carolyn Heilbrun, *Toward a Recognition of Androgyny* (New York: Alfred A. Knopf, 1973), 164.

39. Jane Marcus, in " 'No More Horses': Virginia Woolf on Art and Propaganda," *Women's Studies* 4 (1977):284n, points out that those revealing and damningly silly photographs of men decked out in full power garb in the original 1938 edition of *Three Guineas*—photos "central to the book's argument"—were not reprinted in subsequent paperback editions.

40. For an analysis of the feminist dimensions of the Ceres allusion, among others, see my *Continuing Presences: Virginia Woolf's Use of Literary Allusion* (University Park: Pennyslvania State University Press, 1979), 52–53.

1897:
Virginia Woolf
at Fifteen   *Louise A. DeSalvo*

"the first really lived year of my life"

On Saturday, 1 January, 1898, after having kept a diary for most of 1897, Virginia Stephen bade the diary and that year farewell:

> Here then comes the "Finis" what a volume might not be written round that word—& it is very hard to resist the few sentences that naturally cling to it. . . . Here is a volume of fairly acute life (the first really *lived* year of my life) ended locked & put away. And another & another yet to come. Oh diary they are very long. . . .
>
> *The End of 1897*[1]

Eighteen ninety-seven was the year Woolf wore stays for the first time. The year her half-sister, Stella Duckworth, married and died. The year Woolf experienced a recurrence of symptoms associated with the illness that would plague her throughout her life. The year she acquired a writing desk—too high to write at, but one in which she could store her writing supplies. The year she read no fewer than fifty weighty volumes—including a ten-volume set of Lockhart's *Life of Sir Walter Scott,* her father, Sir Leslie Stephen's, *Life of Henry Fawcett,* and Miss Mitford's *Notes of a Literary Life.* It was the year she attended King's College, London. The year she discovered how the moment was enriched and preserved by the process of writing it down. The year she watched the procession for Queen Victoria's diamond jubilee. The year she attended performances of *Mariana*, with Elizabeth Robins; of Shakespeare's *Hamlet* and *As You Like It;* of Gounod's *Faust.* A year with numerous visits to the zoo; walks through Kensington Gardens, to Battersea Park, to the Round Pond, along the Serpentine; visits to the National Gallery, the National Portrait Gallery, Carlyle's House. A year in which she discovered the pleasures, and the perils, of ice skating and bicycle riding. A year in which one could catch a glimpse of the woman that the girl would become.[2]

Peter Blos has described the work of adolescence as successfully negotiating the following related changes: loosening parental ties and replacing them, at least in part, with "the love of the self or its potential perfection: and with the friendship, sometimes passionate, sometimes transient, of peers"; working out the effects of traumas by confronting them internally; contradicting a "distortion of the family history that was coercively forced on the child" in order to restore the "integrity of the senses"—that is, critically reevaluating parents or their societal representations; developing an emerging sexual identity.[3]

Virginia Woolf, during her adolescence, would negotiate some of these changes more successfully than others; with some she would have enormous difficulty because of the interference of events beyond her control, such as Stella Duckworth's death, or because of the constraints imposed upon her because of her illness. What is striking nonetheless is the energy with which the fiteeen-year-old Virginia Stephen tried, often against all odds, and with amazing success considering those odds, to effect the changes in the self essential for a productive and a profitable adulthood. The 1897 diary provides an invaluable record of Woolf in the process of trying to make those changes, in the process of preparing herself for adulthood.

Take, for example, the history of Woolf's attempts to loosen her ties to her family. On 13 October 1896, Stella Duckworth took her half-sister to see Dr. Seton because Woolf had an anxiety attack—her pulse was 160 and she was in an excited state. A week later, on Wednesday, 21 October 1896, the two went to see Dr. Seton again. This time the recommendations were firm: Woolf would have to give up her lessons entirely until January at the very least, and she would have to spend at least four hours a day outside the house.[4] Although she began to do some Latin with her sister Vanessa by the beginning of March, and even some Greek,[5] much of 1897 passed without her having a normal schedule, a routine of activities designed to prepare her for a meaningful adult life.

Seton's cure itself, though no doubt well-intentioned, might have become the cause of Woolf's continuing anxiety and frequent bursts of temper throughout much of the early part of 1897. Deprived of the routine and the rigor of work, she was also forced to be out of the house for four hours a day, usually with Stella Duckworth. Stella seems to have assumed almost complete responsibility for Woolf's care during this year. It is no wonder Woolf grew increasingly ambivalent and even hostile toward Stella as the year progressed. As Adeline Stephen remarked, "it's bad for Stella to have Ginia always with her!"[6] It was also, no doubt, bad for Virginia to be always with Stella.

Woolf's 1897 diary describes a daily round of activities, often to the nearby Zoo and to Kensington Gardens, to the galleries and museums, often to the workhouses that Stella visited, as she followed in her mother Julia Stephen's footsteps as an "angel of mercy."[7] This daily round of activities seems harrying and exhausting—anxiety-producing rather than anxiety-relieving. On a typical Monday, 25 January 1897, Woolf's fifteenth birthday, Woolf records a walk around the Round Pond after breakfast with her father; a trip with Stella to see about a book for Jack Hills, Stella's fiancé; a trip to Regent Street for flowers and fruit for Jack; a trip to visit with Jack and take him the flowers and fruit; a trip to see Miss Hull in Marleybone Road; a trip to buy an armchair, which was to be Stella's wedding present from the Stephen children; and, finally, the birthday celebration itself. If Seton intended to calm Woolf down by this regimen, this daily round of activities hardly seems the way to accomplish it. In fact, Stella Duckworth herself had to go to the doctor for what was described as a case of the "fidgets." And Violet Dickinson once referred to the generally held opinion that Stella's death was in part linked to exhaustion, just as Julia Stephen's had been.[8]

Denied an identifiable purpose in her fifteenth year, it must have been extremely difficult for Woolf to develop the notion of herself as an evolving, purposeful human being, especially when one realizes she spent so much time in the constant company of family members. She describes trips to the zoo with Vanessa; meeting Vanessa and walking her home; walks with her father or her half-brothers; errands run with Stella; trips to museums and the theater with the family. But rarely, if ever, before Stella's illness does Woolf describe the family permitting her the conditions that would enable her to loosen the ties that bound her to them. She was almost never alone before Stella's illness, except for the time she spent reading. And she rarely records being with young women her own age. She watched Vanessa and her brothers Adrian and Thoby establishing friendships outside the household, largely as a result of their going to school, and she was irritated and lonely when they closeted themselves with their peers. But Woolf, probably because of their fear for her sanity, was kept very close to the family and, until Stella's illness and death, was supervised virtually every moment of her day.

Seton's regimen removed from Woolf's life any semblance of structure, any meaningful work, any serious preparation for adulthood. In reading the 1897 diary, one is struck again and again with how Woolf was forced to become an observer—a voyeur of her family's activities, of *their* meaningful work, which Seton denied *her* in his attempt to cure her. She watched her sister Vanessa go to her art lessons, heard her talk about becoming a painter, and, later in the year, watched her "come out"; Adrian, going to and from Westminster, getting a microscope; Thoby, coming and going from Clifton, where he was becoming somewhat adept at Latin; her father, doing the work that would lead to *Studies of a Biographer,* talking to Henry James and his other illustrious friends; Stella, preparing for her wedding to Jack Hills; her half-brothers, George and Gerald Duckworth, on their endless social rounds; Gerald, later in the year, thinking about beginning his press.[9]

This "watching" was no doubt important to Woolf's development as a novelist. Yet there was something fundamentally unwholesome and potentially damaging in her being denied her lessons and a life that would define her as a person in her own right, with an emerging though fluid identity—as Vanessa had the identity of a painter in embryo and Adrian that of a scientist. Woolf's later comments about the significance of work in *A Room of One's Own* and elsewhere become even more significant when viewed against the imposed vacuity of much of this year, a vacuity that Woolf herself was aware of and railed against from time to time. She could barely conceal her resentment of Vanessa as she entered, for example, that once again "Nessa went to her _____ drawing."[10] In her 17 March entry, after describing yet another walk through Kensington Gardens, her second of the day, she wrote sardonically:

> I went in to the gardens and looked at the flowers—the almond trees out, the crocusses going over, . . . the other trees just beginning to seed. . . . I shall turn into a country clergyman, and make notes of phenomena in Kensington Gardens.

Seton's advice regarding Virginia Woolf echoed the cure prescribed for Leslie Stephen in 1840 when, as a boy, he was made to give up poetry after manifesting symptoms that his mother thought were associated with precocious genius.[11] It is likely that Woolf identified herself and her ailment with her father and his early illness, and perhaps even with the family's

history of madness, as evidenced in the pitiful histories of J. K. Stephen and
Laura Stephen. J. K. was hopelessly in love with Stella Duckworth; he
violently pursued her during Woolf's childhood, and one day, rushing
"upstairs to the nursery at 22 Hyde Park Gate, drew the blade from a sword
stick and plunged it into the bread." He died hopelessly insane (QB 1:36). [12]
Laura, Leslie Stephen's and Minny Thackeray's daughter, was a constant
reminder of this family history. In 1897 she was twenty-seven years old, in-
curably insane or mentally defective, unable even to recognize Leslie Stephen
when he visited her at Brook House, Southgate, where she lived, a constant
source of anguish and despair to him. [13] Given this history, Woolf would have
had good reason to fear that she too might be becoming irrevocably insane.
But what seems fairly certain from the 1897 diary is that Seton's cure itself
exacerbated Woolf's illness, making her and her family perhaps overreact to
anxiety as symptomatic of even more serious illness, and that because they
treated her as if she were seriously ill she probably acted sicker than she really
was.

Deprived of school and of the companionship of peers, Woolf had nothing
against which to judge herself other than the measure of her family, no way
to determine where she stood in relation to young women her own age in
terms of social, intellectual, and emotional growth, no mirror outside the
family that could reflect a less distorted image of herself and her feelings, no
companion who could share that she too experienced rages, disappoint-
ments, griefs, and fears. She was exceedingly and excessively dependent upon
the goodwill and good wishes of Stella, Vanessa, and Leslie. Without them
she had no one. If they were angry with her and withdrew their affection or
attention, she had no one her own age to console her. But for them, in this
year she was almost totally alone. And when deprived of their company,
when they went about their own business, she was frequently incapacitated
because she had been denied the chance to become self-sufficient or to use
friendships outside the family as a bulwark against the hard times she might
encounter within it. On 30 June, with Stella ill, Vanessa occupied with her
drawing, her father employed at his work, an entry reads:

> Nessa went to her drawing—but the rest of the morning is rather
> vague—I went in to Stella for the first time, & found her very well—then
> afterward I may have brought strawberries, or I may have taken a solitary
> walk in the park, both of them the usual employments of mine nowadays.

Woolf's lassitude is evident on the page, as is her tendency to describe her days in terms of what other people did and her activities in relation to theirs. In Woolf's diary there is none of that egocentric tendency one often finds in the diaries of adolescents. Here, instead, the tendency is for Woolf to first describe other family members, what they did and how they felt, then to fill in some information about herself.

The conditions imposed upon Woolf by Dr. Seton and complied with by the family certainly were not conducive to her loosening family ties, to experimenting with a way of being that was separate from their definition of her. Nonetheless, the diary records how Woolf kept fighting to do this throughout the year and how the family often defined these attempts as symptoms of Woolf's illness rather than as healthy though sometimes desperate efforts at separation. In February, for example, plans were being made for Stella Duckworth and Jack Hills to go on a holiday together. Woolf was to accompany them. As soon as the plan was conceived, Woolf voiced her opposition to going, opposition that soon took the form of outbursts of temper when the family would not heed her refusal (2/6). One can well understand Woolf's reluctance to go, considering she had been Stella's constant companion since Seton's regimen had been imposed in November 1896. On 1 February she wrote:

> A terrible idea started that Stella and I should take lodgings at Eastbourne or some such place, where Jack is going next week—Impossible to be alone with those two creatures, yet if I do not go, Stella will not, and Jack particularly wishes her to go—The question is, whether Nessa will be allowed to come too—If so it would be better—but goodness knows how we shall come out of this *quandary* as Vanessa calls it.

Later on the page, she records that she cannot protest *"too* strongly against going.'' On 2 February, Woolf recorded that she told Jack that she *"could not"* go with him and Stella alone. On 5 February, one learns that Woolf lost her battle—she and Vanessa would have to accompany Jack and Stella to Bognor on the following Monday and that nothing could now stop what Woolf called the ''whole thing most horrible'' (2/5).

Although Woolf is not explicit about what she means by the ''whole thing most horrible,'' one can read between the lines. The family—primarily Leslie Stephen—wanted Woolf to act as a kind of chaperone for the twenty-eight-year-old Stella and Jack—just weeks before their wedding. One can imagine how confused and enraged Woolf must have become, given that since November she had been treated as ill and very carefully supervised. For the family now to ask Woolf to assume the awesome responsibility—given the nature of their conventions—of chaperoning Stella and Jack was to redefine her suddenly, and self-servingly, as mature and capable. That Stella and Jack would not be allowed to make the trip without Woolf suggests either that Leslie Stephen did not trust them alone together or that he wanted them chaperoned for appearances' sake. In this context one can well understand and sympathize with Woolf's reluctance to go, and then with her horror at the prospect of being alone with the two of them. For she knew her father well, and one suspects she realized she was being entrusted with seeing to it that Stella maintained her chastity until her wedding, a terrifying responsibility for an adolescent so recently defined as incapable of even being alone. But the family did not hear Woolf's pleas to be spared this charge, did not listen to the message that could be expressed only as rage. She lost the battle, and she and Vanessa (a concession to Woolf) accompanied Stella and Jack on the trip, which was a disaster. (I shall describe this trip more fully later in this essay.)

When Stella returned from her honeymoon she was seriously ill. With Stella bedridden, Woolf seems to have taken on some of her household responsibilities. She records visits to the workhouse, a trip to High Street to buy a chair for George Duckworth, a visit to the bank to retrieve Stella's and Jack's silver, visits to sit with Stella, and, often, rides in the park with her.[14] Stella's illness allowed Woolf some time alone, but it seems she was not fully prepared emotionally for this opportunity. Stella's illness also might have permitted Woolf to redefine herself as a potentially capable human being, for now the family seems to have expected from her the kinds of services it had expected from Stella.[15] It might have been too much too soon, however, because Woolf also began to record accidents that she noticed on her trips about town—a hansom overturned (5/8), a runaway horse (4/13). And it is important that she began to record them at the same time she was required to take on running many errands for the household. Woolf's psyche seemed to have been telling her she was not yet ready to turn from invalid to "angel in the house." The family's expectations following the onset of Stella's illness seem to have put Woolf in a double bind: she was now expected to act responsibly, whereas formerly she was treated as ill. The new responsibilities made her feel both capable and anxious. Yet if she showed her anxiety the family would again curtail her activities and inhibit her new freedom. It is also significant that Stella had to be sick before Woolf was redefined as capable. This too must have confused her. Stella, who had been Woolf's protectress, was now the reason she had to accept responsibilities before she was emotionally ready. It is no wonder Woolf was ambivalent about Stella—that she worried constantly about her health but also began to record irritation and then outright hostility toward Stella and her illness.

On 6 May, with Stella bedridden, Woolf records that she brought home

> Something else which I cannot remember—a catalogue of the classes at King's College . . . which I may go to. After lunch I talked to father about it, and decided to begin next autumn if I begin at all. In the afternoon we went to the workhouse.[16]

In 1897, bringing the King's College catalog home was Woolf's most serious attempt to separate from her family in a healthy, socially acceptable, and non-self-destructive way. But Leslie Stephen demurred. How Woolf was capable of going to the workhouse and running household errands yet incapable of attending King's College is difficult to understand, unless Leslie Stephen needed a substitute for Stella and, Vanessa being occupied with her art lessons, found Woolf the alternative. Woolf must have believed she *was* capable of attending classes or she would not have brought the catalog home. One wonders what damage would have been done had Leslie Stephen allowed his daughter, who at the time was devouring Macaulay at a volume every few days, to try out her newly developed sense of self. Instead of having her capabilities verified, she was forced to see herself as incapable once again—but only incapable of going to school, not of working for the family. And she seems to have responded with those same symptoms she had manifested in November.

On Sunday, 9 May, Seton examined Woolf again. The regimen of no lessons was reinstated. It was during this time that Woolf recorded the dangers she observed while running errands. Almost immediately after Leslie Stephen's refusal to allow her to go to King's College, Woolf recorded, on 8 May—"we saw a hansom overturned in Piccadilly—I saw it in mid air''; on 13 May, while buying sponge cakes for Stella's tea, "I heard a stampede in the street outside—shouting—as the stampede became more violent—& then a crash. Evidently the runaway had collided . . . one horse on the ground and a second prancing madly above it—a carriage was smashed up, & a waggon turned over on to its side.'' Woolf's response both to the requirement that she run errands and to the covert message of Leslie Stephen's refusal was classically self-protective and phobic: venture outside the protection of the family, and all manner of dangers await you. Yet Woolf's fears had not prevented her from trying to venture out in a wholesome way.

On 11 May Woolf wrote:

> Father had taken up Dr Setons notion that I should be healthfully
> employed out of doors—as a lover of nature—& the back garden is to be
> reclaimed—That will be a truly gigantic work of genius—nevertheless
> we will try. Accordingly, a fork, a spade, a hoe & a rake were ordered. . .
> & tomorrow I begin operations.

Woolf was reading, according to her diary entry, the very difficult fifth
volume of Macaulay's history of England. To contemplate the spectacle of
the fifteen-year-old reader of Macaulay deprived of her lessons, not allowed
to go to King's College, and forced to become a gardener to cure her nervous symptoms is a spectacle so ludicrous and so pathetic that the humor and
the pathos did not escape Woolf herself.

Whether Woolf's mental state was as precarious as the family seemed to
think is of course sheer speculation. But they seem to have had less difficulty
dealing with Woolf's illness than with her emotions—her moments of anger
and anxiety, her rages, her "tantrumical" self. They seemed to prefer to define her as incipiently insane, than as emotional, as not having fully resolved
the complicated feelings surrounding her mother's death—ambivalence;
anger at being abandoned; grief; self-chastisement for not being able to put
those feelings to rest; subsequent ambivalence at Stella's illness; and rage at
not being allowed to go to school. Defining an adolescent as sharing a family
tendency toward madness, after all, absolves a family of guilt and responsibility. Instead of seeking a cause for Woolf's anxiety in the complex
constellation of family interactions, it was far easier to see the anxiety as inherited. Then one need do nothing about it, because it was inescapable, in-
curable, the family curse. Julia Stephen, Virginia Woolf's mother, wrote in
her pamphlet *Notes from Sick Rooms* that "in illness we can afford to ignore
the details which in health make familiar intercourse difficult" and, even
more significantly, that the "ordinary relations between the sick and the
well are far easier and pleasanter than between the well and the well."[17]

There was a tendency in the Stephen household, especially in Leslie and
Julia Stephen, to explain emotional unpleasantness as emotional illness. It
was probably easier and less cumbersome for the family, and for Leslie
Stephen, preoccupied with their own lives and with their own grief and sense
of loss at Stella's marriage, to treat Woolf as ill than to take on the difficult
emotional work, the difficult familial intercourse, necessary to help her
understand her anger, her sadness, her rage, and see through them to the

potentially powerful emerging woman beneath. Instead of allowing emotions to surface appropriately and then dealing with them, the family allowed, encouraged, even required emotions, especially unpleasant ones, to be held in check, to be repressed. This is evident in many of Woolf's diary entries. At the time of Stella's wedding, for example, Vanessa and Virginia vowed they would show no grief, despite their sadness at losing Stella. They would be "calm and most proper behaved, as if Stellas marriage were nothing at all touching us" (4/5). When emotions surfaced inappropriately, as repressed feelings often do, they were defined as symptoms of insanity. Then a meaningless, dependent, carefully circumscribed existence was imposed that itself caused Woolf to regard herself as incapable. In fact, Virginia Woolf's life during her fifteenth year very much resembled the life of the animals she observed on her frequent visits to the zoo. It is no wonder she began to describe herself and her emotions in animallike terms—her stubbornness, the "stubbornness of a mule"; her ardor, the "ardour of a marmoset (my new title)" (3/29). For those animals that were caged and restrained, that paced to and fro, peered at by visitors, were very much like Woolf, who was also caged and restricted, who was watched for symptoms of illness, for signs of irritation, for indications of bad behavior. And when Woolf, like a zoo animal, tried to break away, even harsher restraints were imposed.

Nonetheless, Woolf did the best she could. She carved out an identity for herself, as a historian in the making, despite the odds against her, and she did it largely as a result of her own efforts, though Leslie Stephen helped her. By the end of the year she had persuaded her father she was able to attend classes (10/16). But even before Woolf went to King's College, one can see her educating herself to become a historian or perhaps even a biographer. Not only was she reading, she also tried writing various works throughout the year, and they seem to have been historical or biographical ones.

In an 1893 letter to Julia Stephen, written when Woolf was eleven, Leslie Stephen stated:

> Yesterday I discussed George II with "Ginia." . . . She takes in a great deal and will really be an author in time, though I cannot make up my mind in what line. History will be a good thing for her to take up as I can give her some hints.[18]

In 1897 Leslie Stephen continued to encourage his daughter to become a historian or a biographer—to follow in his footsteps. For her birthday he

presented her with Lockhart's ten-volume life of Sir Walter Scott—the
"nicest present I have had yet" (1/26). Reading lives was, for Leslie
Stephen, a form of moral instruction. He once wrote that he was studying
Thackeray's life and was ashamed of himself for worrying, "for I am at least
far better off than he was."[19]

Leslie Stephen had been working on his biography of Scott for the *Dictionary of National Biography* in 1896; Julia Stephen had especially liked the
works of Scott (MB 86). The Scott was a gift that allowed Woolf to forge a
link with both her father and her mother. Reading about the life of a successful literary figure who had his share of difficulties no doubt provided
Woolf with a role model, and probably also an emotional education. For
Woolf, like Scott, had to navigate between two cultures—that of her mother
and that of her father, as Scott in his novels consistently described the clash of
civilizations or cultures, the tug of conflicting loyalties, between the
Jacobites and Hanoverians, between the Scots and the English.

The extent to which reading history and biography gave Woolf a sense of
purpose and structure otherwise denied her during this very difficult year is
evident from her 18 May entry, written when Stella was seriously ill.

> I went for my now usual much to be dreaded drive in the Park with Stella.
> I have now got Carlyle's French Revolution—the 5th volume of
> Macaulay being restored to its place. In this way I shall become surfeited
> with history. Already I am an expert upon William (Hear Hear!) & when
> I have mastered Cs. 2 vols. I shall be eligible for the first B. A. degree.

The formal education denied Woolf because of her illness she provided for
herself by reading. Reading history and biography, even believing herself
eligible for the B.A., must have done a great deal for her during this year.
And the extent to which she read history—in contrast to other types of
works—is evident from a list of the works she was reading. In January, for
example, of the eight or so volumes she records, six are works of
history—*Three Generations of English Women* (vols. 1 and 2); Creighton's
Queen Elizabeth; J. A. Froude's *Thomas Carlyle* (vols. 1 and 2); the first
volume of Lockhart's *Life of Sir Walter Scott.* This preference for history and
biography manifests itself throughout the year. In February she continued
the Scott and the Creighton and read *Essays in Ecclesiastical Biography,* by Sir
James Stephen. In March she read Campbell's *Life of Coleridge,* Carlyle's *Life
of John Sterling* (which had provided her father with the model for his life of
Henry Fawcett),[20] and Pepys; in April, Caesar, Macaulay's *History of*

England, Carlyle's *French Revolution,* and Miss Mitford's *Notes of a Literary Life;* in June, Carlyle's *Oliver Cromwell's Letters and Speeches,* Cowper's *Letters,* a *History of Rome;* in August, her father's *Life of Henry Fawcett;* in September she continued Carlyle's *French Revolution* and read his letters.

In addition there were works of fiction and poetry that she either read or heard her father read aloud to the family. In January Leslie Stephen was reading *Esmond* and *The Antiquary* aloud, and Woolf was reading *The Newcomes* and *The Old Curiosity Shop.* In February she continued *The Newcomes* and read *A Deplorable Affair;* in March she read *Felix Holt,* among others; in April her father recited "The Rime of the Ancient Mariner," and she was reading *Barchester Towers;* in May her father read "Love in the Valley," by Meredith, and she was reading something by Henry James, *Caleb Williams,* and *The Scarlet Letter;* in July she read both *Shirley* and *Vilette;* in August *Vanity Fair* and *Adam Bede;* in September *Jane Eyre* and *Nicolas Nickelby.* During the year she attended performances of *Mariana,* with Elizabeth Robins; of *Hamlet* and *As You Like It;* and of *The White Silk Dress,* among other performances.

Although Woolf was diligent in recording the works she was reading, she rarely if ever entered extended comments about them, other then referring to them, for example, as "my cherished Macaulay" (5/1), "my beautiful Lockhart" (1/30). She does note that reading relieved her anxiety. When Stella was seriously ill and Woolf was reading Macaulay, she wrote: "After all books are the greatest help and comfort" (5/1). Perhaps reading history and biography, in addition to providing her with information, did for her what it did for her father: demonstrated that there were people who not only had more difficult lives than she but overcame immense personal unhappiness and affliction to succeed, not despite them, but because they generated idiosyncratic lenses through which to view the world. Reading history and biography also extended the range of her perceptions beyond the confines of her family, allowing her, while being raised as a young woman in a Victorian household, to measure herself and the way she was treated against other kinds of experiences, particularly the experiences of men. In this year the range and depth of Woolf's historical reading are an indication of how she developed the probing mastery of historical processes that is evident in everything she wrote, but especially in *Orlando, Three Guineas,* and *The Years,* and of how she developed an understanding of the way societal and historical forces impinge upon people's lives. Reading fiction no doubt also extended Woolf's view, but in a different way. Through fiction she probably learned about the ways people interacted and was thereby able to see her own life from the perspective of other alternatives.[21] In addition to reading history and biography, it seems that Woolf was trying her hand at the form.[22]

During the months when Woolf was deprived of her lessons and Stella was ill, one of Woolf's primary consolations was reading. Reading in effect became her refuge, her solace in grief, her substitute for the friendships she did not have. It was the way she carved out an identity for herself as a human being, the way she secured her privacy, the way she began to determine the life she would choose for herself as a woman. The extent to which Woolf was influenced by the works she read in this year is indicated by the facts that she wrote about virtually every one in her maturity; that she used many of the literary allusions in her novels; and that they provided part of the historical background for her numerous essays, biographies, and novels.[23]

To describe fully the influence these works had upon the mind and the manner of Virginia Woolf the novelist, the biographer, and the essayist would require many pages. But the extent to which she was enriched by her reading of history and fiction in 1897 can be indicated briefly by observing how she referred later in life, for example, to reading Carlyle and her father's *Life of Henry Fawcett,* and to hearing her father read Meredith's "Love in the Valley" and Scott's *The Antiquary,* integrating them into her mature work.

Carlyle was the historian to whom Woolf returned again and again in 1897. On 29 January Leslie Stephen took his daughter to visit Carlyle's house in Chelsea, and the trip might have been prompted by her reading Froude's *Carlyle.* Her entry describing the visit reads:

> Went over the house, with an intelligent old woman who knew father and everything about him—We saw the drawing room, and dining room, and Cs. sound proof room, with double walls—His writing table, and his pens, and scraps of his manuscripts—Pictures of him and of her everywhere.

In a very important sense, reading Carlyle and trying to understand his works and his character might have been a way for Woolf not only to train herself to become a historian and biographer, but also connect herself with her father, to try to penetrate his increasingly impenetrable facade. For Carlyle's early childhood and manhood were very much like those of Leslie Stephen—both were bullied at school; both flirted with careers in the ministry; both were athletic coaches and teachers; both had marriages that allowed their masterful, irritable, melancholy, and often difficult natures to assert themselves; both worried about money; both took on extremely am-

bitious projects and suffered through them—Carlyle, *The French Revolution,*
Stephen, the *Dictionary of National Biography;* both shared similar views of the
historical process, though Leslie's were no doubt derived from Carlyle; both
revered the heroic in men; both detested softness; neither recovered from the
death of his wife (MB41).

In 1897, for Woolf as for her character Jacob in *Jacob's Room,* "Carlyle was
a prize." According to the critic Beverly Ann Schlack, many of Carlyle's attitudes are at the core of *Jacob's Room.* Carlyle's denunciation of materialism
and industrialism as destructive of human personality; his attitude toward
the hero as divinity are echoed in the novel. And the novel illustrates as well
Carlyle's contention that "the uttered part of a man's life, let us always
repeat, bears to the unuttered, unconscious part a small unknown proportion. He himself never knows it, much less do others."[24] This of course
became the core of Woolf's method—in the history, novels, and biographies
she wrote in her maturity—and the impact of Carlyle upon her work has
never been fully assessed.

Leslie Stephen's *Life of Fawcett* had immense personal significance for
Woolf. Stephen had had great difficulty in writing this life because of his
closeness to Fawcett.[25] But the model of Fawcett's life must have been important for Woolf to read in this formative adolescent period, especially since
her father had written it. Blinded in a shooting accident in 1858 while at
Cambridge, Fawcett overcame this handicap and went on to hold a pro-
fessorship of political economy and to run for Parliament in 1860. Although
he was defeated in that year, he finally won a seat in 1865. He advocated
widening the scope of elementary education and took special interest in the
rights of women. He married Millicent Garrett, leader of the British
women's suffrage movement, who was a founder of Newnham College,
Cambridge, one of the first English university colleges for women.[26] At this
stage of Woolf's life, afflicted as *she* was, it must have been inspiring to read
of Fawcett's successes—and of his commitment to educational reform and
women's suffrage—and to learn of Millicent Garrett's efforts. Their marriage was probably an enriching model. Millicent Garrett helped her husband
overcome the handicap of his blindness; he supported her through the emotional difficulties of working for women's rights. Learning of this no doubt
widened Woolf's sense of what marriage could be like: mutually supportive,
mutually enriching. At its best, the marriage of Leonard and Virginia Woolf
resembled that of Millicent Garrett and Henry Fawcett much more than it
resembled that of her parents. The model of Millicent Garrett and her sister,
Mrs. Garrett Anderson (whom Woolf met in 1897, when she accompanied

Stella to see that crusading physician)[27] and the crusade for women's suffrage and educational opportunities also gave Woolf an alternative to emulating Stella and Julia Duckworth as "angel in the house."

Woolf referred to George Meredith's "Love in the Valley" in her first published novel, *The Voyage Out.* In that novel Rachel Vinrace and Terence Hewet are two English tourists at a South American resort. They fall in love, but Rachel Vinrace dies of a mysterious illness before they can marry. Hewet is an erstwhile novelist. One of his novels is about silence. This novel in progress, which he reads to Rachel Vinrace, deals with the relation between men and women, with how an ideal wife has become remote and distant. The couple in Hewet's novel "shouted *Love in the Valley* to each other across the snowy slopes of the Riffelhorn" (VO 296).[28] Meredith's poem deals with the same issues as Woolf's *The Voyage Out;* the lovers in the poem are very much like Rachel and Terence; and the specter of death haunts both *Love in the Valley* and *The Voyage Out.* Two inconsecutive stanzas from the Meredith poem illustrate the relationship between it and *Voyage:*

> Hither she comes; she comes to me; she lingers,
>   Deepens her brown eyebrows, while in new surprise
> High rise the lashes in wonder of a stranger;
>   Yet am I the light and living of her eyes.
> Something friends have told her fills her heart to brimming,
>   Nets her in her blushes, and wounds her, and tames. —
> Sure of her haven, O like a dove alighting,
>   Arms up, she dropped: our souls were in our names.
>
> Soon will she lie like a white frost sunrise.
>   Yellow oats and brown wheat, barley pale as rye,
> Long since your sheaves have yielded to the thresher,
>   Felt the girdle loosened, seen the tresses fly.
> Soon will she lie like a blood-red sunset.
>   Swift with the to-morrow, green-winged Spring!
> Sing from the South-West, bring her back the truants,
>   Nightingale and swallow, song and dipping wing.[29]

But what is especially significant in the context of 1897, and in the context of how Woolf used the poem later, is that Leslie Stephen read it to the family while Stella was seriously ill (5/26), less than a month before she died, so that the work has very personal and private associations with Stella's brief marriage to Jack Hills, which was haunted almost from its very beginning by the specter of death. Woolf's first novel, dealing with the short-lived romance of Rachel and Terence, might have been a way for her to work out her grief at Stella's death, and, at least in this one sense, Stella Duckworth might have been the model for Woolf's heroine Rachel Vinrace.[30]

In 1924 Virginia Woolf published an essay entitled *"The Antiquary"* in the *New Republic*. It is likely that she began the essay on or about 16 October 1924.[31] On 17 October Woolf wrote the diary entry recording her inspiration for *To the Lighthouse*—"I see already the Old Man" (WD 64). Beginning her review of *The Antiquary* probably brought up memories and unresolved issues from 1897—the year Leslie Stephen read the work aloud to his children—most particularly, from 27 January, when Woolf records, "Father began the Antiquary to us" through Wednesday, 31 March, when she records that either he or she completed the novel. This is the period when Woolf's freedom was curtailed, when she accompanied Stella and Jack to Bognor against her will. So much of *To the Lighthouse* explores the emotional confluence of the events of 1897—the life-giving yet stifling and inhibiting presence of a mother figure, then her sudden death and absence; the lovable yet irritatingly infantile, dependent father figure; the need to come to terms with these two as parents and with the absence of the mother and continuing presence of the father while simultaneously trying to construct an identity derived from each and yet separate from both. All these reflect Woolf's situation in 1897. And it is fascinating to note that one of the prototypes of the characters of the Antiquary, according to Lockhart's life of Scott, which Woolf read during this year, was John *Ramsay* of Ochtertyre.[32]

Woolf referred to *The Antiquary* in "The Window" section of *To the Lighthouse*. Mrs. Ramsay comes into a room where Mr. Ramsay is "reading something that moved him very much. He was half smiling and then she knew he was controlling his emotion. He was tossing the pages over. He was acting it—perhaps he was thinking himself the person in the book. She wondered what book it was. Oh, it was one of old Sir Walter's she saw" (TTL 176).

Later Mr. Ramsay is described as reading about "poor Steenie's drowning and Mucklebackit's sorrow" (TTL 180). Thoughts of his wife, his family, and himself beome intermingled with his response to the Scott novel:

> This man's strength and sanity, his feeling for straightforward simple things, these fishermen, the poor old crazed creature in Mucklebackit's cottage made him feel so vigorous, so relieved of something that he felt roused and triumphant and could not choke back his tears. Raising the

book a little to hide his face, he let them fall and shook his head from side to side and forgot himself completely . . . forgot his own bothers and failures completely in poor Steenie's drowning and Mucklebackit's sorrow (that was Scott at his best) and the astonishing delight and feeling of vigour that it gave him. (TTL 179–80)

This portrait of Mr. Ramsay, a fictional surrogate for Leslie Stephen, was no doubt based upon Woolf's memory of her father's reading *The Antiquary* to the family in 1897. In the Scott novel the scene Mr. Ramsay reads is as follows:

> The body was laid in its coffin within the wooden bedstead which the young fisher had occupied while alive. At a little distance stood the father, whose rugged, weatherbeaten countenance, shaded by his grizzled hair, had faced many a stormy night and night-like day. He was apparently revolving his loss in his mind with that strong feeling of painful grief peculiar to harsh and rough characters, which almost breaks forth into hatred against the world and all that remain in it after the beloved object is withdrawn. The old man had made the most desperate efforts to save his son, and had only been withheld by main force from renewing them at a moment when, without the possibility of assisting the sufferer, he himself must have perished.[33]

In 1897 Leslie Stephen's continuing, unresolved grief over the loss of his wife Julia was still upon him. For Woolf, hearing her father read of Steenie's drowning and Mucklebackit's sorrow, or reading of it herself, probably supplied a fictional analogue with which to comprehend the depth of her father's continuing grief, an analogue she would return to many years later when writing a fictional portrait of him in *To the Lighthouse*. Indeed, beginning her essay on *The Antiquary* might have caused memories of him to surface and even inspired her to begin to think about that intensely autobiographical novel. It is significant that *The Antiquary* itself contains the image of the lighthouse that is central in Woolf's novel. In a scene in which Sir Arthur, Isabella Wardour, and Ochiltree are stranded on the crag in a storm, a lighthouse beam that is temporarily hidden from view is essential to their survival:

> Deprived of this view of the beacon on which they had relied, they now experienced the double agony of terror and suspense. . . . The signal of safety was lost among a thousand white breakers. . . . "My father! my dear father!" his daughter exclaimed, clinging to him.[34]

Woolf singled this out as one of three scenes she commented upon in her 1924 essay. In *The Antiquary*—as in *To the Lighthouse*—the lighthouse beam is associated with a need for parental protection. In *Lighthouse*, as Cam joins her father in their journey to the lighthouse, she, like Isabella Wardour, thinks about her father's ability to protect her from harm:

> Now I can go on thinking whatever I like, and I shan't fall over a precipice or be drowned, for there he is, keeping his eye on me . . . and yet he was leading them on a great expedition where, for all she knew, they would be drowned. (TTL 304–5)

Earlier Cam had thought of Mr. Ramsay's character traits that had poisoned her childhood, and they are the very traits with which Woolf had to live in 1897:

> But what remained intolerable . . . was that crass blindness and tyranny of his which had poisoned her childhood and raised bitter storms, so that even now she woke in the night trembling with rage and remembered some command of his; some insolence: "Do this," "Do that," his dominance· his "Submit to me." (TTL 253)

In the final section of *Lighthouse* Cam recalls her father's reading in her youth, and she associates his reading with her ambivalent feelings about his ability to protect her:

> on he went, tossing over page after page. And she went on telling herself a story about escaping from a sinking ship, for she was safe, while he sat there; safe as she felt herself when she crept in from the garden, and took a book down. . . . About here, she thought, dabbling her fingers in the water, a ship had sunk, and she murmured, dreamily half asleep, how we perished, each alone. (TTL 283–84)

Cam's ambivalence about her father—that she regards him somehow as both protector and prophet of her own solitary death by drowning—probably echoes Woolf's ambivalence about her own father in 1897 as he sat reading *The Antiquary*, while she listened to Isabella Wardour's ambivalence about *her* father in that novel. For in 1897 Leslie Stephen was doing all he knew how to take care of his daughter, to prevent her from falling victim to yet another anxiety attack. In this sense, in ensuring that Seton's orders were carried out, he was her protector and saw to it that she was safe.

But the very nature of those orders, the very gloomy submission to Seton's view of her illness, must have led Woolf to view her father as believing in her fate, which was to perish, alone, by drowning in the sea.

Moreover, Woolf probably shared Cam's ambivalence about fatherly protectiveness because of one important factor in her background. Although Leslie Stephen acted the part of the protective father in 1897, Woolf had earlier been subjected to the sexual advances of her half-brother or half-brothers while Leslie was too overwhelmed with grief at the death of his wife to notice. Her task of establishing a healthy sexual identity as an adolescent was probably confounded by these sexual assaults. One of the archetypes Woolf lived with, therefore, was the archetype of the male as polluter, as despoiler of a woman's life.[35] Stella's death in that year probably reinforced Woolf's fears about the dangers of sexuality.

In *To the Lighthouse,* after the dinner party Mr. Ramsay feels he must read the Scott chapter in *The Antiquary* again. The chapter, chapter 32, opens with the following poem, purportedly written by "Mysterious Mother":

> What is this secret sin, this untold tale,
> That art cannot extract, nor penance cleanse?

The "untold tale" describing "this secret sin" is unfolded at the end of the Scott chapter, immediately after Steenie's sorrow is described. Evelina Neville, crazed and filled with grief and guilt, led to believe she is tainted because she has committed incest with her half-brother, destroys herself by plunging off a cliff. Cam's fantasies of death by drowning, in the context of *The Antiquary,* are also associated with Evelina's suicide. But one wonders how Woolf must have felt in 1897 upon hearing or reading of Evelina's decision to commit suicide because of her guilt over what she thought was an incestuous relationship with a half-brother, an experience Woolf shared. By this time, Woolf had already experienced incestuous relationships with one or both of her half-brothers, Gerald and George Duckworth, either or both of whom might have been in the room while Leslie or Virginia herself read of Evelina's suicide.

What is equally fascinating about Virginia Woolf's use of *The Antiquary* in *To the Lighthouse* is an indication, in her published essay on the novel, that she misread or misremembered the Evelina Neville episode, the one Mr. Ramsay feels he must reread. There is an important inconsistency between the published version of the essay and its holograph draft. In the holograph Woolf writes of the Glenallan episode:

For who breaks in upon that memorable scene? The cadaverous Earl of Glenallan, ~~who~~ the unhappy nobleman ~~who had the~~ who had married his sister, or—but we wrong the ~~lady, who~~ lady who expiated her crime by leaping from a crag. She was his cousin only—& it is we who are most to be pitied, for she ~~pitches~~ us necessitates romance.

The published version, however, is quite different:

For who taps at the door and destroys that memorable scene? The cadaverous Earl of Glenallan; the unhappy nobleman who had married his sister in the belief that she was his cousin; and had stalked the world in sables ever after.[36]

In the short space of less than two months between the holograph and the published text, Woolf's memory has played a trick on her, and it is a very significant one, given her own background. One suspects that Woolf's misremembering *was* in some way connected with her incestuous childhood experiences and perhaps obliquely connected with her dredging up memories from the past as she began to think of 1897, when her father read *The Antiquary*. For in the published essay an episode of suspected incest is rendered as actual incest by Virginia Woolf's faulty memory. When one recalls that Evelina drowned herself because of her guilt at an episode that was not in fact incest, the misremembering becomes even more significant.

Woolf carried her sense of shame and guilt, of anger and grief and impotence in regard to *her* incestuous experiences throughout her life. Cam's association of her father's reading with a lack of parental protection and Woolf's alluding to that chapter in *To the Lighthouse* may reflect Leslie Stephen's failure to protect Woolf when she was subjected to the incestuous advances of her half-brothers. It is horrifying to speculate that Evelina Neville in *The Antiquary* was the model Woolf would emulate many years later when she committed suicide by plunging into the River Ouse. But the similarities between *The Antiquary* and Woolf's life, and her later use of the novel, suggest that *The Antiquary* was immensely important to Woolf—that she used it to understand her father, to explain her own ambivalence about parental figures—but that somehow she projected her own experiences onto Evelina Neville.

When one recalls that the work of adolescence, according to Blos, includes loosening parental ties and replacing them with self-love and with friendships, reevaluating one's parents, and developing an emerging sexual identity, one can witness, through the autobiographical *To the Lighthouse,* how many of those issues remained unresolved for Woolf during 1897—how difficult it must have been for her to negotiate those changes that she managed. That other task of adolescence—confronting unresolved traumas by working through them internally—was made especially difficult for Woolf because of Stella Duckworth's death. It seems clear that by Woolf's fifteenth year she was still longing for her mother and had not yet worked through the ambivalence (the love and the rage) precipitated by her mother's death, compounded by Leslie Stephen's inability to deal with his children's grief. The 1897 diary makes it very clear that Stella Duckworth acted as mother surrogate to Virginia Woolf during her adolescence. And Stella was very much like Julia Stephen—"sweet and noble and affectionate."[37] Like Julia, Stella visited the sick; like Julia, she was self-sacrificing in her relationship with the family and particularly with Leslie. But Woolf's diary also makes clear how difficult it must have been for an adolescent who was not sweet and noble, who was not perfect, to be in the company of someone as good as Stella. Woolf even occasionally alluded negatively to Stella's sweetness and nobility, referring to her mockingly as "Bella."

The letters Leslie Stephen wrote to Stella immediately after her wedding to Jack Hills indicate the extent to which he had perceived her as a substitute for his wife. He writes almost as a bereaved lover rather than as a stepfather.

> I am tired and excited and don't precisely know whether I am standing on my head or my heels. The world seems to have turned topsy-turvy with me since this morning and I feel as I felt once when I picked myself up after a fall—I cannot tell whether I am hurt or healed of a wound or simply dazzled.[38]

If Woolf, as an adolescent in the throes of trying to establish her individuality and her separation from parental figures, perceived Stella as a mother substitute, rather than as a loving half-sister, her ambivalence toward her would have been normal and healthy, since Stella was chiefly responsible for enforcing Seton's orders that Woolf be carefully supervised. Woolf must have resented Stella; one can understand that she might even have hated her. Leslie Stephen did not function as Woolf's overseer during 1897. He seems to have been closeted with his work much of the time, leaving Stella in charge of Virginia and the functioning of the household. Woolf's experience with her father in that year was usually enjoyable; they took walks together; they went to Carlyle's house; they talked about books; he read to the family.

Woolf's resentment of Seton's regimen, therefore, would have been directed at Stella, and one can also imagine her wishing her half-sister would disappear, perhaps even die and leave her free—the common wish of the adolescent who seeks relief from parental overprotection.

In the months preceding Stella's wedding there is hardly a trace of resentment toward her in the diary, except what boiled over in response to the family's desire that Woolf accompany Stella and Jack on their trip to Bognor. One can imagine that Woolf was so imbued with the family notion that one should be grateful to Stella for carrying out Julia's functions that her healthy resentment was never allowed to surface in a wholesome way and be dealt with. Instead, one confronts her resentment of Stella in response to the proposed trip to Bognor with Jack Hills—the trip she described as "the whole thing most horrible."

The trip to Bognor was a disaster, and Woolf probably long resented being forced to go. And there are indications that the trip had real traumatizing effects. The lodgings Stella and the girls took were unfinished. It was windy, "dismal and cold," raining or drizzling the entire time. It was muddy. The sea was black. Jack took lodgings nearby but came over for meals. On Wednesday, 10 February, Woolf describes how Stella and Jack pretended to be walking along with her and Vanessa but "soon turned and went back alone." The couple seems to have been trying to elude them, which exasperated Virginia. Dragged along against her will, probably realizing that she and Vanessa were supposed to chaperone the couple, being sent out for walks in the cold drizzle was more than she could bear. On Thursday, 11 February, she records a day that would surely tax the nerves and health of the most even-tempered. On yet another cold and rainy morning, Jack declared that Virginia and Vanessa must go out, apparently so he could be alone with Stella. Virginia and Vanessa were sent out for a bicycle ride in the country, without a map, carrying biscuits and chocolate as emergency rations. They found the "roads muddier and worse than we have ever ridden on." They were soon covered with mud and soaked to the skin—cold, miserable, and angry. They were jeered at by a group of schoolboys marching along. When they returned for lunch, having been gone most of the morning, Jack asked them to go through the whole torture *again* in the afternoon, but they refused.

Woolf must have been very confused in her feelings toward Stella and Jack. Although memoirs of this year written later in her life describe how happy she was at seeing Stella so happy in a love relationship such as she had never seen before, the diary from that year records mostly resentment, and how difficult, if not impossible, it was for Woolf to be alone with "those two." On 4 April she refers to the wedding as "the beginning of the end." On 5 April she refers to Nessa's and her resolution "to be calm and most proper behaved, as if Stellas marriage were nothing at all touching us." On 9 April Woolf writes that there was "Too much to do to be dismal, though the last evening was in danger of ending unhappily." And finally on 10 April, the day of the wedding, she records:

> Goodness knows how we got through it all—Certainly it was half a dream, or a nightmare. Stella was almost dreaming I think: but probably hers was a happy one.

Shortly thereafter, when the family went to Brighton, Woolf began to record her outbursts of temper—probably at being left once again without a mother. On 13 April she describes being "tantrumical." On 19 April she records, with fascination, the execution of a woman, almost as if she were exorcising her anger at Stella. On 21 April she describes how she broke her umbrella in half. One can imagine that with time Woolf might have worked through her anger at Stella's marriage and in so doing might have resolved her separation from her mother by reliving it in a more wholesome way. Instead, Stella returned from her wedding trip seriously ill. It was extremely difficult for Woolf, ambivalent and resentful at Stella's leaving the family, to confront Stella's illness. If Woolf had harmful or murderous wishes toward Stella, as would have been normal given the circumstances, she might have blamed herself for Stella's illness.

Stella's illness, according to Woolf's diary, made her "miserable" (4/28). She wondered "how is one to live in such a world" (4/28). In the months that followed Woolf turned to books as her only solace. Her feelings toward Stella probably became even more confused when she was required to spend a large part of her time with her. In the months that follow, Woolf's well-being seems tied to Stella's. She writes, for example, on 3 May: "Stella had a very good night & no pain—so everyone went happily to their work as usual." But she seems to increasingly resent Stella. On 20 May she states that she wishes the drives in the park with her "would cease to exist!" By 23 June the constant stream of queries about Stella's illness had so exasperated Woolf that she wrote: I "answered the invariable 'How is Stella?' till I hated poor Bella & her diseases."

On 19 July Stella Duckworth died after an operation performed in an attempt to save her. Curiously, the family did not attend the burial ceremony.[39] In a 1907 memoir Woolf describes the effect of Stella's death as a "shapeless catastrophe" (MB55) and refers to her illness as peritonitis—the same illness referred to in the 1897 diary, diagnosed when Stella came back from her wedding trip. Later, however, when she wrote "A Sketch of the Past," Woolf recorded Stella's death differently: "And directly she came back she was taken ill. It was appendicitis; she was going to have a baby. And that was mismanaged too; and so, after three months of intermittent illness, she died—at 24 Hyde Park Gate, on July 27th, 1897" (MB107).

That Woolf felt unprotected and unmothered after Stella's death is highly likely. On 27 July—the date Woolf misremembered in her memoir as the time of Stella's death—she records in her diary that Seton thought she was flourishing and also the following entry: "I went for a walk (I insisted on the *walk*) with Gerald." It is entirely possible that Gerald Duckworth started up or continued his amorous advances toward Woolf once Stella was dead, just as George Duckworth had begun his after the death of Julia (MB 142–55). It is no wonder Woolf associated the loss of a mother figure with the terror of a certain kind of sexuality.

At the end of Woolf's life she seems to have misremembered the cause of Stella's death—to have forgotten the diagnosis of peritonitis and substituted appendicitis and to have associated the pregnancy with the death. According to a letter Violet Dickinson wrote to Vanessa Bell, this confusion was understandable, because there was a version of Stella's death besides the "official" one, a version Woolf might have heard as she herself convalesced in Stella's house. This other version of Stella's death is recorded in Jean Love's *Virginia Woolf: Sources of Madness and of Art*:

> In 1942, as a very old lady, Violet Dickinson passed on the nurse's interpretation (and gossip) to Vanessa Bell, telling her that Stella had been injured by Jack on the honeymoon. Evidently Vanessa demurred, for Violet went over the matter again, in more detail. The nurse had been quite definite, she insisted; Stella had had some inner malformation that made sexual intercourse difficult. Something—Violet supposed the uterus—that should have been convex was actually concave, or maybe it was vice versa. At a minimum, Violet insisted, Jack had been a "tiring lover." She said also that the difficulty was due in part to Stella's exhaustion at the time of the wedding and honeymoon.[40]

How much of this story Woolf heard or overheard as a girl of fifteen—from the servants or nurses or even from Violet Dickinson herself—is sheer speculation. But if Stella's death was described as resulting from exhaustion, caused in part by her responsibility for Woolf before her illness, then it seems reasonable to assume that Woolf might have felt partially responsible.

Woolf must have been extremely ambivalent about Stella's death. After Stella's death Woolf was permitted to go out more by herself, to take courses at King's College, to live more fully the life that a fifteen-year-old girl in the process of establishing her own identity is entitled to. How frightening it might have been for the emerging woman to register, if indeed she did, a sense of relief at never again having to accompany Stella on her endless rounds or the rides in the park that were a torment to her.

Woolf might also have considered Stella's pregnancy her responsibility. Her careful records of the times she and Vanessa were induced to leave the engaged couple on their own in Bognor might mean that Woolf fantasized about their activities.[41] In *To the Lighthouse* we have the curious example of Prue Ramsay. In the "Time Passes" part of the novel the sixth section begins:

> The spring without a leaf to toss, bare and bright like a virgin fierce in her chastity, scornful in her purity, was laid out on fields wide-eyed and watchful and entirely careless of what was done or thought by the beholders. [Prue Ramsay, leaning on her father's arm, was given in marriage. What, people said, could have been more fitting? And, they added, how beautiful she looked.]

The spring, as virgin laid out, careless of what was done or thought by the beholders, and the following passage, seems to synopsize much of what happened in 1897—Stella at Bognor, Stella's wedding, Stella's submitting to Jack. Two paragraphs later, again in square brackets:

> [Prue Ramsay died that summer in some illness connected with childbirth, which was indeed a tragedy, people said, everything, they said, had promised so well.] (TTL 98–99)

If one is very literal minded one can read the second set of square brackets as evidence that Prue Ramsay was pregnant before she was married—the illness being connected with "childbirth," not "childbearing" or "pregnancy." Given this very literal reading, the virgin scornful of her purity seems to suggest that Prue engaged in sexual intercourse before her marriage, careless of onlookers. Whether or not this is what happened to Stella at Bognor, it does seem that Woolf felt herself partially responsible for Stella's death. But, incapable of even talking about such a horrifying prospect, she kept it to herself and referred to it only through fiction.

Instead of working through the traumatic effects of her mother's death, Woolf experienced another, perhaps even more devastating, trauma in Stella's death, and she might have considered herself partially responsible and felt immensely guilty, especially since she was freer without Stella to superintend her.

The record of that eventful year, 1897, begins to peter out after Stella's death. The family's visit to Painswick, the redecoration of Woolf's room at Hyde Park Gate, Woolf's attendance at King's College, her reading, her writing "a great work" (8/9) are all recorded. But the effect of Stella's death upon Woolf and upon the household is the predominant topic in the sparse and spare entries in the latter part of the year. After Stella's death, Woolf seems to have repressed much. On 9 August, for example, she recorded—as she often did after Stella's death—that she had forgotten to write down what had happened and that she had therefore *"Forgot what happened."*

> This poor diary is in a very bad way, but, strange though it may seem, the time is always so filled up here, that I get very little time for diarising—even if I wished to, which I dont having taken a great dislike to the whole process.

Woolf's last entry for the year, made at the beginning of 1898, concludes with the following words:

> Here is life given us each alike, & we must do our best with it. Our hand in the sword hilt—& an unuttered fervent vow!
>
> *The End of 1897*

These were brave, courageous, defiant, and hopeful words for the young Virginia Woolf to utter at the beginning of 1898, considering the events she had lived through in the previous year, and considering that elsewhere in her diary she recorded that "Life is a hard business—one needs a rhinoceros skin—& that one has not got!" (10/16). She had navigated a precarious time in her life without giving up the notion of herself as an active, energetic human being. For 1897 had been a difficult year for Woolf—a year of enormous growth and profound change. Yet her vision of herself was in part an embattled one. She saw herself as a woman warrior, like Joan of Arc in her commitment to the cause of living her life, and possibly even killing, or dying, for her beliefs. One thing was certain: for Virginia Woolf life was going to be a very sacred, very important, very dangerous battle—a battle she would continue to fight with all the courage she could muster. And, as the 1897 diary indicates, the courage this woman could muster was considerable.

Notes

1. Virginia Stephen Woolf, 1897 diary, entry dated 1 January 1898, the Henry W. and Albert A. Berg Collection of English and American Literature of the New York Public Library, Astor, Lenox and Tilden Foundations. I wish to express my thanks to the Berg Collection and to the author's literary estate for permission to quote from the diary and from Woolf's essay on *The Antiquary*. I would like to thank Lola L. Szladits, curator of the Berg Collection, for her generous and gracious assistance and support. I have made no editirial changes in transcribing Woolf's entries.

I should also like to thank Ernest J. DeSalvo, Arthur Golden, Jane Lilienfeld, Mitchell A. Leaska, Jane Marcus, Frank McLaughlin, and Sara Ruddick for discussions that clarified for me the issues raised in this essay. The views expressed are, of course, my own unless otherwise identified. Throughout the essay I shall refer to Virginia Stephen Woolf by her married surname, "Woolf."

2. These events are recorded in the following entries: stays, 1 April; Stella's marriage, 10 April; Stella's death, 19 July; Woolf's illness, 23 January, 9 May, passim; writing desk, 20 January; fifty volumes, passim; Lockhart, 26 January through 21 February; *Fawcett*, 23 August; *Notes*, 23 May; King's, 16 October; writing the moment down, 6 July; Queen Victoria, 22 June; *Mariana*, 22 February; *Hamlet*, 12 October; *As You Like It*, 2 March; *Faust*, 2 June; zoo, 7 and 12 January; Kensington Gardens, 31 January; Battersea Park, 3 January; Round Pond, 25 January; Serpentine, 17 January; National Gallery, 6 January; National Portrait Gallery, 19 January, 11 March; Carlyle's House, 29 January; ice skating, 28 January; bicycle riding, 8 February.

3. Peter Blos, *The Adolescent Passage: Developmental Issues* (New York: International Universities Press, 1979). For other published descriptions of Virginia Woolf's adolescence, see Quentin Bell, *Virginia Woolf: A Biography*, 2 vols. (New York: Harcourt Brace Jovanovich, 1972); Jean O. Love, *Virginia Woolf: Sources of Madness and Art* (Berkeley: University of California Press, 1977).

4. Stella Duckworth, 1896 diary, Berg Collection.

5. 15 February; 2 March 1897 diary, Berg.

6. 7 July 1897 diary.

7. 28 January 1897 diary. See Mrs. Leslie Stephen, *Notes from Sick Rooms* (London: Smith, Elder, 1883; reprinted, with an introduction by Constance Hunting, Orono, Maine: Puckerbrush Press, 1980).

8. 25 February 1897 diary; Violet Dickinson to Vanessa Bell, quoted in Love, *Virginia Woolf,* 193; QB 1:39; Sir Leslie Stephen, *Sir Leslie Stephen's Mausoleum Book,* with an introduction by Alan Bell (Oxford: Clarendon Press, 1977).

9. Vanessa, 2 March; 16 April; 24 April; 10 June; 16 June; passim. Adrian and Thoby, 6 January; 11 April; L. Stephen, *Mausoleum Book,* 10 April 1897. Father, 21 January; Letter from Sir Leslie Stephen to Stella Duckworth Hills, 10 April 1897, Berg; Frederic William Maitland, *The Life and Letters of Leslie Stephen* (London: Duckworth, 1906); Noel Gilroy Annan, *Leslie Stephen: His Thought and Character in Relation to His Time* (London:Macgibbon and Kee, 1951); Stella, 3 January through 10 April. Her half-brothers, passim; 18 November.

10. 4 June 1897 diary. Hereafter, diary entries will be cited within the body of the text. The first number will refer to the month; the number after the slash will indicate the day (7/4 therefore indicates 4 July.)

11. Maitland, *Life and Letters of Leslie Steven,* 27–28.

12. Jane Marcus, ''From Jack the Ripper to Virginia Woolf,'' paper presented at the Conference on Victorian War and Violence, sponsored by Northeast Victorian Studies Association and the University of Pennsylvania, 11–13 April 1980.

13. L. Stephen, *Mausoleum Book,* 10 April 1897 entry.

14. These events are recorded on 1 July, 7 and 8 April, and 18 April.

15. The diary entries after Stella's illness indicate the extent to which new responsibilities were delegated to Woolf.

16. Woolf's entry for such an important event is curious. She records it in an offhand manner, as if to soften the blow of her father's refusal.

17. Pp. 1–2. I should like to thank Mitchell A. Leaska for describing these passages to me, from Anna Battista's transcription, even before the reprinting of Julia Stephen's pamphlet.

18. L. Stephen, *Mausoleum Book,* xxviii. For an analysis of the effects on her mature work of Virginia Woolf's regarding herself as a historian, see Jane Marcus, ''Thinking Back through Our Mothers,'' in *New Feminist Essays.* For an early work of fiction describing a woman as historian, see Virginia Woolf, *The Journal of Mistress Joan Martyn,* ed. Susan M. Squier and Louise A. DeSalvo, in *Twentieth Century Literature,* Virginia Woolf issue, 25, no. 3/4 (fall/winter 1979).

19. Maitland, *Life and Letters of Leslie Steven,* 5 December 1897 letter from Sir Leslie Stephen to Mrs. Herbert Fisher, 446.

20. Maitland, 13 December 1884, Letter from Sir Leslie Stephen to Mr. Charles E. Norton, 386.

21. For discussions of the effects of adolescent reading upon development, see Louise M. Rosenblatt, *Literature as Exploration*, rev. ed. (New York: Noble and Noble, 1938, 1968); Louise A. DeSalvo, "Literature and Sexuality," *Media & Methods*, September 1979; Frank McLaughlin, "The Place of Fiction in the Development of Values," *Media & Methods*, March 1980.

For specific explorations of these issues, see Jane Marcus, "Enchanted Organs, Magic Bells: *Night and Day* as Comic Opera," in *Virginia Woolf: Revaluation and Continuity*, ed. Ralph Freedman (Berkeley: University of California Press, 1980); and the essays in Virginia Woolf issue, *Bulletin of the New York Public Library* 80, no. 2 (winter 1977). Of these, see particularly the following: Mitchell A. Leaska, "Virginia Woolf, the Pargeter: A Reading of *The Years*"); Margaret Comstock, "The Loudspeaker and the Human Voice: Politics and the Form of *The Years*"; Jane Marcus, "*The Years* as Greek Drama, Domestic Novel, and Gotterdammerung." See also Jane Marcus, "Pargeting 'The Pargiters': Notes of an Apprentice Plasterer," *Bulletin of the New York Public Library*, spring 1977.

22. 31 January 1897 diary.

23. See B. J. Kirkpatrick, *A Bibliography of Virginia Woolf* (London: Rupert Hart-Davis, 1957); Beverly Ann Schlack, *Continuing Presences: Virginia Woolf's Use of Literary Allusion* (University Park and London: Pennsylvania State University Press, 1979).

24. The quotation is from Carlyle's *Sir Walter Scott*, quoted in Schlack, *Continuing Presences*, 41. For an analysis on Carlyle's influence on *Jacob's Room*, see Schlack.

25. Leslie Stephen to Norton, 13 December 1884, in Maitland, *Life and Letters of Leslie Steven*, 386.

26. See Leslie Stephen, *The Life of Henry Fawcett* (London: Smith, Elder, 1885). For an analysis of the impact of the suffrage movement on Virginia Woolf later in her life, see Jane Marcus, "Art and Anger," *Feminist Studies* 4, no. 1 (February 1978). This essay also explores the connnections between Elizabeth Robins and Virginia Woolf. Woolf might have seen a production of *Mariana* with Elizabeth Robins in 1897.

27. Stella Duckworth went to see Mrs. Garrett Anderson before her marriage. The visit is recorded in the 1897 diary on 25 February. A return visit occurred on 5 March that Woolf records as follows: "In the morning Stella and I went to Mrs. Garrett [sic] Anderson. She did not say anything new—" Stella was being treated for "her fidgets" (2/25).

28. *The Voyage Out*, 296. See Schlack, *Continuing Presences*, 14.

29. George Meredith, *Love in the Valley*, in *Poems* (New York: Charles Scribner's

Sons, 1908), 134–35. See Schlack, *Continuing Presences,* 14. For an analysis of the composition of *The Voyage Out,* see Louise A. DeSalvo, *Virginia Woolf's First Voyage: A Novel in the Making* (Totowa, N.J.: Rowman and Littlefield, 1980; London: Macmillan, 1980).

30. See DeSalvo, *Virginia Woolf's First Voyage.*

31. Virginia Woolf, holograph draft of *"The Antiquary,"* in holograph notebook, ''Essays, 1924,'' Berg Collection. On a manuscript page numbered 167 by the Berg Collection, Woolf dated an essay ''52 Tavistock Sq., Oct. 5th.'' On page 187 of the notebook she began a draft of the essay entitled *"The Antiquary."* By my calculations, based upon the possibility that Woolf began a new page each day, she might have started the essay on or about 16 October 1924.

32. That Mr. Ramsay was the prototype for the antiquary is recorded in John Gibson Lockhart, *Memoirs of the Life of Sir Walter Scott* (New York: Houghton Mifflin, 1901), 3:104.

For analyses of *To the Lighthouse,* see Maria Di Battista's essay in *Virginia Woolf: Revaluation and Continuity,* ed. Ralph Freedman (Berkeley: University of California Press, 1980); Mitchell A. Leaska, *Virginia Woolf's Lighthouse: A Study in Critical Method* (London: Hogarth Press, 1970); *The Novels of Virginia Woolf: From Beginning to End* (New York: John Jay Press, 1977); Jane Lilienfeld, ''The Deceptiveness of Beauty''; Mother Love and Mother Hate in *To the Lighthouse,"* *Twentieth Century Literature* 23, no. 3 (October 1977); Sonya Rudikoff, ''How Many Lovers Had Virginia Woolf?'' *Hudson Review,* winter 1979.

33. Sir Walter Scott, *The Antiquary* (New York: A. L. Burt, n.d.), 64.

34. Ibid., 83. Woolf's essay on *The Antiquary* has been reprinted as part of the essay ''Sir Walter Scott,'' in MOE 56–78.

35. See Rudikoff, ''How Many Lovers.''

36. Woolf, ''Essays, 1924,'' Berg Collection; *"The Antiquary,"* in MOE 67–68. To my knowledge, the editors and the readers of the *New Republic* did not catch the misreading; nor have any Woolf scholars or critics. I have read the ''Letters'' to the *New Republic* in the months following the publication of Woolf's essay on 3 December 1924, and none was published regarding Woolf's misreading. For a theory of misreading, see Harold Bloom, *A Map of Misreading* (New York: Oxford University Press, 1975).

37. L. Stephen, *Mausoleum Book,* xxvi. Both Julia and Stella were, of course, acting the role required of women under the Victorian patriarchy, and the effect on their health was disastrous. See Adrienne Rich, *Of Woman Born: Motherhood as Experience and Institution* (New York: Bantam Books, 1977).

38. Sir Leslie Stephen to Stella Duckworth Hills, 10 April 1897, Berg Collection, in *Mausoleum Book,* xxvi.

39. Woolf's entry records: "Stella was buried by mothers side in Highgate. None of us went."

40. Love, *Virginia Woolf,* 193; Love cites two 1942 letters from Dickinson to Vanessa.

41. Stella Duckworth in her 1896 diary was meticulous in recording her and Vanessa's and Virginia's menstrual cycles. The record continues into 1897. The last occurrence recorded for Stella was on 28 January 1897. There is no record for February, March, or April. In May she records the recurrence of Virginia's and Vanessa's cycles, but not hers, indicating that she was pregnant by that date. Whether Stella never menstruated after January 1897 can, of course, not be determined. That the record exists, however, suggests that this might be so and that Woolf therefore might have had reason to fancy that Stella became pregnant on the trip to Bognor, which occurred in February.

Isis Unveiled:
Virginia Woolf's Use of
Egyptian Myth   *Evelyn Haller*

When Virginia Woolf made use of Egyptian materials in her fiction, she was not following an eccentric course. Not only did interest in Egyptology run high in England, but London and Oxford[1] provided the center for its study, the cultural depot for the deployment of linguists and archaeologists, and the dispersal point for its antiquities. To say that Egyptology (together with archaeology and anthropology) came of age in Woolf's country during her lifetime is not to overstate the case. That the young Virginia Stephen herself thought about things Egyptian is shown by her playful reference to Violet Dickinson's lawn in 1907: "I have seen many worthy and delightful people refresh themselves; Coptic scholars digging for vegetable roots [as painfully] as for roots of languages twenty times buried in Egyptian sand. . . ."[2] Thus Woolf was conversant not only with the facts of prehistory but also with their implications, for she had met the classical scholar Jane Harrison in 1904 (L 1:145); in 1912, while her first novel, *The Voyage Out,* was in its final stages, she heard Jane Harrison speak (L 1:498).

The work of prehistorians was a bold undertaking, for it undermined the Victorian world view. Egypt, for example, had appeal for Woolf because it was anterior to Greek culture with its denigration of women and exaltation of male homosexuality. Furthermore, that center of Greek inheritance, Rome, provided a model for empire: "A Roman thought hath struck him," Shakespeare's Cleopatra said of Antony as she felt him slip from her Egyptian toils of grace (1. 2. 92). By "a Roman thought" we are to understand the austere Roman virtue of duty expressed through political imposition. While Shakespeare's play identifies Rome as the model for the extension and permanence of empire, Egypt is the subversive element. A similar imperial vision had informed the Victorian life and letters of Virginia's youth. In those years the work of prehistorians was also challenging the moral imperative of that vision, Christianity, to which she and her immediate family were antipathetic.[3] Prehistory was, moreover, congruent with Darwinism and later with Freudianism (the Woolfs' Hogarth Press published the English edition of Freud) in its demonstration of the idea that people are not rational. Not only did Woolf side with Egypt against imperialism, Christianity, and patriarchy, but she conveyed this preference through her use of Egyptian myth—especially the figure of the subversive and triumphant Isis, about whom the final phase of paganism had crystallized[4] and who also, as Gibbon chortled, subverted the conquerors. Thus, as sand was cleared away from ancient Egyptian monuments with the coming of the British,[5] so there was an emergence of *very* ancient thought that, though revolutionary, had romantic appeal.

While stratigraphic layers—both tangible and intangible—were being removed by prehistorians, Virginia Stephen Woolf was born in 1882, the year of the foundation of the Egypt Exploration Fund by a novelist, Amelia Edwards. Her godfather, James Russell Lowell (1819–91), was involved with the EEF while he was ambassador to the Court of Saint James[6]—a likely interest, since his relative John Lowell (1799–1836) had made a significant collection of Egyptian antiquities at Thebes that passed to the Museum of Fine Arts in Boston. Moreover, a friend of Virginia's youth, Katherine Thynne (1865–1933), was married to Evelyn Baring, Lord Cromer, consul-general in Egypt as well as president of the EEF from 1906 to 1917. Of Katie, "that divine Giantess," Virginia wrote in an early essay, "she was a great lady before; . . . the splendours of the British Residency at Cairo have only developed that side of her . . . she was like a great benevolent goddess." Woolf found this mythic dimension appealing, for she adds, "I wd be a pagan—if I cd."[7]

Such were the outer circumstances, but there were inner needs that not only opened Virginia Stephen's mind to ideas revolutionary though ancient, but also her eyes to their images. As her good friend Vita Sackville-West was later to write: "Who shall explain . . . the bearing of visual experience upon psychical experience?"[8] In a letter from Egypt (29 January 1926) Vita exclaimed that she was "permanently infuriated by the thought of what you could make of this country if only you could be got here,"[9] suggesting that things Egyptian were not alien to Virginia Woolf. Two years before she received Vita's letter, Woolf had used an Egyptian image in a tribute to the loving-kindness of her aunt Anne Thackeray Ritchie: "As life drew on, with its deaths and its wars, her profound instinct for happiness had to exert itself to gild those grim faces golden, but it succeeded'' (CE 4:75).

Virginia Woolf's Egyptian mode of seeing had taken a charge from the dipolar influences of the Egyptian collection in the British Museum, especially the tiers of Isis and Horus statues, and the knowledge she acquired through classical studies under women scholars[10] who did not hold university positions. These influences were to be crucial, for like Pater's Marius, Woolf ''lived much, and as it were by system, in reminiscence.''[11] It follows that one who lived so thoroughly in her own imagination—an imagination formed by art, especially the literary and visual arts of antiquity, who also considered herself an autodidact—would be susceptible to a mythic figure that would order her emotional, intellectual, and, eventually, political needs.

At about the age of sixteen (1898) Virginia began to study Latin and later continued her study of Greek with Clara Pater, Walter's sister—an exquisitely feminine woman who evoked the Pre-Raphaelite world of unrestricting medieval garments, uncluttered space, and delight in nature. When Virginia studied under Janet Case, she found another personality—''too cheerful & muscular''—in a woman scholar: ''a really valiant strong-minded woman, in a private capacity. We strayed enough from grammar to let me see this. She talked on many subjects; & in all she showed herself possessed of clear strong views, & more than this she had the rare gift of seeing the other side; she had too, I think, a fine woman sympathy which I had reason, once or twice to test'' (1903 diary/notebook, Berg, 50, 55). As she grew older, Clara Pater, Janet Case, and Jane Harrison herself would be found lacking in various ways; what continued to matter to Virginia Woolf—as it had to her mentors—was ''the disinterested passion for things in themselves''(p. 112): in this instance, the classics, which would be rewarding, confirming, and challenging as she set about making her own reordering of tradition.

By the time Virginia ''had a passion'' (MB 160) for Pater's *Marius the Epicurean* (dedicated to his sisters), she had certainly encountered literary as well as visual evidence of Isis. By way of reinforcement, Pater's novel not only provides eloquent descriptions of the rites of Isis but draws the reader to what he calls ''the Golden Book,'' a second-century novel by Apuleius that is a major source of information about the Greco-Roman Isis. Moreover, in Pater's *Marius* a writer learns his craft by studying the ''*aurum intextum*: gold fibre'' of Apuleius's ''curious felicity'' (1:57).

That Isiac ritual and iconography were eventually to be at the core of Woolf's method is congruent with a parallel preoccupation in her beloved

Marius the Epicurean: His Ideas and Sensations: "It is . . . in ritual, rather than in abstract moral and metaphysical appeal of religion or in naked mysticism that Pater is interested."[12] These predispositions are in harmony with the findings of prehistorians. As Jane Harrison observed in an essay entitled "Darwinism and Religion": "In the Greek mysteries only we find what we should call a *Confiteor*; and this is not a confession of faith, but an avowal of rites performed. When the religion of primitive peoples came to be examined, it was speedily seen that, though vague beliefs necessarily abound, definitive creeds are non-existent. Ritual is dominant and imperative.[13]

We know Isiac ritual from objects left us such as the sistra and situlae[14] that not only are clustered in cases at the British Museum but are also shown in tomb paintings and in reliefs. Lemprière, whose *Classical Dictionary* is named in *Between the Acts*, provides an excellent key to those literary sources.

Out of these rites and icons Virginia Woolf not only made literature but built necropolis after necropolis; for, in addition to seeking pattern, her art was also a commemoration of her dead—another theme familiar from *Marius*. Appealing as Pater's settings were for Marius's "yearning towards those inhabitants of the shadowy land he had known in life"—climbing the hills on foot among the painted houses "containing gold and silver ornaments . . . wrought armour and vestments" of the Etrurian dead "scattered so plentifully among the dwelling places of the living" (1:161); or seeing in the catacombs the Christian mass that in its loving remembrance of the dead, moves Marius to martyrdom—Woolf had her own course to follow. For to give what Pater called a " 'subjective immortality' . . . for which many a Roman epitaph cries out plaintively" (1:20) to her own dead, she constructed a painted House of Isis that not only accommodated her "scene-making"[15] but corresponds in literary technique to aspects of the House of Cecilia that moved Marius to aesthetic emotion. Indeed, Pater's analysis of the taste that ordered the House of Cecilia can be an epigraph to Woolf's work as a whole:

> All around in these well-ordered precincts, were the quiet signs . . . of a noble taste—a taste, indeed, chiefly evidenced in the selection and juxtaposition of the material it had to deal with, consisting almost exclusively of the remains of older art, here arranged and harmonised, with effects, both as regards color and form, so delicate as to seem really derivative from some finer intelligence in these matters than lay within the resources of the ancient world. (2:95)

As an individual talent inheriting a rich tradition, Woolf not only juxtaposed remains of older literary and visual art through words, but also included more imposing forms: monumental Egyptian stone. In the House of Cecilia Marius had also perceived significant form in such "juxtaposition" of the "fragments of older architecture" that "had put on . . . a new and singular expressiveness, an air of grave thought, of an intellectual purpose, in itself, aesthetically, very seductive" (1:96). By placing aspects of Egyptian monumentality in her work: sphinxes, obelisks, colossi, temples, pyramids, sarcophagi—Woolf builds an aesthetically seductive Egyptian ambience into her novels that makes a cartouche surround the mythic figure of Isis, enabling her to make aesthetic war on imperialism, Christianity, and patriarchy.

I am arguing that for personal and political reasons—many of them anguished—Woolf chose early in life to become a woman of letters and in her craft to eschew male-dominated systems of thought for one informed by the oldest, most enduring, and most coherent female myth: that of Isis. Woolf was, however, to build upon the received myth by emphasizing Isiac roles of artist, intellectual, and peace-gatherer. Moreover, she developed this bent with increasing literary and political sophistication,[16] admitting along the way important parallel influences such as Joyce's use of Homeric myth in *Ulysses.*

In that vintage year of 1922, Forster's book on Alexandria also appeared, and the discovery of the twice-sacked tomb of a minor boy king reinforced British interest in archaeology as well as in Egypt itself. Meanwhile, Woolf was aware of Eliot's assertion that the "mythical method" Joyce had employed in *Ulysses* (1922)—an approach he had used himself in "The Wasteland" (also 1922)—was "a step toward making the modern world possible for art."[17] She, however, avoided what she discerned as the principal weakness in Joyce's method: that "it never embraces or creates what is outside itself and beyond"(CE 2:108). Thus, throughout her lifetime and especially in its final months during the Second World War, her writing shows evidence of a "need to equate the instinct to create with the instinct of self-preservation and communal survival."[18]

Since the skeleton key of the myth of Isis opens *Between the Acts* to a splendor of golden light like that which radiated from Tutankhamen's tomb, it is probable that this consummate use of the matter of Egypt was unlikely to have occurred in a single burst that was both sudden and delayed. Working back from *Between the Acts*, one can discover this material throughout her fiction: indeed, it is woven into the text of *Melymbrosia,* an early version of her first published novel, *The Voyage Out* (1915), wherein we find allusion to Thoth, the ibis-headed god of writers, who is mentioned directly in Joyce's *Portrait of the Artist* (1915). Given her own self-portrait of the artist as a

young woman in *Moments of Being,* one can see that Woolf was in effect going to encounter for the millionth time the reality of experience and to weave
on the loom of her psyche the uncreated *consciousness of her sex.* When one
reads Woolf with Egyptian myth in mind, the pattern is obvious, for she was
putting her stamp on her work as explicitly as we can see the Isis Pharia (Isis
as Guardian of the Lighthouse) struck on an Alexandrian coin.

Her good friend Vita Sackville-West knew of Virginia's rapport with
things Egyptian, for she wrote from Egypt of her desire to put Virginia "in
the sun" among an alphabetical list of objects. The key words from Vita's
long list that are most strikingly present in Woolf's work are: "alabaster . . .
camels . . . colossi . . . donkeys . . . desert . . . Egyptians . . . hieroglyphics
. . . Horus . . . Isis . . . lotus . . . mummies, mud . . . Nile . . . Osiris, ob-
sidian, obelisks; palms, pyramids, parrokeets; quarries; Ramses, ruins . . .
sarcophagi . . . sand, shadows, Sphinx; temples . . . Tut-ankh-aman
. . ."(29 January 1926, Berg).[19]

An Overview of Isiac Myth

Among the alphabetical Egyptian entries Vita listed while she was thinking
of Virginia were Isis, Horus, and Osiris. While Isis takes her origins from
the Egyptian cow goddess Hathor—horns of both the cow and the moon
survive in her representations—political, indeed, theocratic aspects of the
goddess loomed large throughout the four thousand years of Egyptian
history, for "every Pharaoh was the incarnation of the youthful Horus, and
therefore was the son of Isis." The consort and brother of Isis was Osiris, at
whose loss the tears of Isis caused the rising of the Nile: "The river that
seemed dead as Osiris was reborn as the living water, Horus, emerging to re-
juvenate the whole land: and the Lord, the human embodiment in control of
it all was the Pharaoh. . . . At death the King of Egypt sped away like the
spent Nile. Henceforth as Osiris he held sway over . . . the shadowy
kingdom of the dead." The distinction between these male and female principles in Egyptian thought is most graphic in that "Osiris from this aspect
was the deity of vanished life, whereas his consort Isis . . . was a force which
produced living things and therefore enjoyed immortality in the land of the
Nile where every year her son Horus was reborn under the name of 'fresh
water.'"[20] Isis, therefore, was the stable, life-giving, female factor—the
horizontal line of the triangle, as Plutarch termed her. While pharaohs came
and went and her brother and consort died each year to be reborn as Horus
with the flooding of the Nile, Isis remained constant, the source of life. By

Greco-Roman times Isis had attracted the names and attributes of all beneficent female goddesses—as well as a number of sky-god attributes—to body
forth the final flourish of the pagan spirit in the seven centuries preceding the
imperial triumph of Christianity under Constantine. The historian Gibbon,
whom Woolf admired, dwelt upon the irony of Christianity's subsuming
images of Isis and the infant Horus as models for the Madonna and Child:
"The religion of Constantine achieved, in less than a century, the final conquest of the Roman Empire: but the visitors themselves were insensibly subdued by the arts of their vanquished rivals."[21] Not only was Gibbon's view
of Christianity one with which Woolf was sympathetic, but the latter portion of the statement could serve as epigraph to Woolf's view of Western
culture and, more specifically, to her own ironic use of the anti-Madonna.[22]

Considerable information on Isiac iconography and ritual is to be found in
Lemprière's *Classical Dictionary,* which was first issued in 1788,[23] and has
been frequently reissued and revised. This reference book not only is named
in the text of *Between the Acts* but is introduced by a pun fiercely allusive to
Isis's gathering of the pieces of Osiris's body: "he [Bart] muttered, bringing
the scattered bits together. Lemprière would settle it"(BA 25).

In his summary of seven classical authorities, Lemprière writes of Osiris:
"He took particular care to civilize his subjects, to polish their morals, to
give them good and salutary laws and to teach them agriculture." These
aspects of Osiris remind one of British colonial administrators in Woolf's life
as well as in her fiction.

Of all her novels, *Between the Acts* has the most palpable Egyptian ambience. For example: "All was sun now. The view laid bare by the sun was
flattened, silenced, stilled" (BA 65). Visually, the landscape of Pointz Hall
has two dominant objects: the spire of Bolney Minster and Hogben's Folly.
While the mode of emphasis of the former suggests the Quaker designation
for church as "steeple house,"[24] both forms evoke the obelisk of Egyptian
landscape reinforced by the punning name of the country house itself:
"points hall." "Obelisk" was one of the words on Vita's list. Two obelisks
were prominent in Anglo-Egyptian relations. One, a red granite obelisk
with a repeated inscription in hieroglyphics and Greek, had been discovered
on the Island of Philae in 1815 and brought to Kingston Lacy, a country
estate in Dorsetshire. Together with the Rosetta stone, it gave Champollion
evidence that hieroglyphics were more than a system of picture writing: they
had over the centuries become increasingly phonetic.[25] The other prominent
obelisk, Cleopatra's Needle, had been brought to London through the

generosity of Sir Erasmus Darwin, who was also to aid Amelia Edwards in founding the EEF. Woolf mentions Cleopatra's Needle in a draft of the 1910 portion of *The Years* as representing, among other things, the contrast of the long stretch of prehistory, with "our civilization . . . but the thickness of one green leaf on the top."[26]

The pageant at Pointz Hall, which marshals through tableaux two millennia of English history (it can be surveyed in an afternoon), occupies the central space of the novel. The song the costumed villagers sing in winding procession, "Digging and delving . . . for the earth is always the same, summer and winter and spring; and spring and winter again; ploughing and sowing, eating and growing; time passes" (BA 125), corresponds to the rites of a significant June day in Greco-Roman Alexandria when a festival celebrated the day "when the star of Isis, Sothis, arose, this being regarded as New Year's Day. The rising marked three events simultaneously: the birth of a new year, the summer solstice, and the beginning of the inundation."[27] The presence of this ancient festival can be discerned throughout the novel, but most specifically in the final panels as Miss La Trobe composes her next play. Between her initial vision of "two figures, half concealed by a rock" and their words unheard but alluded to in the final sentence, there is an allusion to the inundation of the Nile: "From the earth green waters seemed to rise over her. She took her voyage away from the shore"(BA 210–11). Lemprière states that "the Egyptians believed that the yearly and regular inundations of the Nile proceeded from the abundant tears which Isis shed for the loss of Osiris." Abundant tears had flowed during the pageant as metaphorically assigned rain down the cheeks of both Isa and Miss La Trobe. Isa, moreover, had searched for her husband Giles and repeatedly lamented the loss of her ideal lover Rupert Haines.

Miss La Trobe's "voyage away from the shore" (BA 211) suggests another festival: the Navigium Isidis (the Sailing of the Ship of Isis), "the extension of her power beyond Egypt."[28] Pater, following Apuleius, describes how on one of the "first hot days" from many harbors "on the Mediterranean, the *Ship of Isis* went to sea, and every one walked down to the shoreside to witness the freighting of the vessel . . . its launching and final abandonment among the waves, as an object really devoted to the Great Goddess, the new rival, or 'double,' of ancient Venus" (1: 105,107). Classical sources also refer to "the procession on the banks of the Nile at Philae as the water begins to rise"; processions in honor of Isis feature mirrors similar to the spirit and fact of the mirror dance that closes the pageant at Pointz Hall. Apuleius has described the mirror bearers in Isiac procession; and the British

Museum keeper contemporary with Woolf, Wallis Budge, informs us that, judging from the monuments, "it seems as if their movements consisted of a series of short, sharp jerkings of the legs and arms, and leaping into the air."[29] Compare this interpretation with Woolf's description of the mirror carriers of the dance that concludes the pageant at Pointz Hall: "Out they leapt, jerked, skipped. Flashing, dazzling, jumping" (BA 184).

Behind the drama and pageantry of Alexandrian Isis-worship lies the massive endurance of Egyptian art itself: an art that looks toward death. Consider in this context two references to "the time of the Pharaohs" that occur in panel seven (BA 30–31); a humorous reference in panel nine to the ancestor who about 1750 wished to be buried "in the same grave" with "his famous hound" (BA 36), in the context of Herodotus: "All persons bury their dogs in sacred vaults within their own 'city,' "[30] and again in panel nine a subtle reference to the art of the Egyptians through the alabaster vase holding the distilled essence of silence. The passage seems idiosyncratic until one places it in a context of tomb art,[31] comparing it with the banks of alabaster bowls in the British Museum or with the alabaster bowl found in Tutankhamen's tomb—a site Virginia Woolf would have been aware of through Vita's having seen it and also through the intensive and prolonged publicity the tomb-opening received. The first volume of Howard Carter's book appeared in 1923, with illustrations and a compelling reference to the golden light he saw on opening the twice-sacked tomb of a minor boy king. *Between the Acts*, moreover, is suffused with the color yellow. This dominance of yellow can also be connected with a convention in Egyptian art whereby the skin of men is represented as red brown, while that of women is generally yellow, according to *The British Museum Guide to the Egyptian Collections*.

The purpose of this exquisite though monumental contrivance of theme and structure is to perpetuate eternally the memories of significant women and men from Woolf's life through iconographic and ideographic condensation: principally, her mother, Julia Stephen, through syncretic Greco-Roman myth wherein Isis Pharia was guardian of the lighthouse at Alexandria, for example, and her brother Thoby through the mythic figure of Osiris, especially as lawgiver. As early as 1925 Woolf considered "a new name" for her books "to supplant 'novel' " and pondered "elegy" (WD 79–80). Through her novels she built, in effect, necropolis after necropolis. In *Between the Acts*, perhaps more than in *To the Lighthouse*, Woolf wrote an elegy using what Eliot called the mythical method to control, to order, and to give shape and significance not only to the immense panorama of the

futility and anarchy that is contemporary history, but also to her own uncanny and haunting memories of her dead. As Howard Carter wrote in *The
Tomb of Tut-ankh-amen*: "This art was for the dead to look upon—to show
that they were not forgotten, and to perpetuate their memory eternally."[32]

Woolf was to rely on conventions of ancient and Alexandrine art without
recourse to belief in the afterlife as such; God most certainly does not exist in
Woolf's view of the universe, but what does exist for her most palpably is
belief in an order both imposed by and discoverable through art. She defines
what she calls a hidden pattern: "we—I mean all human beings—are connected with this hidden pattern; that the whole world is a work of art; that
we are parts of the work of art" (MB 72).[33] This statement resembles the
description of her day-to-day service to art that she outlined in her "Letter to
a Young Poet": "to find the relation between things that seem incompatible
yet have a mysterious affinity, . . . to rethink human life into poetry and so
give us tragedy again and comedy by means of characters not spun out at
length in the novelist's way, but condensed and synthesized in the poet's
way" (CE 2:191). It was therefore a poet's way that Woolf emphasized for
what was to be her last completed novel. In using the mythical method,
Woolf not only chose as referent the maternal, loving, and beneficent Isis
whom Frazer describes as the flowering of civilization,[34] but suggests her
name in that of the central character, Isa.[35]

Another Isiac character, Lucy Swithin, carries about with her "an Outline
of History" (BA 8) that alludes to one of the most popular books of the
twentieth century: H. G. Wells's *Outline of History*, which discusses Isis.
Though the Adlington translation (1566) of Apuleius's *The Golden Ass* is included among books the Woolfs owned, [36] Virginia's Latin was equal to the
original. Since Apuleius himself had witnessed the ceremony of initiation
into the order of the servants of Isis at Rome, in his recreation of this event
we have an early and reliable source of information on her worship. He con-
structs a scene in which Isis speaks of her diversity of manifestations: "I am
she whose godhead, single in essence, but of many forms, with varied rites
and under many names, the whole earth reveres" (book 11, chap. 5). At the
end of a catalog wherein she names those who worship her as Diana, as
Venus, as Juno, as Prosperine, as Ceres, she cites "the Egyptians, which are
excellent in all kind of ancient doctrine, and by their proper ceremonies ac-
custom to worship me, do call me by my true name, Queen Isis."[37]

By the time Apuleius wrote his novel, Isis had become associated with the
sea itself. Egyptian symbols of the abundance of life[38] such as the fish pond
and the lotus—that is, the water lily—as well as the swallow, abound in *Be-*

tween the Acts, thereby increasing the sense of Isiac presence. The sistrum and
the situla (rattle and breast-shaped small pail) of Isiac ritual are alluded to not
only by the tennis racket and cup handed to Isa on a memorable occasion, but
also in her attempts to describe the sweet unrest the memory causes:

> since the words he said, handing her a teacup, handing her a tennis rac-
> quet, could so attach themselves to a certain spot in her; and thus lie be-
> tween them like a wire, tingling, tangling, vibrating—she groped . . .
> for a word to fit the infinitely quick vibrations of the aeroplane propeller
> that she had seen once at dawn at Croydon. Faster, faster, faster, it
> whizzed, whirred, buzzed, till all the flails became one flail and up soared
> the plane away and away. (BA 14–15)

As Isa thinks of Rupert Haines, an emblem of Osiris—the flail—enters the
pattern of association. Vita Sackville-West had drawn Woolf's attention to
the recurrence of water and buckets in her novels, and Woolf agreed that
these were her most common images for childhood. When William Dodge
admires Isa's beauty in the greenhouse she stands against hydrangea, which
means "water vessel" (OED). Similarly, Isa's versifying takes as its main
subject the moon, as does Bart's recitation of Byronic moon poetry soon after
her entrance in the novel. Critics have not been enthralled with Isa's incantatory moon and water verse. Indeed, it is not of an excellence to stand on its
own; rather, its purpose is to heighten the sense of Isiac presence. Similarly,
the prominence of cows—they save the pageant at a crucial moment—twice
described as having "great moon-eyed heads" (BA 140), recalls Isis's origins
in Hathor, the ancient Egyptian cow-goddess.

Consistent with Woolf's readings of Jane Harrison and Walter Pater, the
figure of Isis in *Between the Acts* appears primarily through instances of Isiac
ritual: the temple-opening ceremony of morning; the afternoon worship of
sacred water; incubation through which the divine healer, Isis Medica, was
thought to effect cures or provide answers to problems after the suppliant
had slept within her temple precincts; the reenactment of the search for
Osiris when Isis became a swallow and for whom her tears brought about the
overflowing of the Nile that in turn brought renewal of life—all these are
used provocatively in the panels that structure the novel. These panels,[39]
which cause "the somewhat disjointed quality"[40] of *Between the Acts*, are a
strategic use of the late classical rhetorical mode of parataxis. By representing
reality through a series of panels or icons,[41] especially in the opening portions
of *Between the Acts*, Woolf balances the density of her "encyclopedic style."[42]

The technique itself is suggested in the opening sentence of the novel, with its reference to "the big room with the windows open to the garden" (BA 3). Consider parataxis as a series of medieval stained or painted windows or as a series of frescoes such as Chaucer describes in *The Book of the Duchess*: "For hoolly al the story of Troye / Was in the glasynge ywrought thus" (326–27); "And alle the walles with colours fyne / Were peynted, bothe text and glose, / Of al the Romaunce of the Rose" (332–34). Moreover, Pater made reference to "the old miniature-painters' work on the walls of the chambers within" the House of Cecilia (2: 98). These paintings on walls and windows are the visual analogue to a rhetorical device used not only by Chaucer and his predecessors over more than a thousand-year span, but also by their inheritor, Virginia Woolf.[43]

As Pointz Hall is modeled on the House of Cecilia,[44] the novel itself is a metaphoric painted House of Isis; not only are there selections from the remains of older visual and literary art, but these are juxtaposed by means of a paneled or paratactic structure reminiscent of paintings on the walls of ancient houses or tombs. Thus we have a series of thirty-three panels, each panel depicting a dominant aspect of the matter of Egypt—usually an image of Isis. To examine the principal panels as they occur in chronological order[45] in *Between the Acts* is to apply Joseph Frank's advice for the reading of *Ulysses*: "these references must be connected by the reader and viewed as a whole before the book fits together in any meaningful pattern."[46]

The opening panel provides an ambience for the entrance of Isa as a conflation of the Roman Juno and the Alexandrian Isis. Her appearance is foreshadowed ironically by the obtrusive presence of the limited and vicious Mrs. Haines, who refers to cows—an animal associated not only with the Egyptian Isis but also with Juno, who had "assumed the nature of that animal when the gods fled into Egypt in their war with the giants," according to Lemprière. The "goose-faced woman" recalls in her appearance as well as in her mannerisms one of the birds sacred to Juno and also to Isis.[47] The cesspool, a subject Mrs. Haines considers indelicate,[48] is to be on the Roman road, according to Isa's father-in-law. Isa's appearance is set in a tight cluster of allusion: her dressing gown with peacocks—especially when she is enthroned "on her three-cornered chair"—suggests an image of Juno with peacocks at her sides. The moon poetry intoned by Bart recalls Isis's role as a moon goddess and establishes the Greco-Roman link with Isis that is confirmed by iterated reference to her pigtails: according to the *Oxford Classical Dictionary,* Isis is shown "in her most Hellenic form . . . with serene, ideal, and typically Greek features, with no head-dress, but a curl or braid of hair hanging down each side of her face.'' Juno, a first manifestation of Isis in *Between the Acts,* was a guardian spirit of women from birth to death. Indeed, Roman women were wont to refer to their ''juno'' as Roman men referred to their ''genius.''[49] Isa's majestic entrance quickly involves reference to her son George, whose name suggests Horus as that of Isa suggests Isis but is more appositely related to the recently recurrent name of English kings. The English cry ''The king is dead; long live the king!'' is not unlike the Egyptian notion that each pharaoh is Horus reborn. Isa's thoughts turn to Rupert Haines, the gentleman farmer of ravaged face. Her iterated memory of their limited acquaintance focuses on a tennis racket and a cup he has handed her in the past. These objects suggest dominant iconographic accessories of Isis: the sistrum (a twanging instrument of wires set in a oval frame) and the situla (a small pail). It is significant that there is no other indication of athletic interests on the part of the bovine Isa. ''Her body like a bolster'' (BA 16) also suggests herms, discussed by Jane Harrison in *Mythology,* and more appositely the Canopic jars that held embalmed viscera—a procedure necessary to ''the continued well-being of the deceased in the after-life.''[50]

In this first panel Woolf also makes use of the ultimate condensation of the hieroglyph or ideogram: in slightly more than two pages there are five references to Isa as a seated figure, including her reluctance to be anything other than a seated figure. These allusions relate to the ideogram for Isis: ''She who bore the Pharaoh, who gave him his power with her milk, and who was the Mother Throne, was personified by Aset Isis as she was named by the Greeks.'' It is, for example, by the shape of the throne on her headdress that one distinguishes Isis from her sister Nepthys in Egyptian art. Thus the opening of *Between the Acts* introduces the non-Olympian Isis that vitally appealed to those who were uneasy with the exhortations to civic virtue promulgated by Rome. As Witt sums it up:

> It was her capacity to feel deeply, and in particular to express so poignantly human grief . . . that more than any other factor enabled her to win the hearts of men in the Greco-Roman world whom the traditional Olympian theology had quite often alienated. It was especially as the kind, warm-hearted wife, sister and mother, nursing her child at home, that Isis appealed to those who embraced her faith.[51]

To read ''calligraphs'' requires visual orientation. While on the one hand they simplify meaning, on the other they both amplify and eternalize meaning. ''Like a monument, they tend to summarize a particular concept in one

or two grand 'gestures.' ''[52] Thus the mythic dimension as well as the paratactic structure of *Between the Acts* makes the events of everyday life that compose this elegiac novel significant if not larger than life.

The second panel presents the elderly Lucy Swithin in an echo of the
temple-opening rite wherein a white curtain was drawn to reveal Isis as
widow—that is, as a statue clad in robes and jewels. Lucy's married name
"Swithin" has a folkloric association with deluge: "If it rain on Swithin's
day, it will rain for forty days." This in itself suggests the yearly inundation
of the Nile, brought on, the Egyptians thought, by the tears of Isis mourning
the lost Osiris. When the icon of Lucy as Isis is given, it is both specific and
general: "So she sat down . . . like any other old lady . . . a ring on her
finger and the usual trappings of rather shabby but gallant old age, which included in her case a cross gleaming gold on her breast'' (BA 10). Moreover,
she unconsciously mimes the divinity her imaginative ideal did in fact imitate: '' 'I might have been—Cleopatra,' Miss La Trobe repeated. 'You've
stirred in me my unacted part,' she meant'' (BA 153). As Lemprière expresses a fact on which Shakespeare drew: "Cleopatra, the beautiful queen of
Egypt, was wont to dress herself like this goddess, and affected to be called a
second Isis.''

Aspects of the subordinate figure of Osiris—Isis's husband and brother as
well as her cyclically reborn son Horus—are shared among Rupert Haines,
Bart Oliver, Giles Oliver, and George. Thus the garden setting[53] of the third
panel introducing the child George in the context of his grandfather and his
grandfather's dog provides a mingling of motifs. In art Horus is often represented with a lotus blossom resting on his forehead. George's moment of being in which he gazes into the chalice of a yellow flower, seeing it both whole
in itself and then as part of what lies beyond and therefore as part of everything, parallels a moment of being that Woolf herself experienced in
childhood (MB 71). Woolf's memory of her own experience, however, does
not include either by physical perspective or by intimation the emphasis on
"hall" and "yellow light" that suggests the infant Horus's view of the temple ceremonies as they are given in standard sources of Isiac myth and ritual.

When Bart fashions a crumbled newspaper into a beak over his nose (BA
12), resembling the Seth monster to tease his grandson, he not only intrudes
upon George's moment but makes the child howl. This small incident is an
ironic icon in that it is a reversal of the prototypical source for the legend of
Saint George and the dragon[54] in which Horus overcame Seth to avenge the
death of his father Osiris.

Bart is, however, primarily an Osiris figure. His lifework, serving the empire in India, bears strong resemblance to that of many men of Woolf's family and acquaintance, including Leonard. "After he had accomplished reform at home," Lemprière writes, "Osiris resolved to go and spread cultivation in other parts of the earth." Moreover, Bart's role, his past, and his dreams of India, including as they do both a cascade and sand, allude to an inscription found on "some ancient monuments," which Lemprière quotes: "I am Osiris, who conducted a large and numerous army as far as the deserts of India and . . . the streams of the Ister . . . diffusing benevolence to all the inhabitants of earth." Sohrab, Bart's Afghan hound, recalls in its appearance Anubis, who is represented as a man with the head of a dog because he accompanied Osiris to India clothed in a sheep's skin. The burden of the incident—charged with yellow—is akin to the myth of Horus as the youthful sun, born anew every morning.

To rapidly survey strategic points in succeeding panels: the fourth shows Isa looking into a tripartite mirror, thereby evoking the idea of the *diva triformis* (Diana or Hecate), with allusions to the mirrors and mimed hairdressing of the procession in honor of Isis; the fifth places Isa in the library with her father-in-law Bart, where a function of Isis is attributed to her: extending the life of her follower. In the sixth panel the similarities between the barn and an ancient temple are specified, providing an implied contrast to the far more recent Christian church. While electric light is needed for the church—indeed, it is for that purpose that the pageant is being held—the barn as temple is "a hollow hall, sun-shafted" (BA 26), which recalls the scene in *Marius* where Flavian and he read Apuleius (1:55–56). Through the emphasis on paper roses, Isis's rescue of Lucius from his metamorphosis into an ass is evoked as well.

The seventh panel returns to the library—consider the Great Library of Alexandria—where there are three references to "the Pharaohs" and their "time." It is also in this panel that Lemprière is referred to as an authority.

To summarize the Isiac content of the remaining panels that Woolf has constructed by mythical method is only to hint at the golden treasury of tomb art contained iconographically and ideographically therein; for example, Isa and Mrs. Manresa are of an age, and both have bolsterlike bodies. Isa thinks of Mrs. Manresa as as "old strumpet." Here Woolf is borrowing from the tradition in which Nepthys is a whore. Much of Isa's anger toward her is aroused by Mrs. Manresa's obvious interest in Giles—yet another aspect covered by accumulated Isiac myth. Lemprière, taking as his source Plutarch's *De Iside*, writes that she "became enamoured of Osiris her brother-in-law, and introduced herself to his bed." The compromising greenhouse visit can be viewed in this frame. Isis and Nepthys with the mutilated body of Osiris—or on each side of the body of the deceased on mummy cases—corresponds through irony to Isa and Mrs. Manresa flanking Giles in his bloodstained tennis shoes. Again their similarity in bodily configuration as well as their nearness in age adds to the visual import of the passage. "Isis and Nepthys make Osiris hale."[55]

Allusion to the ritual drama of the dismemberment and resurrection of Osiris or to the ritual of "overthrowing Apep" from the Book of the Dead[56] or to the rites of initiation of priests of Cybele described in Lemprière—these are other layers to the palimpsest of this panel of Giles's bloodstained tennis shoes and to the earlier panel with the incident that caused it, though Quentin Bell notes that this "horrid spectacle" was one Woolf had "actually noticed at the time."[57] But so commodious had Woolf's art become that she could use this incident to make an emblem of the Second World War as well as to accommodate myths of Isis and Osiris.

The ritual of afternoon worship of sacred water is evoked by Isa's vision of "water surrounded by walls of shining glass" after her incantatory "A beaker of cold water, a beaker of cold water" (BA 66). It is also emblematic of her desire for Rupert Haines, who is "lost" to her, as Osiris.[58] Isa's uncle, with whom she stayed when she was an ailing child, sounds much like a priest of Isis, for he was a clergyman "who wore a skull cap" and who "made up poems, walking in his garden, saying them aloud."[59] More revealingly, Isa adds, "People thought him mad . . . I didn't" (BA 51).

The panel wherein Lucy Swithin takes William Dodge away from the slumbering company on the terrace into the house itself contains reference to the Isiac ritual of incubation in which the divine healer was believed to effect miraculous cures after the patient had slept within the temple precincts.[60] Lucy in this panel is not only Isis Medica but also Lady of the House of Life.

Isis as creator is realized in the playwright Miss La Trobe, for her name alludes to another treasure in the British Museum, in this instance in its Natural History Department: the La Trobe gold nugget, acquired in 1856, which "was and still is the largest and best formed crystallized gold known."[61] The La Trobe, a mass of gold cubes, some more than half an inch in size, could serve as an emblem of *Between the Acts*: the mass of the novel is itself structured by the juxtaposed cubes of the pageant and of paratactic strategy. The structure of *Between the Acts*, I am arguing, was the fulfillment of a specifically cubistic method. Recall Woolf's relief and pleasure at Basil de Selincourt's review of *The Years:* "now since de Selincourt sees it . . . my intention in *The Years* may not be so entirely muted and obscured as I feared"

(WD, 14 March 1937, 278). The reviewer had written: "The novel consists entirely of tiny cubes of live experience."[62] Miss La Trobe's name, therefore, reflects her precious value. Moreover, the sign for gold was sometimes associated with Isis, and gold was used in her ceremonies whenever possible.[63]

Not only life is controlled by the figure of Isis in the novel, but also creativity: immediately before Miss La Trobe receives inspiration for her next play, the tree she had hidden behind becomes a colossal sistrum:

The whole tree hummed with the whizz they made, as if each bird pluck-ed a wire. A whizz, a buzz rose from the bird-buzzing, bird-vibrant, bird-blackened tree. The tree became a rhapsody, a quivering cacophony, a whizz and vibrant rapture, branches, leaves, birds syllabling discordant-ly life, life, life, without measure, without stop devouring the tree. (BA 209)

The "bird-vibrant" tree recalls the sound of the sistrum as Pater describes it: "a noise like the jargon of innumerable birds and insects awakened from tor-por and abroad in the spring sun" (1:107).

The cycle of nature continues: the "green waters seemed to rise over her," the inundation having begun not only to the sistrum rattle of the "bird-buzzing" tree but also by the sistrum rattle of "the latch of the iron entrance gate" to Miss La Trobe's cottage (BA 211). At the pub the curtain is red, the color of Isis; "The acrid smell of stale beer saluted her," evokes one of Isis's appellations, for she was "Lady of Beer." Conversation about "Bossy" —also a nickname for cows—stops as La Trobe enters; she looks through the smoke (resembling incense) "at a crude glass painting of a cow" (BA 212); Witt, basing his description of the Sailing of Isis's Ship on the account given by Apuleius, refers to a votive gift placed on the ship as "the picture of a cow."[64] It is in this highly concentrated or, if you will, consecrated ambience that La Trobe creates: "The mud became fertile." She sees the "two scarcely perceptible figures." Then a reference back to the colossal sistrum: "Sudden-ly the tree was pelted with starlings" before she hears "the first words" (BA 212).

Isa's "Yes, yes, yes, the tide rushed out embracing. No, no, no, it con-tracted" (BA 215) in answer to Lucy's question, "Did you feel . . . what he said: we act different parts but are the same?" compares the ambiguity of life with the cycles of the Nile. This penultimate portion of the novel contrasts with the oversimplified "yes I said yes" of Molly Bloom in Joyce's *Ulysses*.

Rather than the acted upon and passive Molly, we have a coda to both the figure and the idea of Isis, the acting and active source of life, stated in allusion to her work of the annual inundation of the Nile—a poetic statement of Woolf's "hidden pattern," here perceived as resolution by imposing on fleeting insight the monumental forms of Egyptian myth. As she had written earlier in an ecstatic passage suggestive of Isis and Horus: "Mysterious figures! Mother and son. . . . Wherever I go . . . I see you. . . . If I fall on my knees, if I go through the ritual, the ancient antics, it's you, unknown figures, you I adore" (MOT 70). For Woolf's netting of "life itself," we find within the cartouche of the matter of Egypt the serene and maternal figure of Isis holding the sistrum of creativity in her hand and wearing on her head the solar disk resembling the moon in its fullness.

The Aset hieroglyph

Notes

1. See T.E.Peet, "The Present Position of Egyptological Studies," an inaugural lecture delivered before the University of Oxford, 17 January 1934 (Oxford: Clarendon Press, 1934), passim.

2. Virginia Woolf, "Friendships Gallery," ed. Ellen Hawkes, *Twentieth Century Literature* 25 (1979): 289.

3. As evidence of Woolf's awareness of this conjunction, see the Victorian scene of the pageant in *Between the Acts,* which ridicules the fusion of the desire to spread Christianity with the desire to spread empire. My argument is epitomized by the minister's "clasping his fossil" while he prays (BA 164–74, esp. 171).

4. See the entry in the *Oxford Classical Dictionary,* for example: "Not only are statues and monuments of her [Isis's] worship found in all parts of the Roman Empire and her symbols quite commonly used on . . . jewelry, but many grave reliefs and tombs show representations of her symbols, particularly the sistrum and the situla. The deceased, if a woman, was frequently portrayed on the funeral monument in the costume characteristic of the deity."

5. Francis Steegmuller, ed. and trans., *Flaubert in Egypt: A Sensibility on Tour,* a narrative drawn from Gustave Flaubert's travel notes and letters (London: Bodley Head, 1972), 141.

6. In its *Proceedings,* the death of Lowell, the first American vice-president, is described as "an unspeakable loss" to the fund. Indeed, Margaret S. Drower, chair of the Committee of the Egypt Exploration Society (the EEF's later name), observes, "After the British Museum, the largest and best collection of antiquities was shipped

there [to the Boston Museum of Fine Arts] every year." *Excavating in Egypt: The Egypt Exploration Society: 1882–1982,* ed. T.G.H. James (London: British Museum Publications, 1982), 22.

7. 1903 holograph notebook of Virginia Woolf, Hyde Park Gate 66BO299, 56. With permission from the Henry W. and Albert A. Berg Collection, the New York Public Library, Astor, Lenox and Tilden Foundations. Hereafter cited as 1903 diary notebook, Berg.

8. Vita Sackville-West, "To Egypt," in *Passenger to Teheran* (London: Hogarth Press, 1926), 38.

9. Vita Sackville-West to Virginia Woolf, 29 January 1926, also with permission of Berg Collection.

10. For a discussion of the chronology of Woolf's women tutors, see Perry Meisel, *The Absent Father: Virginia Woolf and Walter Pater* (New Haven: Yale University Press, 1980), 17–33.

11. Walter Pater, *Marius the Epicurean: His Sensations and Ideas,* 2 vols. (London: Macmillan, 1910), 1: 154. Subsequent citations will be included in the text.

12. Ian Fletcher, *Walter Pater,* Writers and Their Work, no. 114 (London: Longmans, Green, 1959), 24.

13. Jane Harrison, *Alpha and Omega* (London: Sidgwick and Jackson, 1915), 152.

14. A sistrum is a metal rattle consisting of a handle and a frame fitted with loosely held rods. The situla is a breast-shaped pail.

15. "This apparent autonomy of sense images comprised what she came to call her scene-making ability. Her mind seemed automatically to sum up complex situations, not in words, but by means of relatively simplified scenes. She believed that her scene-making ability was her 'natural' way of thinking and remembering—'marking the past.' She cultivated it by adopting it as a method in writing, trying to think first in images and scenes and then to describe the scenes in words." Jean O. Love, *Virginia Woolf: Sources of Madness and Art* (Berkeley: University of California Press, 1977), 218. See also MB 122.

16. The parallel influence of her Aunt Caroline Emilia Stephen's Quakerism, to which Violet Dickinson also converted (QB 1:82) is relevant, especially in light of its foundational encouragement of women to speak.

17. T.S. Eliot, "Ulysses, Order, and Myth,"*Dial* 75 (1923); 480–83.

18. Brenda Silver, ed., "Anon" and "The Reader": Virginia Woolf's Last Essays, *Twentieth Century Literature* 25 (1979):381.

19. I am grateful to Louise DeSalvo for bringing this important letter to my attention.

20. R.E. Witt, *Isis in the Graeco-Roman World* (Ithaca: Cornell University Press, 1971), 15, 18. The Egyptology Department at the British Museum recommended this book early in my research.

21. Edward Gibbon:*The History of the Decline and Fall of the Roman Empire*, ed. J.B. Bury (London: Methuen, 1900–1913), 2:215.

22. See my essay "The Anti-Madonna in the Work and Thought of Virginia Woolf," in *Virginia Woolf: Centennial Essays*, ed. Elaine Ginsberg and Laura Gotlieb (Troy, N.Y.: Whitston, forthcoming).

23. *Lemprière's Classical Dictionary of Proper Names Mentioned in Ancient Authors with a Chronological Table,* new ed. (London, 1788; 1st Routledge ed., 1879; rev. 1949; London: Routledge and Kegan Paul, 1972).

24. A pageant is held in *The Years* to raise funds for a new steeple.

25. For a step-by-step account of the mystery and its solution, see E.A. Wallis Budge, *Egyptian Language: Easy Lessons in Egyptian Hieroglyphics with Sign List* (London: 1910; rpt. New York: Dover, 1976),12–17. On the basis of her reference to "Coptic scholars" in 1907, Woolf might well have been familiar with this material at least in outline, for knowledge of Coptic, that is, New Egyptian, was essential to the first deciphering of the hieroglyphics. Moreover, her interest in language as language is evidenced in her comparison of ancient and modern Greek in the diary she kept during her travels in Greece in 1906 (British Museum MS Ad. 61837, 46–47).

26. Unpublished typescript draft of *The Years*, Monks House Collection, University of Sussex Library. Cited by Susan Squier in "A Track of Our Own" in this volume.

27. Witt, *Isis,* 19.

28. Ibid.

29. Wallis Budge, *The Dwellers on the Nile: The Life, History, and Religion of the Ancient Egyptians* (1926; rpt. New York: Dover Publications, 1977), 133.

30. Quoted by E.A. Wallis Budge, *The Gods of the Egyptians*, 2 vols. (1904; rpt. New York: Dover Publications, 1969), 2:66.

31. There were two major exhibitions of Egyptian art in London during Woolf's lifetime, at the Burlington Fine Arts Club in 1895 and 1922. Bernard V. Bothmer, "Revealing Man's Fate in Man's Face," *Art News* 79, 6 (summer 1980): 125.

32. Howard Carter, "Preface," *The Tomb of Tut-ankh-amen* (London: Cassell, 1923), 7.

33. Compare Vita's observation: "We fumble, knowing that somewhere round the corner lies the last, satisfying coordination. Meanwhile, certain queer comings together, such as are made by rhythm, or by pattern, or by light and shadows, do produce a natural harmony: a harmony suggesting that the part does probably fit, somewhere, into the whole" ("To Egypt," 38).

34. James George Frazer, *The Golden Bough*, 2d ed. (London: Macmillan, 1907) 4:346ff.

35. Jane Marcus has cited the mythic dimension of Isa: "Given the preoccupation

with motherhood in Virginia Woolf's life and writing, a great shaft of light is shed on her final mother figure, Isa, who is less a person than a myth, caught in a tangled web of sexual fantasy and violence, producing cannon-fodder for history's wars with the bed as the eternal battlefield." "Some Sources for *Between the Acts*," *Virginia Woolf Miscellany*, no. 6 (winter 1977), 2.

36. *Catalogue of Books from the Library of Leonard and Virginia Woolf* (Pullman: Washington State University Library, 1975).

37. Apuleius, *The Golden Ass, being the Metamorphoses of Lucius Apuleius*, trans. W. Adlington (1566), Loeb Classical Library (London: William Heinemann, 1922), 546–47.

38. Witt, *Isis*, 23.

39. Consider what Virginia Stephen wrote in 1906 of the view from the Parthenon from what had been the vantage of the Great Statue: "She looked straight through the long doorway, made by the curved line of the columns, and saw a slice of Attic mountain and sky and plain, a shining strip of the sea. It is like a panel let into the Parthenon to complete its beauty." Typescript of diary from 14 September 1906 to 23 April 1909. This selection is dated 14 September 1906, 9–10; MH/A7. Berg Collection.

40. James Naremore, *The World without a Self* (New Haven and London: 1973), 220.

41. Leila Luedeking, curator of modern literary collections at Washington State University, suggests that "this re-enacting in a pageant form of the old method of story-telling in tableaus is directly related to what Bloomsbury painters were doing with their many portraits enclosed in mirrors or in windows or doorways" (correspondence, 18 February 1980).

42. Avrom Fleishman, *Virginia Woolf: A Critical Reading* (Baltimore: Johns Hopkins Press, 1975), xi. Earlier Nancy Bazin suggested that Woolf was moving in the direction of T.S. Eliot's provision of footnotes for the reader of "The Wasteland," though she did not so help "the reader of *Between the Acts* recognize her many allusions." *Virginia Woolf and the Androgynous Vision*, (New Brunswick, N.J.: Rutgers University Press, 1973), 221.

43. See Auerbach's explanation of parataxis in *Mimesis*, trans. Willard R. Trask (Princeton: Princeton University Press, 1953).

44. Pointz Hall not only resembles a Roman villa, since it is a "homely . . . whitish house with the grey roof, and the wing thrown out at right angles" (BA 6), but it is disposed in a hollow (BA 8) like the House of Cecilia. Moreover, the name Woolf assigns the family dwelling in Pointz Hall—Oliver—evokes the "old flower garden . . . set here and there with a venerable olive-tree" that Marius sees there (2: 98).

45. As Hugh Kenner observes of Joyce's *Ulysses,* "But only with Butler's help [*The Authoress of the Odyssey*] can we discover a clear Homeric correspondence at the very beginning, where the correspondences ought to be plain if they are going to work" *The Pound Era* (Berkeley: University of California Press, 1971), 47. A similar attribution may be made to Lemprière.

46. "Spatial Form in Modern Literature," rpt. from *Sewanee Review* in *Criticism: The Foundations of Modern Literary Judgment,* rev. ed., M. Schorer, J. Miles, and G. McKenzie (New York: Harcourt Brace, 1958), 384.

47. Witt, *Isis,* 236. The hieroglyph for "goose" is also that for "son." Budge, *Egyptian Language,* 66.

48. Woolf takes a swipe at Joyce with the discussion of the cesspool. While it probably alludes to what Witt calls "a bizarre" Pompeian fresco of Isis-Fortuna juxtaposed with a man relieving himself painted on a wall leading to a lavatory, the panel gains in humorous effect from the toilet scene in *Ulysses.* See *Pompeii A.D. 79,* catalog compiled and written by John Ward-Perkins and Amanda Claridge (London, 1976), 58.

49. Wm. Smith, *A Classical Dictionary of Greek and Roman Biography, Mythology and Geography,* rev. by G. E. Marindin (London: John Murray, 1904).

50. *British Museum Guide* (1971), 147.

51. Witt, *Isis,* 15, 19.

52. For these terms and many helpful insights on Egyptian art and writing (the terms are not mutually exclusive) I am indebted to Othmar Keel, *The Symbolism of the Biblical World: Ancient Near Eastern Iconography and the Book of Psalms,* trans. Timothy J. Hallett (New York: Seabury Press, 1978), 7–8.

53. Budge describes numerous small stelae with reliefs of Horus used as talismans by the Egyptians, who placed them in their gardens and "even buried them in the ground to protect themselves and their property from the attacks of noxious beasts, and reptiles, and insects of every kind." *Gods,* 2:267.

54. See Budge, *Gods,* 1:489.

55. Witt, *Isis,* 288 n.24.

56. E. A. Wallis Budge, *Egyptian Magic* (1901; rpt. New York: Dover Publications, 1971), 78–84.

57. Quentin Bell, "Introduction," *Between the Acts* (London: Folio Society, 1974), 8.

58. "Osiris, reborn as Horus, was the river's living power and in this sense . . . the Egyptians could 'speak of Osiris as water.' " Witt, *Isis,* 165.

59. Blackman refers to a relief at Karnak depicting "musician-priests wearing close-fitting skull-caps . . . singing." Aylward M. Blackman, "On the Position of Women in the Ancient Egyptian Hierarchy," *Journal of Egyptian Archaeology* 7 (1921): 21.

60. Witt, *Isis*, 54.

61. Peter Bancroft, *The World's Finest Minerals and Crystals* (New York: Viking Press, 1973), 28–29.

62. Basil de Selincourt, "Infinity in Experience: Virginia Woolf's New Novel," *Observer*, Sunday, 14 March, 1937.

63. A congruent pictograph would show Isis kneeling on the sign for gold. See Witt, *Isis*, plate 1, facing 73.

64. Witt goes on to mention glass paintings specifically. See Witt, *Isis*, 177, 309 n.20.

Political Aesthetics: Virginia Woolf and Dorothy Richardson   *Diane Filby Gillespie*

The customary distinction between art and politics in Virginia Woolf's work is breaking down. Woolf not only introduced her concern with social and political issues, especially as they concerned women, into works noted for artistic integrity,[1] but also marshaled her artistic acumen behind her polemic essays and books.[2] Do her aesthetic choices themselves have social and political implications? Here difficulties emerge. One critic describes Woolf as a representative of the "female" phase of women's relationship with their society. This phase of *"self-discovery,* a turning inward freed from some of the dependency of opposition, a search for identity,'' leads to the development of a "female aesthetic." Dependent on the "annihilation of the narrative self," this aesthetic is as self-destructive as women's traditional self-abnegation and passivity.[3] It is, in other words, devoid of political significance. Another critic, in contrast, sees Woolf's aesthetic choices as examples of feminist assertion and affirmation. His focus on the form Woolf uses in *Mrs. Dalloway,* however, is based on an idealization of the feminine as Clarissa Dalloway represents it.[4] Apparently what constitutes feminist behavior needs further examination.

Kate Millett uses the term "politics" to refer to "power-structured relationships, arrangements whereby one group of persons is controlled by another."[5] "Sexual politics" refers to men's control over women. Art has been linked with sex by critics who have evaluated women's art by a different set of criteria and, in a different way, by women writers who consciously have evolved a feminine aesthetic to counter a controlling one defined as masculine. In cases such as these, aesthetic politics or, perhaps more accurately, political aesthetics, becomes a subcategory of sexual politics. To reflect in style as well as in content the values society has inculcated in women is not merely to withdraw into a sphere dominated by those values; it is to rebel in a tangible way against the status quo manifested in art as in society. To shift the emphasis, for example, from an all-knowing, frequently male authorial voice to the dramatized inner life of an individual character is to give that character increased integrity and autonomy. When the character is a woman, the shift is especially important. It is liberating. It requires, moreover, neither flattering men nor adopting their methods. Both Woolf and Dorothy Richardson, one of her contemporaries, take aesthetic stances of this sort. Each woman's work illuminates the other's; both help to define political aesthetics.

The critical difficulty arises because Woolf and Richardson polarize art and politics and yet, ultimately, transcend that polarization. Woolf's comments on politics versus the arts occur in her letters, diaries, and novels. Her assumption is that politics, as Millett later suggests, does involve power relations among groups; it is clear to Woolf that environment has been decisive in making women what they are: men traditionally have controlled the property and the educational institutions in England and thus have controlled women. (TG 17–18) Among the politically active people with whom Woolf was surrounded for much of her life, however, she often heard not confessions of the desire for power but, rather, professions of humanitarian motives. Woolf remained suspicious both of politicians' motives and of the efficacy of their methods. "It seems to me more and more clear," she says in a diary entry in 1919, "that the only honest people are the artists, and that these social reformers and philanthropists get so out of hand and harbour so many discreditable desires under the disguise of loving their kind, that in the end there's more to find fault with in them than in us" (WD 17). She ultimately cannot decide whether sitting on committees and councils and being interested in political issues improves or harms one's character, but she is reasonably certain that such activities rarely benefit the public in any substantial way (L 2:51,76).

Woolf's era of suffrage agitation, however, presented the woman writer not only with the usual conflict between the traditional female role and art but also with the perhaps more difficult choice between political and artistic rebellion. Either commitment had implications for the other; in either case the woman must sort out her attitudes toward the fact that she is a woman and that, as such, she has a world view different from that of the men who dominate both society and art. In either case she can limit her effectiveness by anger and bitterness, or she can transcend self-consciousness. At the level of such transcendence, the polarity between art and politics no longer exists; activity in either area is more likely to be successful. Political aesthetics and aesthetic politics both mean the harmony, balance, and wholeness that result from a large injection of women's values into male-dominated and thus one-sided spheres of activity.

Woolf often does not see such wholeness in the women politicians she knows. Among her acquaintances who were involved with the suffrage movement and other social-political questions were Janet Case, Margaret Llewelyn Davies, Lilian Harris, Ray Strachey, Elizabeth Robins, and Beatrice Webb. Woolf admired some of these women, who at times involved her in their activities. But just as often they made her feel ineffectual, uncomprehending, or defensively superior. She cannot see how hours spent "writing names like Cowgill on envelopes" or going to hear suffrage speakers will accomplish anything; it only wastes time (L 1:422, 437–38). Ray Strachey especially makes her "feel like a faint autumnal mist—she's so effective, and thinks me such a goose" (L 2:63; cf 65). But Woolf is not envious. Political activity may make men "dry dogs" (L 1:217), but it makes women, like Strachey, "floppy, fat, untidy, clumsy, and making fewer concessions than ever to brilliancy, charm, politeness, wit, art, manners, literature and so forth." She is "full of news upon women's future of course but, my God," Woolf exclaims, "if *thats* the future what's the point in it" (L 2:357).

This and other comments indicate the extent to which political activity and art seem to Woolf mutually exclusive. "You'll never like my books," she writes to Margaret Llewelyn Davies, "but then shall I ever understand your Guild? Probably not" (L 2: 399). In fact, to Woolf, it is not artistic but political activity that is more often out of touch with reality, that becomes "all phantasies and moonshine, only mudcolored moonshine." She cannot see how Leonard and others like him "see anything solid" in such concerns and begrudges them the time they spend (L 2:585). Mud is an image, familiar in political parlance, that Woolf associates with politics on more than one occasion. "I think politicians and journalists must be the lowest of Gods creatures," she writes, "creeping perpetually in the mud and biting with one end and stinging with the other" (L 1:332).

The theme of politics versus the arts recurs in the novels. Two examples suffice. In *To the Lighthouse* Lily Briscoe feels a momentary kinship with Mr. Carmichael, the poet, because "some notion was in both of them about the ineffectiveness of action, the supremacy of thought" (TTL 292). The best example, however, is the contrast between Richard Dalloway and Rachel Vinrace in *The Voyage Out*. Dalloway, a politician who is opposed to women's suffrage, defends his career by contrasting it to that of the artist:

> We politicians doubtless seem . . . a gross commonplace set of people;
> but we see both sides; we may be clumsy, but we do our best to get a
> grasp of things. Now your artists *find* things in a mess, shrug their
> shoulders, turn aside to their visions—which I grant may be very
> beautiful—and *leave* things in a mess. Now that seems to me evading
> one's responsibilities. Besides, we aren't all born with the artistic faculty.
> (VO 44–45)

Rachel, an accomplished pianist, defends the artist against charges of ir-
responsibility. The politician may slightly improve the material well-being
of certain people, but he ignores their minds and feelings just as he ignores his
own. Dalloway retorts that women do not and ought not understand
politics. (VO 66–67). As her discussion of the subject in *Three Guineas* reveals, Woolf agrees; women ought not understand the kind of political activity that has done both England and the world so little good. As for the
vote, Terence Hewet in *The Voyage Out* sums up what undoubtedly is
Woolf's opinion: as long as even well-educated women see men as larger
than life, they are unlikely to do anything with the vote should they get it.
(VO 212). As Woolf emphasizes throughout *A Room of One's Own*, financial
and intellectual independence are more important. Without them, women
will not have the courage to express their values even if given the forum.

Woolf tempers her negative remarks on politics in a number of ways and
on a number of occasions, partly because she corresponds with people who
have that orientation, partly because she has a sense of humor, and partly
because she is sympathetic, although she does not seem to know why. She
wonders in her diary what she would be like if she were immersed in such activities (WD 17). The most interesting passage in this connection, however,
occurs in *To the Lighthouse*. Lily Briscoe recalls a lecture on brotherly love she
heard Charles Tansley deliver during the war. She wonders how anyone so
ignorant of painting and so adamant about the inferiority of women artists
can speak on such a subject. To this extent we have again the alienation of the
artist from the more public-spirited person. Yet Lily goes on to admit that
Tansley had admirable qualities. She realizes that, just as he distorts the
image of women for his own purposes, so she distorts his. For her he is a
scapegoat. Everyone, however, has feelings of inferiority and as a result
forms ''grotesque'' images of other people. (TTL 293) Woolf comes close
here to a definition of the human tendency to describe one's values and

activities in opposition to those of other people, to defend one's own choices by caricaturing those of others. She does this herself when she attacks politicians and their motives and methods, sometimes biting and stinging as energetically as she accuses them of doing. She does it too when she attacks the aesthetic positions of some writers, like the Edwardians, and identifies with those of others. However, like Lily Briscoe, she is increasingly conscious of the human condition in general, less preoccupied with differences than with similarities among groups, less angry about unjust opinions of women and more aware of universal injustices, less negative about politicians and more aware that their attitudes, like those of artists, can be ranged upon a continuum with acceptance of the status quo at one end and, toward the other, varying degrees of rebellion against it.

Because of Woolf's interest in women's situation and because of the charge that she withdrew from the arena of political and especially suffrage activity, the similarities in her presentations of women politicians and women artists are especially important. None of the feminists Woolf sketches briefly in her fiction is wholly admirable. In *Mrs. Dalloway,* for example, Sally Seton, a potential writer or painter, defends women's suffrage. She denounces Hugh Whitbread as the uninformed, unthinking, unfeeling representative of all that in British middle-class is responsible for the situation of women. Apparently, however, she is productive artistically only in her youth and does no more than talk about women's rights. She marries a bald cotton manufacturer and has five sons. Unlike Sally Seton, Evelyn Murgatroyd in *The Voyage Out* wants to effect social reforms, not just talk about them. She wants to replace inferior, brutish men in positions of power with superior, noble women. She assumes antagonism rather than cooperation between the sexes (VO 247–48). Julia Hedge in *Jacob's Room* also is angry and bitter. Instead of insisting on women's superiority, however, she imitates with vengeance the methods of men. Waiting for her books in the British Museum, she swears and thinks bitterly of the men's names ranged all around the dome and then fervently of the enormous intellectual task to which she must apply herself for the sake of the cause (JR 106).

Mary Datchet in *Night and Day* is Woolf's most ambitious attempt to understand the feminist. Mary, somewhat like Evelyn Murgatroyd, is determined to accomplish much. Politically radical, she directs her desire to mobilize, organize, and wield power toward a thorough reconstruction of the suffrage society to which she belongs. At home in committee rooms, where issues seem to her to have right and wrong sides and where her commanding attitude impresses the other members, she enjoys vanquishing her opponents. Woolf presents neither Mary Datchet's commitment to the suffrage movement nor her mastery of traditionally masculine skills, however, as wholly admirable. When Katharine Hilbery visits Mary at the suffrage office, she concludes that she will not join the movement, perhaps because, as her father observes, "the sight of one's fellow-enthusiasts always chokes one off. They show up the faults of one's cause so much more plainly than one's antagonists" and destroy the illusions one can maintain in private (N&D 100). The meager Mr. Clacton with his passion for detail and order and the exuberant but disorganized Mrs. Seal, who run the suffrage office, are not inspiring representatives of the movement. The suggestion that Woolf shrank from affiliating herself formally with a movement that had so many unimpressive advocates as well as so many ugly, demeaning, and bizarre aspects probably is, at least in part, correct.

Mary Datchet bears some guilt by her association with others in the movement; still, Woolf finds common ground with her. She is complex as Woolf's more briefly sketched feminists are not. In Mary's life not only public issues but also private and emotional ones are important, as her love for Ralph Denham, her delight in her independent life and intellect, and her sensitivity to her surroundings reveal:

> There were few mornings when Mary did not look up, as she bent to lace her boots, and as she followed the yellow rod from curtain to breakfast-table she usually breathed some sigh of thankfulness that her life provided her with such moments of pure enjoyment. She was robbing no one of anything, and yet, to get so much pleasure from simple things, such as eating one's breakfast alone in a room which had nice colours in it, clean from the skirting of the boards to the corners of the ceiling, seemed to suit her so thoroughly that she used at first to hunt about for some one to apologize to, or for some flaw in the situation. (ND 77)

Mary has a room of her own; she is observant and sensitive; and she has private moments of insight that balance her public, political self. When she laughingly tells Ralph, "Men are such pedants—they don't know what things matter, and what things don't" (N&D 90), she voices Woolf's assessment of the major differences between male and female writers, the difference in values. Mary, moreover, is not subservient to traditions. "What was the good, after all," she thinks, "of being a woman if one didn't keep fresh, and cram one's life with all sorts of views and experiments?" (N&D 79). Her observation echoes a theme to which Woolf continually returns in

A Writer's Diary. She affirms her love of change, her related conviction that truth is elusive, relative, or multiple, and her desire to experiment with contrasting styles and subjects. The side of Mary Datchet, then, that accepts and imitates male values and behavior is complicated by a side that has all the characteristics Woolf thinks necessary for the woman artist. By the end of the novel Mary is a whole person who could function effectively in either sphere. Like Lily Briscoe and Woolf herself, Mary Datchet transcends her anger at the injustices done to women and focuses on more general human problems. She moves beyond suffrage to socialism.[7] Had she been an artist she would have established the right priorities, too, and attained the perspective necessary to accomplish something of value as Lily Briscoe does when she completes her painting and Orlando does when she completes her poem.[8]

The characteristics and attitudes of the feminists in Woolf's fiction parallel those of the various kinds of women writers she defines in her essays. She notes that the restrictions placed upon female artists affect them in dangerous ways. Some women accept the idea that they lack intellect and artistic ability. Either they give up art altogether or they content themselves with tasteless and naively egotistical self-expression.[9] Other women respond, like many feminists, with anger and bitterness to the view that they are intellectually and aesthetically inept. Some consider themselves superior and write in a defensively feminine manner; others try to prove their equality by imitating the thought and expression of men. In either case, self-consciousness diminishes effectiveness. Woolf cites many instances of women writers whose work is marred by anger and bitterness, among them Olive Schreiner,[10] Lady Winchilsea, (ROOM 61–63), the Duchess of Newcastle (ROOM 64), and Charlotte Brontë (ROOM 72). On the other hand, she compliments Jane Austen and Dorothy Osborne because they write as women without the debilitating consciousness that they are doing so (ROOM 65–66, 71). On the whole, Woolf thinks that the woman artist slowly is achieving the detachment necessary for the production of significant art (CE 2:145).

Woolf's aesthetic statements are well known. The extent to which these statements reflect the spirit of her age, however, is less widely acknowledged. The reverberations between her work and Dorothy Richardson's are a case in point. Woolf was familiar with the early volumes of Richardson's *Pilgrimage;* she reviewed the fourth part, *The Tunnel,* in 1919 and the seventh, *Revolving Lights,* in 1923. These reviews cannot be dismissed lightly.[11] In her published criticism, Woolf treats Richardson kindly; yet privately she classifies her with the female artists who angrily and self-consciously try to produce a feminine art. The "damned egotistical self," she says in a diary entry in 1920, "ruins Joyce and Richardson to my mind" and makes them too "narrow and restricting" (WD 22). Her remark explains the comment in the review of *Revolving Lights* that Miriam, Richardson's largely autobiographical character, "points too didactically" to small things that interest her (CW 125). Just as Woolf links Richardson and Joyce, so Richardson links Woolf and Joyce. In the 1938 foreword to *Pilgrimage* Richardson alludes to them as independent travelers in the same aesthetic direction. In private letters, however, Richardson describes Woolf as essentially a masculine writer who, in her attempts to deal with life, is off base. Richardson's response is to the despair she senses in Woolf's last book, presumably *Between the Acts*.[12] Each woman therefore treats the other as both comrade and rival.

Woolf's reading and reviewing of *The Tunnel* and *Revolving Lights* occurred during the years when she turned from the relatively traditional form of her first two novels to her more experimental methods. Moreover, these reviews read like early versions of her much-quoted essays on fiction, "Modern Fiction" and "Mr. Bennett and Mrs. Brown." The ideas developed in these essays are not merely responses to Richardson's artistic method. They are also paraphrases and amplifications of ideas that Richardson's developing artist-character, Miriam Henderson, encounters or advances in the two sections of *Pilgrimage* Woolf reviewed. In *The Tunnel*, for example, Miriam confronts Hypo Wilson, a character based on H.G. Wells.[13] His attitude toward the novel is the product of a world view that Miriam rejects. She is distressed by his beliefs that God is merely man's invention, that man evolved from the ape until he discovered science, and that science will order chaos. Women, Wilson thinks, reproduce the men who implement science, and writers describe reality as the scientist sees it.[14] His values emerge both in his manner of conversation and in the advice he gives Miriam. Listening to him talk, she first is impressed by his charm and his authoritative manner. Yet she resents his condescending tone and is convinced that somehow what he says is wrong (T 2:119). Hypo is dogmatic; he tells rather than asks and subordinates rather than involves his listeners. He has a penchant, moreover, for epithets that classify and label, and his typical and appropriate gesture is the "minatory outstretched forefinger" (T 2:113, 118). To converse with him, Miriam discovers, she must be false to her feminine values. She has "to be brilliant and amusing to hold his attention—in fact to tell lies. To get on here, one would have to say clever things in a high bright voice" (T 2:113). To a certain extent Miriam conforms to expectations; then she reproaches herself for giving in, partly because she senses in Hypo Wilson a recognition of something more in life than his scientific world view allows. She also senses that he fears and denies that something (T 2:124). Constantly Miriam tries to win his admission of a reality different from and more fundamental than his (RL 3:360).

The end product of Miriam's pilgrimage is not adjustment to society and its values; rather, it is a demand that society adjust to her view of reality. She must communicate, however, what that view is, and she must do so in a way that does not contradict it. She hesitates when on various occasions Hypo Wilson urges her to take advantage of her ability to observe closely and write up her experiences (T 2:129). She is afraid of writing like Edna Prout, another friend of Wilson's. Miriam is amazed to find that he is reading the proofs of Miss Prout's latest novel, but she is aghast when she realizes that Miss Prout has included people they both know. She is offended, however, not by the use of the author's experience but by the attitude toward that experience. People are violated, life itself is violated by the reduction to absurdity of everyone and everything except the superior author. Miriam, who reads the manuscript, concludes that both author and characters are ruthless and exploitative and that both engage in a lot of futile fuss that betrays a false definition of reality (RL 3:342, 348–49). Men and the women who imitate them "weave golden things; thought, science, art, religion, upon a black background," Miriam thinks. But "they never *are*. They only make or do; unconscious of the quality of life as it passes" (RL 3:280).

In *Revolving Lights* Miriam juxtaposes to art as men have defined it women's sensitivity to and ability to create atmospheres. In fact, Miriam insists that among men creativity is the exception while among women it is the rule. Women's art, she says to Hypo Wilson, is "as big an art as any other. Most women can exercise it, for reasons, by fits and starts. The best women work at it the whole of the time." Men, however, preoccupied with mere appearances rather than with the subtle relationships among things that constitute atmosphere, thrive on but remain oblivious to women's creative activity (RL 3:256–57). To Miriam the fact that women are creators of atmospheres provides one answer to the charge that they are inferior because they have not achieved in art. She points to the public nature of men's accomplishments as opposed to the private nature of women's. She notes, moreover, that the material of women's art, unlike men's, is people. Nevertheless, she is equally concerned with pointing out the similarities between the art of the two sexes. Women's art, like men's, requires consciously learned skills and self-discipline as, indeed, Woolf's Orlando discovers when she changes sexes. Female artists, like male artists, must rest now and then from the strain of their work. Miriam compares the male artist's insistence that he occasionally must get away from his work, sometimes into dissipation, with the woman's occasional need to be "nothing to nobody, [to leave] off for a while giving out any atmosphere" (RL 3:258), as Woolf's Mrs. Ramsay must do in *To the Lighthouse.*

Miriam herself does not set out to master woman's art. She learns from observing and even from trying her hand that the products of such art are intangible; they cannot be read or framed or played upon a musical instrument; consequently they go unrecognized and unvalued by the men who most need the kind of sensitivity and awareness they represent. Miriam's developing aesthetics is an attempt both to retain the curiosity about individuals and sensitivity to relationships inherent in woman's art and to find a suitable way to express them. She has to learn that often a very fine line exists between the art of creating atmospheres and an artificial, essentially hypocritical feminine social role. She admires woman's ability to see value in everyone, but she hesitates to encourage woman's tendency to quote man's opinions and thus perpetuate his inability to see that value. There is a difference, moreover, between the subdued inspiration growing out of a sensitivity to the inner life and to relationships among people that every woman can exercise if she chooses, and the flamboyant, superficially clever posing growing out of a knowledge of men and their limited view of woman as body. Miriam wants an art form that will enable both men and women to distinguish between woman's art and its deterioration into woman's artifice.

Miriam can neither imitate novels written by men nor retreat into woman's art if she wants to change Hypo Wilson's view of what is real as well as the view of the society he represents. Her comments throughout *Pilgrimage* form the basis for a contrast between masculine and feminine realism in the novel. In essence, masculine realism reflects a partial, analytical, and often negative world view. Assuming that life is primarily in the state of becoming, it emphasizes change. External facts, sequences of events, and continual productivity are most valuable. No relationship of importance exists between man and anything called "God." The individual too is relatively unimportant; he is valuable primarily as a part of one or more groups arranged in neat hierarchies. To the others in these groups he relates physically or verbally. The artist relates with his superior verbal skill and communicates to other people his extensive knowledge of this world of facts and groups. His attitude toward his readers and often toward his characters is condescending and coercive. Self-consciously proud of his talent and avidly seeking admiration, he produces clever phrases and aesthetic structures that call attention to themselves and to his ability.

Feminine realism, on the other hand, reflects an all-encompassing, synthetic, fundamentally affirmative world view. It intuits that life is primarily changeless and stable, in the state of being. In this context a person's inner sense of living fully, joyfully in the all-inclusive present moment is most valuable. Life so experienced has a dimension that might be called spiritual. Such insight, which is the primary reality, is achieved not in conversation or in physical contact with other people, but in silent and usually solitary contemplation, enhanced at times by one's surroundings or by a similar awareness in someone else. Far more significant than any group to which he or she belongs is each individual's awareness or lack of awareness of this dimension. To foster it in others and to share it by means of her art is the task of the feminine realist. Such communication is not achieved by a superior person imparting knowledge to an inferior. It is achieved by equals collaborating in the discovery of a reality to which everyone has potential access. The feminine realist does not call attention to her skill and provide a barrier between the reader and the reality she perceives. Instead, she makes her awareness fully accessible in every element of her art.

Miriam's developing aesthetics in *Pilgrimage* defines the way Richardson presents her. Miriam's mind determines all characteristics of the book. Richardson is confident enough in the vital sense of reality her method creates to dare to present without commentary all of Miriam's vacillations, exaggerations, and weaknesses along with her certainties and strengths. She is confident enough in the potential sense of reality within her readers to dare to appeal directly to it by eliminating most of the conventional props supporting the limited view of reality prompting masculine realism. Whether her confidence was justified is another question. Woolf's own comments suggest that it was not. The similarities between a number of ideas Miriam expresses in *Pilgrimage* and Woolf's ideas are clear. Whether Woolf took ideas from Richardson or merely found in her work the expression of what she thought and felt herself is, in the final analysis, irrelevant. More important are the similarities of their views on the novel in theory, their divergences in practice, and the metaphysical differences accounting for the divergence, all of which contribute to an understanding of political aesthetics.

In her 1919 review of *The Tunnel,* Woolf says that Richardson's method "demands attention, as a door whose handle we wrench ineffectively calls our attention to the fact that it is locked." Nevertheless, Woolf defends Richardson's choice of method and recognizes that it is the product of a realization that traditional forms are inappropriate for the material she wants to present. Woolf cites two brief comments from *The Tunnel* as clues to

Richardson's method, Hypo Wilson's prediction that "him and her" will be eliminated from the novel, and Miriam's remark that "to write books knowing all about style would be to become like a man." Appropriately, Woolf notes, in the work containing these remarks,

> "him and her" are cut out, and with them goes the old deliberate business: the chapters that lead up and the chapters that lead down; the characters who are always characteristic; the scenes that are passionate and the scenes that are humorous; the elaborate construction of reality; the conception that shapes and surrounds the whole. All these things are cast away, and there is left, denuded, unsheltered, unbegun and unfinished, the consciousness of Miriam Henderson. (CW 120)

In this manner, Woolf says, Richardson presents reality more vividly and directly than she could have with traditional methods (CW 121).

In her 1923 review of *Revolving Lights,* Woolf credits Richardson with consciously developing, if not inventing, "the psychological sentence of the feminine gender." More flexible and sensitive than the masculine sentence, it enables Richardson to present honestly "states of being" rather than "states of doing." Miriam, Woolf says, "is aware of 'life itself'; of the atmosphere of the table rather than of the table; of the silence rather than of the sound" (CW 125). Woolf recognizes that reality as Richardson defines it is the individual consciousness responding to, distorting, even ignoring facts and events, not the facts and events themselves. Even more frequently, reality is the individual consciousness registering and interpreting cues from the outer world, like atmospheres and silences, not usually included in novels. Woolf perceives in Richardson's work a significant shift in values, from outer to inner, from emphatic to subtle. With a shift in values has gone a shift in characterization. And a more sensitive stylistic instrument, a more flexible sentence, has become necessary.

Two months after her review of *The Tunnel,* Woolf published in the *Times Literary Supplement,* the same periodical where the review appeared, an unsigned essay entitled "Modern Novels." This essay was revised and published in 1925 in *The Common Reader* as "Modern Fiction." Seven months after her review of *Revolving Lights,* Woolf published in *The Nation and Athenaeum,* again the same periodical where her review appeared, an early, shorter version of "Mr. Bennett and Mrs. Brown." This essay was rewritten and delivered as a lecture in May 1924.[15] Although in her diary Woolf condemns both Joyce and Richardson for egotism, in "Modern Fiction" she singles out Joyce as one young writer who attempts to convey the "proper stuff of fiction," who follows her injunction to "record the atoms as they fall upon the mind in the order in which they fall, [to] . . . trace the pattern, however disconnected and incoherent in appearance, which each sight or incident scores upon the consciousness" (CE 2:106–7), who perceives that the traditionally unimportant may be more real than the traditionally great. Richardson she does not mention. Yet the value system and corresponding method that Woolf advocates in these essays suggests Richardson's as Woolf herself describes it. Both women insist upon a shift from material to spiritual, from outer to inner reality in the presentation of characters. Both consider the conventional novel form, with its emphasis on love and its neatly devised structure of exceptional external events labeled comic or tragic, an obstruction to inner, everyday reality.

Yet Woolf is not satisfied with Richardson's method. Her charge is the perennial one against it: it lacks "art."[16] "We have to decide," she says in her review of *The Tunnel*, "whether the flying helter-skelter resolves itself by degrees into a perceptible whole." The work disappoints her in this respect, just as the work of the hypothetical Mary Carmichael disappoints her in *A Room of One's Own* (ROOM 95). Its surface is "vivid," but Woolf is afraid that it is still surface, that it somehow lacks significance. She is aware, however, that her criticism may be unreasonable and that her discomfort with Richardson's method suggests a certain contradiction:

> We want to be rid of realism, to penetrate without its help into the regions beneath it, and further require that Miss Richardson shall fashion this new material into something which has the shapeliness of the old accepted forms. We are asking too much; but the extent of our asking proves that *The Tunnel* is better in its failure than most books in their success. (CW 122)

When it comes to her own art, Woolf does ask "too much." That she does so indicates the major differences between the two women's views of art and of what it can accomplish in society. Woolf insists upon changes in both the content and the form of the novel, but she does not attack traditional or contemporary art as an ordering force in the face of a potentially terrifying and meaningless chaos. She does attack, however, the particular ordering mechanisms extant in the novel, because they are based upon the view that external facts and events constitute reality. In other literary forms, like poetry and drama, and in other art media, like painting and music, she finds

methods of ordering her material more appropriate for the expression of a
character's inner life. Her material prompts a selection from a wider variety
of established and contemporary literary and artistic forms than those within
the province of the traditional and contemporary novel; but critics trained in
the arts as defined in a society dominated by masculine values find these
forms, whatever experimental combinations Woolf makes of them, comprehensible and explicable. Possibly for this reason John Cowper Powys, one
of the minority who prefers Richardson's work to Woolf's, accepts Richardson's own evaluation and dismisses Woolf as having used the "methods of
men."[17] Using those methods, however, has turned out to be more politic
than Richardson's more thoroughgoing rejection of them: Woolf is credited
with ideas about the novel and women's situation that were not hers alone,
and those ideas, by way of her works, are seriously considered.

Both Woolf and Richardson were convinced that a general reassessment of
social values and even a redefinition of many of the words that express them
was necessary. Richardson however, attacked "art" itself. She challenged
the value it has been accorded in a male-dominated culture obsessed with
various distorting and incomplete systems, categories, and forms, a culture
driven continuously toward action and production. She looked for and found
sufficient order and pattern in the inner life itself. It is a source of aesthetic
pleasure to which the so-called work of art need not, indeed cannot, add. Her
material, the developing consciousness of Miriam Henderson, determines
whatever form her art has. Fundamentally more optimistic, sane, and certain
than Woolf, [18] Richardson actually applied to her fictional method the implications of their shared belief that such a thing as the art of life exists and
that all people are potential artists. Instead of continually experimenting
with form, as Woolf did, Richardson did not begin *Pilgrimage* until she was
certain of her world view and of the form appropriate to its expression. Once
sure, she did not deviate.

Richardson's interest in aesthetics, like Woolf's, is closely related to her
interest in social and political issues, particularly the British women's suffrage movement. Like Woolf, too, Richardson was both repelled by and attracted to political activity. In one of her autobiographical sketches she ad-
mits that for a brief period in her life she was totally preoccupied with the suffrage issue.[19] As usually the case with Richardson, a judicious counterpoin-
ting of her published opinions and those of Miriam Henderson in *Pilgrimage*
provides the most comprehensive statement of her position. Like Katharine
Hilbery in Woolf's *Night and Day,* Miriam does not formally join the movement. Unlike Katharine, however, Miriam objects to women's voting

because it is unfeminine. Women have the ability, she thinks, to balance and synthesize all points of view. Voting and joining political parties requires them to deny this ability by taking sides (RL 3:394). But Miriam objects mainly to the feminists' lack of faith in women. Women, she insists, do not need emancipation. As a group they have been restricted by laws that are insults; but never have they been mastered, made subject, or victimized in any essential way. She objects, moreover, to the feminists' adoption of the mistaken male notion that women are among the chaotic forces in need of civilization. On the contrary, women possess within themselves the only real civilization, and the civilization of the external world with which men concern themselves is retarded because men refuse to recognize and to include all that women represent (RL 3:394). Miriam thus undermines the environmental emphasis of the feminists, their assertion that women are the products primarily of the restrictions imposed upon them by a male-dominated society and value system.

In this way her position deviates from Virginia Woolf's. As Woolf does later in *Three Guineas,* Miriam's friend, Michael Shatov, distinguishes between opinion and fact. "It is a matter of indisputable *fact,*" he says, "that in the past women have been subject" (D 3:219). "If you believe that," Miriam declares, "it is impossible for us to associate. Because we are living in two utterly different worlds." She insists that she cannot live cheerfully regarding herself "as an emancipated slave, with traditions of slavery for memory and the form of a slave as an everlasting heritage" (D 3:219). Her own generalizations about women as individuals, she says, are justified, whereas men's generalizations about women as a group are not. Unlike men, she generalizes not about the potential and achievements of a group but about the existence of individual, untouched, unrecognized inner lives. What she does, she tries to explain, has something in common with Christianity—meaning not, as Shatov is quick to point out, the unenviable position of women in Christian countries, but rather the fact that "Christ was the first man to see women as individuals" (D 3:220–21).

In spite of her impatience with its environmental emphasis, Miriam at times defends the suffrage movement even as carried on by the militants. Unpleasant agitation seems necessary to bring about reforms; pleasant requests have no impact (DH 4:482–84). Throughout her indirect relationship with the militant suffrage movement via her friend, Amabel, Miriam consistently emphasizes one additional and crucial point: the militants cannot be stereotyped as strange, unfeminine creatures with neither experience of nor qualifications for the traditional woman's role.[20] Some of them are from those social classes with the strongest sense of tradition (DLH 4:247; CH 344, 323). Amabel herself does not fit the stereotype of the suffragette in either appearance or attitude. She is an extremely attractive woman and even plays the traditional charming, flattering feminine role to an extent that at times seems to Miriam incompatible with suffrage activities (CH 4:343). Yet Amabel's refusal to imitate masculine ways of thinking and behaving in spite of her involvement with the suffrage movement is the main reason Miriam defends it. Amabel is not remade when she enters the world of public group action; instead, she brings to that world her own values and inner certainty. Marching in a suffrage parade, Amabel seems to Miriam

> to invite all the world to march with her, to help and be helped. Certain in the way a man so rarely is certain, whole where he is divided, strong where he is weak. Deeply ensconced within her being, and therefore radiant. And it was she, and others here and there in the procession, particularly those the general public was not prepared for, matronly, middleaged, and obviously gentlewomen, who gave it the quality that shamed into so blessed a silence the pavement-scoffers and the gutter-wits; and who were so deliberately ignored by those of the newspaper men who still went on with their misrepresentations to support the policy of their employers. (CH 4:345)

When Amabel is arrested, Miriam admires her willingness "to pay for effectively stating the desire and the right of women to help in the world's housekeeping" (CH 4:351). That phrase, "the world's housekeeping," underscores again her emphasis on women's bringing their own values into the larger world beyond the home.

The alternatives at present available do not allow them to do so. In the working world of men they are treated as inferiors and made to conform to the values of that world. They contribute little of their own view of reality. Miriam's attitude reflects, as usual, Richardson's. In a number of reviews of books on the position of women and in a series of letters to the editor, Richardson affirms a socialist view of woman's role in society. Instead of being responsible to a single man, subject to his whims and eccentricities, victimized by any accidents that may befall him, a woman ought to be responsible to the larger society, which in turn is responsible for her well-being and that of her children.[21] Such a relationship between women and their society implies that their insights, values, and abilities are acknowledged, that "wisdom," "the ability to see," is no longer divorced from "the ability to do.'' The domination of the former by the latter has not had admirable results. Richardson does not see women as the saviors of the world, but she does think that the world would benefit from an influx of ''the dynamic power that has been, so far, almost universally shortcircuiting in the home.''[22]

To Richardson the Quakers are a microcosm of the larger society she envisions.[23] Except among them, however, the proper relationship between men and women is very little in evidence. In *A Room of One's Own* Woolf describes a trip to the British Museum to see what had been written on women. Her experience is anticipated by Miriam's in *The Tunnel* a decade earlier. Woolf is amazed at the numbers of books she finds and at the suppressed and disguised anger behind many of them. She temporarily becomes angry herself, especially at the continual assertions of ''the mental, moral, and physical inferiority of women.'' Such assessments of her sex do not correspond to her sense of herself. Nor does the elevation of the male sex correspond to her experience of men (ROOM 31–32). Similarly, Miriam, who looks up ''women'' in the index of her employer's encyclopedia, is enraged by the charges of women's mental, moral, and physical inferiority. Her anger, however, abates less quickly than Woolf's. Throughout most of the rest of *Pilgrimage,* she is preoccupied with turning the entire male value system upside down, with elevating as superior what has been deemed inferior, with redefining as virtues in form as well as in content what have been considered vices, with recording everything the way it would have been recorded had women wielded the pens from the beginning (T 2:251; D 3:218). As in Woolf's work, the women politicians and artists who are treated sympathetically have much in common. What Amabel does when she marches in the suffrage processions, Miriam plans to do when she writes. Both women take their values into spheres previously dominated by men: politics and art. In so doing they transcend the apparent differences between these activities.

Political aesthetics, then, means tangible declarations of the value of individual inner lives, especially those of women, in forms that challenge prevailing social and aesthetic criteria. Richardson's challenge was more thoroughgoing than Woolf's, and as a result Woolf's work has had the greater impact. But, whatever their differences, the aesthetic positions of these two women writers hardly represent a withdrawal into self-destructive traditional femininity. Admitting the weaknesses of that tradition, they have both found ways to isolate and embody the strengths. That those embodiments still are provoking controversy, Woolf consistently and Richardson increasingly, indicates a degree of success. The political aesthetician can wield power and affect values long after death.

Notes

1. See Herbert Marder, *Feminism and Art: A Study of Virginia Woolf* (Chicago and London: University of Chicago Press, 1968), 2. Marder's study is preceded by other discussions of Woolf's feminism. See, for example, Mary Kelsey, "Virginia Woolf and the She-Condition," *Sewanee Review* 39 (1931): 425–44, and E.D. Pendry, "Feminism, Fiction and Virginia Woolf," in *The New Feminism of English Fiction: A Study in Contemporary Women-Novelists* (Tokyo: Kenkyusha, 1956). The tendency of women to make a social-political issue the content of their art is part of a tradition: denied the pulpit, the lectern, and the political platform, women have used literature as a forum for their opinions. These works of social criticism and reform often had little merit as art. See Vineta Colby, *The Singular Anomaly: Women Novelists of the Nineteenth Century* (New York: New York University Press, 1970), 10–12, and Ellen Moers, *Literary Women: The Great Writers* (Garden City, N.Y.: Doubleday, 1976), 20–41.

2. See Jane Marcus, " 'No More Horses': Virginia Woolf on Art and Propaganda," *Women's Studies* 4 (1977): 264–89.

3. Elaine Showalter, *A Literature of Their Own: British Women Novelists From Brontë to Lessing* (Princeton: Princeton University Press, 1977), 13, 33; "Virginia Woolf and the Flight into Androgyny," 263–79. Showalter's definition of Woolf's position within three phases of women's relation to society echoes that of E.D. Pendry. These two books, as well as Sydney Janet Kaplan's *Feminine Consciousness in the Modern British Novel* (Urbana: University of Illinois Press, 1975) emphasize what the authors see as Woolf's and Richardson's, inadequacies. The two most recent ones, Showalter's and Kaplan's, are assertions of independence from influential writers like Woolf based on the assumptions of a more "enlightened" contemporary feminism.

4. O. P. Sharma, "Feminism as Aesthetic Vision: A Study of Virginia Woolf's 'Mrs. Dalloway,' " *Women's Studies* 3 (1975): 61–73.

5. Kate Millett, *Sexual Politics* (Garden City, N.Y.: Doubleday, 1970), 23.

6. J.B. Batchelor, "Feminism in Virginia Woolf," in *Virginia Woolf: A Collection of Critical Essays,* ed. Claire Sprague (Englewood Cliffs, N. J.: Prentice–Hall, 1971), 173.

7. Margaret Comstock, in " 'The Current Answers Won't Do': The Comic Form of *Night and Day,*" *Women's Studies* 4 (1977): 153–71, provides a sound ap-

proach to Mary Datchet's role in the novel. For a brief view of this character in the context of other suffragettes in fiction, see Susan Higgins, "The Suffragettes in Fiction," *Hecate* 2 (July 1976): 31–47. Showalter also includes a chapter entitled "Women Writers and the Suffrage Movement."

8. For a more complete discussion of the women artists in Woolf's fiction, see my "Virginia Woolf and the 'Reign of Error,' " *Research Studies* 43 (December 1975): 222–34, and "Virginia Woolf's Miss La Trobe: The Artist's Last Struggle against Masculine Values," *Women & Literature* 5, 1 (spring 1977): 38–46.

9. "The Sad Years," *TLS,* 29 August, 1918, 403; "Women and Fiction," CE 2:147–48.

10. "Olive Schreiner," *New Republic,* 18 March, 1925, 103.

11. Jean Guiguet, for example, in her preface to Woolf's *Contemporary Writers,* disagrees with critics who think Woolf is indebted to Richardson. Woolf was stimulated, Guiguet insists, by what she disliked about other writers, not by what she liked. Leonard Woolf also objects to a link between his wife's work and that of Richardson or Joyce. She wrote "The Mark on the Wall," he says, early in 1917, before she read either *The Tunnel* or the manuscript of *Ulysses. See Downhill All the Way* (London: Hogarth, 1967), 59. Certainly influences are difficult to document; nevertheless, to view the work of any writer in an aesthetic vacuum is as much a disservice as a service; reactions to criticism more favorable than deserved often are more unfavorable than deserved. Michèle Barret, in her introduction to *Virginia Woolf: Women and Writing* (New York and London: Harcourt Brace Jovanovich, 1979), briefly considers Woolf's preoccupation with the experiments of Dorothy Richardson and Katherine Mansfield.

12. See Richardson's unpublished letters to John Cowper Powys, 24 April 1940 and July 1941, as well as an unpublished letter to Henry Savage, January 1950, in the Beinecke Rare Book and Manuscript Library, Yale University.

13. Gloria Glikin, "Through the Novelist's Looking–Glass," *Kenyon Review* 31 (1969): 297–319, discusses Richardson's portrait of H.G. Wells as Hypo Wilson. As Glikin points out, Wells acknowledged Richardson's portrait of him in his *Experiment in Autobiography.*

14 *The Tunnel* 2:122. All references to Dorothy Richardson's *Pilgrimage* are to the four–volume J. M. Dent edition (London, 1967). The following abbreviations are used in the text: T, *The Tunnel* (1919); D, *Deadlock* (1921); RL, *Revolving Lights* (1923); DLH, *Dawn's Left Hand* (1931); CH, *Clear Horizon* (1935); DH, *Dimple Hill* (published with the first collected edition in 1938).

15. For the publishing history of these essays, see Samuel Hynes, "The Whole Contention between Mr. Bennett and Mrs. Brown," *Novel* 1 (fall 1967): 36, 38–40.

16. Woolf is not alone in suggesting that *Pilgrimage* lacks art. Indeed, this charge

probably is one of the major reasons for the critical neglect of Richardson's work. Reviewers and critics too numerous to mention charge that *Pilgrimage* lacks selection and significance, plot, interpretation, a hierarchy of values, meaning, even characterization and setting.

17. *Dorothy M. Richardson* (London: Joiner and Steele, 1931), 7. Similarly, Caesar Blake in *Dorothy Richardson* (Ann Arbor: University of Michigan Press, 1960), 187, distinguishes between Woolf's " 'art' novel" and Richardson's " 'life' novel."

18. Richardson, in her essay "Compensations?" *Focus* 6 (July 1928): 3–7, indicates a dislike for both "cheerful resignation" and "horrified Schopenhaueresque revolt." Instead, she bases her optimism upon a recognition of permanence in a world preoccupied with change and dissolution. This recognition she associates with women. As Shirley Rose points out in "Dorothy Richardson: The First Hundred Years: A Retrospective View," *Dalhousie Review* 52 (1973): 93, Richardson's optimism, "in contrast to the twentieth-century artists' general preoccupation with moral and physical decay may be responsible in part for the critical neglect of her work."

19. "Data for Spanish Publisher," ed. Joseph Prescott, *London Magazine* 6 (June 1959): 19.

20. May Sinclair, a somewhat older contemporary of Woolf and Richardson, emphasizes this point in her reply to Sir Almroth Wright, a medical man who denounces the women participating in the movement as sexually frustrated, neurotic, hysterical, and degenerate. See *Feminism* (London: Women Writers' Suffrage League, 1912).

21. See "The Reality of Feminism," *Ploughshare,* n.s., 2 (September 1917): 242–43; "Letter to the Odd Man," *Ye Crank and the Open Road* 5 (March 1907): 147–48; "Notes about a book purporting to Be about Christianity and Socialism," *Ye Crank and the Open Road* 5 (June 1907): 314.

22. "Talent and Genius: Is Not Genius Actually Far More Common Than Talent?" *Vanity Fair* (N.Y.) 21 (October 1923): 120.

23. See Richardson's *Quakers Past and Present* (London: Constable, 1914), 72, 75–80.

An Uneasy Sisterhood:
Virginia Woolf and
Katherine Mansfield   *Ann L. McLaughlin*

"I was jealous of her writing," Virginia Woolf wrote in 1923, shortly after the death of Katherine Mansfield, the brilliant New Zealand short story writer, who died of tuberculosis at the age of thirty-four. Mansfield's writing, Woolf said, was "the only writing I have ever been jealous of. . . . The feeling so often comes to me now—" she continued. "Yes. Go on writing of course: but into emptiness. There's no competitor. I'm cock—a lonely cock whose crowing nothing breaks—of my walk" (DVW 2:227–28).

Woolf's confession that Mansfield's was the only writing of which she was jealous suggests that Mansfield's vision had deep importance for Woolf. That her death made Woolf feel she had been deprived of a crucial audience implies that the affinities she felt between their work gave her an important sense of support, even of sisterhood, though it was often uneasy.

Although Woolf pronounced some of Mansfield's stories "cheap" (L 4:366) and overpraised, ideas and techniques from Mansfield's work reappear in Woolf's novels as though they had taken root in her consciousness to flower again years later in a fuller, more articulate form. But it is not the direct influence of Mansfield on Woolf that is important. It is the striking parallelism in their writing experiments that shows why, despite her jealousy of Mansfield, Woolf felt deeply alone after her death.

Woolf and Mansfield met early in 1917, and that April Woolf wrote to her sister, "I'm going to see Katherine Mansfield, to get a story from her, perhaps" (L 2:150). The story was "Prelude," and it became the second publication of the Woolfs' new Hogarth Press.

"Prelude" is a long, plotless story about a New Zealand family that conveys an atmosphere rather than presenting a sequence of events. The story dwells on ambivalences and incipient changes within its characters rather than depicting the development of neat, coherent personalities. Tumultuous emotions boil beneath the bland surface of family life in "Prelude" as individuals struggle for independence within the group's conformity. The family members' need of independence was to become one of Woolf's central themes. Ten years later in *To the Lighthouse* Nancy broods on her need "to escape the horror of family life" (TTL 112). Aspects of Beryl, the restless young aunt in "Prelude," who is full of inarticulate longings, appear in many of Woolf's young women, from Cam Ramsay in *To the Lighthouse* to Delia Pargiter and Kitty Malone in *The Years*.

"I want to write a kind of long elegy,"[1] Mansfield confided in her *Journal* during the weeks when she was beginning "Prelude." The elegy was to be for her beloved brother, recently killed in the war. Fifteen years later Woolf turned to her diary after finishing *The Waves* and noted, "I have been sitting these 15 minutes in a state of glory, and calm, and some tears, thinking of Thoby [Woolf's dead brother], and if I could write Julian Thoby Stephen 1881–1906 on the first page. I suppose not" (WD 169).

Like the feelings that inspired "Prelude" and *The Waves*, the feelings about the style of these works were also similar. "I want to write... perhaps not poetry," Mansfield mused. "Nor perhaps in prose. Almost certainly in a kind of *special prose*."[2] Telling Ethel Smyth of her progress with *The Waves*, Woolf reported, "I am writing to a rhythm and not to a plot. Does this convey anything? And thus though the rhythmical is more natural to me than the narrative, it is completely opposed to the tradition of fiction" (L 4:204).

Linda Burnell, the mother of the family in "Prelude," lies in bed staring at the strangely animated–looking flowers on the wallpaper. "Things had a habit of coming alive like that. Not only large substantial things like furniture, but curtains and the patterns of stuffs and fringes of quilts and cushions. How often she had seen the tassel fringe of her quilt change into a funny procession of dancers with priests attending."[3]

Woolf was to explore this sense of a world of things and how that world related to the human world in her important short story "The Mark on the Wall," which she wrote just a few weeks after reading "Prelude." In it Woolf describes the meanderings of her mind much as Mansfield described Linda's. She tells of waking from a nightmare to lie "worshipping the chest of drawers, worshipping solidity, . . . worshipping the impersonal world which is a proof of some existence other than ours (HH 45). Human relationships with this impersonal world, which fascinated Linda, would become one of Woolf's major themes.

Annie Beauchamp, Mansfield's mother, was Mansfield's inspiration for her picture of Linda Burnell, who is caught in her ambivalent feelings about her roles as wife and mother. This fact may have added to Woolf's determination ten years later to portray Julia Stephen, her mother, in all her complexity and ambivalence as Mrs. Ramsay in *To the Lighthouse*.

In August 1917, Mansfield wrote a note thanking Woolf for her hospitality when she visited the Woolfs at Asheham. Excited about her friendship with Woolf and all they seemed to share, Mansfield inserted this pronouncement, "we have got the same job, Virginia, and it is really very curious and thrilling that we should both, quite apart from each other, be after so very nearly the same thing. We are, you know; there's no denying it."[4]

At first Woolf seems to have neither denied nor agreed with Mansfield's contention. But two years later when she wrote her famous essay, "Modern Fiction," "Prelude" must have contributed to her thoughts about the possibilities and responsibilities of a new fiction. "Life is not a series of gig lamps symmetrically arranged"; she said, "life is a luminous halo, a semi-transparent envelope surrounding us from the beginning of consciousness to the end. Is it not the task of the novelist to convey this varying, and this unknown and uncircumscribed spirit, whatever aberration or complexity it may display" (CR 154). Mansfield's "Prelude" answers this question positively. It does not present a line of gig lamps. Instead it reveals halos around its curiously vivid characters, whom we both know and do not know, especially Linda in her aberration and complexity.

If Woolf felt admiration and envy for Mansfield's writing innovations, she felt distaste at times for Mansfield's personal style. The day after Mansfield had dinner with the Woolfs to celebrate the first page proof of "Prelude," Woolf wrote in her diary.

> We could both wish ones first impression of K. M. was not that she stinks like a—well civet cat that had taken to street walking. In truth, I'm a little shocked by her commonness at first sight; lines so hard & cheap. However, when this diminishes, she is so intelligent & inscrutable that she repays friendship . . . We discussed Henry James, & K.M. was illuminating I thought.[5]

Woolf's comments imply a strong attraction and revulsion for her young dinner guest and belie her own insecurities. Mansfield had married briefly, had miscarried one illegitimate child, had had an abortion, and was currently living with John Middleton Murry, a young critic and poet. Whether or not

Woolf knew all these facts, she must have had the uneasy sense that Mansfield was far more experienced than she in certain areas. Her condescension barely masked her curiosity and her half-envious feelings.

Woolf and Mansfield became close friends despite their different personal manners and saw each other often during the fall of 1918 and the spring of 1919. Woolf visited Mansfield at her house in Hampstead, since Mansfield was confined to bed much of the time because of her tuberculosis. Their letters during this period speak of their writing, their journal-keeping, their writer friends, and the books they were reading and reviewing. Mansfield described the approach of spring, announced the birth of two kittens to her adored cat, and enclosed a diagram of the cat family tree.

Woolf could sympathize with the depressions that often followed Mansfield's bouts of pain and fever. Sickness and the threat of it were a major part of both women's lives, a subject of their writing, and a bond between them. It affected their marriages, since both needed patient, protective husbands. Leonard Woolf's extraordinary capacity for steady, conscientious care proved far more supportive to Virginia, however, than John Middleton Murry's anguished and erratic concern for Mansfield.

Woolf's friendship with Mansfield in this period may well have inspired several of her own short stories. "An Unwritten Novel," "The Mark on the Wall," and "Kew Gardens" are often grouped as some of Woolf's most important early writing, since they reveal the vision she would follow. It is significant that parallels with Mansfield's early stories can be seen in all three. "An Unwritten Novel" is remarkably like an early Mansfield story, "Journey to Bruges." In both stories a lone young woman observes an older woman who is a fellow-traveller; in Mansfield's story they are on a boat, in Woolf's on a local train. In both the observer indulges in a fantasy about the other woman's life, and at the end of both stories she is startled to discover that her conjectures are wrong. In both stories the discoveries lead to a meditation on the mysteriousness of life and the impossibility of ever really knowing others. Although there is no evidence that Woolf read "Journey to Bruges," its similarity to "An Unwritten Novel" reveals an inherent affinity in the ways Woolf and Mansfield approached experience.

In his biography of Mansfield, Antony Alpers suggests that Mansfield proposed that Woolf write "Kew Gardens." Although the actual letter has not been found, in a similar letter, written the same day, Mansfield suggests details that Woolf followed. She proposes that different pairs of people walk in the garden, "some of them seeming so extraordinarily 'odd' and separate from the flowers, but others quite related and at ease." There would be "pauses," she said, when the flowers " 'come in' as it were."[6] The story, which may well be the result of Mansfield's direct suggestions, shows Woolf's growing fascination with the relationship between the human and the surrounding nonhuman world; a fascination Mansfield's writing continued to inspire. We have already seen how Linda's fascination with the world of things in "Prelude" seemed to inspire Woolf to write her third important story of this period, "The Mark on the Wall."

In late 1919, after Mansfield left for Italy in the hope that its climate would ease her respiratory problems, tension and jealousies began to beleaguer their friendship. Depressed and lonely, Mansfield wrote a surprisingly cool review of *Night and Day,* Woolf's second novel. The book *"reeks"* of intellectual snobbery, Mansfield wrote to Murry.[7] She was angry at Woolf's seeming obliviousness to the war and disappointed by what she felt was her retreat into a traditional style. Mansfield confessed that she was uncertain about her appraisal, however, and jealous of Woolf's life. "How I envy Virginia; no wonder she can write. There is always in her writing a calm freedom of expression as though she were at peace—her roof over her, her possessions round her, and her man somewhere within call. Boge, what have I done that I should have *all* the handicaps."[8]

Though Woolf was not jealous of Mansfield's life during these hard years of sickness and restless travel, she was envious of Mansfield's success and critical of her work. In 1922 she wrote a friend that Mansfield's collection *Bliss and Other Stores* was "hard" and "shallow" and "so sentimental" that she had "to rush to the bookcase for something to drink. Shakespeare, Conrad, even Virginia Woolf. But," Woolf added, "she takes in all reviewers" (L 2:514–15).

Although Woolf announced in the same letter that she would not read *The Garden Party and Other Stories,* Mansfield's third collection, it is the group of Mansfield stories that echoes most clearly in her own work. "At the Bay," one of the most important stories in the collection, is a sequel to "Prelude." It begins with a description of the sea at dawn, before the family stirs. Returning to her concept of the nonhuman world, Mansfield shows that larger circle that encloses the sleeping human one. The story begins, "Very early morning. The sun was not yet risen . . . there was nothing to mark which was beach and where was the sea."[9] Ten years later Woolf began *The Waves* with a look at the predawn sea, a description that seems to echo some of Mansfield's phrases. "The sun had not yet risen. The sea was indistinguishable from the sky" (W 7). As in "At the Bay," the focus in *The Waves* shifts to the sleeping children within the house. Mansfield ended her story with a return to the sea, completing her frame of the nonhuman world. Woolf's final sentence in *The Waves*, "The waves broke on the shore" (W 297), completes her own nonhuman frame. These striking similarities between "At the Bay" and *The Waves* reveal the affinity Woolf felt for Mansfield's poetic diction as well as for her framing concept of the nonhuman world. Woolf developed that concept further in the "Time Passes" section of *To the Lighthouse*, explored it in depth in *The Waves*, and returned to it in the chapter prologues in *The Years*.

The fullness with which Mansfield described children, revealing their moments of terror and rebellion as well as their times of gaiety, may have reminded Woolf of similar moments in her own childhood, since there were marked similarities in the family experiences upon which both writers drew. Like Woolf, Mansfield adored her remote and beautiful mother, who died relatively early, and feared her stern Victorian father. Both writers lost beloved brothers, whom they saw as inspirations to their writing, and both were members of large, bustling households in which they often felt vulnerable.

Mansfield's experiments with the child's perspective may have stimulated Woolf's later writing about children, for Mansfield-like children keep appearing in her fiction. Susan in *The Waves*, the young Cam Ramsay in *To the Lighthouse*, and Rhoda Pargiter in *The Years* all show much of Kezia's combination of sensitivity and stubbornness. Susan's fury, as she tears off the calendar pages at school while awaiting the release of the holidays, is akin to Matilda's anger as she rushes out of the house determined to leave New Zealand in "The Wind Blows."[10] The scene of the Flanders boys on the beach in *Jacob's Room*, where Jacob stubbornly carries home the sheep's jaw, is reminiscent of the one in "At the Bay" where the Trout boys dig intently for a squashed boot buried in the sand.

Mansfield's longing for a child, and her lack of one, helped make her own childhood memories vivid and accessible, as similar feelings did for Woolf later on. "Things happened so simply then, without preparation and without any shock," Mansfield wrote in her journal, remembering the birth of a sibling. "They let me go into my mother's room (I remember standing on tiptoe and using both hands to turn the big white china door-handle) and there lay my mother in bed with her arms along the sheet."[11] This habit of carefully recalling the actual sensations of childhood, rather than giving a sentimental copy, was one in which Woolf also engaged. Years later, musing on the child's "curious focus," she remembered the "great black space" under the nursery table "with the table-cloth hanging down in folds" (MB 78).

The disturbed mind, which Mansfield portrayed in Linda and other characters, was another perspective Woolf experimented with later on. Mansfield developed Linda, with her escapist fantasies and anagogic longings, more fully in "At the Bay" than she had in "Prelude." In *Jacob's Room*, which Woolf wrote two years later, there are echoes of Linda in Mrs. Jarvis. Subtly distorted perspectives such as that of Edna, the tense, frightened young girl in "Something Childish but Very Natural," are akin to that of Rhoda in *The Waves*, since both characters experience social and sexual terrors.

Bertha, the overexcited heroine of "Bliss," who suffers her own sexual fears, views her dinner party from a somewhat manic perspective and recognizes her husband's infidelity at the end. Woolf confided in her diary that she threw the story down in disgust and confronted the fact that Mansfield was "content with superficial smartness," for her whole conception was "poor" and "cheap" (DVW 1:179). One explanation for Woolf's violent reaction to "Bliss" is her feeling that, in depicting Bertha's slightly hysterical sense of reality, Mansfield assumed a superior, almost ridiculing stance. Believing mood shifts and mental states to be serious and potentially terrifying, Woolf turned to that subject with intense insight in *Mrs. Dalloway*, where the manic Septimus Smith conveys her own experience of mental suffering.

"The Daughters of the Late Colonel" is in the same collection of Mansfield stories that Woolf announced she would not read, but it too has clear echoes in her work, especially *The Years*. The late colonel's daughters are aging spinsters, like Eleanor Pargiter, another colonel's daughter.[12] The sisters' feelings, which seem both comic and poignant at the end of the story as they attempt to face their changed reality, have certain reflections in Eleanor's emotions at the end of *The Years*, despite her greater depth and development.

Writing to Woolf about Chekhov, Mansfield once said that "what a writer does is not so much to *solve* the question but to *put* the question."[13] This questioning quality, which is so typical of Mansfield's best stories, appears at the end of "The Daughters of the Late Colonel," where Constantia hears a barrel organ outside and wonders, "What did it mean? What was it she was always wanting? What did it all lead to? Now? Now?"[14] Constantia's questions seem to have lingered in Woolf's mind, for twenty-two years later she had Eleanor Pargiter, in a similar mood of wondering, ask at the end of *The Years*, "And now? And now?" (Y 434–35). Such questions about life's direction and the elusive feeling of the present constitute another strong affinity between Woolf's and Mansfield's writing.

"The Garden Party," another late Mansfield story, presents the absurd, almost existential juxtaposition of horror and gaiety, which Mansfield had often experienced in her own life. Laura, the heroine, discovers in the midst of the party that a carter has been killed accidentally. She visits the bereaved family, feeling that her gesture of sympathy is awkward. But afterward when her brother inquires about her visit, she says that it was "simply marvellous." " 'Isn't life,' she stammered, 'Isn't life'—But what life was she couldn't explain."[15]

The essential problem in *Mrs. Dalloway* is similar, though Woolf develops it far more extensively. When Clarissa learns of Septimus Smith's suicide during her party, she too is confronted with the mysterious quality of life. Alone at her window, she hears the clock striking and knows she must return to the party. "But what an extraordinary night! She felt somehow very like him—the young man who had killed himself. She felt glad that he had done it; thrown it away . . . . He made her feel the beauty; made her feel the fun" (MD 283–84). Mansfield simply touches on this eerie sense of exhilaration at life's inherent paradox in "The Garden Party" and other stories, while Woolf explores it at length in all her novels.

"The Fly," one of Mansfield's last and most famous stories, impressed Woolf so much that she made several direct references to it in her own writing. In Mansfield's story an office boss acts out his sense of blind victimization by torturing a fly. In Woolf's story "The New Dress" Mabel Waring takes solace from remembering, albeit inaccurately, that the fly survives. She feels victimized as she waits alone at a dance and thinks, "That wretched fly—where had she read the story that kept coming into her mind about the fly and the saucer?—struggled out" (HH 55–56). In *The Years* Eleanor reflects that Duffus, the caretaker for her apartment, is like "a fly struggling to haul itself up out of a saucer" (Y 98).

Mansfield's precise observation of the dying fly demonstrates a characteristic of her writing, which Woolf continued to appreciate even when she was sharply critical of Mansfield. "She possessed the most amazing *senses* of her generation," Woolf wrote a friend, "so that she could actually reproduce this room for instance, with its fly, clock, dog, tortoise if need be, to the life, she was weak as water, as insipid, and a great deal more commonplace when she had to use her mind" (L 3:59).

Critical as Woolf was of Mansfield's intellectual powers, she had good reason to feel suddenly alone when her friend died. In many areas of their writing, such as poetic diction and the plotless story, the perspective of the child, the meditative mind, and the frame of the nonhuman world, Mansfield and Woolf were indeed working at the same job. Mansfield's death at thirty-four left Woolf to continue that job alone. She was, as she said, a lonely cock of the walk "whose crowing nothing breaks" (DVW 2:228).

"Am I already forgetting her?" (DVW 2:226) Woolf asked herself a week after Mansfield's death. Woolf's writing supplies a strong negative answer, for in the end she was able to give many of Mansfield's brilliant innovations a new and larger life in her own work.

Notes

1. *The Journal of Katherine Mansfield,* ed. J. Middleton Murry (New York: Alfred A. Knopf, 1927), 44 (hereafter *KM Journal*).

2. Ibid.

3. *The Short Stories of Katherine Mansfield* (New York: Alfred A. Knopf, 1941), 234 (hereafter *KM Stories*).

4. *The Letters of Katherine Mansfield, vol. I,* ed. J. Middleton Murry (New York: Alfred A. Knopf, 1929), 71 (hereafter *KM Letters*).

5. DVW 1:58. Mansfield may have become accustomed to rather theatrical makeup because of her work as a mimic. She supplemented her meager income by giving imitations of well-known people at London parties. Lady Ottoline Morrell once said that Mansfield "had rather a cheap taste . . . . slightly 'Swan and Edgar.' " Lady Ottoline Morrell to Rosamund Lehmann, 22 May, 1931. King's College Library, Cambridge. Permission to quote from the above was kindly granted by Mrs. Julian Vinogradoff.

6. Antony Alpers, *The Life of Katherine Mansfield* (New York: Viking Press, 1980), 250. "Kew Gardens" also has echoes of Mansfield's story "A Dill Pickle," in which the couple reminisce on an early meeting in Kew Gardens. As she parts from the man, the woman stares at the glove in her hand with an intensity that is akin to that of the man in "Kew Gardens," who remembers how he once stared at a silver buckle on the shoe of a woman to whom he was proposing. The snail, Mansfield's recurrent image for the harsh realities that underlie the beauties of life, figures importantly in both "The Mark on the Wall" and "Kew Gardens."

7. *Katherine Mansfield's Letters to John Middleton Murry, 1912–1922,* ed. John Middleton Murry (London: Constable, 1951), 388 (hereafter *KM Letters to JMM*).

8. *KM Letters to JMM,* 419–20.

9. *KM Stories,* 263.

10. "The Wind Blows" appeared in *Signature* in October 1915 as "Autumn II" and was later included in *Bliss.* Mansfield explained to Murry why she had included it: "As to 'The Wind Blows,' I put that in because so many people had admired it (Yes,

Clarissa Dalloway's
Respectable Suicide   *Emily Jensen*

Virginia Woolf's *Mrs. Dalloway* presents one day in the life of Clarissa Dalloway, a day that begins with her going to pick up the flowers for a party she is giving that evening and ends about 3:00 A.M., while the party is still going on. Not much to hang a novel on, but with the memories and associations that lace the narrative, we acquire an intricately woven image of the woman who figures at the center. As others have observed,[1] she is a woman who is both enthusiastically involved in the process of living and simultaneously terrified of some interruption to that involvement.

It is my thesis that Clarissa Dalloway's fear of interruption is the most important feature of her personality and, concomitantly, that the event that is the source of that fear is the most important fact of her life. In that historic interruption of "the most exquisite moment of her whole life" (MD 52), Clarissa agrees to deny her love for Sally Seton, decides marriage to Peter Walsh is impossible, and chooses instead to marry Richard Dalloway and become respectable. No simple girlhood crush,[2] Clarissa's love for Sally Seton is a profound reality that permeates her adult life. Through its metaphoric structure, the novel reveals that Clarissa felt her only real love for Sally Seton, denied that and married Richard, not Peter Walsh, because Richard would demand less of her emotionally (MD 10) and would provide the means for a respectable life. Crippled by heterosexual convention, her life thereafter, her "process of living," is her "punishment" for having denied herself that love. She identifies with Septimus Smith as one who committed suicide to preserve the "treasure" of his homosexual feelings, and whose madness is the overt expression of her more guarded emotional life, a life in which she balances contempt for herself as the perfect hostess and praise for it's 'Autumn II,' but a little different). Virginia, Lytton and queer people like Mary Hamilton and Bertie all spoke so strongly about it I felt I must put it in." *KM Letters to JMM*, 515.

11. *KM Journal*, 50–51.

12. In "The Daughters of the Late Colonel," Josephine is aware of an enlarged photograph of her dead mother, wearing pagoda-shaped earrings, that hangs over the piano and makes her mother seem eerily remote. In *The Years*, Delia Pargiter stares up at the portrait of her mother as a white-robed girl holding a flower basket and thinks it grotesquely incongruous, since her real mother is dying upstairs. In both the story and the novel the sound of a barrel organ fills its hearers with sudden longing.

13. *KM Letters* 1:204.

14. *KM Stories*, 483.

15. *KM Stories*, 548–49.

her ability to be the perfect hostess.[3] Both Peter Walsh, who sees through her (MD 255), and Miss Kilman, through whom she sees herself, help expose the delicacy of that balance. While Clarissa's choice in itself—to deny her love for Sally, break off with Peter, and marry Richard—is not by definition self-destructive,[4] the way it is presented in *Mrs. Dalloway* suggests that it is destructive for Clarissa Dalloway. It is, in fact, on a par with Septimus Smith's more obvious suicide, as stated by Clarissa's specific identification with him at the end of the novel: "she felt somehow very like him—the young man who had killed himself" (MD 283). How she feels like him can be clarified by examining the verbal network in the novel—phrases and images that by repetition take on the nature of a metaphor—and by examining her responses to other characters.

The novel begins with an image that initiates a number of verbal strains, each of which is played upon later on:

> What a lark! What a plunge! For so it had always seemed to her, when, with a little squeak of the hinges, which she could hear now, she had burst open the French windows and plunged at Bourton into the open air. How fresh, how calm, stiller than this of course, the air was in the early morning; like the flap of a wave; the kiss of a wave; chill and sharp and yet (for a girl of eighteen as she then was) solemn, feeling as she did, standing there at the open window, that something awful was about to happen. (MD 3)

"Plunge . . . Bourton . . . this . . . solemn . . . ; something awful was about to happen." Thus, on the first page of the novel, the dichotomies in Clarissa's life are established: "Bourton" versus "this" and "plunging" into life versus the "solemn" fear "that something awful was about to happen." That Bourton represents both Sally and Clarissa's love for women becomes clear in the extended memory sequence occasioned by Clarissa's discovery that Lady Bruton had asked Richard to lunch without her; that fact "made the moment in which she stood shiver" (MD 44), recalling to her mind other moments. First she recalls her many failures with Richard, but then her moments of success with women, when "for that moment, she had seen an illumination, a match burning in a crocus; an inner meaning almost expressed" (MD 47). Woolf insists that we perceive Clarissa's awareness that it is with women that she has experienced her most intense moments of passion by telling us so outright: "It was over—the moment. Against such moments (with women too) there contrasted (as she laid her

hat down) the bed'' (MD 47). Of course it is Clarissa's need also not quite to
see what she sees—''an inner meaning almost expressed''—for, as will become clear later, she spends a good deal of her time attempting to justify to
herself having chosen ''the bed'' of her current life over those intense
moments. In either case, whether for the reader's benefit or Clarissa's, it is
superfluous to say ''with women too,'' since the entire passage concerns
women; it is, in fact, inaccurate, since men are not included at all.

> But this question of love (she thought, putting her coat away), this falling
> in love with women. Take Sally Seton; her relation in the old days with
> Sally Seton. Had not that, after all, been love? (MD 48)

Certainly the intensity of the lengthy passage that follows can leave no
doubt in our minds or in Clarissa's as to the nature of her feelings for Sally
Seton: ''But all that evening she could not take her eyes off Sally . . . [MD
48]. Sally it was who made her feel, for the first time, how sheltered her life
at Bourton was. She knew nothing about sex—nothing about social problems . . . [MD 49]. She could remember standing in her bedroom at the top
of the house holding the hot water can in her hands and saying aloud, 'she is
beneath this roof . . . she is beneath this roof!' [MD 51].'' Hot water can,
indeed. For despite Clarissa's disclaimer that the words carry no meaning for
her anymore, doing her hair in the present does begin to bring back the old
feeling:

> ''if it were now to die 'twere now to be most happy.'' That was her feel-
> ing—Othello's feeling, and she felt it, she was convinced, as strongly as
> Shakespeare meant Othello to feel it, all because she was coming down to
> dinner in a white frock to meet Sally Seton! (MD 51)

It is neither insignificant nor unrelated (as very little is in this novel of delicate
weavings, tiny stitches overlaying other stitches to form a textured pattern)
that Septimus Smith survives the war and the loss of his friend Evans to
discover that he has lost the ability to feel; in his case, as in Clarissa's, the feeling that is lost is for a person of his own sex. Nor is it unrelated that both of
them call upon Shakespeare: while Clarissa identifies with Othello's passion
for Desdemona, Septimus focuses on the meaning behind Shakespeare's
words, that ''love between man and woman was repulsive'' (MD 134).
Taken together, these allusions give us the quality of the feeling subsequently
lost and the homosexual nature of it.

For both Clarissa and Septimus, the feeling is lost by an interruption: war cuts short Septimus's feeling for Evans, and, because he does not understand the meaning of that relationship, he participates in what becomes a frustration of his ability to feel at all, aided certainly by the advice of Dr. Holmes that he owed a duty to his wife (MD 139). Thus two bastions of masculine power and authority—the military and the medical profession—converge to inhibit Septimus's feeling. Peter Walsh, a man whose "good opinion" (MD 53) Clarissa wanted, interrupts Clarissa's feeling for Sally Seton. They were all walking on the terrace at Bourton when

> she and Sally fell a little behind. Then came the most exquisite moment of her whole life passing a stone urn with flowers in it. Sally stopped; picked a flower; kissed her on the lips . . . . There she was alone with Sally . . . .
> "Star-gazing?" said Peter.
> It was like running one's face against a granite wall in the darkness! It was shocking; it was horrible!
> Not for herself. She felt only how Sally was being mauled already, maltreated; she felt his hostility; his jealousy; his determination to break into their companionship. . . .
> "Oh this horror!" she said to herself, as if she had known all along that something would interrupt, would embitter her moment of happiness. (MD 52–53)

"She had burst open the French windows and plunged at Bourton into the open air" (MD 3) and smashed headfirst "against a granite wall in the darkness." The clash of imagery from the open air and flapping waves of the first scene to the granite wall of this scene is tactile in its intensity and telling in its effects on Clarissa. Why, then, does she say the horror is "not for herself" but only for Sally, who indeed had managed to upset most of the residents at Bourton by her unconventional behavior. Yet Clarissa understands their relationship as having sprung "from a sense of being in league together, a presentiment of something that was bound to part them (they spoke of marriage always as a catastrophe)" (MD 50), and certainly that is what lies on the other side of the granite wall for both of them. One reason Clarissa might see Peter's interruption as more horrible for Sally than for herself is that in this lovers' triangle, it is Sally with whom Peter is competing for Clarissa's love. This is clear both from Clarissa's father's equal dislike of Peter and Sally (MD 62, 90) and from Peter and Sally's memory of their intimacy when Peter was courting Clarissa (MD 285, 292). More important, however, is that Clarissa had been expecting some such cessation of her moment with Sally: the horror for her, in fact, is the recognition that what she had feared all along does happen. Even in Clarissa's tryst with Sally where they both talked of marriage as the catastrophe that would separate them, the protectiveness "was much more on her side than Sally's" (MD 50). This is so largely, no doubt, because of Clarissa's view of Sally as a woman who dared "say anything, do anything" (MD 48), rather than as a woman who cared enough about social convention to know that any passion she felt for another woman would not be allowed, "not in this world. No" (MD 17), as Clarissa says in another context about loving Miss Kilman.

But Clarissa does care enough about convention to know "that something would interrupt, would embitter her moment of happiness." Sally's perception of this quality in Clarissa is particularly acute: in the final scene of the novel she tells Peter that "Clarissa was at heart a snob . . . . And it was that that was between them, she was convinced" (MD 289–90). Because Clarissa does care about convention and respectability, she is relieved on one level when Peter interrupts her moment with Sally:

> Yet, after all, how much she owed him later . . . . She owed him words: "sentimental," "civilized"; they started up every day of her life as if he guarded her . . . . "Sentimental," perhaps she was to be thinking of the past. (MD 53–54)

Thus ends Clarissa's impassioned memory of her past with Sally, "the most exquisite moment of her whole life" carefully packed away and—thanks to Peter—labeled "sentimental" and presumably also not "civilized." Or, what is more likely, because loving Sally is not accepted as "civilized," it is best for Clarissa to see it as "sentimental." And the words that condemn Clarissa's love for Sally to a memory of exquisite moments lost are not far removed from those words that Sir William Bradshaw worships in Septimus Smith's case: the twin goddesses, Proportion and Conversion. Proportion is his term for conventional heterosexual life (men should be like him, women like Lady Bradshaw), and Conversion is the means by which it is maintained: "she feasts on the wills of the weakly, loving to impress, to impose, adoring her own features stamped on the face of the populace" (MD 151). It is not at all surprising that Septimus jumps out a window to avoid Bradshaw, and Clarissa reckons "one wouldn't like Sir William to see one unhappy. No; not that man" (MD 278). The authoritarian words that condemn both of them are parallel in that "sentimental" is the other side of "civilized" in the same way that Conversion is the other side of Proportion: for the socially elite, the educated and refined Clarissa, labeling behavior "sentimental" is just as condemning, hence as effective in changing it, as the more direct method of conversion is for the masses. While Septimus must be institutionalized to acquire Bradshaw's "sense of proportion" (MD 150), Clarissa has Peter's words to "guard" her every day so that instead of plunging "at Bourton into the open air" and risking the threat of a granite wall to impede her, she "plunged into the very heart of the moment . . . of this June morning" (MD 54); that is, she gave up Sally, broke off with Peter, married Richard, and became the respectable M.P.'s wife who gives parties to enhance Richard's position (MD 116), all the while trying to convince herself that "this" is the life she wants.

That this respectable life represents a choice with suicidal implications becomes clear in Clarissa's final scene in the novel, the scene that brings together all the verbal strains begun earlier. She is alone in a room away from the party, and she is thinking of Septimus Smith's suicide and its relevance to her own life.

> A thing there was that mattered; a thing wreathed about with chatter, defaced, obscured in her own life, let drop every day in corruption, lies, chatter. This he had preserved . . . .
>   But this young man who had killed himself—had he plunged holding his treasure? "If it were now to die, 'twere now to be most happy," she had said to herself once, coming down in white. (MD 280–81)

While the literal context makes it clear that Clarissa's "thing that mattered" and Septimus's "treasure" are synonymous, the verbal associations clarify that both refer to the integrity of homosexual love and of the selves involved in that love.[5] Thinking of his treasure immediately calls up Clarissa's moment with Sally, inherent both in the line from Shakespeare and in the partial repetition of that intense moment, "coming down to dinner in a white frock to meet Sally Seton!" (MD 51).[6] Clarissa's assessment of her denial of that moment and therefore denial of her love for Sally Seton is bitter in its self-revelation: to admit that that love was "defaced, obscured in her own life, let drop every day in corruption, lies, chatter" is devastating, given that the life Clarissa chose to live out, to make up, to build up, was that of a hostess creating the perfect environment for her invited guests; with the blinders off she sees it for what it is: banal chatter, a life of corruption and lies. Further, using "plunge" to describe Septimus's suicidal leap recalls the other times

Clarissa uses the word, always to describe an enthusiastic leap into life, whether life at Bourton, this moment, or the drawing room. As used here, the word implies that there is no difference between his leap into death and hers into the life she has chosen; both are suicidal.

It is not surprising that the question Clarissa had asked herself earlier in the day—What had she done with her life? (MD 63–64)—here enters her consciousness with an increased sense of terror to it:

> Then (she had felt it only this morning) there was the terror; the overwhelming incapacity, one's parents giving it into one's hands, this life, to be lived to the end, to be walked with serenely; there was in the depths of her heart an awful fear. (MD 281)

Nor is it surprising that she consoles herself by being thankful to Richard, who, by providing her with the context for a respectable life, makes it possible for her to ignore the question generally. The thought process is the same as that she employed earlier when, in her horror at the memory of Peter's interrupting her moment with Sally, she consoled herself by being thankful to him for that deed. Similarly, in that earlier scene, she is thankful to her servants "generally for helping her be like this, to be what she wanted, gentle, generous-hearted" (MD 58). The difference in this final scene in the novel is that the argument fails to convince even Clarissa. We may have had doubts all along but here she begins to waver:

> Even now, quite often if Richard had not been there reading the *Times,* so that she could crouch like a bird and gradually revive, send roaring up that immeasurable delight, rubbing stick to stick, one thing with another, she must have perished. But that young man had killed himself.
>
> Somehow it was her disaster—her disgrace. It was her punishment to see sink here a man, there a woman, in this profound darkness, and she forced to stand here in her evening dress. She had schemed; she had pilfered. She was never wholly admirable. She had wanted success. Lady Bexborough and the rest of it. And once she had walked on the terrace at Bourton.
>
> It was due to Richard; she had never been so happy. Nothing could be slow enough; nothing last too long. No pleasure could equal, she thought, straightening the chairs, pushing one book on the shelf, this having done with the triumphs of youth, lost herself in the process of living. (MD 281–82)

A marvelously rich passage, it conveys in full the struggle that goes on in Clarissa's mind. First there is the consolation of Richard's conventional life: It is because he is "there reading the *Times*" that she can make a life out of being a hostess, creating warmth by "rubbing stick to stick," and, if he were not there providing that excuse, "she must have perished." She would have perished as Septimus Smith had perished by going mad in retreat from the heterosexual convention being imposed on him. In this sense his madness is the overt expression of the battle that is constantly raging in Clarissa's mind. He retains dead Evans and his love for him by fantasizing his presence—"the visions, the faces, the voices of the dead" (MD 220)—but that fantasy keeps clashing with the reality of the "doom pronounced in Milan . . . [that he is] to be alone forever" (MD 220). Clarissa, on the other hand, in a perfectly respectable female role, creates life for other people, "rubbing stick to stick" in such a way that she can live it vicariously

"But that young man had killed himself." And this time, with the fact of Septimus Smith's suicide preying upon her, the usual consolation does not hold. If he killed himself to avoid perishing in his frustrated homosexual love, what has she done? Well, she too has suffered: "it was her punishment to see sink here a man, there a woman, in this profound darkness, and she forced to stand here in her evening dress." It is her punishment to be the respectable hostess, standing by while others go down around her in the same darkness that contains the granite wall of Peter's mocking interruption to her own homosexual love. While before that darkness seemed a physical description, here it connotes ignorance, prejudice, a profound lack of consciousness—an attitude maintained in the interest of Peter's revered "civilization" and Sir William Bradshaw's worshiped "Proportion."

And Clarissa is sufficiently aware of those imperatives, in fact controlled by them, that she feels "forced" to live the lie: although it is her choice—"she had wanted success. Lady Bexborough and the rest of it"—it is not a choice that has any reality for her. Caught in a bind of which she is fully conscious, she participates totally in the only option she sees as viable for her, leaving Sally and her love for her forever trapped in the past: "And once she had walked on the terrace at Bourton." A deceptively simple sentence, it carries the solemn weight of an entire life. In the novel it closes the sequence of imagery begun on the first page with the "plunge at Bourton into the open air" and continued with the subsequent interruption of Peter's insolence that felt like a granite wall. Its resonances pervade the novel.

And "it was due to Richard;" Clarissa's pause (indicated by the semicolon) is our pause, and we realize with her the ambiguity, for it is "due to

Richard'' as he represents respectable conventionality that she denies her love
for Sally Seton. But then, the pause over, it is her happiness, her not having
to face the fact of that denial, that becomes his due. Yet, determined as she is
to convince herself otherwise, the loss comes through: "no pleasure could
equal . . . this having done with the triumphs of youth, lost herself in the
process of living."

One would think this would be an end on it, now having accepted the loss
of self as an essential piece of her present "happiness," but that consolation
fails her also. She goes to look at the sky, to find "something of her own in
it," a familiar "dusky sky, turning away its cheek in beauty" (MD 283), and
comes face to face instead not only with an "ashen pale" sky that is "new to
her" but with the old woman in the room opposite, staring at her. This too
is new. Before, the old woman had been there, moving about her room, and
Clarissa had watched her. The woman's stare signals a change in Clarissa's
attitude toward Septimus Smith's suicide: "she did not pity him" (MD
283). With Big Ben striking, "with all this going on," with her recognition
that she is like Septimus," she felt glad that he had done it; thrown it away''
(MD 283). Of course we have been preparing for this from the initial identification of Big Ben as symbolic of the interruption Clarissa fears: "a particular hush, or solemnity; an indescribable pause; a suspense (but that might
be her heart, affected, they said, by influenza)[7] before Big Ben strikes" (MD
4–5). Thus when Clarissa identifies the old woman with Big Ben, thinking,
"gigantic as it was, it had something to do with her. Down, down, into the
midst of ordinary things the finger fell making the moment solemn" (MD
192–93), the old woman becomes one more representation of the loss of
Clarissa's "most exquisite moment of her whole life," her love for Sally
Seton. With that staring her in the face in the figure of the old woman, it is
no wonder she is glad Septimus Smith killed himself. Perhaps Clarissa's
subsequent lines—"he made her feel the beauty; made her feel the fun" (MD
284)—seem to confuse the issue until we notice the "but" beginning the
sentence immediately following: "But she must go back. She must assemble" (MD 284). It is the beauty and the fun of the life she has denied herself
that Septimus's suicide calls up, not the life she must go back to and must attend both the party and herself to meet it.

And "assemble" she does. The process described in this final scene as the
ratiocinations of a mind in struggle with itself and its unconscious associations is revealed metaphorically in the novel through other phrases that capture our attention when repeated. If the pause before Big Ben strikes comes
to represent Clarissa's fear of interruption, hence also her denial of the self
that loves women,[8] "the leaden circles [that] dissolved in the air," the

brilliant synesthetic phrase that accompanies the striking of Big Ben, conveys both the solemnity, the weight, the significance of that denial and the subsequent refusal to acknowledge it. The fact of Clarissa's self-denial "dissolves in the air" as she turns in gratitude to the men in her life who make respectability possible. It is her way of not "perishing," of not going mad as Septimus Smith has done.

The other recurrent phrase in the novel is the line from a song in Shakespeare's *Cymbeline*: "Fear no more the heat o' the sun."[9] The Shakespearean source is critical, partly for its associations with the other Shakespearean allusions in the novel, but also for its *Cymbeline* context. It is the first line of a song being sung to a woman (Imogen) who is posing as a man (Fidele), thought to be dead when in fact she is alive. Clarissa? The portrait does suggest to me Clarissa, who "did undoubtedly then feel what men felt" (MD 47) in response to women, and who does question the quality of her life in comparison to Septimus Smith's death. The first four lines of the song present the general theme:

> Fear no more the heat o' the sun,
>   Nor the furious winter's rages;
> Thou thy worldly task hast done,
>   Home art gone, and ta'en thy wages.

Sung for one who is thought to be dead, the song calls for an end to one's fear of life and whatever it brings, imaged as the extremes of summer and winter, because one has done one's "worldly task" and, regardless of what that is, dies. Clarissa repeats enough of the first line to call up the song four times in the novel; Septimus uses it once. The first time it appears, triggered in the literal context by an open page of a book in a shop window, the full pattern of associations is established, a pattern developed in the subsequent repetitions of the phrase. The pattern begins with a question—"What was she trying to recover?" (MD 12)—moves to a statement of her present needs—"How much she wanted it—that people should look pleased as she came in" (MD 13)—then to a wish that "she could have had her life over again" because "she had the oddest sense of being herself invisible; unseen; known . . . not even Clarissa anymore" (MD 14). The pattern concludes with an acceptance of her present life and the "worldly task" she has taken on; her phrase "that is all" (MD 15) implies that that is all she sees as possible for her. The Shakespearean line is thus established as a metaphor of Clarissa's mental process throughout the novel; the novel captures a day in which Clarissa confronts the question whether hers is a meaningful life, admitting on the one hand that it is a sham that annihilates her as a person but, on the other, consoling herself by saying that nothing else is possible, given her need for respectability—''Lady Bexborough and the rest of it.''[10]

The second time the refrain appears, it is in the context of the respectable but meaningless life Clarissa has opted for:

> ''Fear no more,'' said Clarissa. Fear no more the heat o' the sun; for the shock of Lady Bruton, asking Richard to lunch without her made the moment in which she stood shiver. (MD 44)

When the present moment rocks as if in the wake of a boat, the imperative to ''fear no more'' is ominous, threatening. This present moment, this life of corruption and lies and chatter, is after all what she has chosen over a more meaningful, more honest life, and if it does not sustain her, what is left? Yet there is in the line, particularly as it calls up the *Cymbeline* context, a kind of resigned acknowledgment that life is over—for Clarissa, meaningful life—and that there is not much point in fussing about the daily tremors that rock one's mooring: she made her bed, and now she must lie in it.

In the third repetition of the line, the focus is on the conclusion to the pattern established earlier: ''that is all.'' More importantly, the crux of Clarissa's conflict emerges here; she is sitting contentedly, mending her dress for her party, when she thinks,

> the whole world seems to be saying ''that is all'' more and more ponderously, until even the heart in the body . . . says too, That is all. Fear no more, says the heart . . . , committing its burden to some sea, which sighs collectively for all sorrows . . . . And the body alone listens . . . to the wave breaking, the dog barking, far away barking and barking. (MD 58–59)

Convention so effectively declares what is possible for Clarissa that she accepts the limitation as her own emotional reality and, having accepted that, she need ''fear no more'' because for her the possibility of a meaningful life is over. The heart commits its burden to the sea of sorrows; only the body objects. In a curious separation of heart from body, conditioned responses from honest feelings, only the barebones natural feelings are capable of hearing ''the waves breaking, the dog barking.'' Clarissa's subtle distinction in feeling suggests the level on which her internal conflict occurs: trained for respectability, she participates in the role laid out for her even to the point of expressing the emotions appropriate to that role. Yet in conflict with this is the physical body that is alone in tune with the sounds of nature imaged in the wave and the dog's barking.

As elsewhere in the novel, Clarissa's conflict is clarified through a comparison with Septimus Smith, who is responsible for the fourth instance of the "fear no more" refrain.

> His hand lay there on the back of the sofa, as he had seen his hand lie when he was bathing, floating, on the top of the waves, while far away on shore he heard dogs barking and barking far away. Fear no more, says the body; fear no more. (MD 211)

Unlike Clarissa, Septimus does achieve communion with nature—actually floating on the waves and hearing the dogs barking—admittedly by an utter distortion of reality that is nonetheless real enough for him that he will kill himself to protect it. For Septimus, it is nature versus human nature—"Nature. . . breath[ing] through her hollowed hands Shakespeare's words, her meaning" (MD 211–12)—and human nature imposing rules of heterosexual conduct in the figure of Dr. Holmes who "seemed to stand for something horrible to him" (MD 213). And we recall the image of Septimus and Evans, "a case of two dogs playing on a hearth-rug" (MD 130); it is a strange image on first reading until we see its relation to the texture of the whole: Shakespeare's words decrying heterosexuality and, in so doing, presenting nature's meaning as imaged in the dogs. For both Clarissa and Septimus, what is natural is disallowed, and the "fear no more" refrain begins to carry the meaning of their apparently separate responses to that denial: Septimus appears to retain his love for Evans through visions and voices of the dead, while Clarissa more obviously denies hers for Sally Seton, accepting conventional heterosexual life as all that is possible for her; in the process, she refuses the body and its natural feelings, which is exactly what Septimus does in asserting that he has lost his ability to feel. Of course, to Peter's eyes, she too achieves a communion with nature in her green mermaid's dress at the party, "lolloping on the waves . . . all with the most perfect ease and air of a creature floating in its element" (MD 264). However, I suspect that the distorted reality of Septimus's vision reflects on Peter's equally distorted vision of Clarissa's reality.

The final appearance of the refrain marks the resolution of the paradox Clarissa lives:

> she did not pity him, with all this going on. There! The old lady had put out her light! The whole house was dark now with this going on, she

repeated, and the words came to her, Fear no more the heat of the sun. She must go back to them. But what an extraordinary night! She felt somehow very like him—the young man who had killed himself. (MD 283)

Representing Big Ben and the interruption of Clarissa's love for Sally, the old woman puts out her light, leaving all in darkness, presumably the same darkness of ignorance and prejudice in which Clarissa earlier feels it is her punishment to watch others sink. Here she capitulates; she will go back to the party, "fearing no more," because for her, as for Septimus, it is all over: "Home art gone and taken thy wages."

Clarissa's self-destructive ambivalence—her acceptance of heterosexual convention at the expense of her natural feelings because of her need for respectability—is revealed thus through the verbal network of the novel, through her identification with Septimus Smith and through her own thought processes. It is also revealed in her love/hate response to Doris Kilman. When Miss Kilman first enters Clarissa's consciousness (and the novel), she appears as "one of those spectres with which one battles in the night" (MD 16), Clarissa's image for guilt. As such, Kilman reminds Clarissa of the choice she made to deny her love for women and marry respectably. Clarissa had begun in fact by thinking of Miss Kilman in relation to her daughter, Elizabeth, speculating about the nature of their mutual devotion. Yet, given Kilman's poverty, social class, and religious fanaticism, it is easy for Clarissa to identify the guilt she provokes as having to do with social class; Clarissa seems to feel guilty that she has opted for an empty, selfish life of social vanity over a more productive, socially conscious life. Yet,

no doubt with another throw of the dice, had the black been uppermost and not the white, she would have loved Miss Kilman! But not in this world. No. (MD 17)

The most salient characteristic of "this world" as it is presented throughout the novel is its determined confirmation of heterosexuality, from Richard's disapproval of Shakespeare's sonnets for the homosexual relationship implied in them (MD 113) and his joshing denial that there is anything more than a schoolgirl crush between Elizabeth and Miss Kilman (MD 15, 266), to Bradshaw's support of "Proportion" and Peter's defense of "civilization." To flip the dice the other way around would indeed make it a world in which loving Miss Kilman, or simply loving women, would be possible for

Clarissa. Thus the real guilt Kilman fosters in Clarissa is her awareness that she has denied herself exactly what she sees Kilman living out, and in her own house, the citadel of respectability. Unknown to Clarissa but obvious to the reader is the similarity between Kilman's feeling for Elizabeth and Clarissa's for Sally; while Clarissa appropriately quotes Shakespeare ("if it were now to die 'twere now to be most happy"), Kilman expresses her passion in her own words:

> She was about to split asunder, she felt. The agony was terrific. If she could grasp her, if she could clasp her, if she could make her hers absolutely and forever and then die; that was all she wanted.(MD 199–200)

The words differ, but the content and the intensity are essentially the same. It is no wonder Clarissa finds it difficult to accept Richard's assessment that the whole thing is a phase "such as all girls go through" (MD 15).

Ultimately Clarissa does sense the meaning of her love/hate feelings for Miss Kilman. In the midst of her successful party, when her pleasure at the ambience she has created begins to wane, she thinks of Kilman:

> Kilman her enemy. That was satisfying; that was real. Ah, how she hated her—not, hypocritical, corrupt; with all that power; Elizabeth's seducer; the woman who had crept in to steal and defile (Richard would say, What nonsense!). She hated her: she loved her. (MD 265–66)

Whereas she is aware that the feelings she derives from being the successful hostess are vicarious—"but after all it was what other people felt" (MD 265)—Clarissa's response to Kilman is hers, and it is real. She hates Kilman for the power she has, and that power is Kilman's ability to love women (and teach history) and in the process to defy the heterosexual norms that so inhibit Clarissa. Yet she loves her for exactly the same reason; the colon separating "she hated her" from "she loved her" insists on the equivalence of the two. Indeed, a powerful dilemma.

The question we must ask is the same one Clarissa asks herself in response to Septimus Smith's suicide: at what cost to herself does she maintain her respectable life? Certainly there is the guilt for a wasted life, as imaged through Kilman and as called up by the solemn pause before Big Ben strikes each hour, by the old woman who lives opposite, and finally by Septimus Smith's suicide. These offer a fairly constant reminder of the self she has denied in choosing respectability. Yet she manages to counter these generally with the consolation that she does well what she has chosen to do: she gives smashing parties, she makes it possible for others to enjoy themselves, and she accepts her vicarious pleasure as what is possible for her, even to the extent of feeling thankful to Richard for providing the context in which her self-sacrifice is seen as respectable. Of course, if we listened to Peter and Sally in the novel, we would question Clarissa's assessment of her respectable life: Peter laments that "with twice [Richard's] wits, she had to see things through his eyes—one of the tragedies of married life" (MD 116), and Sally, having predicted that Dalloway "would 'stifle her soul' (she wrote reams of poetry in those days), make a mere hostess of her" (MD 114), wonders at the party "how could Clarissa have done it—married Richard Dalloway? . . . And then all this" (MD 288), waving her hand to indicate Clarissa's smashing party. Yet they obviously have their own biases: as Peter says, his life was ruined when Clarissa dropped him:

> One could not be in love twice, he said. And what could [Sally] say? Still it is better to have loved (but he would think her sentimental—he used to be so sharp). (MD 292)

Indeed, "what could she say?" It is not only the clichéd line that is "sentimental"; it is also Sally's love for Clarissa, labeled earlier by Peter as "sentimental" (MD 54). Both of them are still in love with Clarissa, as revealed here and also in the last line of the novel—"For there she was" (MD 296)—which, though it appears as Peter's perception, calls up Clarissa's scene with Sally: "There she was alone with Sally" (MD 52). With such personal feelings at stake, their judgment of Clarissa's life, which has excluded both of them, might well be seen as suspect.

Yet basically Clarissa agrees with Peter and Sally. Despite her persistent attempts to console herself for having chosen the life she has, her imagery for that life belies her. It is a narrow bed in an attic (MD 46) where she sleeps badly, unable to "dispel a virginity preserved through childbirth which clung to her like a sheet" (MD 46). So much for her personal, sexual self. It is not surprising that when Peter drops by in the morning she feels threatened by exposure: she "summoned to her help the things she did; the things she liked; her husband; Elizabeth; her self, in short . . . all to come about her and beat off the enemy" (MD 65–66). For Clarissa there is no self but those things.

But then there are the parties where she reigns as the perfect hostess; admittedly, she must compose her self to play that role:

> That was her self when some effort, some call on her to be her self, drew the parts together, she alone knew how different, how incompatible and composed so for the world only into one centre, one diamond, one woman who sat in her drawing-room and made a meeting-point. (MD 55)

Taken alone, this description suggests a self that is at worst artificial, hard, different from the real self. But, because Clarissa takes some credit for creating this self, it does not seem so bad. However, the image that comes to her mind when the party is actually going on is substantially different; the image is

> this post that she felt herself to have become, for oddly enough she had quite forgotten what she looked like, but felt herself a stake driven in at the top of her stairs. Every time she gave a party she had this feeling of being something not herself. (MD 259)

It is one thing to feel unreal, or artificial, as the hostess of a social gathering; it is quite another to feel oneself "a stake driven in at the top of the stairs," forced into that deadly posture, no doubt, by her own inability to survive outside the norms of conventional society. And a dead stake is not much different from a dead stiff in the morgue, justifying in graphic terms Clarissa's sense that she was "somehow very like him—that young man who had killed himself" (MD 283). It is thus appropriate that, from Clarissa's point of view, Septimus impales himself on "rusty spikes" (MD 280) in his suicidal leap from the window; that image calls up Clarissa's image of the stake, both phallic and both suggesting respectability in a culture defined by male prerogative: to attempt survival outside the heterosexual norms of that culture is to die at the stake, classic punishment for social deviants."[11]

"And once she had walked on the terrace at Bourton" (MD 282). With the imagery of the narrow bed, the attic, and the stake defining the limitations of her present life, that walk on the terrace seems particularly rich, its loss especially poignant. Sally loved her then,

> and she felt that she had been given a present, wrapped up, and told just to keep it, not to look at it—a diamond, something infinitely precious. (MD 52–53)

It is a self, Clarissa's real self, and Clarissa knows all too well about the female

ego and what happens to it as a woman matures. Oh, she composes another
"diamond" self, "one woman who sat in her drawing-room" (MD 55), but
that one seems brittle, impenetrable, unlike the one she is given whose "radiance burnt through, the revelation, the religious feeling!" (MD 53). And
this "infinitely precious" diamond is another image for the thing that mattered, that thing "wreathed about with chatter . . . let drop every day in
corruption, lies, chatter" (MD 280). It seems to me that Clarissa's question
whether Septimus preserved the "treasure" by killing himself comes out of
her full awareness that, in her life of respectability, she has not. Certainly she
has preserved her sexual integrity: it is significant that she retains a "virginity" in an attic bedroom, an image that recalls the "bedroom at the top of the
house" (MD 51) in Bourton where she first experienced her passion for Sally. And it is equally significant that she married Richard, not Peter, for
Richard allows her her virginal attic bedroom, whereas with Peter "everything had to be shared" (MD 10). But this kind of self-denying virginity is
no more effective in sustaining her love for Sally than are Septimus Smith's
visions and voices of the dead Evans; Evans is in fact dead and, for Clarissa,
Sally might as well be: at best Sally is a ghost out of the past whom Clarissa
has avoided over the years and whose married name she cannot even
remember. Clarissa's approval of Septimus's literal suicide reveals the extent
to which she understands the self-destruction involved in her own life. She
recognizes that she has committed her own kind of suicide: she has in fact
committed one of the most common of suicides for women, that respectable
destruction of the self in the interest of the other, firmly convinced that in
this world where the dice fall with the white on top, "that is all" that is
possible.

Notes

1. See especially Reuben Brower, "Something Central Which Permeated:
Virginia Woolf and 'Mrs. Dalloway,' " in *Virginia Woolf: A Collection of Critical
Essays,* ed. Claire Sprague (Englewood Cliffs, N.J.: Prentice-Hall, 1971), 51–62.

2. It is a popular assumption that the relationship between Clarissa and Sally is a
girlhood friendship, similar no doubt to the phase "all girls go through" (MD 15),
to quote Richard. See, for example, John Lehmann, *Virginia Woolf and Her World*
(New York: Harcourt Brace Jovanovich, 1975), 50.

3. Cf. Lee R. Edwards, "War and Roses: The Politics of *Mrs. Dalloway,*" in *The*

Authority of Experience: Essays in Feminist Criticism, ed. Arlyn Diamond and Lee R. Edwards (Amherst: University of Massachusetts Press, 1977), 160–77. While I agree with some of the polarities Edwards posits in the novel, (wars vs. parties; authority vs. individuality; "abstract, hierarchical" value systems vs. a "celebration of the spontaneity and variability of life"), I do not agree that Septimus and Clarissa represent polarities or that Septimus's suicide to preserve the "integrity of feeling" is a nonsolution while Clarissa's life as the perfect hostess represents a "mode of being which enhances feeling" and is thus a positive solution.

4. It is in fact more common in fiction that the heroine must end any liaison with a woman in order to achieve fulfillment in marriage.

5. With this interpretation I am thus identifying the "integrity of the soul" or the "integrity of feeling" referred to by several critics.

6. I do not think we need bother about Clarissa's apparent ambiguity in "this he had preserved" versus "had he plunged holding his treasure?" since we are following a mind as it naturally moves, not a linear, logical argument.

7. This diagnosis is perhaps as accurate as that one imposed on Septimus: shell shock.

8. The gender of the clock is obviously appropriate, given the symbolic value it carries.

9. William Shakespeare, *Cymbeline,* 4.2. 258ff.

10. Cf. Marilyn Schauer Samuels, "The Symbolic Function of the Sun in *Mrs. Dalloway,*" *Modern Fiction Studies,* 18, no. 3 (autumn 1972): 387–99. Although I agree with Samuels's interpretation that there is a quality of life that Septimus seeks to preserve in death, I do not agree with her conclusion concerning the *Cymbeline* line "that this quality cannot be destroyed and may indeed be preserved by death" and that this is one of the "meanings which, enlightened by Septimus, Clarissa now attributes to the line."

11. I would like to thank Jane Marcus for drawing my attention to this detail.

Virginia Woolf and
the Women's Movement   *Naomi Black*

It is generally accepted today that Virginia Woolf was a feminist. However, it also seems to be generally accepted that her feminism was not political, and that she had no significant relationship with the organized women's movement of her day.[1] The comments of her brother-in-law, Clive Bell, are typical. After noting that "Virginia was, in her peculiar way, an ardent feminist," he went on to say, "In political feminism—the Suffrage Movement—she was not much interested." Her only activism, he recalled, was going "once or twice . . . to some obscure office" to stuff envelopes for what he identifies as the Adult Suffrage League.[2] His son, Quentin Bell, who was Virginia Woolf's biographer, was only one of many to echo this assessment.

Certainly Virginia Woolf's own comments on feminism and feminists did much to encourage these views. The activists of the movement were not exempt from her awareness of how ridiculous and futile human beings could be, especially when they were committed to a cause. And in a famous passage in *Three Guineas* she rejected the very word "feminist" as "an old word, a vicious and corrupt word, that has done much harm in its day and is now obsolete." She urged that it be burned and banned (TG 184).

Yet there can no longer be any doubt of her commitment to even the most political versions of feminism. Specifically, her involvement with the women's movement is emerging with the availability of new archival material concerning both her and the relevant British organizations. This material accordingly casts new light on the origins of Virginia Woolf's feminism and on her feminist writings.

My discussion here will focus on *Three Guineas*. It has not been appreciated how that book includes both the author's continuing beliefs and also the beliefs and the specific policy demands of certain women's organizations. Only the hostile reactions to *Three Guineas* register awareness of the importance of its arguments. The book sold well and was praised by feminists, but it has repeatedly been attacked and misunderstood. The most virulent contemporary review, by Q. D. Leavis in *Scrutiny,* described the book as "babblings," "unpleasant self-indulgence" motivated by class bias and "sex hostility." But Q. D. Leavis's almost hysterical essay also included an awareness of some of the implications: "Then there are the unfortunate men . . . . They must from the start share the work of tending their offspring. A thorough-going revolution in their wage-earning pursuits, and so a regular social reorganization must follow."[3]

Today's feminists will recognize the argument about role assignments and will agree that the consequences would be revolutionary. That was the central message of a book that one critic called "neurotic"[4] and another dismissed as "therapeutic," "the product of a very odd mind" (QB 2:197, 204). It was also the message of an important element in the feminist tradition. Although Virginia Woolf did not invent this sort of feminism, she was able to articulate it distinctively.

The allegedly antifeminist passage from *Three Guineas* cited above shows Virginia Woolf's typical complexity and irony. In it she went on to say that women like Josephine Butler should not be labeled feminists, because they were "fighting the tyranny of the patriarchal state"[5] rather than merely seeking women's rights (TG 186). Such a statement is not a disavowal of feminism, but a distinction among its different varieties, opting in favor of the one with the most radical ambitions and the largest goals. Virginia Woolf's feminism was what has been called "social" feminism, and the organizations with which she was associated were social feminist ones. And this was important both for her and for them.

Here we encounter a series of difficult problems of definition. How are we to interpret the notions of feminism and of the women's movement? The answer is that we are in effect dealing with a system of beliefs that can be described in both personal and organizational terms. All feminists share the desire that women not be judged inferior or lacking by male standards. Along with this goes the conviction that women have a distinct history and interests separate from those of men. Feminist organizations make up the largest part of the women's movement; they are groups of women who actively seek to ensure that women not be disadvantaged in comparison with men. This is their minimum goal, and they often want much more.[6] Such organizations work through modes of influence we now recognize as political, using lobbying and other pressure-group tactics as well as attempting to influence public opinion through a range of conventional and unconventional means. The women's movement thus includes far more than the suffrage organizations, just as feminism means far more than civil rights.

Within the various manifestations of the women's movement, feminist organizations have historically been inspired by two sets of beliefs: what has been called "political" or "equal rights" feminism as differentiated from the "social" or "maternal" feminism that has already been referred to. Both have been important throughout the industrialized world, and they still coexist today. The better known is the equal rights feminism that achieved its greatest visibility in the suffrage campaigns of the early twentieth century; it still animates important segments of the American women's movement, such as the campaigns for the Equal Rights Amendment. For this sort of feminism, the basic argument for women's rights is that women are essentially the same as men, or would be if given the chance. It is the position of John Stuart Mill's *Subjection of Women.* Equal rights feminist organizations seek to abrogate the legislative and other arrangements that prevent women from sharing the opportunities to which all human beings are entitled. Q. D. Leavis was referring to this viewpoint when, in her review of *Three Guineas,* she wrote approvingly of "women's right to share interests and occupations that have sometimes been considered suitable only for men."[7] By the late nineteenth century the vote had come to be the major symbol of women's disadvantages. In an argument about justice, suffrage stood for equality. The furthest extension of such a position is the belief that any differential treatment of women is a demeaning handicap; equal rights feminists sometimes oppose any form of maternity leave or benefits.

Even in the great suffrage coalitions, however, most activists did not advocate woman suffrage mainly for symbolic reasons, or even as a citizen's tool for self-protection. For the large majority of the women's movement the arguments for improving women's status were based on beliefs about the *differences* between men and women. Among those holding these views there are disagreements about whether women's distinctive qualities are innate or whether they are the cumulative product of women's experiences with childbirth, child-care and homemaking. In either case, social feminists believe that women have produced a set of values and practical skills that are excluded, along with women, from the larger society that is organized and run by men. The female virtues are nurturant, cooperative, and peaceful. The female skills produce orderliness, safety, and security. An authoritative public role for women is therefore necessary to improve the defective social system. The vote was the necessary instrument for women's public service, which would transform the state. In the late nineteenth and early twentieth centuries such arguments persuaded extremely conventional women that it was proper to act aggressively to obtain a public role. Today it persuades many feminists of the necessity for women to play a far larger part in politics than they have yet.

An important part of the social feminist rationale has always been the relationship of women to violence, especially to war. Some social feminists argued, against all evidence, that females or mothers were somehow constitutionally incapable of violence. A more moderate view, widely accepted among suffragists, was that women's previous training and experience, what we would call socialization, would keep a government run by women from being imperialist or warlike. Among those who accepted this argument, it was one of the most compelling reasons for the participation of women in public life. In 1916 Virginia Woolf expressed the connection in a letter as follows:

> I grow steadily more feminist owing to the Times, which I read at breakfast and wonder how this preposterous masculine fiction [the war] keeps going a day longer—without some vigorous young woman pulling us together and marching through it. (L 2–76)

The majority of the British suffrage movement accepted social feminist arguments, even if sometimes accompanied by equal rights ones. Even the militant suffragettes, the members of the Pankhursts' Women's Social and Political Union, believed in the distinctiveness and superiority of women's values and capabilities, though they were far from eschewing warlike behavior. Certainly most of the members of the very large coalition of non-militants, the National Union of Women's Suffrage Societies, accepted such arguments. So did the Women's Co-operative Guild, which united the wives of relatively prosperous working men. These were the women's organizations with which Virginia Woolf was associated.

Given her legend as the precious invalid lady of Bloomsbury, it is surprising to discover how many social or political associations Virginia Woolf belonged to. Typically, women participate in far fewer groups than men do. As late as 1977, an international survey found that only 6 percent of the women questioned in Britain were active in as many as two organizations.[8] At one time or another in her life, Virginia Woolf seems to have been active in at least four: the "adult suffrage" group for which she worked in 1910, the Women's Co-operative Guild, the British Labour party (including here both the Fabians and the Rodmell Labour party), and the Village Institute of Rodmell. The last two are not feminist organizations, though the Village Institutes are women's organizations of some importance. In addition, Virginia Woolf had close connections with the London and National Society for Women's Service, one of the sucessors to the nonmilitant National Union of Women's Suffrage Societies.

Virginia Woolf's memberships thus place her squarely in the middle of the organizational network of social feminism in Britain. The leaders of these groups represent a dimension of the British intellectual aristocracy that has not yet been investigated. The names are familiar in the history of social change: Strachey, Rendel, Garrett, Fawcett, Davies, and Llewelyn Davies. Here we have the mothers and sisters, the daughters and wives of the patriarchs and their debunking offspring. Virginia Woolf knew them all and worked with many of them.

The overlapping of personal and organizational connections shows most clearly in the group for which Virginia Stephen probably did her suffrage work of addressing envelopes and attending meetings. She seems to have belonged to an "extremely shadowy organisation" called the People's Suffrage Federation. The PSF used a Mecklenburgh Square address, close to where Virginia Stephen then lived, was run in large part by Margaret Llewelyn Davies, and included on its executive committee her old Latin teacher Janet Case. As published and unpublished letters show, at the beginning of January 1910 Miss Case inspired her former pupil to write and offer to do some suffrage work. Miss Case took the offer to Miss Llewelyn Davies, who passed it on to Mrs. Vaughan Nash, also on the executive committee of the People's Suffrage Federation. Rosalind Nash wrote back suggesting that Miss Stephen might like to do some writing or research for the "People's Suffrage."[9] This circumstantial evidence, along with the little information we have about the beliefs and activities of the PSF, makes it reasonably certain that it was the suffrage group to which Virginia Stephen belonged.

The People's Suffrage Federation seems to have been essentially an umbrella organization composed of the women's auxiliaries of the labor movement: the Women's Co-operative Guild, the Women's Labour League, and the Women's Trade Union League. Its executive board included founders and leaders of these groups along with some of their supporters from the British Labour party and the Co-operative Movement. Its most distinguished political participants were Arthur Henderson, M.P., future foreign minister, and Margaret Bondfield, prominent in women's trade unions and later to be Britain's first woman cabinet minister. Although Virginia Woolf correctly identified the group's goal as complete adult suffrage, in practice it was a woman suffrage group, able to use the desirability of adult suffrage as an argument for working with the other woman suffrage organizations.

The year of Virginia Stephen's suffrage work, 1910, was the peak of cooperation among the woman suffrage groups, by then very numerous. Even the militant Women's Social and Political Union called a truce for about ten months in order to help mount a substantial parliamentary offensive. Asquith's governing Liberals had refused to make woman suffrage a government bill, so all-party agreement was necessary if any women at all were to get the vote. The People's Suffrage Federation seems to have had the role of urging Labour members of Parliament not to accept any franchise changes that did not include women, as well as of encouraging them to support any possible partial enfranchisement of women alone. The PSF could also hope to show the public, Parliament, and even the prime minister that women of the working class supported the cooperative suffrage efforts.

Very little is known about what the PSF actually did. As its spokesman, Arthur Henderson played a significant role in the parliamentary maneuverings that finally failed to produce the hoped-for all-party bill for a degree of woman suffrage. PSF activists led by Henderson induced the British Labour Party Congress of 1912 to instruct the Labour M.P.s not to accept any franchise measure that did not include women. There are scattered references to it in the records of the Women's Labour League, but none later than 1913. For the moment, its main claim to fame should be the high probability that it was the organization for which Virginia Woolf did what she regarded as her only real "political" work.[10]

The second organization important for Virginia Woolf was a major constituent of the People's Suffrage Federation, the Women's Co-operative Guild. The WCG was an important part of Virginia Woolf's life from at least 1913, when she attended the annual congress that she was to write about in 1930 in her "Introductory Letter" to *Life as We Have Known It.*

We know that Virginia Woolf also attended guild conferences in 1916 and 1922, and that from 1916 to 1920 she organized and chaired meetings of the local guild at her house at Richmond.[11]

The Women's Co-operative Guild still exists, though it has now changed its name to Co-operative Women's Guild, a reflection of its shift away from feminist concerns. Before the war it achieved the considerable membership of 87,000 and hoped for 100,000; after the war it declined steadily and now has fewer than 17,000 members. As the centenary of the 1883 founding approaches, this is clearly a dying organization, in even worse trouble than the declining Consumer Co-operative Movement as a whole.[12] In spite of its early importance as an example of the radical political involvement of working-class women, it is still known mainly for the connection with Virginia Woolf. But in the early years of the century, when Virginia Stephen encountered it, the WCG was a major suffrage and reform organization, cooperating with the nonmilitant suffragists. It had started as a women's auxiliary to the consumer cooperative movement, designed to enlist wives of cooperators into active support of the cooperative stores. For the founders, another motive was adult education for barely literate married working-class women. By 1889, when Margaret Llewelyn Davies became general secretary, the group had already developed a strong momentum of its own, pushing for a more extensive and egalitarian role for women within the cooperative movement and in the larger society. By 1914 it was self-confident enough to defy the Co-operative Congress's demand that the WCC forgo support of reform in divorce legislation; for four years it managed without its customary subsidy.

The Women's Co-operative Guild's interest in woman suffrage grew directly out of its basic social feminist beliefs. Its ample publications supply some of the clearest examples of social feminist views about the nature of politics. These are particularly interesting because of the role the WCG played in the People's Suffrage Federation, of which Margaret Llewelyn Davies was a founder. For instance, a pamphlet entitled "Why Women Should Have the Vote" made the following typical statements:

> Politics is nothing but the art of helping the life of the people—helping the home . . . . Employment, the wages question, housing, education, old-age pensions, temperance, public health in all its branches, public economy—everything in one way or the other touches the purse-bearer and home-maker in her daily work, her spending power, and her care for the members of the family, young and old. By giving her the vote, fresh life will be put into the movements for reform.

In another suffrage pamphlet, dated 1908, Margaret Llewelyn Davies wrote:

> What are the questions with which a vote—the tool of the citizen—are concerned? Peace and war, education, labour problems, the drink traffic, free trade, taxation, and the housing question are among them.[13]

The questions claimed as "women's issues" thus included the domestic ones, the working-class issues of wages, the economic concerns that follow from a commitment to cooperation, and the problems of "peace and war." In the thirties, the last category came to dominate the WCG's activities, as its members insisted on a completely pacifist response to world problems.

A recent and well-reviewed account of pacifism in interwar Britain expressed surprise at the overlap between pacifism and feminism; the book did not even mention the Women's Co-operative Guild and seemed unaware of the ideological links it epitomized.[14] The WCG's stubborn and consistent opposition to the use of force was based on a fairly simple belief that women had the obligation to oppose war. Their condemnation of militarism extended even to the Boy Scouts, the Girl Guides, and the Church Lads' Brigades, as well as to Armistice Day celebrations and the League of Nations' sanctions policy. In the summer of 1938 the Guild Congress passed a resolution undauntedly opposing rearmament; this was the summer before the Munich Agreements, when war was visibly approaching. "The Co-op women as usual were magnificent," wrote Virginia Woolf to Margaret Llewelyn Davies. "I had seen the resolution—they beat the Labour Party hollow" (L 6:250). As late as March 1939 the WCG was calling for repeal of the Conscription Bill. Unlike the other sections of the labor movement, it never gave positive endorsement to the war effort. After the war it continued at the far left of the Labour party, pacifist, antinuclear, anti-NATO, anti-American, and anti-Europe.

In her "Introductory Letter" to *Life as We Have Known It* Virginia Woolf spelled out how a social feminist group could develop international interests and a pacifist orientation, both as an extension of domestic concerns. The account began with a description of the room where the first members of the WCG met, "remote from boiling saucepans and crying children." In the earliest version of the piece, first published as a separate essay in 1930, the account continued.

> And then that room became a place where one could make, and share with others in making, the model of what a working woman's house should be. Then as membership grew and twenty or thirty women made a practice of meeting weekly, that one house became a street of houses; and if you have a street of houses you must have stores and drains and post-boxes; and at last the street becomes a town, and a town brings in questions of education and finance and the relation of one town to another town. And then the town becomes a country; it becomes England; it becomes Germany and America; and so from debating questions of butter and bacon, working women at their weekly meetings have to consider

the relations of one great nation to another . . . [They were] as
only for baths and wages and electric lights, but also for co-opei
dustry and adult suffrage and the taxation of land values and div
reform. It was thus that they were to ask, as the years went by, 1
and disarmament and the sisterhood of nations. (CE 4:146)

The second version, published in 1931 with the guildswomen's n
omitted the chain of expanding interests. The final international
were summed up as follows:

Thus in a year or two they were to demand peace and disarmament and
the spread of Co-operative principles not only among the working people
of Great Britain, but among the nations of the world.[15]

"The spread of Co-operative principles" was the WCG's recipe for world
peace; we can regret the second version's loss of the phrase "the sisterhood of
nations."

What Virginia Woolf seems to have got from the WCG is some doctrinal
and organizational support for pacifism. She clearly had enormous admiration for both the middle-class leaders and the working-class members of the
group. The "Introductory Letter" also shows a sophisticated, rather rueful
awareness of how different she was from both these groups of women. This
awareness reappears in *Three Guineas,* where her recommendations are
carefully addressed to women like herself, who were neither activists nor
wage earners. Perhaps she also drew from the WCG the idea of the power
that can be exerted by a group of "outsiders" with integrity and a disdain for
praise or subsidies.

This integrity was shared by the third organization with which Virginia
Woolf was involved, the group of nonmilitant suffragists who worked so pa-
tiently for more than fifty years to gain access to political influence. Their
greatest pride was their retention of democracy and decency within their
organization; they felt this was one of the most important contributions
women could make to public life. The People's Suffrage Federation had been
an umbrella group of labor suffragist groups, and the Women's Co-operative
Guild was also basically a working-class organization, though with middle-
class leaders. In contrast, the National Union of Women's Suffrage Societies
(NUWSS) was mainly middle class. It shared the social feminism of the PSF
and the WCG, though there were equal rights feminists as well among its
membership. Headed by Mrs. Henry (Millicent Garrett) Fawcett, the group

had in its heyday more than four hundred constituent self-governing societies; it was able to hold as many as fifty public meetings at the same time and to muster parades and demonstrations of ten to fifteen thousand persons. The association had its origins in the first women's rights clubs organized in the 1860s. Its descendant, rechristened the Fawcett Society in honor of its most important president, is still in existence. For Virginia Woolf, its significance is once again in relation to arguments about the relation of women to war.[16]

The NUWSS supported the First World War, but reluctantly. The final decision was made at the urging of Maria Vérone, the most active internationalist among the French feminists; she told a public meeting of the NUWSS council, "The more pacifist we are, the more we should demand today the destruction of German militarism."[17] The organization then used war service as a demonstration of what women could do if allowed a public role. The NUWSS also issued a typically social feminist statement about the war, justifying its support, and continuing as follows;

> Suffragists will be unworthy of the political power which they have claimed . . . if they do not now strive with all their mind and soul to understand the causes of this recurrent madness, so that they may heal it . . . Until women learn to *think* as women (and not merely *feel* as women), they will not affect much. "Men must work and women must weep," wrote Charles Kingsley in his poem *The Three Fishers* . . . . The modern woman must drive back her tears; she has work to do, as always, in meeting the situations created by men, but she also has a great new pioneer work to do in making her womanly thought prevail, in conquering the repulsive idea that womanly thought is cowardly thought, and the equally repulsive idea that it is womanly for a woman to echo the sentiments of men.

This statement is echoed in all the versions of *Three Guineas,* which was first published under the title "Women Must Weep."[18]

After the war the NUWSS produced two successor groups, both of which have some importance for Virginia Woolf. In 1919 Millicent Garrett Fawcett and a group of followers including Ray and Philippa Strachey established the London and National Society for Women's Service, which kept control of what had been the International Women's Suffrage Association's library. This became the Marsham Street or Women's Service Library of which Virginia Woolf was so fond. We have only indirect and fragmentary evidence of Virginia Woolf's associations with the Society for Women's Service, but it begins to look like a fairly extensive connection. We know that she wrote at least one article for their journal, the *Woman Leader,* and that she at least considered giving them the manuscript of *A Room of One's Own* to sell. In 1930 on the occasion of a celebration for Ethel Smyth she gave at Women's Service House a speech entitled "Professions for Women"; it was the first version of *Three Guineas.* Some unpublished correspondence confirms how intensively Virginia Woolf used the library and the services of the librarian, Vera Douie, in preparing the final text of *Three Guineas* in 1937 and 1938. This correspondence also shows that from May 1938 until her death Virginia Woolf had a standing arrangement with the library to purchase books they requested. In addition, her published letters included references to her having asked friends to subscribe to the library, as well as her agreement to serve on some kind of committee at Women's Service House.[19] Certainly *Three Guineas* includes the specific policy goals of the Society for Women's Service. Ray Strachey summed them up as "the economic equality of women, and . . . both practical work and propaganda on equal pay and opportunity." In the twenties the group was concerned to obtain complete equality in the franchise, and in the thirties a major campaign was for equality of treatment of women in the civil service, an important issue in *Three Guineas.*[20]

There is no evidence that Virginia Woolf had anything to do with the other, larger descendant of the NUWSS, called after 1918 the National Union of Societies for Equal Citizenship. Under future M.P. Eleanor Rathbone, this group developed a "new feminism" very close in many ways to Virginia Woolf's beliefs; the Society for Women's Service followed more an "equal rights" logic, though the two groups agreed in support of many issues. Eleanor Rathbone argued that women should avoid being assimilated into a male version of society and should concentrate on their qualities as women. Accordingly, one of her group's priorities was what was first called the "national endowment of motherhood." Women were to be subsidized for performing the social service that only they could perform, reproduction. This policy, also a central goal of the Women's Co-operative Guild, was finally enacted in a much reduced form as mothers' allowances.[21] It appears prominently in *Three Guineas.*

In a memoir written in 1939–40 Virginia Woolf included "the Vote" among the major influences on her (MB 80–81). We may speculate that the vote was significant in part because it was the issue that first brought her into contact with other feminists. Certainly the People's Suffrage Federation, her suffrage group, was connected with the other organizations that were to be important for her. In turn, the Women's Co-operative Guild and the dif-

ferent stages of the National Union of Women's Suffrage Societies seem to
have provided a major part of the arguments and the specific policy measures
of Virginia Woolf's feminist writings.

The social feminist image of the transformed world is a radical one.
Virginia Woolf thought she was incapable of working out the details of how
to produce it. In a letter to Ethel Smyth she typically presented herself as a visionary: "But then of course I'm not a politician, and so take one leap to the
desirable lands" (L 6:478). She thought her role was to supply the vision. Yet
in her feminist works she included the specific measures that the women's
movement of her time thought were necessary stages along the road to the
"desirable lands." The list is a long one, and it corresponds point by point
with the practical demands made by organized groups of feminists; many of
them are still being asked for today. In *A Room of One's Own,* the least concrete of her feminist writings, Virginia Woolf asked on behalf of women for
economic independence and privacy, as well as for control of marriage and of
reproduction (Shakespeare's sister) and the opportunity for advanced education. This last includes both access on equal terms and the possibility of such
essential related conditions as travel and leisure. The "Introductory Letter"
to *Life as We Have Known It* endorsed working women's demands such as the
vote on equal terms with men, reformed divorce laws, minimum wages, and
modernization of household equipment. In *Three Guineas* she added a
women's party in Parliament, a women's newspaper, progressive education
(nonhierarchical and including the history of women), pensions for single
women, salaries for wives, and childbirth anesthesia. The last should probably be seen as equivalent to today's demands for more humane childbirth arrangements in which mothers have a larger role; the preceding point looks
like wages for housework but is probably mothers' allowances. In addition,
Three Guineas included sustained argument for the full and equal admission of
women to the senior, influential, and well-paid professions; she discussed the
church and the civil service at length. In the interim, women should be admitted on equal terms to the existing traditional educational institutions. As
she measured and counted the precise level of women's share in, for instance,
scholarships at Cambridge, the reader may sense an advance warning of affirmative action techniques, though this would be anachronistic for 1938.
Virginia Woolf was listing the measures rich women could help bring about,
along with the public policies that women's organizations thought possible
and campaigned for. One of her major concerns was to produce some rich
(and thus powerful) women who would see such changes as urgent.

In a way, the critics of *Three Guineas* were correct in thinking that the
book is not really about preventing war. The solution to war is easy:

pacifism. But according to Virginia Woolf only women are pacifists, and mainly for the wrong reasons and in the wrong ways. What would a truly pacifist *society* be like? In 1938 the vocabulary was lacking to express the answer that such a society would have to be nonsexist. The use of the term "fascist" was misleading. Its opposite was "democratic," but since the days of Aristotle the notion of democracy had been able to coexist very comfortably with complete subordination of women. However, whatever the terminology used, the existence of violence is not the main reason for wanting to end such a society and to reform the family that is its constituent unit. Instead, it is what a peaceful egalitarian society would be like in positive terms. And for her goal the pacifist, supposedly apolitical Virginia Woolf gave a description very like that of Thomas Hobbes. The purpose of government, wrote the author of *Leviathan*, (L 6–379) is "to live delightfully." Virginia Woolf called it "the life of natural happiness " (L 6–379)[22]

Viscountess Rhondda, who had been a militant suffragette, wrote in response to *Three Guineas* to say that she was sure that women were as capable of violence as men: "in my heart I find, it seems to me, such echoes of all the pride, vanity and combativeness I ever see in men." Virginia Woolf wrote back as follows:

> [Such feelings] are in us of course; I feel them pricking every moment. But again they have so little encouragement in us; surely, with the great example of what not to be blazing in front of us, we can damp them down before they get a hold. If we emphasise our position as outsiders and come to think it a natural distinction it should be easier for us than for those unfortunate young men.

Virginia Woolf compared herself to her "old half brother . . . who shot and rode and owned several acres." Even more to the point, she reminded Lady Rhondda of how even that wealthy peeress had encountered difficulties as a woman trying to break into the world of journalism:

> But isn't that too a proof of what I say—I mean, as a woman shut out from so many of the newspaper sanctuaries you have to fight to enter; and thus don't think, as those within naturally do, how to shut others out. (L 6:236–37)

Virginia Woolf was demonstrating what the real meaning could be for the "Outsiders' Club" she suggested as the solution to the problems of co-option. This association without rules and officers, and therefore without hierarchy or status, suggests a forerunner to the structureless consciousness-raising groups of the present women's movement. It would operate as a network of support structures within which, like Virginia Woolf and Lady Rhondda, women could remind each other of what their shared history and personal experiences meant. Feminists who read *Three Guineas* wrote and asked if they were "outsiders." Of course, responded Virginia Woolf, who felt herself to be one. She also made it clear that she thought of the women's movement as a first approximation to the Outsiders' Club. Perhaps her experiences with the movement were one of the bases of her confidence that the cause of women would triumph.

In a letter written a year before her death, Virginia Woolf speculated on how the outsiders could try to bring about the conditions they so much wanted in the postwar world:

> sharing life after the war: pooling men's and women's work [and] the possibility, if disarmament comes, of removing men's disabilities. Can one change sex characteristics? How far is the women's movement a remarkable experiment in that transformation?

Wondering if it would be possible to "alter the crest and spur of the fighting cock," she found the impact of the war encouraging, for it had removed a great deal of the lure and glamour of militarism. She ended hopefully:

> It looks as if the sexes can adapt themselves; and here (thats our work) we can, or the young women can, bring enormous influence to bear. So many of the young men, could they get prestige and admiration, would give up glory and develop whats now so stunted. (L 6:379–80)

Virginia Woolf thus pushed the ideas of the social feminists to their natural conclusion, the transformation not just of women's role, but also of society and finally of men. In Q. D. Leavis's violent response to *Three Guineas* she lamented its impact on the existing civilization. Virginia Woolf's point was just that: the need to end civilization as we know it, to the extent that it depends on fascism in the family and in the state, the unpaid devotion of women in the home, the exploitation of women in the workplace, and the implicit structure of values that favors competition, hierarchy, and violence. "But what about *my* civilization?" she asked (DVW 4:298).

Virginia Woolf thus bridged the older and the newer, present-day women's movements. The new movement is likely to think that feminism began in the past few years. But when its members respond to Virginia Woolf's message, they are also implicitly recognizing their relation to the groups that were the context and in part the source of her feminism. The values of social feminism that she accepted still form a major part of the beliefs of feminists today. To begin with, she articulated the older and continuing beliefs: the emphasis on the differences between men and women, the belief that male domination has deformed public life, the hopes for the results of women's influence on public life, the importance of the specific reforms the movement has supported and continues to support, and the notion of women as nurturers and therefore peacemakers. She also added a number of concerns that were not as important for the older movement or were even alien to them, but which are of increasing importance today: hostility to the patriarchal family, fears of co-option and assimilation, sexual issues, and the reliance on the women's movement as a continuing source of support for women even after legal equality has been acquired. The older and the newer movements do not interpret the continuing issues in the same way; necessarily, views have changed about the nature of sexuality and maternity, about education and women's history, and about fascism and war. But there are clear continuities of both ideas and organizations.

Virginia Woolf's feminism was political because it responded to notions about power and social structure, and because it reflected a specific organizational and programmatic history. The vehemence of attempts to represent this sort of feminism as apolitical and marginal shows just how essentially radical it is. War and the patriarchy continue, if perhaps with rather less support than before the days of the women's movement. There is a long way to go yet before women even have their own rooms, which mean economic independence and political equality. The equal rights feminists had this as their goal. The social feminists wanted more, no less than the creation of a permanently peaceful society of equals.

Virginia Woolf certainly did not expect to see society transformed in her time; she would be saddened but not surprised to see how little has changed. But to want to end war is not to be apolitical.

Notes

1. Although Berenice Carroll argues persuasively that Virginia Woolf's work (including the fiction) incorporates a coherent political program for a society

transformed in terms of "female" values, she underestimates and in part misinterprets Woolf's relationship to the women's movement of her time. " 'To Crush Him in Our Own Country': The Political Thought of Virginia Woolf," *Feminist Studies* 4, no. 1 (February 1978): 99–129. In " 'No More Horses': Virginia Woolf on Art and Propaganda," *Women's Studies* 4 (1977): 264–89, as in her more recent work, Jane Marcus also argues for the political and feminist dimensions of Virginia Woolf's writing, emphasizing the role played by her notions about capitalism and the class struggle.

2. Clive Bell, *Old Friends* (New York: Harcourt Brace, 1956), 101.

3. Q. D. Leavis, "Caterpillars of the Commonwealth Unite!" *Scrutiny* 7 (September 1938): 209, 204, 205, 209, 211.

4. Herbert Marder, *Feminism and Art: A Study of Virginia Woolf* (Chicago: University of Chicago Press, 1968), 174.

5. In the articles cited above, Berenice Carroll and Jane Marcus give different interpretations of Virginia Woolf's remarks about feminism; for Carroll, it means Virginia Woolf is rejecting "all labels, dogma, and hierarchical or bureaucratic organization" (121), and for Marcus Virginia Woolf is making the "premature and optimistic" assumption that "the only freedom that matters, the economic, has been achieved" (268).

6. The definition of feminism used here is close to the one used by Linda Gordon in *Woman's Body, Woman's Right: Birth Control in America* (New York: Grossman, 1976). For a useful account of social feminism see J. Stanley Lemons, *The Woman Citizen: Social Feminism in the 1920's* (Urbana: University of Illinois Press, 1975).

7. Leavis, "Caterpillars of the Commonwealth," 211.

8. Jacques-René Rabier, *European Women and Men in 1978: A Comparison of Attitudes towards Some of the Problems Facing Society* (Brussels: Commission of the European Communities, 1979), 203.

9. The description of the PSF is from George Dangerfield, *The Strange Death of Liberal England* (New York: Capricorn, 1961), 163. The address 34 Mecklenburgh Square is to be found on PSF pamphlets in the possession of the Fawcett Library in London. For the most substantial description of the PSF, including the list of its executive committee, see A. J. R., ed., *The Suffrage Annual and Women's Who's Who* (London: Stanley Paul, 1913), 99–102. The letter from Rosalind Nash and the sequence of events described here are referred to by Quentin Bell (QB 1:161); the relevant letters by Virginia Woolf are in L 1:421, 422, 426. The letter by Rosalind Nash (dated 19 January 1910) is in the University of Sussex Library. The PSF is sometimes referred to as "The People's Suffrage Federation for Adult Suffrage."

10. There are brief references to the PSF in most of the standard accounts of the suffrage battle, with a tendency to confuse it with the earlier Adult Suffrage Society

founded by Arthur Henderson and Margaret Bondfield, as, for instance, in Norbert C. Soldon, *Women in British Trade Unions, 1874–1976* (Dublin: Gill and Macmillan, 1978), 74. The complicated story of how the British labor movement came to accept that woman suffrage could precede full manhood suffrage is best explained in Constance Rover, *Women's Suffrage and Party Politics in Britain, 1866–1914* (London: Routledge and Kegan Paul 1967), and Jill Liddington and Jill Norris, *One Hand Tied behind Us: The Rise of the Women's Suffrage Movement* (London: Virago, 1978). See also Lucy Middleton, ed., *Women in the Labour Movement* (London: Croom Helm, 1977), especially Middleton, ''Women in Labour Politics,'' and Margherita Rendel, ''The Contribution of the Women's Labour League to the Winning of the Franchise.'' In Middleton, see also Jean Gaffin's ''Women and Cooperation'' for the best published source for the early years of the Women's Co-operative Guild; there is also some useful material in Liddington and Norris.

11. For the conferences, L 2:99, 530; there are many other references to the guild's showing serious involvement, such as L 2:152, 356, 534–36.

12. See Jean Gaffin and David Thoms, *Caring & Sharing: The Centenary History of the Co-operative Women's Guild* (Manchester: Co-operative Union Ltd., 1983).

13. Pamphlets in the collection of the Fawcett Library, London.

14. Martin Ceadel, *Pacifism in Britain* (Oxford: Clarendon, 1980), 84.

15. ''Introductory Letter'' to Margaret Llewelyn Davies, ed., *Life as We Have Known It* (London: Hogarth, 1931), xxxvi.

16. The most extensive account of the NUWSS is to be found in Ray Strachey, *The Cause: A Short History of the Women's Movement in Great Britain* (London: George Bell, 1928).

17. Ray Strachey, *Millicent Garrett Fawcett* (London: John Murray, 1931), 289 (my translation).

18. Cited from the *International Women's News* in Arnold Whittick, *Woman into Citizen* (London: Atheneum with Frederick Mueller, 1979), 296; see also the statement of the Women's Social and Political Union cited by Whittick on p. 297. ''Women Must Weep'' appeared in the *Atlantic Monthly* 161 (May 1938).

19. The Fawcett Society had to move three times and was bombed; its remaining records, at the Fawcett Library, have not yet been sorted. There are nine unpublished postcards and two unpublished letters by Virginia Woolf that are relevant, as is a typescript by Vera Douie, ''Women's Service Library: The First Sixteen years, 1925–1942,'' n.d.; pp. 7–8 refer to Virginia Woolf's donations: they are also documented in the correspondence, which includes carbons of thank yous. See also L 5:136, 6:234, 236, 473; DVW 2:53 and appendix 2.

20. Ray Strachey, *Millicent Garrett Fawcett* (London: John Murray, 1931), 336.

21. Jane Lewis, *The Politics of Motherhood: Child and Maternal Welfare in England, 1900–1939* (London: Croom Helm, 1980).

22. Sterling Lamprecht, ed., *Thomas Hobbes's "De Cive"* (New York: Appleton, Century, Croft, 1948), 143. For a more detailed discussion of Virginia Woolf's political feminism, see my essay "Virginia Woolf: The Life of Natural Happiness," in Dale Spender, ed., *Feminist Theorists* (London: Women's Press, 1983).

A Track of Our Own:
Typescript Drafts
of *The Years* *Susan Squier*

In 1933 Virginia Woolf's work on her ninth novel was interrupted by an odd, Wildean coincidence. Manchester University decided to award her a Doctor of Letters; the honor would no doubt have pleased many people, but to Woolf it was "Mumbo Jumbo." She was determined to refuse it, and that determination plunged her into a vexing, embarrassing social tangle, forcing her to defend her position to strangers and friends alike. The beginning was an awful dinner party: meeting by chance a Mrs. Stocks of Manchester University, Woolf found herself listening, captive, to a lengthy description of the university's pleasure in conferring the degree. When she finally found the courage to explain that she intended to refuse it, a general argument began in which her only ally was her sister, Vanessa Bell. The assembled company drew a distinction between university honors, which were permitted, and state honors, which must be refused. Against them, Virginia and Vanessa simply stated "the silliness of honours for women." Later Woolf speculated in her diary that perhaps she and Vanessa lacked the "publicity sense." That would explain why such an honor left her cold. "Nothing would induce me to connive at all that humbug. Nor would it give me, even illicitly, any pleasure (WD 189–90)."

Arguments were only the stormy beginning, however. Then there came the necessary polite letters: to the vice-chancellor of the university; to Shena, Lady Simon, with whom it had been arranged that the Woolfs would stay when they came to Manchester for the award. To both Woolf pleaded a well-established aversion to honors of any kind for writers, but a letter written on the same day expands on the reasons for her refusal. Addressing her close and combatant friend the composer Ethel Smyth, Woolf describes her views on

honors for women—views shared with Vanessa, but in which she differed
dramatically from her correspondent. Her handwriting is feeble, she explains, because she has been writing letters, refusing an honor of the sort
Smyth thinks one should accept. But Smyth, she writes, half-jokingly, is "a
base honour corrupted woman—going up to 'honour' women, when the
only honour is blue blank air, no more and no less." "What's the point of
this honour worship?" she asks Smyth, rhetorically. "Mumbo Jumbo!" (L
5:172). To honor women verbally without contributing economically, to
honor women with merely the "blue blank air" of applause and an audience
and a podium, seems to her so much superstition—primitive and unlikely to
advance the real cause of a feminist civilization.

In her diaries and letters, Virginia Woolf had long speculated on what *was*
likely to advance it. In 1916 the agony of World War I had moved her to
dream of a "vigorous young woman" who could unite England against the
"mudcoloured moonshine" of patriarchal politics and the "preposterous
masculine fiction" of war. (L 2:76,582) That image surfaced seventeen years
later in the manuscript Woolf was working on when Manchester University
offered her the honorary degree. The novel that was interrupted by that odd,
mirroring coincidence was Virginia Woolf's second venture into the realm of
realism. After *Night and Day* (1919), she once again hoped in *The Years*
(1937) to combine fact and vision, to explore the relation between the individual and society. This novel, her ninth, traced the fortunes of the
Pargiter family from 1880 to the "present day," or 1937, when the novel
was published. Though the novel focuses mainly on Eleanor, the unmarried
daughter who acts as Colonel Pargiter's housekeeper when her mother dies,
it introduces us to other characters in the Pargiter family as well. And as the
male Pargiters have a variety of roles in patriarchal society, so the female
characters enact a whole range of responses to the question Woolf was considering—in art—when the episode of the Manchester honorary degree
replicated it in life: What is woman's right relation to the institutions of
patriarchal society?

There is Eleanor's rebellious cousin, Kitty Lasswade, daughter of an Oxford don, who dreams of freedom in the north of England but capitulates by
making a socially advantageous marriage to Lord Lasswade. And Peggy
Pargiter, Eleanor's niece, a doctor whose training has taken the deadening
toll on spirit and sense of which Woolf warned in *Three Guineas,* the feminist
essay written as a companion piece to *The Years.* And Eleanor's other cousin
Sara Pargiter, a quasi-Cassandra whose apocalyptic world view is often eerily
accurate. And Maggie, Sara's sister, who has escaped conventionality

without forfeiting her chance for a happy, egalitarian marriage. And finally, there is Rose Pargiter, whose childhood experience of being molested by a drunken man has led to an adult commitment to militant suffragism—Rose, the very image of that vigorous young leader Woolf dreamed of in 1916. A political novel in the feminist sense of the word, *The Years* traces the changes that befall the Pargiters, male and female, as England moves from empire to nation threatened by fascism and as women move from the protected prison of the Victorian family to the freedom of the modern public domain.

Woolf's original plans for this novel were ambitious—and innovative: it would combine fictional excerpts from an imaginary novel tracing a typical English family, the Pargiters, from 1800 to 2032, with interpolated essays exploring the issues and ideas those "chapters" raised. If her formal intentions were complex, so were her thematic ones; she hoped the novel would "come, with the most powerful and agile leaps, like a chamois, across precipices from 1880 to here and now" (WD 183). Sadly, Woolf finally abandoned her experiment in commingling life and art—only one month before the "odd coincidence" of the Manchester University honorary degree—revising the novel to omit the nonfiction essays. Still, we are left not only with the excellent edition of that first draft, compiled by Mitchell A. Leaska in 1977, but with many of the themes from those omitted essays, which have been dramatized in the remaining fictional scenes. Woolf's massive revision of the novel midway through its composition (in February 1933) provides readers with the rare opportunity to see the unfolding process of composition. Furthermore, the publication of *The Pargiters,* the "essay-novel" portion of Woolf's early draft of *The Years,* was also accompanied in 1977 by publication of " 'Two enormous chunks': Episodes Excluded during the Final Revisions of *The Years.*"[1] Their editor, Grace Radin, has discovered in those massive last-minute deletions the pattern of Woolf's revision—a consistent movement away from direct denunciation of the sexism in British society—anticipated in her earlier decision to turn from the more straightforward address of an "essay-novel" to the indirection of fiction. Ultimately, as Radin and others have pointed out, much of the overt socio-political commentary was omitted from *The Years* and appeared instead in the novel's companion piece, *Three Guineas* (1938).

In February 1933 Virginia Woolf completed the first major revision of what was then called *The Pargiters.* Deciding to leave out the "inter-chapters," she had moved from treating the issues in essays to embodying them in the fiction itself. And so on 25 March of that year she was speaking as Elvira Pargiter, condemning women's willingness to accept the honors bestowed by patriarchal society, when life and art combined in the "odd coincidence" of the Manchester University honorary degree.

> It is an utterly corrupt society I have just remarked, speaking in the person of Elvira Pargiter, and I will take nothing that it can give me etc. etc.: Now, as Virginia Woolf, I have to write—oh dear me what a bore—to the Vice Chancellor of Manchester University and say that I refuse to be made a Doctor of Letters. . . . Lord knows how I'm to put Elvira's language into polite journalese. What an odd coincidence! that real life should provide precisely the situation I was writing about. I hardly know which I am, or where: Virginia or Elvira: in the Pargiters or outside. (WD 189)

Eight pages of Woolf's unpublished typescript draft of *The Years*, held in the Monks House Collection at the University of Sussex Library, consider the same issue raised simultaneously by art and life in March 1933. In that frustrating confusion two individuals played significant roles as foils to Woolf: Vanessa Bell acted the supportive sister, helping Woolf develop her own argument for refusing the degree, and Ethel Smyth played the friendly opponent, whose sympathies—though feminist—nonetheless lay with accepting such honors.

The passage presents us with a similar fictional scene, in which Elvira Pargiter and her sister Maggie frame a letter to their cousin Rose, debating women's responsibilities to patriarchal British society. Originally the passage formed part of the "1910" chapter of *The Years*, falling roughly in the middle of the novel. It opens on a spring evening—6 May 1910. Year, month, and day all mark crucial turning points in the lives of the Pargiter family, of women as a group, and of the nation as a whole. The Pargiter households are beginning to dissolve; Digby Pargiter's death has brought about the sale of his house and the dispersal of his children, and within a year Colonel Pargiter's death will force a similar decampment. During 1910, of course, "human character changed," but, more specifically, the spring of that year saw a change in women's behavior.[2] After the General Election, the Women's Social and Political Union adopted a calmer posture toward the government in an attempt to encourage Parliament to pass the Conciliation Bill, which would guarantee women's suffrage. During the spring and summer of that year violent prosuffrage demonstrations ceased and a new peaceful, more unified mood reigned. Finally, 6 May 1910 marked the end of a reign as well. On that day King Edward VII of England died, and the crown passed to George V. It was a time of transitions, and the sense of an ending figures vividly in Maggie and Elvira's conversation. In the characterization, setting, and imagery the sense of a beginning, if more ambiguous, is present as well.

These previously unpublished typescript drafts complete our picture of Virginia Woolf's movement from the "essay-novel" experiment she titled *The Pargiters* to the novel of political criticism entitled *The Years*. In addition to revealing Woolf's fictional treatment of the real-life drama played out by Virginia Woolf, Vanessa Bell, and Ethel Smyth in 1933, the pages reveal Woolf's view of the nature and extent of women's obligation to Britain's current patriarchal society and her hopes for the feminist civilization of the future. Finally, they show Woolf using the materials of fiction—characterization, setting, and image—to reveal conflicts of an ideological nature.

A note about the text: these pages are held at the University of Sussex Library, Falmer, Brighton, where they may be studied by scholars working on Virginia Woolf, subject to the permission of Mr. Adrian Peasegood, curator. They are held in two files: MHPB 4 and MHPB 15.2. Page numbers and internal chronology suggest that the pages form one sequence whose original length was approximately twenty pages: the first group, pages 361 through 367, has two pages missing (363 and 365); the second group comprises page 380 (and its second-draft form, page 3'0380) and page 381. Since there is no evidence that Woolf intended either their division or their order within each group, I have used the page number at the top left of each page and the internal evidence to establish a coherent order. In my editing I have normalized Woolf's spelling and punctuation but as a rule have followed her additions and deletions; the few exceptional deleted passages I have included in the text are indicated by brackets. Finally, I have noted any substantial gaps in the typescript sequence with asterisks. In the final version of *The Years,* Elvira's name was changed to Sara.

Text

Elvira lay back on the sofa now and again looking into a book which she opened and shut. "But Maggie look here," she said after a time; "We may be Englishwomen; perhaps we can't help it. Passports, you know. Magdalena Pargiter, British subject—what about that?"

"On I daresay," said Maggie, "on passports. Yes and what about Eton and Harrow, Oxford and Cambridge—that sort of thing?'' She pinned the hem of the long strip of silver stuff that lay on her knee.

''That's true,'' said Elvira. ''That's a blessed and undeniable fact, Maggie. That's what I shall say next time Rose comes to lunch. I shall say, Look here Rose, Two women who are completely without education, who have never eaten, drunk, smoked or otherwise misconducted themselves, who have never dipped even the tips of their little fingers in the golden coffers of the royal mint can't be English; and what's more won't be.[3] That's what you'd say to Rose isn't it Maggie?''

''I merely say,'' said Maggie, absentmindedly, pinning her hem, ''that if you haven't taken any money you needn't behave like a fool. Gold lace; Eton and Harrow match and so on.'' She mumbled; a reserve of pins was between her lips. ''If you haven't swallowed the bribe, you needn't be a dam'd ass. You needn't pay the piper.''[4]

''Throw me a pen,'' said Elvira, ''and I'll write to her—'' She dipped her pen in the ink and began,

My dear Rose—

She paused, ''Rose,'' she reflected, ''coat and skirt; very square, very solid; bites her underlip. You see Maggie, I writing to Rose become Rose; I adapt myself to Rose; I become terse, emphatic for example, to the point.''

My dear Rose—

* * *

''I shall now take a drink of coffee and begin a new paragraph. It's very exhausting, being Rose.'' She sipped her coffee and then threw herself back on the sofa with her hands behind her head. She murmured,[5] ''an interminable and wonderful procession, from one end of time to the other, The Pargiters [*sic*]. And time past is but a rose-leaf on top of what's to come. Our civilization, Maggie, is but the thickness of one green leaf on the top of all Cleopatra's Needle; what's to come. So that in twice twelve thousand years a man, looking in at this window, into this den, this cave, this little antre scooped out of the mud and filled with dung will hold his nose and say, 'Pah, they stink.' To blow one's nose in a pocket handkerchief will be an act of criminal indecency. Nasty things, noses, hands, fingernails.'' She held her hand up in front of her and looked at it. ''And there you sit,'' she added, looking at her sister, ''Magdalena Pargiter, you savage, on the sixth of May Nineteen hundred and ten stitching curtains.''

''It's a dress, not a curtain,'' said Maggie.

''For a party?''

"Yes. Tomorrow."

"Tomorrow and tomorrow and tomorrow," Elvira murmured. She was silent. "And what did the man in gold lace say to the lady on his left when you went to the party, Maggie?" she asked.

"Oh, I can't remember," said Maggie. "They just went off together, into a little room,—"

"Just raising his finger—so—he beckoned," said Elvira. "And the lady in diamonds got up. And they went into a little room opening out of the big drawing room with shaded yellow lamps, one chair and a convenient sofa. And he turned down the lamp and stooped to unlace his boots, which were tight, patent leather, undoing the buttons on his uniform, he said. . . . But you know, Maggie, in those circumstances the greatest of poets seldom put long speeches even into the mouths of kings. However, to finish the letter.[6] Well, what comes next?"

"We hope Uncle Abel's gout is better and send him our best love. Then sign your name, Elvira Pargiter."

Elvira dipped her pen in the ink. "We hope Uncle Abel's gout is better," she began, and, waving her pen in the air, "It's a tremendously exciting affair, Maggie," she broke off. "Here we are, following the procession through the desert, with nothing but a clump of trees on the horizon, and the spears of savages and hyenas howling; and now we are come to this rock; this formidable and craggy mountain; and rubbing our eyes and taking a look round, we wave our hands to the assembled company, wave our swords in the air, blow them a kiss and make off [on a track of our own]."

"All right," said Maggie. "Finish the letter."

"We hope Uncle Abel's gout is better," Elvira wrote, "and send him our best love. Affectionately yours, Elvira Pargiter."

* * *

" 'That's our bus,' said Rose. 'Not this one. That one.' " She imitated Rose's voice again.

"Very sensibly," said Maggie. "If she wants to do the business,[7] she must go catch a bus and go to a room—"

"With a carved doorway on the ground floor," Elvira interposed.

"But as for all this nonsense," Maggie continued, "these meetings, this waste of time. . . ."

"Oh, but a meeting's a very queer thing, Maggie. It's beautiful. Like a trunk of stone lying in pale greenish light in a desert. Nothing grows. No flowers. 'Where are the eyes and the mouth?' I said, passing my hand over

that assembly of ten grown people sitting on hard chairs; the surface is
eyeless, impersonal. Then there were voices outside, trailing away, inaudible; cabs rushing; children shrieking; and ten grown up people—''

''It's so simple,'' Maggie interrupted her. ''What Rose ought to say is:
Give me whatever the sum is—the weekly books come to fifteen shillings a
head; not counting washing. Then there's the children. Give me or let me
earn whatever's a fair sum to live on—''

''Which could be decided by both houses of Parliament sitting in full bot-
tomed wigs,'' Elvira added.

''Give me,'' Maggie continued, ''a fair sum to live on, and then, Rose
should say—brushing aside all this nonsense—we'll—''

''Pull down the old world and build another!'' Elvira exclaimed.

''We'll live like reasonable human beings. We don't want gold lace,[8] and
Eton and Harrow and muskets, Rose should say.''

''She might put it this way,'' said Elvira. '' 'Milord Duke (addressing the
Prime Minister) what with child birth and chastity, and looking after old
gentlemen who have shot off half their fingers in the wars (like my sister
Eleanor) and sitting in a dark room for a million years—a room that smells of
cabbages, furniture—(you remember the smell of Abercorn Terrace, Maggie?) we, the undersigned have inherited a tradition, Milord—if not an
education, still a civilisation—which in our opinion it would be a thousand
pities to swop for yours. For whereas—here she should begin a new
paragraph with a capital W— 'For Whereas the gentlemen of England (see
Whittaker's Almanac) never stir a finger save for money; and are educated
thereto (see Edward, my brother, teaching undergraduates), we the undersigned have for countless ages worked without pay; Rose's income being
precisely twelve pound ten a quarter. Hence her coat and skirt.' Perhaps
that'll go in a post script,'' she said, looking for her letter to Rose.

''What's the use of letter writing?'' said Maggie, yawning. ''And it's bed
time now. This'll have to do as it is,'' she said, taking the dress which she
had been making and holding it against herself.

*   *   *

This unpublished passage from the typescript drafts of *The Years* considers
three issues Woolf herself debated: women's rights and duties in a patriarchal
society and their means for achieving a feminist one. Dialogue and mock
debate delineate the differences in position between Elvira, Maggie, and Rose
Pargiter—three characters whose opinions resemble those of Woolf herself,
her sister Vanessa, and her friend Ethel Smyth. Furthermore, those issues

were actually debated in 1910, when the Women's Social and Political Union revised its methods in fighting for women's rights, moving from militance to pacifism in hope of achieving parliamentary support for the Conciliation Bill. Elvira and Maggie seem to be most sympathetic to the pacifist, socialist suffragism of Sylvia Pankhurst and her followers. The sisters agree that only if women have taken the bribe of economic or educational support must they in turn support the British government, at peace or at war. They agree, too, in seeing such patriotism as perilously close to prostitution. The lady in diamonds enacts the circle dance that Woolf would later name "subconscious Hitlerism" (DM 245). When the man in gold lace, who is the prime minister, beckons, she comes to him loyally prepared to pay with her sexual favors for the privileges she has received. So the society that oppresses women by making them sexual objects and restricting their powers hands out illusory privileges, thus gaining women's support in oppressing others abroad.

However, the woman who does not take the bribe (like Woolf herself at the time this passage was written) need not behave "like an ass" by prostituting either her person or her politics. Instead she may join the procession down "a track of our own" to a society of our own—built on a different model from the competitive, privileged one of Colonel Pargiter and his peers. Maggie and Elvira play on the word "procession," formerly royal and patriarchal, now practiced by the suffragists in huge marches. Their different personalities cause them to envision different outcomes. Prophetic Elvira hopes the procession will lead to a decisive break with the past, as women "pull down the old world and build another," while conciliatory Maggie hopes only that people will forgo the bad old ways ("gold lace and [power and] Eton and Harrow and [Oxford and] muskets") to live "like reasonable human beings."

In contrast, the sisters' view of Rose Pargiter shows her to be a fervent patriotic suffragist like Ethel Smyth, biographer and bedfellow (ideologically and, it was rumored, actually) of the more militant Emmeline Pankhurst. Virginia Woolf called Ethel Smyth a "jolly good fellow," and the gathering of Pargiters at the end of *The Years* sings Rose's praises in the same words. Perhaps feeling it weakened her unified presentation of women's grievances against patriarchal society, Woolf omittted this debate between feminists over means and ends from the final draft of "1910." Instead, the published chapter looks outward, exploring the variety of women's responses to male society, and takes a resigned rather than combative tone. In the original draft Elvira plans a letter setting forth women's case against sexism in society. Maggie's response is a dubious question, "What's the good of writing letters?'' Yet her comment at least suggests the possibility of a more forceful response to women's oppression; in the final version, a similar comment expresses alienation from male society without allegiance to any alternative way of life. In thin, reedy tones, Sara has been singing a pompous eighteenth-century march, but she breaks off in discouragement to ask, ''What's the good of singing if one hasn't any voice?'' While Sara's question may suggest women's almost biological aversion to the violence such a march tune celebrates, abstention rather than protest is its mode. Woolf also revises the original focus on the feminist civilization to come, replacing it with an indictment of the masculine society of the present—for which there seems to be no alternative. ''Bring up your children on a desert island where the ships only come when the moon's full!'' Sara exclaims. ''Or have none?'' suggests Maggie (Y 190).

Yet the full moon of feminist civilization is rather carefully explored in the original version, contained in these typescript pages from the University of Sussex Library. Woolf relies on both imagery and setting to suggest the conflicts and possibilities attendant on its creation. Although both Elvira and Maggie seem to anticipate change, in the context of their conversation such change still seems problematic: while they dream of a society in which social conventions no longer shackle women, Maggie continues to sew her conventional evening dress for the inevitable party. Yet we must realize that for Virginia Woolf such domestic labor had ambiguous value: she frequently used scenes of such traditional ''female'' work to explore radical feminist ideas. In part this strategy follows from her determination not to ''take it for granted that life exists more fully in what is commonly thought big than in what is commonly thought small'' (CR 155). So she eavesdrops on sewing rooms and washhouses, as earlier writers loitered near the House of Lords, in search of significance. But there is a further reason for Woolf's frequent attention to domestic scenes in her fiction: she felt that women's household drudgery, while clearly a product of oppressive patriarchal culture, had nonetheless two important qualities supporting feminist aims. First, through its very banality domestic labor guarantees privacy. Throughout Woolf's works, women appreciate the pleasant safety from male interruption that distasteful work ironically provides. Even Clarissa Dalloway's alarm at being found sewing by Peter Walsh hints at her appreciative anticipation of the privacy such work usually affords. And, when women enjoy such privacy—and at few other times—they are free to engage in a wide-ranging satirical critique of the society that has banished them to kitchen, washhouse, or sewing room.

Woolf understood that the experience of isolated domestic work could create solidarity among women. This is not to suggest, of course, that such drudgery *always* nurtures a feminist outlook in Woolf's fiction; we need only remember the shrine that Crosby, the servant in *The Years,* builds to her employer, "Almighty, all-powerful Mr. Martin" to see that drudgery may also encourage hero worship. Yet the issue here, as so often in power relationships, is identification. If the domestic drudge identifies with her oppressors, her condition will nurture only alienation—from her peers as well as from the exploitative master. Both Kitty Lasswade and Crosby experience that alienation in *The Years,* though they occupy opposite ends of the social scale. Crosby scorns the other inhabitants of her rooming house; Kitty Lasswade despises rich society women. Both feel more at home with the masculine, privileged society that has banished them—Crosby to her rooming house, Kitty to a cottage on her son's estate.

But if the domestic drudge profits from her exclusion, she learns to trust and identify with her peers; the result, in time, is a strong sense of belonging, to which Woolf gave shape in her dream of a "Society of Outsiders" (TG 106). That group, drawn together by insights born from oppression, struggles to transform not only the individual life, but the whole of society by breaking down class barriers. But perhaps the most striking and extended exploration of the ironically liberating effect of women's exile to domestic labor appears in two little-known essays published in 1931 and 1932, "Great Men's Houses" and "The Docks of London," in which Woolf reveals how the space women fill with their domestic duties in the home reflects their place in society.[9] In "Great Men's Houses" she describes the plan of Thomas Carlyle's home, showing that the forms of one's labor, rather than family or class ties, determine one's place in society. And gender determines the forms of one's labor. Because both Mrs. Carlyle and her maid are responsible for the hot baths, clean rooms, and meals that Carlyle required to write his history, both women occupy the same space in the home. While the great man fills the top floors (Woolf describes Carlyle writing "up in the attic under a skylight"), the women cluster in the lower regions: kitchen, washroom, scullery, basement. Woolf's spatial analysis has a sociological conclusion. Just as women's domestic tasks keep them in the lower regions of the home, so they limit them to the lower regions of society. But separated from men as they are in their domestic, feminine area, so women may come to share a separate vision of a feminist future in which female effort will not be limited to supporting male genius.

Woolf's spatial analysis of power relationships expands, in "The Docks of London," to show that women and women's work are segregated not only in the private home but in the public sphere as well. Part of the Thames waterfront becomes London's scullery in that essay. Woolf's later choice of that same unfashionable area for Maggie and Sara Pargiter's home in *The Years* has thematic rightness, for that novel portrays women's domestic work as source of a radical vision for the future. Feminist and domestic drudge are explicitly yoked in *The Years,* where the artist becomes "charwoman to the world," presenting a radically cleansed structure for human relationships.[10]

Spatial presentation of power relationships was also Woolf's technique in these early draft pages of "1910," where Elvira's vivid sculptural thinking gives us two monuments, two images for two civilizations: the "colossal Wreck" whose desert ruins mark the patriarchy, and the spire of Cleopatra's Needle, which marks the transition to the feminist society of the future. Elvira's first monument is a response to the suffrage meeting she attended with Rose, and it compactly expresses that meeting's faith; the impending fall of male, patriarchal civilization. "Oh, but a meeting's a very queer thing, Maggie. It's beautiful. Like a trunk of stone lying in pale greenish light in a desert." Her simile invokes Shelley's broken monument of Ozymandias, standing in the desert. The inscription on its pedestal reads, "My name is Ozymandias, King of Kings,/Look on my Works, ye Mighty, and despair!" and like the "traveller from an antique land," Elvira encourages us to recognize that motto's irony, for "Nothing beside remains. Round the decay / Of that colossal Wreck, boundless and bare / The lone and level sands stretch far away."[11] Elvira's simile suggests that one day the patriarchal civilization that currently oppresses women and excludes them from power will have left no more traces than the kingdom of Ozymandias. In its place a new civilization will have arisen, whose duration and influence will make the old one seem "but the thickness of one green leaf on top of all Cleopatra's Needle."

Like the monuments in the published version of *The Years,* Cleopatra's Needle is in one sense a British imperialist figure of conquest, for this needle-shaped stone on London's Victoria Embankment was presented by Egypt to the British Empire in 1878.[12] Celebrating the British dominion over Egypt, it recalls a powerful queen who was far from a feminist monarch; the image at first seems merely to combine imperialism and nationalism, British rule and the reign of Cleopatra, one form of oppression and another. Yet when we consider Elvira's image in context—the brief sisterly conversation that Woolf omitted from the published version of *The Years*—we find a more interesting group of associations. Needle-shaped, named for a queen, the image of Cleopatra's Needle suggests the female solidarity born in private domestic labor like the needlework with which Maggie is absorbed while she and Elvira dream of a feminist society.[13] And it furthermore suggests that a king may someday fall to a queen; that the male, patriarchal civilization will pass away, to be succeeded by a feminist, egalitarian one.

In its mingled meanings, the image of Cleopatra's Needle exemplifies the quality of conflict that may have prompted Virginia Woolf to omit these typescript draft pages from the published version of *The Years.* In imagery, setting, and characterization, these pages explore issues that were raised in 1933 by Manchester University's decision to award Woolf an honorary degree. Just as Woolf then debated with Vanessa Bell and Ethel Smyth whether women had a duty to refuse the honors of patriarchal society, so in these pages Elvira and Maggie frame the terms of an imaginary debate with Rose on woman's obligations as British subjects and her proper method of fighting for a feminist civilization. Perhaps Virginia Woolf felt this scene fragmented the focus of her splendid feminist novel: admittedly these pages are concerned less with the general relation between women and patriarchal society than with specific tactical disagreements within the women's movement. Yet to contemporary feminists they are compelling precisely for that reason: they speak to our concerns *from the inside,* by exploring the conflicts at the heart of change.

Acknowledgments

My thanks to Jane Marcus for urging me to study these drafts, to Elizabeth Inglis of the Manuscripts Section, University of Sussex Library, for her assistence in obtaining photocopies of them, and to Quentin Bell for permission to publish them.

Notes

1. Grace Radin, " 'Two Enormous Chunks': Episodes Excluded during the Final Revisions of *The Years,"* *Bulletin of the New York Public Library* 80, no. 2 (winter 1977): 221–51.

2. Virginia Woolf, "Mr. Bennett and Mrs. Brown," *The Captain's Death Bed and Other Essays* (New York: Harcourt Brace Jovanovich, 1950), 94–119, esp. 96.

3. Two women who are completely without education, who have never eaten drunk or smoked or whored—excuse the word I shall say—for she blushes—at the public cost; cant be English;/ deleted passage.

4. /"What Maggie says is, Elvira repeated, is, "If you dont take the bribe you neednt be an ass. Like Papa she added./ deleted passage.

5. /"Marching on, marching/ deleted passage.

6. /She took up the page she had written and read out "It would be incumbent upon us to accept the teaching of the Archbichop *[sic]* of Canterbury . . . and that I may say with the utmost emphasis we are not prepared to do"/ deleted passage.

7. /end corruption/ deleted passage.

8. /power and/ /Oxford and/ deleted phrases.

9. *The London Scene: Five Essays by Virginia Woolf* (New York: Frank Hallman, 1975). I examine the political and aesthetic significance of Woolf's spatial vision in the "London Scene" essays in a chapter of my book *Virginia Woolf and London: The Politics of City Space.*

10. For further treatment of this theme in *The Years*, see Jane Marcus, *"The Years* as Greek Drama, Domestic Novel, and Gotterdammerung," *Bulletin of the New York Public Library* 80 no. 2, (winter 1977): 276–301, and Margaret Comstock, "The Loudspeaker and the Human Voice: Politics and the Form of *The Years," Bulletin of the New York Public Library* 80, no. 2 (winter 1977): 252–75.

11. Percy Bysshe Shelley, "Ozymandias," in *Norton Anthology of English Literature, vol. 2,* ed. M. H. Abrams (New York: W. W. Norton, 1979), 690–91.

12. Woolf borrowed the image of Cleopatra's Needle from Oliver Strachey, who himself borrowed it from Sir James Jeans, F.R.S. Quite characteristically, Woolf subverted Strachey's sexual and Jeans's scientific use of the image, making it instead symbolize the enduring feminist civilization of the future (DVW 4:65, 66).

13. It may even be a form of insurrection when women dare to make and wear their own dresses. In her fifties, Virginia Woolf still remembered with anguish George Duckworth's criticism of the evening dress she made as a young girl "of a green stuff bought erratically at a furniture shop . . . because it was cheaper than dress stuff; also more adventurous." Duckworth told her to "tear it up," sensing "some kind of insurrection; of defiance of social standards" (MB 130). Jane Marcus has suggested that even the colors women choose to wear may be significant: the dress Duckworth despised was green, like Mrs. Dalloway's dress—the color of hope. The colors of the Women's Social and Political Union were purple, white, and green, symbolic of bravery, purity, and hope.

Theater of War:
Virginia Woolf's
Between the Acts   *Sallie Sears*

The universe of *Between the Acts*[1] is a universe of words—words more palpable than people; "words like sweets" on the tongue (BA 10); "coarse words descending like maggots" (BA 203); "words the defilers, . . . words the impure"; a universe of interrupted speech, repetitions, quotations, abortive communication, fragments of sentences, truisms, homespun verses, "talk" (both audible and silent), and talk *about* words, talk, and speaking;[2] a universe whose central events are the verbal performances of the not-very-well-executed pageant and of the audience during and between its acts; a universe in which rooms empty of all these "talk producers" stir in the spectral narrator (who is fond of taking us into such places) an eloquence, even lyricism, that the characters themselves do not inspire and of which they are incapable.

Yet if we are asked to engage with anything, it is not with the characters' feelings but with their language. One of the striking features of *Between the Acts,* indeed, is the degree to which it distances us from the lives it parades before our eyes. The world we enter ("the airy world of Poyntz Hall")[3] is a conspicuously stylized, "literary" one;[4] the atmosphere "that of an interlude, fantastic and unconstrained";[5] the characters are puppetlike, one-dimensional; even the sympathetic ones hover on the verge of caricature, caricaturing one another. The narrator is remote, sardonic, disengaged. Under her gaze the characters flash into being as birds ("Mrs. Haines . . . a goosefaced woman with eyes protruding as if they saw something to gobble in the gutter" (BA 3), animals, or both ("so indigenous was she that even her body, crippled by arthritis, resembled an uncouth, nocturnal animal, now nearly extinct—clapped and laughed aloud—the sudden laughter of a startled jay") (BA 93–94). As such images suggest, the concern for human suffering that informs even so scathing a novel as *The Years* has receded into the outer reaches of emotional space—a distance that, like the "light above the clouds," is itself a subject of interest to the mind that does the distancing (the light "pure blue, black blue; blue that had never filtered down; that had escaped registration. It never fell as sun, shadow, or rain upon the world, but disregarded the little coloured ball of earth entirely") (BA 23). From the perspective of that mind, the characters' triumphs (such as they are) and failures alike seem vaguely absurd, the whole human spectacle a sham.

Yet their circumstances are grim enough. The novel takes place on a day in June 1939, the month Hitler was "busy supervising the completion of plans to invade Poland"[6] for the war that, to Woolf, signaled the "complete ruin" both of European civilization and of her own "last lap" (WD 289). England is in jeopardy; the characters themselves, though privileged, are distraught, lonely, unsatisfied. The "ghost of convention" haunts their lives, rising to the surface at the slightest touch, crippling their capacity to act or even to see that they have options. "Given his choice," Giles (a stockbroker) "would have chosen to farm. But he was not given his choice. So one thing led to another; and the conglomeration of things pressed you flat; held you fast, like a fish in water. So he came home for the week-end, and changed" (BA 47). Though these characters sense things are amiss, they hardly know what, or why. Nor do they care to. Self-conscious, divided, wavering, they imprison themselves in specious fantasies, mute resentments, unrealizable longings. Some pine for persons they cannot have or hardly know; some conjure up times in which things were, must have been, or might become better. A few attempt to comfort one another. One (La Trobe) tries to make the group take an honest look at its own spiritual state. Such efforts change very little, for the characters are incapable of purposeful action and resist the knowledge that might lead to it. Among their favorite strategies for deflecting the truth is to theatricalize it. They pose, wear masks, act parts, posture, declaim, exaggerate ("Blood seemed to pour from her shoes. This is death, death, death . . . when illusion fails" [BA 180], La Trobe cries when the audience's attention wanders). Throughout the novel they seem to be speaking lines. Some write bad poetry, reciting it silently. Others trivialize great poetry by quoting snatches in banal contexts. Emotions vaporize in self-conscious "renditions" of whatever substance they may initially have had. Banalities take on a strange power to stir feeling (" 'The father of my children.' It worked, that old cliche; she [Isa] felt pride, and affection" [BA 48]). Even the characters' fantasies are literary. Isa poeticizes all feelings—love, loneliness, lust, despair—including suicidal ones ("O that my life could here have ending" [BA 181]). Everything their minds touch upon either recedes into the distance, disappears, or becomes a fiction—like the world of the narrator, though a mimic version, and mangled with pretensions she does not have; like a work of art, though not a very good one.

I rather believe with Faulkner, "The past is never dead, it is not even past." And this for the simple reason that the world we live in at any moment is the world of the past: it consists of the monuments and the relics of what has been done by men for better or worse; its facts are always what has become. (Hannah Arendt)

That the characters seem imprisoned in a bad script is not accidental. Their strategies of denial and deflection find their counterpart in the novel's representation of human life as a spectacle, a dream, a fantastic and not very well put together drama. The novel itself, however, is far from being haphazard. To the contrary, every stroke is deliberate, from the opening paragraphs that juxtapose human and animal realms (one character is "goosefaced," another "swanlike"; a cow "coughs," a bird "chuckles"), dehumanizing the characters and humanizing creatures, to the disquieting ending of the novel, which makes clear that the whole work (not just the pageant) is to be understood as a play within a play; an interlude in some "larger" cosmic drama, the progress of which is not into the future but into the prehistoric past of humankind. In *this* drama the characters we have regarded as (representations of) "real" people are shown to have been fictional all along; actors indeed, but in the scenes and entr'actes of a play whose final curtain rises to reveal the present dissolving into the dark night of the past, the "night before roads were made, or houses" and the "hero" (Giles) and "heroine" (Isa), whose love/hate mating ("Before they slept, they must fight; after they had fought, they would embrace. . . . But first they must fight, as the dog fox fights with the vixen, in the heart of darkness" [BA 219]), will initiate this transformation, like savages on a rock.

"We pour to the edge of a precipice," wrote Woolf in 1940; "We live without a future" (WD 325, 350). In the greenhouse, Isa and Dodge somewhat melodramatically echo these sentiments ("The doom of sudden death hanging over us. . . . There's no retreating and advancing" [BA 114]), as does the narrator, whose artistry surpasses that of her fictional counterparts ("The future shadowed their present, like the sun coming through the many-veined transparent vine leaf; a crisscross of lines making no pattern'' [BA 114]). For all its "airy" atmosphere the novel sees this "future" everywhere implicit in the quality of present existence. The violence at the heart of the characters' shenanigans is incontestable, betraying itself in incident after incident: little George's ecstasy on entering the luminous inner darkness of a flower is a result of its literal destruction—"Membrane after membrane was torn" [BA 11]; in fury at his own impotence, Giles stomps to death the "monstrous inversion" of a toad—ribs crushed, oozing blood—unable to die, caught in the throat of a snake that cannot swallow it[7] ("The mass crushed and slithered. . . . his tennis shoes [were] bloodstained and sticky. But it was action. Action relieved him. He strode to the barn, with blood on his shoes" [BA 99]); Isa keeps visualizing the bloody details of a rape story. Seeking solace from "the old brute, her father-in-law" ("his veins swollen, his cheeks flushed" [BA 13]), who with his dog ("hairy flanks [sucking] in and out . . . a blob of foam on its nostrils") has terrified her son (or, in Bart's words, "destroyed the little boy's world" [BA 202]), Isa turns to the library: "There they [Keats, Spenser, Tolstoy] were, reflecting. What? What remedy was there for her age—the age of the century, thirty-nine, in books?'' Yet like a person with a "raging tooth" in a chemist's shop staring at the bottles "lest one of them may contain a cure, she considered: Keats and Shelley; Yeats and Donne" (BA 19); history, biography, science. "None of them stopped her toothache. For her generation the newspaper was a book" (BA 20). But if the newspaper is a book for Isa's generation it is hardly a remedy. Isa picks up the *Times* and reads about a woman dragged by the Whitehall guard to the barracks, "where she was thrown upon a bed" and stripped. The woman screams, hits one of the troopers "about the face" with a hammer (BA 20). That story, with its interlocked themes of politics, war, and rape (that "conscious process of intimidation by which *all men* keep *all women* in a state of fear"),[8] dramatizing that "every avenue of power" in patriarchal society is "entirely in male hands,'"[9] haunts Isa throughout the day and presages the brutal lovemaking between herself and Giles and the novel's conclusion[10]—a scene that both initiates and symbolizes the work's vision of a collective return to the savagery of the past.[11]

It is no accident that it is a *sexual* skirmish that initiates humanity's return to the dark night of the past. As in *The Years* and *Three Guineas*, Woolf's indictment of civilization is feminist as well as pacifist; nor are the two separable, in her view.[12] Though none of the characters come off unscathed

by the novel's sardonic vision of human existence, there are nevertheless important differences between the female and male characters. In spite of
moments of warmth and affection, the males in the novel are the
"separatists," the destroyers, the conformists, and, of course, the holders of
power. Like Old Bart's dog ("Either he cringed or he bit" [BA 18]), when
they are not brutal they are craven, passive, or repressed. For all their faults
the women, at least by impulse, are the "unifiers," the visionaries, the artists, the healers, the seekers of harmony, nonconformists, restorers of peace,
givers of joy ("Pleasure's what they want" [BA 43], says Mrs. Manresa of
the villagers); the dreamers, the darers, the truth-tellers, and, to the extent
that there are any, the activists. Not all are likeable; some are vicious; few are
more than momentarily effective. None escape the narrator's irony. But they
alone are capable of actions that do not hurt or damage something. However
flickeringly, it is their imaginations that keep alive the sense of the past, the
continuity of culture, the interdependence of all living creatures, and what
slender hope exists for a better world. In the persons of Miss La Trobe and
Mrs. Swithin ("the maid and mother in modern dress"), the values Woolf
regarded as a function of the "training" women receive, Jane Marcus points
out, become associated with "the double aspect of the ancient mother goddess" in whose figure "the death and rebirth of the earth" were celebrated.[13]
But her powers have faded if her image has not: males rule hearth, country,
and globe in the novel. The war that embodies the values of *their* training is
already under way. Though the male characters too are miserable with the
world as it is, they tend to do little but fret. When they do act it is apt to be
violent, as when Old Bart terrifies his grandson. Their memories are sterile,
their dreams without hope.[14] Bart's vision of the past takes him to a garden
of death and comes as he sleeps; Lucy's brings a teeming forest into her room
and is a work of "imaginative reconstruction," a creative act. Wakened by
the birds, she spends "the hours between three and five thinking of
rhododendron forests in Piccadilly; when the entire continent, not then . . .
divided by a channel, was all one; populated . . . by elephant-bodied, seal-
necked, heaving, surging, slowly writhing and, she supposed, barking
monsters; the iguanodon, the mammoth, and the mastodon; from whom
presumably, she thought, jerking the window open, we descend" (BA 8–9).
At the center of this vision is movement, sound, vitality; oneness and continuity in the midst of variety; the primeval energy and evolutionary potential of life; its monstrous and wondrous forms before "Man, the hunter" in-
truded. Death is at the center and in every detail of Bart's dream. Its
backdrop is racist and imperialist. In a land without water, beside the

maggot-eaten bones of an animal, Bart clenches a gun. Nature is extinct. The only living things in the scene are human, the helmeted white "explorer" and the "savages" on whose land he stands.

As in her other novels, Woolf places the burden of hope upon the women characters. They are the sole counterforce to a society that rewards its dominant members—"gun slayers, bomb droppers" (BA 187), stockbrokers, landholders, Indian civil servants—and disenfranchises and devalues the rest. In no novel, however, is her celebration of women so muted or so skeptical. Isolated and self-isolating, pursuing and eluding one another throughout the day, male and female characters alike in *Between the Acts* try to make something happen but cannot. Nor in their hearts do they hope to. Like ghosts, they can no longer touch anything real in themselves or each other. (Even their voices are "disembodied.") Most are in a state of frustrated lust, yearning, rage, despair and make strenuous efforts to deny, escape, or trivialize this state. Those who by contrast (Lucy Swithin, "Old Flimsy") seem content, wander vague and unfocused throughout the long day that comprises the time of the novel ("She [Lucy] seemed to see them for the first time. Was it that she had no body? Up in the clouds, like an air ball, her mind touched ground now and then with a shock of surprise" [BA 116]).[15]

The real preoccupation of *Between the Acts* is the spiritual condition in which such strategies of evasion result. The condition is general: it characterizes the entire society, indeed the age (it is no accident that Isa, the "heroine," is thirty-nine, "the age of the century" [BA 19]). And it reveals itself not in the characters' "feelings" but in the subjects that haunt their minds, dominate their conversation, and mirror the misrule of their beings:[16] language, death, silence, emptiness, nothingness, fictionality, performance, the failure of art, the passage of time, the eruption of irrepressible but "discordant," meaningless life; the chaos of history, the omnipresence of the past, the obliteration of the present, the absence of the future, the dimming of perception, the evasion of feeling, the repudiation of responsibility, human unconnection broken by brief moments of warmth, the paralysis of the will, the failure of action, the breakdown of communication, the burden of consciousness ("what we must remember: what we would forget" [BA 55]),[17] the "leaden duty...to others" (BA 67) that kills desire.

Language, Mind, and World

It is above all in the medium of language that the characters take flight from the realities of their experience. As their responses to the pageant indicate, their first effort is to *not* hear, speak, understand. What they cannot deflect by "larding, stuffing or cant" (BA 187) they simply abort. Conversations trail off, fix upon trivialities, fade in and out ("She spoke too low at first; all they heard was . . . *reason holds sway*" [BA 123]). Characters stop listening; speak when no one is there ("[The swallows] 'come every year,' said Mrs. Swithin, ignoring the fact that she spoke to empty air" [BA 103]); fail to complete what they are saying (" 'It is time,' said Mrs. Swithin, 'to go and join—' She left the sentence unfinished, as if she were of two minds and they fluttered to right and to left, like pigeons" [BA 74]). Those who (like Giles) do face some painful truth about their lives (that their spouses are unfaithful, their jobs meaningless, their friends boring, their country imperiled) keep their perceptions to themselves. Among the subjects everyone conspicuously avoids is the war.[18] Giles arrives home "enraged" that sixteen men have been shot across the channel, but rather than speaking he jerks his chair:

> Thus only could he show his irritation, his rage with old fogies who sat and looked at the view over coffee and cream when the whole of Europe—over there—was bristling . . . with guns, poised with planes. . . . as for himself, one thing followed another; and so he sat, with the old fogies, looking at the view. (BA 53–54)

Those who do speak up typically face obstacles of various sorts; nature itself abets the enterprise of silence ("The wind blew away the connecting words of their chant" [BA 80]; "His first words [the breeze had risen; the leaves were rustling] were lost" [BA 191]).

Even when words are not "lost" to the ear they may be lost to the mind, as when Streatfield ("their representative spokesman; their symbol; themselves" [BA 190]) finally succeeds in making the audience hear him ("at last a whole sentence emerged; not comprehensible; say rather audible" [BA 191]). What is "audible" is in fact characteristically incomprehensible. Obscuring awareness, disrupting communication, its powers are negative, absurd:

> What an intolerable constriction, contraction, and reduction to simplified absurdity he [Streatfield, trying to explain the pageant] was. . . . Of all incongruous sights a clergyman in the livery of his servitude to the summing up was the most grotesque and entire. He opened his mouth. O Lord, protect and preserve us from words the defilers, words the impure! (BA 190)

The few "authentic" (and coherent) communications that take place in the novel are in fact not audible. Most, furthermore, are hostile, as when Isa "overhears" Giles thinking about Dodge, the homosexual: "A toady; a lickspittle . . . a teaser and twitcher . . . not a man to have straightforward love for a woman—his head was close to Isa's head—but simply a—At this word, which he could not speak in public, he pursed his lips" (BA 60). In fact, however, he has not spoken *any* of these words aloud, including the "acceptable" ones. (The unacceptable one he cannot say even to himself. Nevertheless, Isa knows what the word is.) If, as in this instance, these silent utterances are "understood" by an equally silent auditor,[19] the understanding and the communion remain tacit. Speech is frozen; dialogue is soundless. What R. D. Laing calls the "false self"—the self visible to the world (hence objectively "real") but dishonest in what it makes visible—is, though audible, incoherent; the "real self," though coherent, is mute. Encased in the language the characters use to keep reality at bay—a language that is false, inappropriate, theatrical—the gestures of that self leave little trace.

When painful subjects break past such inhibitions, speakers and listeners alike automatically turn off. Their attention flags; their thoughts wander; they interrupt themselves and one another. "Serious" talk quickly turns commonplace. When it doesn't, they help it to:

And what about the Jews? The refugees . . . The Jews . . . People like ourselves, beginning life again . . . But it's always been the same. . . . My old mother, who's over eighty, can remember . . . Yes, she still reads without glasses. . . . How amazing! Well, don't they say, after eighty . . . (BA 121; elisions in original. Note that the conversation is back on "safe" ground immediately.)

Even those who want to speak openly to others cannot. Words fail them, or courage.

Moved by Lucy Swithin's kindness, Dodge longs to pour out his anguish:

"At school they held me under a bucket of dirty water, Mrs. Swithin; when I looked up, the world was dirty, Mrs. Swithin; so I married; but my child's not my child, Mrs. Swithin. I'm a half-man, Mrs. Swithin; a flickering, mind-divided little snake in the grass, Mrs. Swithin . . . but you've healed me. . . ." So he wished to say; but said nothing. (BA 73)

Like Mr. Ramsay seeking to embrace his dead wife, the characters grope in vain for living contact. All that is granted them is the momentary awareness of a lack, an absence, an incapacity, a lost vocabulary: " 'We haven't the words—we haven't the words,' Mrs. Swithin protested. 'Behind the eyes; not on the lips; that's all.' "

" 'Thoughts without words,' her brother mused. 'Can that be?' " (BA 55); a passing sense of their own ineptitude ("I can't put two words together. I don't know how it is—such a chatterbox as I am with my tongue, once I hold a pen" [BA 61]; "Contemplating the idiot, Mr. Streatfield had lost the thread of his discourse. His command over words seemed gone" [BA 194]).

To the extent that it contributes to their world what little honesty and coherence it will tolerate, silence is a positive force in the lives of the characters. It is the medium of what little conscious life and real communication they allow, the medium in which they are most truthful—the only one in which they allow themselves to be direct (" 'Or what are your rings for, and your nails . . . that little straw hat?' said Isabella, addressing Mrs. Manresa silently and thereby making silence add its unmistakable contribution to talk" [BA 39]). But the impact of such "contributions" is negligible: if the characters prefer on the whole not to speak aloud, they also would on the whole rather avoid the truth, even in their thoughts, than face it. Whether "audible" or not, the language they prefer is a mode of oblivion. Rather than being the vehicle by which thought "finds itself" (a phrase of Cassirer's), apprehends reality, shares its findings, language is the medium in which thought loses itself, falsifies its impressions, takes flight from the world, trivializes spiritual life. Such language is an instrument of severance, distortion, desolation. It is in the service not of "being," but of what Woolf calls moments of "non-being"—of unconsciousness, forgetfulness, failures of consciousness; moments when the mind and the world it makes "visible" to itself are obscured, dimmed, wrapped, as Woolf puts it, in "nondescript cotton wool" (MB 70); moments like the state of death Isa imagines as she strips a leaf of Old Man's Beard, "shrivelling the shreds in lieu of words, for no words grown there, nor roses either" (BA 208).

Upon occasion, words are both audible and "felt"—do in fact connect people, have some palpable impact (instead of being lost, unheard, "drowned out"). Rather than being the vehicle of mental life, however, words on such occasions mimic the attributes and processes of the material universe. As in primitive thought, these words have an immediate physical impact rivaling that of the external world. "Thing-like," alive; "active" not inert, they assert themselves with uncanny force: in mindless bursts of energy, as objects with sensuous, even erotic, properties that the characters taste and touch; that have density, color, sound; that "harden" or melt and dissolve like candies ("they were talking—not shaping pellets of information or handing ideas from one to another, but rolling words like sweets on their tongues; which, as they thinned to transparency, gave off pink, green, and sweetness" [BA 10]—the content is idle chitchat). There are words that reverberate like chimes; words with kinetic power and perfected form ("The words [some lines of Byron] made two rings, perfect rings, that floated them, herself and Haines, like two swans down stream" [BA 5]); words that vibrate between two characters, attaching them viscerally, sexually, like some uncanny umbilical cord (" 'In love,' she must be . . . since the words he said, handing her a teacup . . . could so attach themselves to a certain spot in her; and thus lie between them like a wire, tingling, tangling, vibrating [like] the infinitely quick vibrations of [an] aeroplane propeller" [BA 14–15]). These words—we never learn what they were—constitute Isa's total erotic experience with Haines; she does not encounter him again.

Words on such occasions may take on sinister as well as sensuous powers; they besmirch ("words the defilers . . . words the impure" [BA 190]); turn loathsome ("coarse words descending like maggots" [BA 203]); hurt ("pellets of information" [BA 10]); distance rather than connect people ("Her words peppered the audience as with a shower of hard little stones. Mrs. Manresa . . . felt as if her skin cracked when she smiled. There was a vast vacancy between her, the singing villagers and the piping child" [BA 78]); become conscious, accusing ("The words rose and pointed a finger of scorn at him" [BA 149]), hostile, dangerous ("Words this afternoon ceased to lie flat in the sentence. They rose, became menacing and shook their fists at you. This afternoon he wasn't Giles Oliver come to see [the pageant]; manacled to a rock he was, and forced passively to behold indescribable horror" [BA 59–60]).

Whether their effect is sinister or sensuously pleasurable, the words that palpably affect the characters have an uncanny existence of their own. With few exceptions they are more "real," more active, tangible, and vital than the actual objects, activities[20] or persons[21] that make up the world of Pointz Hall. Like almost all utterances in the novel, however, such words sever themselves from "thought" as such; they may have "charge," but they do not have meaning ("Words of one syllable sank down into the mud. She [La Trobe] drowsed; she nodded. The mud became fertile. Words rose above the intolerably laden dumb oxen plodding through the mud. Words without meaning—wonderful words" [BA 212]). Compared with the characters, though, they do have life. When the characters are not spectral they are mechanical, false, lifeless; with "glazed" "china faces" (BA 156); "plated" (BA 202); "stuffed" rather than flesh and blood (BA 40); or vague, limp, fizzled ("What word expressed the sag at his heart . . . as the retreating Manresa . . . ripped the rag doll and let the sawdust stream from his heart?" [BA 202]). Silence, distance, isolation, remoteness, vacancy, incoherence, absence; "disembodied voices," "bodiless eyes"; inaudible, broken, "abortive" communications; pursuits of persons pursuing others (all in vain); ritualized gestures and unconsummated desires: these are the qualities, attributes, and activities that "fill" the characters' world, shape their experience, reflect their spiritual state.

The narrator alone has a language and a sensibility capable of transforming this state into something resembling beauty; she is drawn to its possibilities of artifice, stillness, cold perfection—qualities the novel has, qualities of her own style, qualities she celebrates when she takes us, ghostly spectators, into the empty room to look at the painting whose costumed, slightly artificial figure leads "the eye up, down, from the curve to the straight, through glades of greenery and shades of silver, dun and rose into silence" (BA 36). The room itself resembles the painting it holds (which looks "at nobody" but draws its viewers "down the paths of silence" [BA 45]). "Empty, empty, empty; silent, silent, silent. The room was a shell, singing of what was before time was; a vase stood in the heart of the house, alabaster, smooth, cold, holding the still, distilled essence of emptiness, silence" (BA 36–37).

The characters, however, know nothing of the aesthetics of silence or alabaster perfection. Preempting their attention in vampire fashion, the lure of nonbeing saps their lives of color, vibrance, vitality. (Even their names suggest something elusive, insubstantial—"Dodge," "Trixie," "Giles," "Candish," "Old Flimsy," "Sands.") So far as their language goes, whether it is an instrument to deflect or replace thought and the world or whether words (like the characters) are ghostly (unheard, inaudible) or (unlike the characters) preternaturally vivid, alive, sensuous, the effect is finally the same: to give life to hallucination, to deaden, drain, and inauthenticate reality.

The Pageant and the Audience

What cure indeed for such a world? Yet in the figure of Miss La Trobe the novel explores at some length the possibility of the artist as an ameliorating force for social change, specifically a female artist who is a sexual and social outcast (she is a lesbian, a loner, a drinker, not much liked) in the community—itself a microcosm of society as a whole—that gathers at Pointz Hall. La Trobe is author and director of the pageant that is the novel's main event and the purpose of the gathering. Though it sparks some joy, the pageant for the most part fizzles ("What idea lay behind, eh? What made her indue the antique with this glamour—this sham lure, and set 'em climbing . . . up the monkey puzzle tree?" [BA 97]). Yet it is both a daring and a clever work. In spite of the local setting and amateur cast, it is also an ambitious one, at least in intent. Its author is out to do more than "entertain" her audience—a fact that, when people begin to sense it, they do not like. The collision between her efforts and their response is the source of what "drama" there is in the novel and is the concern of this section.

La Trobe of course does hope to entertain the group. But though she wishes to please ("delight") the audience, she also seeks to make it recognize in the "mirror" of the present, the images of the past, and the abyss of the future its own nature revealed and arraigned. Like Artaud,[22] she wishes to enchant her audience in order to unblind—and, in so doing, change—it. Unlike Artaud, however, she cannot find a way to do both at once. To the extent that she achieves either goal, it tends to be at the expense of the other. She has in fact a number of hopes for her work that, for various reasons, do not pan out: she hopes to tap the hidden potential of the spectators, to "twitch the invisible strings" within them so that they may find revealed their "unacted part" (BA 153) ("the dream of the unlived life," as Rilke puts it), the awareness of which they have suppressed. So far as we know, she achieves notable results with only one person, Lucy Swithin ("Old Flimsy"), who confesses that her unacted role is Cleopatra! (The scene is touching but, like much in the novel, also tongue in cheek.) To cleanse the audience's perception and awaken its conscience, La Trobe tries at the end "to expose them, as it were, to douche them, with present-time reality." "But something was going wrong with the experiment. 'Reality too strong' " (BA 179). The audience balks even at matters of decor that seem far out: "Swathed in conventions, they couldn't see, as she could, that a dish cloth [as a turban] in the open looked much richer than real silk" (BA 64). She has better luck (though not consistently) stirring their feelings than educating their taste. She wants to "brew" and sustain emotion ("the emotion must be continued" [BA 139]). Among the emotions she does brew is intoxication (BA 94), but her aim is at least in part political: she wishes to make the spectators "see" that their behavior and their values are implicated in the world events taking place; that the corruption of previous ages is manifest in all three.

The goal is political, but the route is pleasure. By intoxicating her audience she hopes to stir its sense of oneness; that Dionysiac rapture in which, as Nietzsche puts it, "the individual forgets himself completely. . . . expresses himself through song and dance as the member of a higher community."[23] In that state perhaps she can make it "see" what before it did not ("'for one moment she held them together—the dispersing company. Hadn't she, for twenty-five minutes, made them see?'' (BA 98). In part she hopes the results will, if not "cure," offer some respite to their (and perhaps her own) pain (a "vision imparted was relief from agony . . . for one moment" [BA 98]). Her major aim in seeking to enrapture and awaken the audience, however, is to make something different *of* its members than the murderers, thieves, and liars that, in the pageant's final speech, she tells them point blank they are.

They are quick to elude the spell; the amateurishness inevitable in local pageantry helps them: "Every moment [of delay] the audience slipped the noose; split up into scraps and fragments" (BA 122). (Though chance events occasionally abet La Trobe, they are few, and they are occurrences of "nature."[24] The human performers are less helpful, forgetting lines, mumbling, and so forth. Nor is nature always on the author's side ("the wind blew their words away" [BA 124]; "half their words were blown away" [BA 78]; "The breeze blew gaps between their words" [BA 139]).

All her aims, in fact, more or less fail. She comes closest to "enchanting" her audience by strategies least apt to unblind it: devices too conventional to upset the spectators' equilibrium or challenge the commonplaces that rule their behavior and cloud their consciousnesses. When, more faithful to the stringent nature of her vision, her strategies are bolder, the audience balks. It prefers traditional techniques and has traditional expectations. Up to a point these are appropriate. For the pageant as a genre is deeply rooted in local history and custom—a fact La Trobe exploits by imitating fragments of the literary past—the style, subject, themes, and rhetoric of "the poets from whom we descend by way of the mind" (BA 68) (and, occasionally, of political oratory). But her borrowings have a thrust. They are not simply imitations, they are parodies. In spite of its traditional and festive mask, the pageant does not celebrate English character, history, "destiny," consciousness, or progress, it indicts them[25]—and the civilization of which Nazi Germany no less than England is a part. Nor is La Trobe's approach "traditional." The *form* of her pageant (as well as its props, technology, and other accouterments) unmistakably betrays its modernity. Exploiting the diversity inherent in the pageant as a genre,[26] she achieves effects that are increasingly daring and innovative. Her "conventional" touches are in fact few: aesthetically as well as politically, the work is radical. She fragments episodes, even single speeches; a demonic (and unreliable) machine solilo-quizes, chants nursery rhymes, makes unbearable noises, falls silent when it isn't supposed to, gets nasty with the audience; the costumes are "pop art" (made from ordinary domestic materials—scouring pads, cardboard, silver paper, "six-penny dish cloths" [BA 62]). Random intrusions, "chance" events, cacophonous noises (John Cage: "It goes without saying that dissonances and noises are welcome in this new music")[27] choreograph themselves into the production (parodying the notion of cosmic purpose and design), for the most part with the artist's blessing. Fragments of scenes represent and imply entire works being parodied (including their form, style, world view).[28] Truncations of the plot, deafening shouts, omissions and deliberate obfuscations cut a "knot in the centre" (BA 91) both of the scenes being performed and of the audience's understanding of them.[29]

Though there are moments when the pageant delights the audience, it grows increasingly restive. Its sensibilities are offended by what it considers the crazy tricks and sheer wantonness of the technique; it grows increasingly suspicious about the point ("message") and meaning of the pageant (which the preacher, Streatfield, tries to sum up, but cannot). What little the au-dience does understand, it resents. Petulant, evasive, fitful, it rejects the work's attempt to include them in its indictment of the human condition in general. That underlying motive, moreover, becomes increasingly pointed. As the acts progress, the "unmasking" of the fictions each age sustains about itself becomes more blatant; the critique of these grows more scathing; the innocence of the past is shown to be more and more suspect; the present becomes more and more obviously a hidden target in the pageant's exposure of "historical" epochs; the audience increasingly is implicated—both on-tologically and morally—in the entire spectacle.

These changes reflect themselves in the pageant's progressively daring technical innovations. By the final act ("The Present Time. Ourselves") dramatic representation and parody alike disappear, to be replaced by a "hap-pening" in which the audience not only is forced to become conscious of itself but [may be] assigned "the same ontological status as the per-formers."[30] There is no "performance" on the stage area at all—not a scene or a skit or an actor—no representation whatever of an imaginary universe.

After an unendurable delay, members of the cast appear flashing mirrors and pieces of mirrors at the audience, forcing those they can to stare at their own reflections. After this an unknown amplified voice ("megaphonic, anonymous" [BA 186]) denounces the spectators as tyrants, liars, thieves. (I will return to this in a moment.)

Paramount among the techniques of happenings is abuse and teasing of the audience ("The audience may be made to stand uncomfortably in a crowded room, or fight for space to stand on boards laid in a few inches of water. There is no attempt to cater to the audience's desire to see everything. In fact this is often deliberately frustrated.")[31] As is the case with "Present Time," happenings are of "unpredictable" duration (the audience "frequently does not know when [they] are over, and has to be signalled to leave." Moreover, happenings, too, have no plot or story, "therefore no element of suspense." The audience becomes part of this plotless performance ("the audience becomes to a certain extent its own spectacle").[32]

So far as "duration" goes, the audience of "The Present Time. Ourselves" does not understand that the act has begun or, even retrospectively, when it began, for nothing gives them a cue. (The reader here has the advantage of knowing La Trobe's stage directions: "try ten mins. of present time. Swallows, cows, etc." [BA 179]). Not only have ordinary dramatic conventions (or La Trobe's freehand versions of these) been abolished, but this has been done "without warning, abruptly." There are no devices that signal "beginnings" (music, voices, actors appearing, etc.): La Trobe's directions in fact specifically forbid music at the act's opening. Nor are the spectators cued to shift their "ordinary" (traditional, conventional) expectations. Except for the "tick" of the disembodied machine, "the horns of cars . . . the swish of trees" (BA 178) and the audience's own chatter, there is no sound. Nor is there anything to see: "Nothing whatever appeared on the stage" (BA 176) (a phrase that is repeated three pages later).

The emotional effect of this misunderstood silence, prolonged wait, empty stage, and absence of cues on the audience is irritation, distress, exasperation ("All their nerves were on edge. They sat exposed. The machine ticked. There was no music" [BA 178]). The spectators feel "strung out," suspended in a no-man's-land between the illusion cast by the previous act and the reality of the present moment ("They were neither one thing nor the other; neither Victorian nor themselves. They were suspended, without being, in limbo. Tick, tick, tick went the machine" [BA 178]). A disagreeable consciousness of "dead time" and of their own unhappiness begins to assail them. They question the purpose of the entertainment, feel trapped, maddened ("They were all caught and caged; prisoners; watching a spectacle. Nothing happened. The tick of the machine was maddening" [BA 176]).

Except for some momentary respites (provided by the shower, the setting up of props that are in fact not used, the playing of a nursery tune (on that soothing patriarchal theme, "The King is in his Counting House, counting out his money / the Queen is in her parlour, eating bread and honey") followed by "A waltz, was it? Something half known, half not" (BA 182), the audience is not let off the hook. Two more assaults upon its composure soon take place: a piece of music (only identifiable as "Very up to date," "Jazz? Anyhow the rhythm kicked, reared, snapped short. What a jangle and a jingle! . . . What a cackle, a cacophony! Nothing ended. So abrupt. And corrupt. Such an outrage; such an insult. And not plain" [BA 183]) and the introduction of the mirrors ("Ourselves? But that's cruel. To snap us as we are, before we've had time to assume . . . And only, too, in parts. . . . That's what's so distorting and upsetting and utterly unfair" [BA 184]; elisions in the original).

In their break with traditional techniques and daring assault upon the audience, these strategies not only anticipate those of happenings but rouse the same ambivalent responses ("Do they [happenings] shock for therapeutic or terroristic ends? Do they celebrate a forward-looking defiance of the ruling myth or a black mass of their own?").[33] In a milder vein, someone at the pageant protests, "It's true, there's a sense in which we all, I admit, are savages still. Those women with red nails. And dressing up—what's that? The old savage, I suppose. . . . [But] the mirrors! Reflecting us . . . I called that cruel. One feels such a fool, caught unprotected" (BA 199). As the force of these assaults accumulates, the attack begins to seem "personal."[34] The audience grows hostile, attributing its discomfort to personal malice on the part of La Trobe ("So that was her little game! To show us up, as we are, here and now!" [BA 186]).

The restiveness of the audience is not without point. The pageant ends with a direct address to the spectators, making its indictment of them explicit and summing up the motifs of the previous acts—the behavior, values, and vices that were the targets of the parodies in those acts, vices called by name for the first time—the "tyrannies and servilities" that both the pageant and the novel represent as common to the present as well as the past, to the audience as well as the characters of the spectacle, to the public life and private life of all classes, all ages, of any epoch, and in any society, England as well as Hitler's Germany, organized by the patriarchal principles, institutions, and politics of what "we mis-call civilization":

Before we part, ladies and gentlemen, before we go. . . . let's talk in words of one syllable, without larding, stuffing or cant. . . . And calmly consider our selves. Ourselves. Some bony. Some fat. (The glasses confirmed this.) *Liars most of us. Thieves too. . . . The poor are as bad as the rich are. Perhaps worse. Don't hide among rags. Or let our cloth protect us. Or for the matter of that book learning; or skilful practice on pianos; or laying on of paint. Or presume there's innocency in childhood. . . . Or faith in love. . . . Or virtue in those that have grown white hairs. Consider the gun slayers, bomb droppers here or there. They do openly what we do slyly. Take for example . . . Mr. M's bungalow. A view spoilt for ever. That's murder. . . . Or Mrs. E's lipstick and blood-red nails. . . . A tyrant, remember, is half a slave. Item the vanity of Mr. H. the writer, scraping in the dunghill for sixpenny fame. . . . Then there's the amiable condescension of the lady of the manor—the upper class manner. And buying shares in the market to sell 'em. . . . O we're all the same. . . . Look at ourselves, ladies and gentlemen! . . . and ask how's this wall, the great wall, which we call, perhaps mis-call, civilization, is to be built by* (here the mirrors flicked and flashed) *orts, scraps and fragments like ourselves?* (BA 187–88)

La Trobe's attack is not limited to the contemporary world. The behavior and values she assails recapitulate the major themes of the preceding acts: unprepossessing physical appearances and whether or not they are acknowledged; language ("larding, stuffing . . . cant") that distorts the truth, disguises motives, rationalizes both political and personal exploitation, hides feelings; lying, thievery, the culpability of the poor ("Each bead . . . a crime" [BA 89]), as well as the rich (Lady Harpy Harridan's plot with Sir S. Lilyliver to swindle her niece); the effort of both to "hide"—either behind their poverty and rags (as when the crone Elsbeth extends her "skinny forearm from her ragged shift" to avoid being tortured) or their "cloth," education, and cultural accomplishments (Sir Lilyliver's inflated rhetoric of polite compliment with which he hides his loathing of Lady Harridan); the debunking of "innocency in childhood" (England as a "child"); of faith in love, virtue in age.

Even references that are clearly contemporary (bomb dropping, profiteering on the stock market, cluttering the environment with ugly buildings) echo major themes of the previous acts: the plunder and piracy of the Elizabethan "age of exploration"; the imperialism of the age that equated "prosperity" with "respectability"—" 'Er Majesty's Empire" (BA 161) (when the shah of Persia, sultan of Morocco, black men, white men, tourists "all of 'em Obey the Rule of my truncheon" [BA 162]; "Let 'em sweat at the mines; cough at the looms. . . . That's the price of Empire; that's the white man's burden'' [BA 163]).[35] However obliquely, the pageant throughout "hovers" over the topics of tyranny, oppression, violence, personal betrayal; sexual, political, and economic exploitation; power relations based on class, gender, race, religion, and state; distorted family and "love" relationships; lives contaminated by "the corrupt murmur; the chink of gold and metal" (BA 156) that is the background music of our civilization; ideologies that rationalize and language that glorifies these practices, disguising their real nature in a variety of clichés, bombast, and other distortions. The various acts mime the rhetoric of patriotism, of love, seduction, class, domestic relations, religion, ethics, "morality," and power politics. But when La Trobe comes to Present Time she allows *no* rhetoric—except what she hopes the audience will "hear" when made conscious of its own conversation. Though her final speech is a peroration of the major themes of the entire pageant, its style is plain, its comments are direct, its thrust is explicit.

Its effect, however, is another matter. La Trobe's satire of the rhetoric, values, manners, social priorities, literary forms, politics, and world view of successive ages of English history is predicated upon the assumption (so crucial to modernists like Brecht, Artaud, Peter Weiss) that an audience that *sees* deplorable truths, hitherto unconscious, hidden, or denied, will not only deplore but seek to abolish the circumstances that brought them into being. La Trobe's pageant is directed toward the moral and political change of the spectators based upon such an awakening of consciousness. As we have seen, however, she is successful only in making them feel attacked, not in having them see—or at least admit—why. They do not understand that the pageant's scathing view of contemporary life (or of the past) is impersonal; that La Trobe is not slandering but seeking to transform them. Between her and her audience tyranny reigns ("I am the slave of my audience" [BA 211]), dialogue fails; the relation is one of servitude, resistance, seduction gone awry. Morally deaf, complacent even in their despair, passive yet recalcitrant, they will not, do not, or cannot hear ("see") what she is saying. The cord is snapped, the frail cord that alone (for Virginia Woolf) justified her endeavors as an artist and seemed to her increasingly presumptuous in the face of the catastrophic war that to her meant the end both of "civilization" and of her own "last lap." Yet she did not and could not stop writing. The tension the novel establishes between La Trobe and her audience—the performance and its reception, the intention and the effect, reflects, I believe, Woolf's own conflict about the value of her work in "an empty, meaningless world" where maniacal events were stripping her not only of an "audience" but of the right to seek one out and, at times, even of the ability to engage in creative activities.[36] Her very identity as an artist seemed threatened:

> Last night aeroplanes (G?) over. . . . It struck me that one curious feeling [as they await news that the French government has fallen] is, that the writing "I" has vanished. No audience. No echo. That's part of one's death (WD 323). [The day Woolf finished "Poyntz Hall" she decided to begin "the next book (nameless) Anon, it will be called" (WD 345).]

Though the war seems "unreal" (a word she repeatedly uses), it reduces all else to insignificance: "These vast formless shapes [the invasion of Holland and Belgium] circulate. They aren't substances: but they make everything else minute" (WD 319).[37] Though she keeps writing, she cannot get over "the odd incongruity of feeling intensely [about her work] and at the same time knowing that there's no importance in that feeling. Or is there, as I sometimes think, more importance than ever?" (WD 320).

Rather than dispelling this "incongruity," the novel reenacts it. Mirroring the commitment to her art its author could neither disavow nor vindicate in a world gone mad, the fictional situation ends in a draw. La Trobe remains undaunted; her effort fails, yet she will go on writing. In spite of her discouragement at the end of the pageant, she is already conceiving in the "fertile mud" of her mind her next work, though how she will overcome the barrier of misunderstanding, outrage, and blank resistance from her next audience is something she does not speak of. Based on the reaction of *this* one, her prognosis could hardly be hopeful.

La Trobe has an intimation that darkness lies ahead not only for herself but for the world. The beginning of her new play turns out to be a double of the ending of the novel—itself the beginning of the "next Act" of the cosmic drama ("He said she meant we all act. Yes, but whose play? Ah, that's the question!"[BA 199–200]), with its entr'actes, we learn we have been watching all along. The curtain of that drama opens (and the novel closes) on the scene that La Trobe has just imagined, a vision of humanity returned to the darkness of its past, the "night before roads were made, or houses" where two savages on a rock are about to speak. La Trobe is a seer. In addition to divining the future, she is the only one in the novel who tries to redeem the present, to rescue it from the scene about to open. As happened with Cassandra, however, nobody listens.

Notes

1. Virginia Woolf, *Between the Acts* (New York: Harcourt Brace Jovanovich, 1970); first published 1941). All subsequent citations are to this edition, referred to as BA.

2. The first and last "actions" (and sentences) in the novel consist not of the characters speaking—not of dialogue—but of the narrator's telling us that they were speaking or have spoken. The novel begins, "It was a summer's night and they were talking . . . about the cesspool" (BA 3). It ends, "Then the curtain rose. They spoke" (BA 219). "They spoke" are the last words in the novel. We never learn what was "spoken."

3. Virginia Woolf, *A Writer's Diary: Being Extracts from the Diary of Virginia Woolf,* ed. Leonard Woolf (New York: Harcourt Brace Jovanovich, 1973; first published, 1954), 282. Hereafter referred to as WD.

4. While conceiving of the novel, Woolf wrote, "it's to be dialogue: and poetry: and prose; all quite distinct" (WD 275).

5. Jean Guiguet, *Virginia Woolf and Her Works,* trans. Jean Stewart (New York: Harcourt Brace and World, 1962, 1965), 453.

6. William L. Shirer, *The Rise and Fall of the Third Reich: A History of Nazi Germany* (New York: Fawcett, 1962), 664.

7. See a discussion of this event in Diane Filby Gillespie's article, "Virginia Woolf's Miss La Trobe: The Artist's Last Struggle against Masculine Values," *Women and Literature* 5, no. 1 (1977): 38–46.

8. Susan Brownmiller, *Against Our Will: Men, Women and Rape* (New York: Bantam, 1976), 5.

9. Kate Millet, *Sexual Politics* (New York: Avon, 1971), 45.

10. I am indebted to Jane Marcus for calling my attention to the mixture of violence and sex in that last scene.

11. Commenting on Woolf's increasingly pessimistic view of the human condition (in "*Between the Acts* and the Coming of War," *Novel: A Forum on Fiction* 10, no. 3 [1977]: 220–36) at the end of her life, Alex Zwerdling remarks, "By the late thirties this precarious faith [in the possibility of human progress] seemed bankrupt, and Woolf was beginning to think of history as retrogressive rather than progressive."

12. In her article "Some Sources for *Between the Acts,*" *Virginia Woolf Miscellany,* no. 6 (1977), Jane Marcus observes that Woolf in the novel finds "the source of history's cycles as Vico did in human sexuality, which perpetually acts out the war between the sexes as the first war, the first drama."

13. Ibid.

14. The rare exceptions to this summary of the male characters are a few working-class males who have rural occupations and are profoundly in touch with the natural world, like Bond (whose name suggests that connection), the cowman, who is "fluid and natural" (BA 77). Though he is "like a withered willow, bent over a stream, all its leaves shed," there is still in his eyes "the whimsical flow of the waters" (BA 28). He speaks "cow language" (BA 28).

15. As Alex Zwerdling points out, Lucy, though "warmhearted" is also "dim-witted," and the novel not only satirizes her but calls "into question the whole benevolent world view in which she believes and which Woolf herself once took rather more seriously." Zwerdling, "*Between the Acts* and the Coming of War," 230.

16. In the first third of the book, the characters *talk* about the following subjects (those that have to do with present events characteristically trail off into associations with the past): the cesspool, local and national history, passage of time, graves, past wars and conquests, past literature, old families, old houses and the deaths of their occupants, weather of the past, each other's empty pieties, domestic trivia (the fish for dinner; false teeth) (the latter leading to the question whether there were dentists in the time of the pharaohs), prehistory, death, dead poets, not having words to express thoughts, the ineffectuality of art. In the same sixty pages the characters *think* about these subjects: the failure of art, the prehistoric past, the killing of fish, childhood, changes through time, nature looking like a picture, the effects of words, suicide, self-disparagement, violence, the pressure of convention, the deadliness of social judgment, ghosts, the burden to conform, loathing others, the war, being trapped in empty work and life, "desire" (in cliches), the burden both of connection and un-connection ("We're too close; but not close enough"), the desire for success, nature as horrible, death. Among the narrator's favorite topics are silence, emptiness, distance, stasis, death.

17. "Once, [Lucy] remembered, [Bart] had made her take the fish off the hook herself. The blood had shocked her—'Oh!' she had cried—for the gills were full of blood. And he had growled: 'Cindy!' The ghost of that morning in the meadow was in her mind" (BA 21).

18. According to *A Writer's Diary* such avoidance was not uncommon in Woolf's circle as the crisis in Europe gathered force. She repeatedly mentions how "unreal" the war seems to herself and her friends: "One ceases to think about it—that's all. Goes on discussing the new room, new chair, new books" (WD 289–90). Unlike the characters, however, Woolf was aware of her own responses, understood perfectly well what was happening in the world, and, in fact, did *not* stop thinking about it.

19. The characters in fact have a knack for sending and receiving silent messages.

20. Characteristic movements of the characters are retreating, withdrawing, dispersing, wandering, floating. Key words describing them are "detached," "bodiless," "cut off," "separate," "far off," "inaudible," "invisible." Characters see each other reflected in or behind glass; have only eyes or faces; drift past, can't hear, each other. Their voices are "stray"—"voices without bodies, symbolical, . . . bodiless voices" (BA 151). The choreography of physical disconnection, isolation, and spectrality is a metaphor for, and enactment of, their spiritual state.

21. Those who seem "vital," like Mrs. Manresa, are parodied; this "wild child of nature," furthermore, suffers an unmasking at the novel's end: "alas, the sunset light was unsympathetic to her make-up; plated it looked, not deeply interfused. And she dropped her hand; and she gave him an arch roguish twinkle, as if to say—but the end of that sentence was cut short" (BA 202).

22. "Impelling men to see themselves as they are," Artaud writes, [the theater] causes the mask to fall, reveals the lie, the slackness, baseness, and hypocrisy of our world . . . and . . . invites [the audience] to take, in the face of destiny, a superior and heroic attitude they would never have assumed without it"—an attitude he explicitly says will alter the way they behave. Indeed, he "defies" any spectator who has seen in the theater "violence and blood . . . placed at the service of the violence of the thought" to "give himself up, once outside the theater, to ideas of war, riot, and blatant murder." Antonin Artaud, *The Theater and Its Double,* trans. Mary Caroline Richards (New York: Grove, 1958), 31–32, 82.

23. Friedrich Nietzsche, *The Birth of Tragedy and the Genealogy of Morals,* trans. Francis Golffing (New York: Doubleday, 1956), 22–23.

24. At one breakdown in the performance the rain "saves" it; at another cows do: lowing in unison, they "annihilated the gap; bridged the distance; filled the emptiness and continued the emotion" (BA 140–41), keeping the illusion alive—for a little while.

25. Jane Marcus points out that "The pageant was and is the perfect form for propaganda, for populist revisions of history." Marcus, "Some Sources for *Between the Acts.*"

26. "Traditionally episodic" ("avoiding complete plot and full characterization"), pageants from 1905 on were used to celebrate local history by means of "dramatic episodes, dancing and processions." "Pageant," *Encyclopaedia Britannica* (Chicago: William Benton, 1969), 17:31–32.

27. "Experimental Music," in *The Discontinuous Universe: Selected Writings in Contemporary Consciousness,* ed. Sallie Sears and Georgianna W. Lord (New York, London: Basic Books, 1972), 45–49.

28. For an elucidation of the paradigmatic nature of the fragment to modernist sensibility, see Erich Auerbach's chapter on Woolf ("The Brown Stocking") in

Mimesis: The Representation of Reality in Western Literature, trans. Willard R. Trask (Princeton: Princeton University Press, 1953).

29. At the end of the Elizabethan "drama," for instance, there is a "medley" in which the actors shout "so loud that it was difficult to make out what they were saying" (BA 90). The "bawling" of the youths and "confusion" of the plot destroy coherence at moments crucial to the audience's comprehension of the "action" and its resolution. This assault on traditional notions of a proper (i.e., "professional") performance—such as clarity of speech and gesture, skillfully coordinated series of scenes—leads Isa to wonder if the plot matters and to conclude, "Don't bother about the plot: the plot's nothing" (BA 91). In "The Age of Reason" (the most elaborate performance), "owing to a lack of time a scene has been omitted" (BA 141). Not surprisingly, it is the climax of the action that has been omitted; it is summarized for the audience on the programs. "We're asked to imagine all that," someone remarks (BA 141). Only Lucy Swithin appreciates the aesthetic possibilities of this demand on the imagination, linking it (as Artaud links modern drama in general) to Oriental theater: " 'Imagine?' said Mrs. Swithin. 'How right! Actors show us too much. The Chinese, you know, put a dagger on the table and that's a battle.' . . . 'Yes, they bore one stiff,' Mrs. Manresa interrupted, scenting culture" (BA 142).

30. Darko Suvin, "Reflections on Happenings," *Drama Review* 14 (1970): 125–44. Virginia Woolf could not of course have known about happenings, though she may have heard about their forerunners, the "provocation performances" put on by the Dadas in the 1920s in Zurich and Paris, which also assailed audiences, though more casually than happenings would do in the sixties in America.

31. Susan Sontag, "Happenings: An Art of Radical Juxtaposition," *Against Interpretation: And Other Essays* (New York: Farrar, Straus and Giroux, 1966), 263–74. One of the "therapeutic" aims posited for happenings, Sontag remarks, is to unclog "the perceptiveness of the participants" and to provide a "cybernated shock" strong enough to purge the audience of its "cozy emotional anesthesia" and some of the "specific frustrations caused by cybernated life."

32. Suvin, "Reflections on Happenings," 140.

33. Ibid., 140.

34. Paranoia begins to surface in "The Victorian Age," which satirizes the age's values ("purity, prosperity, respectability"), institutions, rhetoric, and politics among spectators whose parents were eminent Victorians: " 'Tut-tut-tut,' Mrs. Lynn Jones expostulated. 'There were grand men among them. . . .' Why she did not know, yet somehow felt that a sneer had been aimed at her father; therefore at herself" (BA 164).

35. As Judy Little remarks (citing the same observation by N. C. Thakur) "The Victorian Section strikes again some of the pacifist and feminist themes of *Three*

Guineas and *A Room of One's Own.*'' ''Festive Comedy in Woolf's *Between the Acts,*'' *Women and Literature* 5, no. 1 (1977): 26–37.

36. The war was ''like a desperate illness'' sapping her creative power. Factors closer to home reinforced her doubts about her work. Led by Eliot, the male establishment pronounced *Ulysses* a masterpiece. A month before her suicide, looking at her own volumes, she feels ''shame'' at her own ''verbosity.'' ''Who am I ashamed of? Myself reading them. Then Joyce is dead: Joyce about a fortnight younger than I am. . . . And now all the gents are furbishing up their opinions'' (WD 349). (They were also, of course, furbishing up for battle.)

37. When ''society is in chaos,'' Woolf told the Artist's International Association during the war, the artist is ''besieged by voices, all disturbing,'' such as ''the voice which warns the artist that unless he can show good cause why art benefits the state he will be made to help it actively—by making aeroplanes, by firing guns.'' Society is not only the artist's ''pay master but his patron. If the patron becomes too busy or too distracted to exercise his critical faculty, the artist will work in a vacuum and his art will suffer and perhaps perish from lack of understanding.'' ''The Artist and Politics,'' in *The Moment and Other Essays,* ed. Leonard Woolf (New York: Harcourt, 1974; first published 1947), 225–28. (No date is given for the essay, which, however, mentions Hitler and Mussolini.)

Virginia Woolf
in Her Fifties   *Carolyn G. Heilbrun*

Insofar as that is possible, Virginia Woolf became another person in her fifties. At fifty (more or less) one is either reborn or moribund. Looking back—as one tends to do at fifty, though not too much if one is busy living—Woolf must have felt that her accomplishment was notable. But she also knew she was beginning again. She writes in her diary, after rereading *The Years,* "For my own guidance, I have never suffered, since *The Voyage Out,* such acute despair on rereading, as this time. On Saturday, for instance: there I was, faced with complete failure" (WD 257). She knew that *The Years* was, in a certain sense, a first novel.

Her fifties were not the time of her first awakening; there are more awakenings than births in a life. Endowed with genius, a writer awakens to its possibilities, if she is fortunate, after she has learned her craft. So it was with Woolf. Her love affair with Vita Sackville-West awakened her to her love for women, and to the possibilities embodied in *Mrs. Dalloway.*[1] In discovering this love, Woolf chanced upon the necessary release—as one might turn the dial on a safe, vaguely remembering the combination, hitting on it at last. From the publication of *Mrs. Dalloway* until 1932, Woolf was in what Olivier Bell, editor of the diaries, has called "perhaps the most fruitful and satisfying years of her life" (DVW 3:vii). Then she had to learn a new art, to begin again.

If Vita's was the love that awakened Woolf to her major phase, Ethel Smyth's was the friendship that encouraged her new art.[2] The place of the two women in Woolf's life is reflected in their attitudes toward *Three Guineas.* Woolf expected both to dislike it, but Ethel Smyth replied "Your book is so splendid that it makes me hot" (L 6:232). Vita, on the other hand, accused Virginia of "misleading arguments," which Virginia greatly resented (L 6:240). She didn't mind if Vita didn't agree with her, but she wanted to have it out "with swords or fisticuffs" if Vita did not realize *Three Guineas* was an honest book. "I took more pains to get up the facts and state them plainly than I ever took with anything in my life." "Oh Lord," she continued, "how sick I get of all this talk about 'lovely prose' and charm when all I wanted was to state a very intricate case as plainly and readably as I could" (L 6:243). Woolf had been transformed into a different woman writer than the one Vita had loved.

If Vita's love awakened Woolf to *Mrs. Dalloway,* the writing of *To the Lighthouse* made possible the books that immediately followed it. This transformation was not as profound as the one Woolf underwent in her fifties, but it was essential to it. With the accomplishment of *To the Lighthouse,* Woolf not only was enabled to recognize the fullest possible extent of her genius in *The Waves,* but also freed her submerged gaiety, liberating herself to write *Orlando* and *A Room of One's Own.* Once her struggle with her mother was laid to rest, as Sara Ruddick has pointed out,[3] Woolf was free to write of women and the possibilities inherent in their relationships. *Orlando* was a marvelous jeu d'esprit, a love letter to Vita, restoring to her, as Nigel Nicholson has said, Knole, the inheritance that her birth as a girl had deprived her of.[4] Woolf would have liked, one guesses, to have restored to all women what their talents deserved and their sex denied them. John Graham has written that the second half of *Orlando,* after the change of sex, fails in its use of comedy: the serious elements dominate *Orlando's* "later chapters to its detriment as a work of art." Woolf has, in her own words, failed "to keep the realities at bay."[5] Had she been able to read this comment by one of the best and most sensitive of her critics, she would have recognized it as characteristic of the threat she faced in her fifties. The moment one begins to criticize the destinies of women, even in a less than wholly serious way, the patriarchy (by no means composed entirely of men) feels that art is betrayed. Adrienne Rich was the first, as far as I know, to comment on a note "of dogged tentativeness" in *A Room of One's Own.* "It is the tone of a woman almost in touch with her anger, who is determined not to appear angry, who is *willing* herself to be calm, detached, and even charming in a roomful of men where things have been said which are attacks on her very integrity." Woolf, Rich sensed, while addressing women, was acutely conscious of being overheard by men.[6] But in Woolf's fifties, with great work behind her, she would no longer fear either the expression of her anger or its effects on the men who overheard her.

Significantly, Leonard Woolf shared—indeed, to some extent encouraged—the accepted view of the work Woolf did in her fifties, the work that
did not fear to offend the patriarchy. Leonard Woolf writes: "Four times in
her life she forced herself to write a book against her artistic and
psychological grain; four times the result was bad for the book and twice it
was bad for herself."[7] The four books Leonard Woolf had in mind are: *Night
and Day* (1919), *The Years* (1937), *Three Guineas* (1938), and *Roger Fry*
(1940). Three were written in Woolf's fifties. I shall not discuss *Night and
Day* here, since it does not belong to the period I am exploring and represents
a somewhat different problem (but only somewhat). I believe that *Night and
Day* was an early and premature attempt to grapple with the "assigned
script" of women's lives. In any case, the other three books were written
after what I have called her transformation. They seemed to Leonard, and to
many others, "against her artistic grain" because this is precisely what they
were: a new start, "a raid on the inarticulate." Such an attempt must, of
course, be against the grain in the sense Eliot conveyed in the *Four Quartets.*
Leonard has further muddied the waters by suggesting that in writing *The
Years* Virginia was responding to the accusations of critics that "she could
not create real characters or the reality of everyday life."[8] Such an idea is
simply nonsense: nothing in her history suggests she had such a reason for
writing. It must also be noticed that only *The Years* caused her this terrible
anguish, both in revision and, especially, after publication. She cared little for
the public response to *Three Guineas* or *Roger Fry,* a point to which I shall
return.

But I must digress to say a word about Leonard. His relationship with
Virginia was never an easy one, even in the context of what David Daiches
has called a marriage between a man of great talent and a woman of genius.[9]
The past years have seen harsh criticism of Leonard, some of it—given the
complexities of human life—deserved. I think he was wrong in the judgment
of her work I have quoted. Further, one cannot but feel that to go behind her
back to doctors, to impose upon her a regimem she dreaded, was to decide
too readily that he knew more about her needs than she knew or could
understand. I even believe that Leonard, in failing to understand, as he seemed uniquely qualified to do, the connection between the subjection of women
and the misuse of authority epitomized in fascism, failed in an important intellectual way. But one knows, even today, sympathetic and supportive men
who fail thus. It is not easy to forgive Leonard any of these things, but it is
well to remember that he was backed up in his thought by all the medical
knowledge of his day as well as by Vanessa; and that he was there coping, not

advising from a safe distance, and without the benefit of hindsight. I believe, furthermore, as I shall argue, that Virginia's death was not due to the treatment she received, but to a decision she had taken about life itself, and to the desperate strain of the times. Many have also criticized Leonard for not taking her to Freud or someone among his followers. To be honest about my own bias, let me say that I think, had he done so, Woolf would never have written her novels (she might have written criticism) and would not have lived to undergo the transformation of which I write.[10]

Virginia Woolf, then, began *The Years* with a sense of breaking with the past. She found herself, as she was to write of Roger Fry, "at the beginning of life, not in the middle, and nowhere in sight of the end" (RFB 162). By "nowhere in sight of the end," she meant not that there were an indefinite number of years ahead (she was to write later: "I'm 56; and think that Gibbon had allowed himself 12 years, and died instantly" [WD 289]), but rather that hers was not the condition of old age where one waits and accumulates years. Neither she nor Roger ever faced that. But, picturing death by a bomb, she thinks: "Oh, I wanted another ten years" (WD 340). Nowhere in sight of the end means that one waits not for death, but for the next achievement, the next daring.

I believe Woolf's next achievement was uniquely female. To allow oneself at fifty the expression of one's feminism ("the awful daring of a moment's surrender") is an experience for which there is no male counterpart, at least not for white men in the Western world. If a man is to break out into revolt against the system he has, perhaps for his parents' sake, pretended to honor, he will do so earlier, at a much younger age. The pattern of men's lives suggests that at fifty they are likelier to reveal their egoism than their hidden ideals or revolutionary hopes. I mention this to emphasize what has been so little understood by Woolf's biographers, editors, and, apparently, by Leonard himself: the nature of what happened to her in her fifties.

In Woolf's decision to express her sense of society's deprivation of women, she had two major obstacles to fear. The first, outside herself, was the ridicule, misery, and anxiety the patriarchy holds in store for women who express their anger about the enforced destiny of women. That not even Leonard could understand this condemns not Leonard, but the extensive influence of the system that has served men so well. Even today, after a decade or more of feminism, young women shy away from an emphatic statement of their sense of self. Perhaps only women who have played the patriarchal game and won a self despite it can find the courage to consider facing the pain that the outright expression of feminism inevitably entails. It is worth noting

that, against feminist attitudes, writers and critics who would modulate
their language in other contexts feel free to indulge in tirades. Woolf knew
what she had to fear, but at fifty she thought she had found the courage to
bear it.

The second obstacle was within herself: her own sense of the importance
to literature of separating art and propaganda (to put it in its harshest terms,
which she never failed to do); she saw art and discursiveness as opposed, and
the presentation of "fact" inimical to art. Her sense of art, which had with
the force of a religious principle forbidden "propaganda," was the hardest
obstacle to overcome. Profoundly felt principles are often the bedrock on
which the structure of our sanity rests.

It was this second obstacle, of course, that Leonard spoke of when he said
she was writing against the grain. Or, as Quentin Bell put it, *The Years* "was
a step back, or at least a step in another direction. It could easily be a wrong
direction" (QB 2:195). In no sense was it a step back, but it was a step in the
direction marked for her by the work of Huxley and D.H. Lawrence, whose
writing she recognized as the kind from which, all her life, she had shied
away. She wrote about Lawrence:

> But it's the preaching that rasps me. Like a person delivering judgment
> when only half the facts are there: and clinging to the rails and beating the
> cushion. Come out and see what's up here—I want to say. I mean it's so
> barren: so easy: giving advice on a system. The moral is, if you want to
> help, never systematise—not till you're 70: and have been supple and
> sympathetic and creative and tried out all your nerves and scopes. He died
> though at 45. And why does Aldous say he was an "artist"? Art is being
> rid of all preaching: things in themselves: the sentence in itself beautiful.
> (WD 182–83)

This entry, written a few months before Woolf's fifty-first birthday, must be
read in context. She recalls what she had always objected to in Lawrence,
what in a way would threaten her own sense of herself as an artist should she
imitate it. But after all, if not seventy, she was over fifty and had certainly
been "creative and tried out all her nerves and scopes" in the earlier novels.

Then, just after her fifty-first birthday, she read *Point Counterpoint.* "Not a
good novel. All raw, uncooked, protesting . . . interest in ideas; makes people into ideas" (WD 230). But in a sense perception frees her: Huxley,
younger and less tried than Lawrence, had taken to ideas before taking to art.
This, at least, she could never be guilty of.

It is significant that, when Leonard Woolf edited *A Writer's Diary,* publishing only those sections that revealed Woolf as a writer, more than half the selections were written after Woolf had turned fifty. The first 172 pages cover the years 1918 through 1931. The rest of the book, through page 351, covers the remaining ten years, with only three months of the last year. One might have expected that in the earlier period, the years of her great "artistic" achievements, she would have been exploring her art. In fact, the most interesting introspection about herself as a writer came in the last period, when she underwent an inner debate between her ideas about art and her feminism.

The greatest turmoil surrounded two books: *The Years* and *Roger Fry.* The reasons for this turmoil become clearer if we realize that *Three Guineas,* the book that has most directly annoyed her male editors and, according to Nigel Nicolson, most of her male correspondents (L 6:240), did not cause her any noticeable anguish. For Woolf herself, the battle was over by the time she published *Three Guineas.* Having fought through to the new courage that marked *The Years,* she was free in what she called her "pamphlet" to assume a tone that is far from ladylike, wholly unconciliatory, beyond the charm of *A Room of One's Own*: she was able to indulge the glorious release of letting her anger rip. She reacted with emotion only to Vita's accusation that she had been dishonest. She knew from her hard work on *The Years* that "facts" were difficult to encompass in a novel; soon she would discover that they are sometimes recalcitrant in biography;[11] but in her "pamphlet" she could simply shout them from the rooftops and be glad.

Still, the tone of *Three Guineas,* and its accusation of the connection between the making of war and the treatment of women, *was* angry: Woolf, like all women, had to fight a deep fear of anger in herself. For many years I was made uncomfortable by *Three Guineas,* preferring the "nicer" *Room,* where Woolf never presses against the bounds of proper female behavior—where, it could seem, her art prevailed. I say this to my shame. What prevailed was not her art alone, but her fear (and mine) of arousing the patriarchy to disgust, of acting wholly apart from the "script" assigned to women. For as read in the 1930s *The Years* was easier to live with than *Three Guineas;* for Woolf herself it was otherwise; she struggled with *The Years* and, as her diaries and letters testify, found, in her ability in *Three Guineas* to say the unacceptable, an extraordinary release. She, who had worried so about reviews, did not even bother to read Queenie Lavis through.[12] From first to last, *Three Guineas* was a romp.

"Sunk once more in the happy tumultuous dream," she wrote in her diary; "began *Three Guineas* this morning and can't stop thinking it" (WD 265). And a bit later: "Spiritual temperature went up with a rush: why I don't know, save that I'm having a good gallop at *Three Guineas*" (WD 267). Was *Three Guineas,* she wondered, the achievement of her fifty-five years (WD 271)? She did not mean, I think, the achievement of a lifetime, surpassing *The Waves* or any earlier work. She meant the achievement of being fifty-five, and of finding the courage and relief to utter the forbidden words. The achievement of fifty-five is different, and in its way harder: "But I wanted—how violently—how persistently, pressingly, compulsorily I can't say—to write this book: and have a quiet composed feeling: as if I had said my say: take it or leave it: I'm quit of that: free for fresh adventure—at the age of 56" (WD 278). She had cleared her decks, said what she had always wanted to say, shifted the burden: "now I feel entirely free. Why? Have committed myself, am afraid of nothing. Can do anything I like. No longer famous, no longer on a pedestal: no longer hawked in by societies: on my own, forever" (WD 281). This is the account of a woman who has transformed herself in her fifties.

The transformation had begun with *Flush,* a mock biography of a dog. Perhaps she had in mind a loving parody of Lytton Strachey, whom just then she found newly charming and saw too seldom. She had not liked the mixture of fact and fiction in his *Elizabeth and Essex,*[13] but she was thinking of him with new affection (QB 2:162). And we can hardly doubt that, in working on her biography of a spaniel, she found most tempting the conflict between the doggy fact and doggy fiction or between desire and the demands of an imperious world. She had skirted the issue in *Orlando,* her other lighthearted work: where one's hero changes sex, what other "facts" can one brood upon? But here was a chance to play out the conflict in a canine sphere where few would argue or greatly care. In writing about a dog, she risked being called a silly but not a lout: above all, she would not be feared. She was practicing her scales.

When she had turned fifty in January 1932, Woolf still had before her the task of getting into print the *Second Common Reader*—the memorial volume to the old Virginia Woolf. Bell tells us that she did virtually nothing else for the first nine months of 1932 (QB 2:171). The *Second Common Reader* ends with her essay "How to Read a Book," which closely resembles an essay by her father, also delivered before a school audience.[14] It may have seemed to her, as it surely seems to us, a fitting conclusion to her career as an old-fashioned critic, as her father's literary heir. Once the *Second Common Reader* was finished, she went back to "A Letter to a Young Poet," begun earlier. Here she brought sharply into focus, clarifying it for herself, her sense of isolation, not only from her own generation, but, what is harder, from the young. There is a no-woman's-land discovered by those who expound their feminism late in life. Occupied neither by the friends of their youth, who disdained the fight, nor by the youth of the day, who have not yet taken it up, this land is a lonely place. In her "Letter to a Young Poet," Woolf, in enunciating her separation from the young men of her nephew's generation, expressed her own sense of isolation.[15] Responding to John Lehmann, who had written, "it has never been so hard to write poetry as it is today" (CE 2:185), she must have seen their situation as in some ways analogous to her own. Young poets, she felt, had turned from the world to write wholly of themselves; surely they (like her?) should turn their eyes outward. She easily understood how they felt: "You are rasped, jarred, thoroughly out of temper. And if I am to guess the reason, it is, I should say, that the rhythm which was opening and shutting with a force that sent shocks of excitement from your head to your heels has encountered some hard and hostile object upon which it has smashed itself to pieces. Something has worked in which cannot be made into poetry; some foreign body, angular, sharp-edged, gritty, has refused to join in the dance" (CE 2:185–86). This is an accurate account of what happens to the woman writer when she meets the hard and hostile fact of feminism. Woolf, as she knew, had been fortunate in that the world had allowed her to have her poetry first, but she understood the process young poets struggled with now: "The poet as I guess," she continued to Lehmann, "has strained himself to include an emotion that is not domesticated and acclimatized to poetry; the effort has thrown him off his balance; he rights himself . . . by a violent recourse to the poetical" (CE 2:187). It was not a recourse she would choose.

She did, however, have advice for the young poet, advice similar to what her friend Tom Eliot had written years before. "All you need," Woolf wrote now, "is to stand at the window and let your rhythmical sense open and shut, open and shut, boldly and freely, until one thing melts in another, until the taxis are dancing with the daffodils, until a whole has been made from these separate fragments" (CE 2:191). Perceiving this, Woolf perhaps felt closer in her fifties to Eliot; perhaps she had discovered an affinity with him.[16] She wrote to Vanessa in 1936: "I had a visit, long long ago from Tom Eliot, whom I love, or could have loved, had we both been in the prime and not in the sere; how necessary do you think copulation is to friendship?" (L 6:59). These questions that seemed to cluster around Eliot were the ones she was trying to master in *The Years,* spun out, as she wrote to Lehmann, "in the novelist's way."

Finally, in writing "A Letter to a Young Poet," Woolf faced the fame she

had won, which she knew would be the price of her feminism. The great
poets cared nothing for fame, she wrote. Just look at famous people, she ad-
monished Lehmann and herself, how the waters of dullness spread around
them (CE 194). In seeming to advise on a situation utterly different from her
own, Woolf enumerated the costs of not doing what the world expects of
you. Meanwhile, she played with facts a bit by pretending to be a dog—the
dog, moreover, of a woman whose life was a byword for patriarchal
imprisonment.

Woolf began to write *The Years* at the end of her fiftieth year. As is by now
well known, the novel began to go with great ease, as had *To the Lighthouse*.
She was writing of long-buried feelings, of passions conceived in youth, now
a joy to express at last. The problems began with the revision, and with her
decision to eliminate the feminist ''propaganda'' from the work. I shall not
here retell the whole story of her painful creation of this extraordinary novel.
Suffice it to recognize that an understanding of it awaited feminist criticism,
a discipline as derided, and as undeservedly so, as *The Years* itself. Analysis of
what Woolf had set out to do, and what she ultimately accomplished, became clearer when the manuscripts were consulted. In reviewing here some
of the problems Woolf faced in this revision, I am garnering facts and insights
from the work of recent scholars and critics.[17] My aim is to suggest, in the
light of my own experience of being in one's fifties, how it was that in middle age Woolf found herself uniquely urged toward an artistic act of great
courage. Those professional women of my generation who became frank
feminists in their fifties are few enough, and they had the support of a growing women's movement. This meant practically that, though they would be
derided, they would not be altogether isolated. Woolf had no women's
movement to encourage or support her; her energies were fired by the growing fascist menace in Germany and Italy. What most impelled her, I believe,
was precisely that conviction most derided by her editors: the connection
between totalitarianism and the subjection of women. She was worrying
about the rights of women when, Bell felt, she should have been worrying
about the rights of nations. In choosing to demonstrate the deprivation of
the girls in her generation, Woolf emphasized the connections between
fascism and the patriarchal family. This connection, together with the
presentation of patriarchal family life, was what *The Years* was to embody.
Her terrible struggles with the novel came after the first free writings, in a
revision in which she tried to shape the fiction without the support of the
essay. The result, *The Years,* has been widely misunderstood because its effect
was, after all, a negative: the failure of communication, of solution. Not even

the opening of the professions from which women have been barred—Peggy is a doctor at the end of *The Years*—offers a solution. Woolf understood the fascination "radiated by women who seem to have cut through the constraints and eluded the strictures of the private house,"[18] But she knew that this was a delusion. To change the condition of women, and the condition of the world, one had to change the whole structure, beginning with marriage—the institution conservatives are always most eager to retain. The immense courage behind *The Years* lies here: in the demonstration that there is no solution to the human dilemma, least of all marriage, that traditional haven for one sex conditioned upon the self-mutilation of the other. Woolf looked at marriage, furthermore, with scorn, the only weapon suitable to it; and "scorn is deliberately offensive."[19] She added that offensive behavior is judged heroic only "when carried out on a large scale by men with machineguns."[20]

It has been suggested by Victoria Middleton that *The Years* is "antivisionary," aimed at the very heart of "literary creation itself."[21] This is true only if we are prepared to call "The Waste Land" antiliterary and antivisionary. What *The Years* is, I think, is counter to the visions that had already made Woolf justly famous. When the same critic observes, like Leonard Woolf, that in *The Years* Woolf "chose to work in a mode contrary to her deepest creative instincts,"[22] we recognize how extraordinary it is, in one's fifties, to search out a new creative vein, to allow one's anger to drive one to the discovery of new forms. This measures the terrible daring of Woolf's, and all the best, feminist writing: by its nature it opposes what we have learned from the great art of the patriarchy—that anger is inimical to creation.

All her life Woolf had written against such anger, had, indeed, castigated Charlotte Brontë for this very fault.[23] To discover in one's fifties the courage to go against this conviction is as painful as it is rare. Given the shock of this reversal, it is not surprising that admirers of Woolf's earlier works accuse American critics of overestimating her feminism. As James Naremore has pointed out, Woolf was alone among great modern British novelists in abandoning "nostalgia for the old, predemocratic order of things."[24] She also began to wonder if private values, embodied in women, might not be translated into public values, enacted by men and women.[25] She knew, in any case, that in having given the private values over to women to keep, men had in effect abandoned them. She revealed this in *The Years* and stated it boldly in *Three Guineas*. Her courage was matched only by her relief.

According to Leonard Woolf, Virginia was persuaded against her better judgment to write the biography of Roger Fry. So, at least, it appeared to Leonard and, perhaps at first, to her. But I believe that her assumption of that task was in keeping with the training of the new artist and writer she sought to become. I guess at three reasons why she took on this biographical task, but they are only guesses: perhaps not even she understood them.[26] Above all was the chance to deal with facts, to re-create a life where interpretation must be reconciled with hard evidence: the conflict between vision and fact that she had, in a sense, worked out novelistically in, for example, Lily Briscoe's ideas about painting had now to be confronted in nonfiction as well. Second was the sheer appeal of biography, a form she had always loved, and to which her father, in a sense, had devoted his life. In this biography, moreover, she was writing about a man she had greatly admired, for whom she had felt profound affection. His particular talents and gifts were precisely those she liked to espy in the lives of the "obscure," those who did not fit easily or at all into established institutions. Quentin Bell makes a point of how much she had to suppress, because of pressure from Fry's family, but more important was what she need not fear to unearth. She must have seen the task as a fair challenge. A too-little-mentioned threat to the biographer is that aspect of the subject that is not admirable: the biographer either suppresses it or feels violated by it. The subject of a biography is not like a living friend whom one loves in spite of his or her sinister tendencies: one does not spend one's working hours unremittingly with such a friend.

The third appeal of this task for Woolf must have been the chance to write about a painter, a worker in the visual arts, not in literature (despite Fry's admiration for Mallarmé and its influence on Woolf). Not only was Woolf absolved from recounting painful struggles with literary ideals; she was now enabled to explore her sister's art, which she had previously viewed only as a mirror of her own talents. Bell suggests that Woolf flattered Fry in praising his paintings. Perhaps so. But the writer feels differently toward the painter; ignoring technicalities, she is able to appreciate a kind of vision hidden from, or overlooked by, the art critic. "I could trace so many adventures and discoveries in your pictures," Woolf wrote to Roger Fry. "How you have managed to carry on this warfare, always striding ahead, never giving up or lying down & becoming inert & torpid & commonplace like other people, I can't imagine" (QB 2:181). This seems to me less flattery than notice of something Woolf had learned to admire, to try to emulate: "the perpetual adventure of your mind from one end of the room to the other."

I may as well declare that I do not denigrate *Roger Fry* as others do. It tells us much about Fry, his family (which resembled Woolf's in many ways), his times, his hopes, his achievement. Compared with Frances Spalding's recent biography of Fry, Woolf's seems remarkably perceptive and well written, despite her need to avoid certain facts.[27] Indeed, those who wish a short course in the art of biography could do worse than to study both books. Furthermore, Woolf's biography tells us a great deal about Woolf herself, as is the way with fine biographies: Roger Fry, who—as Kenneth Clark has told us—changed the taste of England,[28] had in doing so left behind him much of the old England that Woolf fought against and would soon recall in "A Sketch of the Past." In allowing her to come to terms both with her past and with what she saw as the inexorable demands of the future, the biography of Fry served to crystallize her new attitudes.[29]

Woolf died shortly after her fifty-ninth birthday. If one is to understand why she ended her life as she did, it is necessary to set down the events of her last year. After she finished *Roger Fry*, Woolf was ill in bed until 28 March, almost exactly a year before her death.[30] In that remaining year Germany invaded Norway, Denmark, Holland, and Belgium; France fell; Italy came into the war on Germany's side. The fear of the invasion of England was real, and the Woolfs, sensibly fearing Hitler's armies, acquired against their advent a lethal dose of morphia from Virginia's brother Adrian. During this year Woolf twice delivered public lectures, always a difficult feat for her, but worse in this time of stress. The Battle of Britain began, with daily air raids and planes fighting over Sussex. Within a month the Woolfs' newly acquired house in Mecklenburgh Square and their old house in Tavistock Square were bombed, the latter left in ruins. Such belongings as they could rescue were moved to Monks House; the Hogarth Press moved to Herefordshire. There was one small, ironic event. Forster, who had so angered Woolf in earlier years by failing to suggest her for the Committee of the London Library (because women were impossible, Leslie Stephen had agreed), now did so: she refused the offer.

Despite the peril and strain of the Battle of Britain, Woolf continued to work on *Between the Acts* and to live in Monks House—largely, compared with her accustomed life in London, in isolation. Between times she wrote "A Sketch of the Past," more detailed by far than any of her previous childhood memoirs, and she began "Anon," her new nonfiction book. In war and middle age, she looked back, trying to organize the past in a new way. In "Anon" the past was history, literature, and the sense of their connections to those whom she had always called the "obscure." She did not wish to write another *Common Reader*, but she was concerned, as Brenda Silver points out, with the battle of the creative instinct's power against "darkness and disruption."[31] Shakespeare and bombs seemed to her at this time, following the advice she had given the "Young Poet, " to be part of the same sentence, the same theme. Yet both the memoir and the nonfiction work were left unfinished. She survived only a month after she completed her novel *Between the Acts.* Why did she kill herself? Why did she lack the strength to survive?

I have already mentioned Leonard's misguided act in going behind her back to consult a doctor; added to this was Vanessa's brutal letter to Virginia—"What shall we do when we're invaded if you are a helpless invalid"—the words of a vigorous person trying to "snap" another out of her despair (L 6:485). These factors were important—coming from the two people she loved most, how could they not have been? But I believe the balance was already tipping away from life.[32]

Woolf *was* in her fifties, a time when one either determines to live as long as possible or begins to count the cost of continued life. I believe she began to reckon as one who has long since determined that life is not worth prolonging at any price. Because Woolf had tried to kill herself before, it has been assumed that her suicide was a symptom of her madness. The excellent article by Susan M. Kenney on this subject, and Nigel Nicolson's introduction to volume 6 of Woolf's letters, should serve to dispel that idea.[33] Woolf's suicide was a free act, a choice; I believe Kenney is right in suggesting that the final choice on the side of life in *Between the Acts* was Woolf's ultimate rendering of the balance of the world, her commitment to the possibility of affirmation. As Kenney well puts it, writing of all Woolf's novels, "She made up for her lack of an integrated, meaningful, and above all comforting vision by literally making it up, creating it not out of conviction or even theory, but out of sheer will and imagination, and she gave it to all her characters . . . . [I]n doing so she was both exerting power over the imagined life, and giving the vision to herself as she existed in her characters."[34]

In the case of Woolf's feelings at the end of *Between the Acts,* however, I do not believe that Kenney's description, perfect for all the other novels, is exact. Woolf's affirmation in *Between the Acts,* as I see it, is an affirmation on the side of life, but, unlike the conclusions of the other novels, it is not a vision of life as she might have lived it. The dichotomy Kenney suggests between Woolf and her characters exists, I believe, up to this last novel: Mrs. Dalloway through Bernard in *The Waves* affirm life in a way Woolf herself could conceive of affirming it, had she had the psychic strength to do so. Her characters did, as Kenney asserts, act for her in ways she might have acted but for the pain. I agree with Kenney that this is what writers do. But I think the vision in *Between the Acts* is a different one: Woolf believed that life would begin again, but not that she would ever be a part of it, even in her imagination. She did not wish to be a part of it, and her characters could not act for her. Thus *Between the Acts* ends with the possibility of a childbirth she had not risked, an act unconnected with herself at that time.

She felt this separation, I believe, because of the state of the world, because of her conviction that civilization was done for, and because her feminism had come too late; she felt it above all because of her isolation, her distance from the London she had loved and from its life. Only those who love large cities and die a bit away from them (though they may cherish country vacations and travel for a month at a time) can know the slow depression that follows exile from a loved city. And when that exile is enforced because one no longer has a home there, because the very city is being destroyed, the country isolation becomes an even greater burden.

Other life might begin again, at the beginning of a new civilization, but not hers. She must have thought with great logic about suicide. Women, of course, can approach suicide with greater freedom from guilt than can men. A man will find another woman easily enough (and Leonard indeed found the companionship of Trekki Parsons), but a man who deserts an aging woman will have abandoned her to loneliness, sadness, and an autonomy she may not be prepared to undertake. This is, perhaps, an odd advantage of womanhood, and one that will, if feminism succeeds, not long prevail. But Woolf might well have thought of it and considered the easier life Leonard might find with another woman. Then, she did not find within herself great powers of renewal. They rarely are present in one's fifties, and they were less so for her now; she had, in any case, never thought of more than ten more years of life—that is the longest extension she ever imagines or contemplates in her letters or diaries. And the battle with what she thought of as "the horrible side of the universe, the forces of madness," seemed to her likely to be lost. As Bell suggests, for her only the feminine as opposed to "the beastly masculine" might have held off the nightmare (QB 2:187). She had done all she could on that behalf, but it must have seemed to her, despite her personal relief in taking up the fight, that it was all too late: "masculine" behavior, extreme to the point of madness, had taken over the world. She chose to end her life before the chance to make that decision for herself could be taken from her.

In 1939 she had recorded in her diary that her friend Margaret Llewelyn Davies "lives too carefully of life." "Why," Woolf asks, "drag on, always measuring and testing one's little bit of strength and setting it easy tasks so as to accumulate years?'' (WD 301). Though Woolf grappled with new ideas, to give her ''brain a wider scope'' (WD 309), the thought of death was never far away. She found herself quoting Arnold on old age:

> The foot less prompt to meet the morning dew
> The heart less bounding at emotion new.
> And hope, once crush'd, less quick to spring again.
>
> (WD 346)

Later she wrote: ''The house is damp. The house is untidy. But there is no alternative. Also days will lengthen. What I need is the old spurt'' (WD 350). It is the voice of Madame de Staël, exiled by Napoleon from Paris. But friends might visit Madame de Staël: Paris was not under bombardment. Woolf tried to cheer herself up, in letters to friends, about the ''snatches of divine loneliness'' and her love for Leonard: ''and my heart stood still with pride that he had ever married me'' (L 6:286). She tried to think of the future for her friends, telling Ethel Smyth that there had never been a woman's autobiography: ''I should like an analysis of your sex life,'' Woolf wrote, reminding Smyth that no woman had yet told the truth. But she knew that even if such an analysis ever came (as it has in our time) she would not be a part of it, not in the flesh. Having totted up the score, she decided that death was the way for her. True, she said in her last note to Leonard that she feared madness again. There had been madness in her past, but madness now was, I suspect, not the heart of the matter; it was simply the easiest way to describe despair, or the clear decision that life in her sixties, given the conditions of her world, was simply not worth the terrible effort it would have cost. She had not, after all, petered out. She had done something wholly new in her fifties—embodied her woman's anger and found a new way to speak about the past—and if the effort exhausted her, she had left behind an affirmation that would last, as her earlier novels would last, long after her life and those terrible times were over.

Notes

1. Although many critics have noticed a change in Woolf embodied in *Mrs. Dalloway,* I am chiefly indebted here to the master's essay of Julie Abraham (Columbia University, spring 1980) on the full implications for *Mrs. Dalloway* of Woolf's discovery of lesbian love.

2. See also Jane Marcus, ''One's Own Trumpet,'' *Chicago Magazine,* June 1979, 201–3.

3. Sara Ruddick, unpublished paper.

4. Nigel Nicolson, *Portrait of a Marriage* (New York: Atheneum, 1973), 208.

5. John Graham, "The 'Caricature Value' of Parody and Fantasy in *Orlando*," in *Virginia Woolf: A Collection of Critical Essays,* ed. Claire Sprague (Englewood Cliffs, N.J.: Prentice-Hall, 1971), 102, 103.

6. Adrienne Rich, "When We Dead Awaken," in *Adrienne Rich's Poetry,* ed. Barbara Charlesworth Gelpi and Albert Gelpi (New York: Norton, 1975), 92.

7. Leonard Woolf, *The Journey Not the Arrival Matters* (London: Hogarth Press, 1969), 40.

8. Ibid., 41. See also Virginia Woolf's letter on *The Years* to Stephen Spender, L 6:122.

9. David Daiches, *Virginia Woolf* (Norfolk, Conn.: New Directions, 1942), 6. Daiches adds that such a marriage "ought by all the laws to have ended in a mess."

10. See also Alix Strachey's essay in *Recollections of Virginia Woolf by Her Contemporaries,* ed. Joan Russell Noble (London: Peter Owens, 1972), 111–18. I base my view on the lives of many women I have known, some highly talented if none a genius of Woolf's kind, whose lives were destroyed, or impaired, by doctrinaire phallocentric Freudian analyses in the 1940s, 1950s, and 1960s.

11. In an essay from those years, "The Art of Biography," Woolf discussed the difficulty of combining fiction and fact in that genre. CE 4:221–28.

12. Queenie Leavis, the Midge Decter of her day, spoke exactly for the patriarchy, as some women have always found it easier to do. The men who edited the Virginia Woolf volume of *The Critical Heritage* still affirm Queenie Leavis, as does Elaine Showalter in *A Literature of Their Own.* Queenie Leavis's criticism is particularly sad because she attacks Woolf on the grounds of class and of Woolf's childlessness, two issues that, above all, should not divide women.

13. See Virginia Woolf's reference to Strachey's *Elizabeth and Essex* in "The Art of Biography."

14. I am indebted here to Katherine Hill, "Virginia Woolf and Leslie Stephen," Ph.D. diss., Columbia University, 1979.

15. Her nephew, Julian Bell, died in Spain on 18 July 1937. Had he died before *The Years* was finished, it is questionable whether Woolf would have found the courage to transform herself. After his death she finished *Three Guineas* and worked on *Between the Acts.*

16. See T. S. Eliot, "The Metaphysical Poets," in *Selected Essays, 1917–1932* (New York: Harcourt, Brace, 1932), 247. If at this time Woolf found herself closer to Eliot, she also found herself further from G. E. Moore and all the sweet principles of his ethics and her youth. When Moore visited Woolf in the thirties, she wondered how she could have revered this man. She was struck by "Moore's lack of what she could only call *mass.*" She could no longer capture the sense of Moore's *force.* Paul

Levy, *Moore: G.E. Moore and the Cambridge Apostles* (New York: Holt, Rinehart and Winston, 1979), 296–97.

17. Important criticism and scholarship on *The Years* can be found in *Bulletin of the New York Public Library* 80, no. 2 (winter 1977). All the articles are important. The article by Grace Radin, "Two Enormous Chunks: Episodes Excluded during the Final Revisions of *The Years,*" is essential to anyone studying *The Years* or the history of its composition and publication. See also Grace Radin's earlier " 'I Am Not a Hero': Virginia Woolf and the First Version of *The Years,*" *Massachusetts Review* (winter 1975), 195–208. Also essential is Virginia Woolf, *The Pargiters: The Novel-Essay Portion of "The Years,"* ed. with an introduction by Mitchell A. Leaska (New York: New York Public Library and Readex Books, 1977). See also James Naremore, "Nature and History in *The Years,*" in *Virginia Woolf: Revaluation and Commentary,* ed. Ralph Freedman (Berkeley: University of California Press, 1980), 241–62. For rare early critical praise of *The Years,* see references in the works cited; also Herbert Marder, "Beyond the Lighthouse: *The Years,*" *Bucknell Review* (1967), 61–70; and "Virginia Woolf's 'System That Did Not Shut Out,' " *Papers on Language and Literature* (winter 1968), 106–11.

18. Sallie Sears, "Notes on Sexuality: *The Years* and *Three Guineas,*" *Bulletin of the New York Public Library,* 80, no. 2 (winter 1977): 220.

19. Beverly Ann Schlack, "Virginia Woolf's Strategy of Scorn in *The Years* and *Three Guineas,*" *Bulletin of the New York Public Library* 80, no. 2 (winter 1977): 146.

20. Ibid., 150.

21. Victoria S. Middleton, "*The Years:* 'A Deliberate Failure,' " *Bulletin of the New York Public Library* 80, no. 2 (winter 1977): 158.

22. Ibid., 162.

23. Michelle Barrett, ed., *Virginia Woolf: Women and Writing* (New York: Harcourt Brace Jovanovich, 1979), 18–19.

24. Naremore, "Nature and History in *The Years,*" 243. See my essay on James Joyce and Virginia Woolf in *James Joyce Centenary Essays,* ed. Hugh Kenner and Thomas F. Staley (Berkeley: University of California Press, forthcoming).

25. See, in this connection, Valerie Saiving, "The Human Situation: A Feminine View," *Journal of Religion* 40 (April 1960): 100–12, and Judith Plaskow, *Sex: Sin and Grace* (Washington, D.C.: University Press of America, 1980). Both authors discuss with brilliance (Plaskow in relation to the theologies of Tillich and Niebuhr) how the Christian ideals are in fact left to women to enact; sins therefore are by definition only male sins, since women already suffer from too much self-abnegation, not too little.

26. Here, and at certain other points, I take issue with Quentin Bell in his interpretation of the facts of Woolf's life. It is important, therefore, to state my belief that he has given the facts fairly and that, where he has prejudices, he has stated them. He

has given us materials no one else could give, or give as gracefully, and if we reinterpret them (and he may find our reinterpretations foolish or wrongheaded) we can do so only because of his enabling work.

27. Frances Spalding, *Roger Fry* (London: Granada Publishing, 1980). Spalding has presented us with many important new facts about Fry. Her writing, however, is unfortunate; she seems oddly drawn to the dangling modifier: for example, "Working so closely together, their drawings became almost indistinguishable" (20).

28. "His influence on taste and on the theory of art had spread to quarters where his name was barely known . . . . In so far as taste can be changed by one man, it was changed by Roger Fry." Kenneth Clark, "Introduction," Roger Fry, *Last Lectures* (Boston: Beacon Press, 1962), ix.

29. See in this connection Virginia Woolf's letters to Benedict Nicolson about her and Roger Fry's world, L 6:413–14, 419–22.

30. The facts in this paragraph are mostly from QB 2:251–52.

31. Brenda Silver, " 'Anon' and 'The Reader': Virginia Woolf's Last Essays," *Twentieth Century Literature* 25, no. 3/4 (fall/winter 1979): 358.

32. L 6:485. Vanessa added: "you must accept the fact the Leonard and I can judge better than you."

33. Susan M. Kenney, "Two Endings: Virginia Woolf's Suicide and *Between the Acts,*" *University of Toronto Quarterly* (summer 1975), 275. The whole article (265–89) is extremely valuable.

34. Ibid.

Three Guineas
Before and After:
Further Answers to
Correspondents   *Brenda R. Silver*

On 12 October 1937 Virginia Woolf recorded in her diary finishing "what I think is the last page of *Three Guineas*. Oh how violently I have been galloping through these mornings! It has pressed and spurted out of me." Thinking back over the history of the book that had been "sizzling" in her since 1931 and how she had forced herself to put it aside, "save for some frantic notes," until she finished *The Years,* she deserved, she felt, "this gallop. And taken time and thought too" (WD 276).[1] In fact, from that fateful moment in the bathtub when Woolf conceived her "sequel to a Room of Ones Own" (January 1931; DVW 4:6), the new work on women had dominated her thoughts and pushed aside her other writing. Although she completed *The Waves* and the second *Common Reader* and drafted parts of *Flush* before sitting down to write her novel-essay *The Pargiters,* she had already begun to marshal her arguments and collect her "facts." (By February 1932, for example, she had "collected enough powder to blow up St Pauls" [DVW 4:77].) After the novel split off from the essay to become *The Years* (January 1933), the essay simmered in the back of her mind until its eruption during 1935, when she began to sketch the book and finally "couldn't resist dashing off a chapter" (DVW 4:346). The turning point was the Labour party conference at Brighton in September/October 1935, where the pacifists were defeated. Between 1935 and the beginning of 1937, when she was finally free of her novel, Woolf devised several scenarios for what became *Three Guineas* as well as continuing to gather facts. All in all, twelve volumes of reading notes made between 1931 and the end of 1937, including three fat scrapbooks of cuttings and quotations, trace Woolf's preparation for the book that she "wanted—how violently—how persistently, pressingly, compulsorily I can't say—to write" (WD 278).[2]

Reactions to *Three Guineas* varied widely. We know that Leonard Woolf did not like it; nor did Vita Sackville-West. Shena, Lady Simon, Ethel Smyth, and Margaret Llewelyn Davies, on the other hand, approved. Many of her close friends were silent, a statement in itself. (Previously she had written her sister Vanessa, "I shan't, when published, have a friend left" [L 6:218].) The most famous public response is probably Q. D. Leavis's attack in *Scrutiny*, "Caterpillars of the Commonwealth Unite!" Even before this article appeared, however, *Time and Tide* had printed an account of the battles waged over the book in the English press.[3] But there were other responses to *Three Guineas* as well: the numerous letters Woolf received from correspondents who felt compelled to refute or support the arguments she had deliberately intended to "[stir] up thought" about the relationship between hierarchy, patriarchy, fascism, and war (L 6:236). On 26 June 1938 she noted "getting the oddest letters" about *Three Guineas*, "which I shall collect, as a valuable contribution to psychology" (L 6:247). These letters, many of them now preserved in the University of Sussex Library,[4] form an essential chapter in Woolf's ongoing dialogue with the culture she had criticized so strongly in the work itself.

Although for the most part we can only speculate about what Woolf might have done with these letters, we can gauge the nature of the debate they generated by examining the issues her correspondents raised in the letters she saved. Shortly after *Three Guineas* was published, she noted that she was "getting a fair bag of the oddest letters" (L 6:239), and she apparently continued to receive these at a steady rate for the next few months. From what I can gather, a great many more letters arrived than those now at Sussex. It is possible that she discarded the ones that simply asked her to explain what she meant—a common request, one surmises, from her moans to Ethel Smyth about the time it took to answer them (L 6:262)—and kept those that led her to call the letters "a valuable contribution to psychology." Despite her moans, Woolf scrupulously answered each of her correspondents, new and old, providing, if only we had the full range of her replies, a sequel to the book that had at one time been called *Answers to Correspondents* (WD 254). Ultimately, however, Woolf's "answer" resides in more than the individual replies; it resides in the direction her thoughts took when she was asked to write an essay on women and peace at the end of 1939, and in her persistent struggle to "fight with the mind," to think "against the current,"[5] to understand and to alter the communal psychology that by that time threatened to destroy life and ideas alike.

To appreciate the full extent of Woolf's dialogue with her culture—and her correspondents—a dialogue that continued long after the book appeared, we must chart briefly the "time and thought" that Woolf gave to the argument of *Three Guineas* as recorded in the twelve volumes of reading notes that she compiled before the publication of her book. The place to begin, perhaps, is the First Essay of *The Pargiters,* the original version of the new book on women, where Woolf introduces her fictional account of "a family called Pargiter": "This novel . . . is not a novel of vision, but a novel of fact. It is based upon some scores—I might boldly say thousands—of old memoirs. There is scarcely a statement in it that cannot be *[traced to some biography or]* verified." (P 9). Woolf's declaration, as she truthfully says, is no "empty boast." As early as January 1931 Woolf had begun to gather cuttings and quotations about women, men, law, sexuality, religion, the Church of England, sports, science, education, economics, politics, and social mores. Her sources included a variety of newspapers and periodicals as well as large numbers of biographies, autobiographies, and social and intellectual histories. If her original idea had been to write "about the sexual life of women," by November 1932, when she had written the first section of the novel-essay, she planned "to take in everything, sex, education, life &c; . . . from 1880 to here & now" (DVW 4:6, 129). Given this goal, it is not surprising to find among her reading notes from this period twenty-three pages on R. H. Gretton's *Modern History of the English People, 1880–1922,* or to discover that these notes appear in the same volume as notes on a biography of Parnell[6] and notes on Montaigne's essay "On Some Lines of Virgil" (HRN, vol. 23). In this last entry Woolf records Montaigne's views about the strength of women's sexuality, the same views that appear in the Fifth Essay of *The Pargiters* (P 109). Moreover, the table of contents for this volume records that it originally contained notes on the biography of Joseph Wright, the philologist and dictionary maker, who we now know probably provided Woolf with the title of *The Pargiters* as well as appearing as a character in it.[7]

But these notes—and others like them—are only the tip of the iceberg; to get the full scope of Woolf's collection of facts during 1931 and 1932 one needs to turn to the first of the three scrapbooks, now at Sussex, in which Woolf pasted the cuttings and quotations that ultimately served as her source for both the text and the notes of *Three Guineas* (MHP/B.16f, vol. 1). Although it is unclear at exactly what point between 1931 and 1938 Woolf decided to create these scrapbooks, the first one is distinguished by containing material that can be dated from 1931 to the beginning of 1933, with a few entries from an earlier date.[8] (For example, Woolf has pasted into this scrapbook two reviews of *A Room of One's Own* and a cutting of her essay

"Two Women: Emily Davies and Lady Augusta Stanley.") Among the entries are quotations that appeared first in the original version of Woolf's speech on professions for women, delivered 21 January 1931—for example, Tennyson in *The Princess;* J. M. Keynes and Vera Brittain in the *Nation and Athenaeum*—and reappeared in both *The Parigiters* and *Three Guineas*.[9] Similarly, other entries from this volume made their way directly or indirectly into the novel-essay before resurfacing in her political tract.

In the beginning of 1933, when Woolf decided to compact *The Pargiter* essays into the fiction (DVW 4:146), she stopped collecting facts with the same energy she had displayed previously—or exhibited again in 1935. At the beginning of that year, Woolf recorded the resurgence of her desire "to write On being despised. My mind will go on pumping up ideas for that" (DVW 4:271). Now, however, the desire to write a book on women intersected with another desire—the desire to write an antifascist pamphlet (DVW 4:282)—so that from 1935 on, when Woolf once more began systematically to gather cuttings and quotations, she focused increasingly on politics, politicians, attitudes toward war, and fascism and on their influence on private lives.

Nine months later, when the Labour party voted to use "all the necessary measures provided by the Covenant" of the League of Nations to prevent Italy from attacking Abyssinia—thereby implicitly accepting the possibility of war[10]—Woolf was catapulted from research into writing. A long diary entry on 2 October 1935 records her complex response to Ernest Bevin's attack on George Lansbury, the pacifist, to Lansbury's own speech ("Tears came to my eyes"), to her distrust of what she saw as a pose in all the men, and to the insubstantial voices of the few women who spoke ("A thin frail protest, but genuine"). "My sympathies," she continues, "were with Salter who preached non-resistance. He's quite right. That should be our view. But then if society is in its present state? Happily, uneducated & voteless, I am not responsible for the state of society." Still not at ease, however, she goes on to ask, "Ought we all to be engaged in altering the structure of society?" (DVW 4:345–46).[11] Two weeks more and the experience bore fruit: "Did I say the result of the L.P. at Brighton was the breaking of that dam between me & the new book, so that I couldn't resist dashing off a chapter" (DVW 4:346). That was 15 October; by 27 October she was "[dashing] off scene after scene" (DVW 4:348).

What were the results of her renewed energy in 1935? A host of reading notes intermingled with snatches of ideas and outlines for the new book, some of them humorous, some not. For example, one notebook opens with an entry headed "Glossary" and shows Woolf creating new words to express new attitudes (MHP/B.16b). It begins with a long, illegible, unpronounceable word—[?Humanno . . .]—followed by the phrase, "of both sexes: but men outnumber women, because they have a family to support." Then Woolf gives some examples of her new vocabulary: "Soldier = Gutsgruzzler. Heroism = Botulism. a hero = Bottle. One who takes honours, (except for admittedly commercial purposes) silly sambo." The entry ends, "Let us substitute for the word feminist the word—to signify one who believes that [women] . . . though now shreds & patches can be brought to a state of greater completeness."[12]

Another entry in this same notebook, headed "The Burning of the Vote. A Comedy. Scene Hampstead Heath," anticipates the tone of the Victorian section of *Between the Acts.* The first page reads:

> Choruses. Songs burlesque,
> [Asquith Enthroned
> mixture of the most absurd Greek names
> with Pot & Pole . . .
>
> Its so much easier to sing of the dawn
> If you're feeling warm
> &c

The second page continues:

> Voices of Victorian mothers wailing.
> The children answering.
> A record breaker passes.
> We will not dine.
>   Joad & Wells.
> May the Lord make us truly thankful.
> But who is the Lord.
> A transparency appears.
> 10,000 a year. The Arch. of Cant.
> The dappled dawn.
> The
> Do not raise monuments.
> Let us not praise famous women.

In stark contrast, other entries in this notebook anticipate *Three Guineas* as it actually emerged. One begins, "The meeting at Brighton. The upshot of it was [men] think war necessary'' and continues in the voice of the letter writer to speculate on women's lack of the only power that counts—force—and to ask what good it does to talk about peace, write letters, or write checks: "all moonshine." A second entry evokes "The horror of war. The Spanish photographs," and the notebook ends with quotations from John Buchan's biography of Francis and Riversdale Grenfell about the glory of being a soldier that reappear in the opening pages of *Three Guineas* (TG 7).

Of the twelve notebooks pertaining to *Three Guineas*, however, the three scrapbooks are by far the most compelling. Only here can we experience the full power of Woolf's devotion to the task of accumulating the facts she needed to support her arguments. For one thing, there is the sheer number of entries; the first scrapbook contains seventy-three, the latter two more than ninety entries each. Then there is the diversity. Interspersed with the cuttings and quotations are a number of manifestos, questionnaires, and letters asking for Woolf's support in some cause, plus a striking—and strikingly negative—description of a service she had attended in St. Paul's.[13] But what impresses me most about the scrapbooks is Woolf's eye for the telling details that reveal the conscious and unconscious attitudes governing behavior—her reading, that is, of the messages encoded in diverse modes of public and private discourse.[14] Spurred by the events of the thirties and her own growing anger, she confronted head-on the destructiveness she had long before attributed to traditional English social structures and values and set out to document its pervasiveness and source. Every book, every newspaper article, became part of her larger vision, even if they were read for completely unrelated ends. A passage from Edmund Gosse's biography of Donne read for the second *Common Reader,* a quotation from Elizabeth Barrett Browning's letters read for *Flush,* verses from her old friend G. Lowes Dickinson's translation of Goethe—all these found their way into the scrapbooks and into her book.

The same insight that influenced her choice of entries also led to their careful arrangement within the scrapbooks. The effect she achieves is that of a collage, the two or three cuttings on a single page often serving as ironic commentary on each other, as well as setting up reverberations that extend throughout the whole. Moreover, the care she took in compiling the entries extended into the creation of the index to each volume. Here every entry is identified by the particular aspect of the cutting or quotation that Woolf wanted to note. A second, shorter index on the cover of each volume provides yet another example of the attention she paid to finding the exact quotation to prove a point.

No wonder, then, that Woolf was pleased when her friends praised the richness of the notes and the excellent use of quotation and was angered by Vita Sackville-West's criticism of her "misleading arguments" (L 6:243). When Shena, Lady Simon wrote to Woolf, "I never imagined you could write a second Room of One's Own which would equal if not surpass . . . the original, & the footnotes raise the whole level of references to a height that no other writer can ever hope to reach" (MHL, 12 June 1938),[15] Woolf responded with some self-disparagement: "It was such a grind, collecting and compressing the notes, slipping in facts and keeping up enough of a dance to lead the reader on so that I couldn't keep my eye on the general aspect, and was much in the dark as to the whole" (L 6:239). But she clearly appreciated this response. Later that summer she appears to have shown Shena her scrapbooks, for in a letter dated 25 July 1938 Shena writes, "Here are two cuttings to add to your collection."[16]

Meanwhile, another friend, Lady Eleanor Cecil—Nelly—had written to Woolf: "I have enjoyed it enormously & maliciously — The best of it is when *you* write something it won't be out of date like a pamphlet but will be there for use whenever the occasion comes — It is 'strong pepper & curry mustard for leading gentlemens' as Mrs. Nansen wrote to me about some speech lately, & I hope the leading gentlemens get it stuffed down their throats again & again — and the backward gentlewomens' too — That is the sad part of the story — If we stuck together as men do – – – wouldn't we have got everything worth having long ago? You have always," she continues, "had an absolute genius for quotation — your exhibits are too amusing & deadly — and your comments — to quote Mrs. Nansen again 'full of Visedom [*sic*] & spirit & truth' " (MHL, 15 June 1938).[17]

Woolf, then, was angered—and one tends to feel rightly—when Vita Sackville-West wrote, "You are a tantalising writer because at one moment you enchant one with your lovely prose and next moment exasperate one with your misleading arguments" (see L 6:257).[18] In her reply to Vita, Woolf was neither modest nor disarming: "It may be a silly book, and I dont agree that its a well-written book; but its certainly an honest book: and I took more pains to get up the facts and state them plainly than I ever took with any thing in my life. However, I daresay I'm reading more into 'misleading' than's there. But Oh Lord how sick I get of all this talk about 'lovely prose' and charm when all I wanted was to state a very intricate case as plainly and readable as I could" (L 6:243).

In fact, the whole disagreement with Vita about *Three Guineas* introduces a number of themes that recur in both the public and private responses to the book and serves as an entree into the issues raised by Woolf's correspondents. For one thing, the letters almost always include praise of Woolf's style, praise that is often qualified negatively by the ability of her prose to gloss over weaknesses in the argument, or associated positively with the reasonableness that Woolf brought to her argument and her ability to slip otherwise unpalatable truths down unsuspecting throats.[19] "My dear Virginia," Philippa Strachey began her letter to Woolf, "I have read it with rapture — It is what we have panted for for years & years — Something that the gentlemen of our acquaintance will be forced to take up on account of its author & will be unable to put down on account of its amusingness until they have reached the bitter end." After commenting on the effectiveness of the argument and declaring the notes "worthy of Beyle," she continues, "Your pen has often before provided me with intense pleasure but this time the pleasure is swollen by all sorts of extraneous currents including the joys of a vent to evil feelings. You don't display these yourself but the exposition of the case for them is extraordinarily comforting to the restrained furies" (MHL, 30 May 1938).[20]

An American woman, writing Woolf from Pasadena, California, put the sentiment this way: "Its cool logic, its irresistible and gruelling humor in picturing the cruel absurdities which have always crippled women's efforts in our pseudo civilization, its rapier like thrusts at the smugly complacent—if often unconscious—masculine assumption that judgment and wisdom are a peculiar endowment of the male, make the reading of your book a real and joyous adventure. Withal, you have done it without a trace of the acrimony and acerbity which so often weaken feminine discussion of the roles which men have imposed on women. It is a masterly performance" (MHP/Letters).

On the negative side, a correspondent with a "knowledge of the labour market" declared: "You probably realise that by virtue of your (literary) seniority the newspaper lords have now given orders to reviewers that your work must be treated with respect. This is an old English custom. Accordingly your last work has been praised but obviously not read. May I suggest, with deference, that you get some brutal minded opponent to read it & criticise it. In its present form, its disingenuousness, apparent suppression of facts, & cheerful acceptance of unverified statements do ill service to the cause you have at heart." The writer's particular concern was Woolf's reiterated use of Ray Strachey's statement, "£250 a year is quite an achievement, even for a highly qualified woman with years of experience" (TG 160). This, the writer asserts, citing statistics, "is untrue" (MHP/Letters).

Vita's criticism of the book was not of Woolf's *facts,* but of the deductions she drew from them: "By my unfortunate allusion to the elegance of your style," she wrote, "I meant that you almost succeeded in convincing one in spite of oneself, until one stopped to reflect afterwards in cold blood. To take an example, I question very much whether any Englishwoman feels that England is not her country because she will lose her nationality if she should happen to marry a foreigner (p. 196). Again, on p. 194, you suggest that 'fighting is a sex characteristic which she cannot share,' but is it not true that many women are extremely bellicose and urge their men on to fight? What about the white feather campaign in the last war? I am entirely in agreement with you that they ought not to be like that, but the fact remains that they frequently are. The average woman admires what she considers to be the virile qualities" (MHL, 23 July 1938).[21]

Vita's two examples bring me to the second recurring theme in the responses to the book: that Woolf's argument and suggestions, particularly her rules for women who enter the professions, her counsel to ignore men's warlike strutting and preening as one ignores an obstreperous child, and her call for women to remain a Society of Outsiders, are impractical—impractical for any number of reasons. One of the most prominent refrains in this criticism, however, states that women are not nearly as disinterested, or pacifist, or willing to work together, or nonhierarchical as Woolf perceives them to be. This response takes many forms. Several correspondents—mostly men, but some women—wrote vividly (and often misogynistically) of women's greed, desire for power, or militaristic tendencies. One man, who identifies himself as an "idealist" and a suffragist with a desire "to see the other side," accuses Woolf of being an "Olympian," in part for failing to see that what appears to be sexual prejudice and opposition is really economic rivalry between the sexes. He then launches into an attack on educating women equally with men when they will only marry and not use their education, and ends by accusing Woolf of supporting "gold-diggers" for suggesting that women have a right to their husbands' salaries: "Supposing," he asks, as part of a much larger argument, "the man is a barrister earning 40,000 a year, & the family lives luxuriously on £16,000 a year; then according to you he should give her £12,000 a year after keeping her in supreme luxury! Forgive my asking Why the hell should he? Are you acting as the giddy gold-diggers' best friend? You don't even stipulate that she need prove to be a good wife to him. Simply that she has a 'spiritual right' to £12,000 a year. (Words fail me here.) 'Because her own work is unpaid.' I only wish my own work were unpaid on similar terms" (MHP/Letters).[22]

Taking a different tack, a male teacher who professes to see little hope for

the "advance of civilization in the attitude, outlook, ambitions or intellec-
tuality . . . of the masses of our male population," writes: "It is no use you
or Mrs. Rance of Woolwich and all those who may be influenced by such
refusing to be Sister Susie knitting socks for soldiers. I suggest that the
women folks in the last War were more enthusiastic for the killing of British
French German etc., soldiers than were any section of our men. . . . You
know Mrs. Woolf the part that women played in the last War — Write a
book indicting them for their blood stained share in it. Who have written
most strongly against War? Our men poets — many of them died in the mud
of Flanders — lousy, rat bitten — and the women (pardon me) who cried
over them dried their tears and found another man — although the one that
bleached in Gallipoli's glare was always to be 'the only one.' Oh heavens,
Mrs. Woolf let's be fair! I believe most sincerely that you want to be fair"
(MHP/Letters).

Other correspondents—mostly women and many of them Woolf's friends
or acquaintances—wrote personally, confessing or admitting that they were
not as free from involvement in the public sphere or political activities or personal ambitions and vanities as they believed she wanted them to be. Often
these correspondents refer to the Outsider's Society and try to decide
whether they could be said to belong. A typical example is the extract from a
letter from Lady Rhondda, editor of *Time and Tide,* to Woolf, printed in the
Letters: "But in my heart I find, it seems to me, such echoes of all the pride,
vanity, and combativeness I ever see in men that I don't need to have it explained — I *know*" (L 6:236). In a long addendum to the original letter, Lady
Rhondda describes in great detail the difficulty of trying to remain an outsider while needing to be considered an insider in order to produce a weekly
review. For this reason, she explains, she is forced to delete women's names
and references to matters concerning women from the publication (MHL, 2
June 1938).

Similarly, Shena Simon writes—and one feels she is serious—that she has
"a confession to make. I am not a complete outsider because I am just
finishing training as an air warden. Whilst I agree entirely with you in
repudiating any responsibility for the present state of the world, I feel that if
war does come I should prefer to be looking after people rather than to be one
of those who had to be looked after." She ends by stating, "However, if —
as is possible — you feel that I have so far fallen short of the standard of the
League of Outsiders — which I admit is the case — that our friendship must
cease, I shall acquiesce though with much sorrow" (MHL, 5 July 1938).

Naomi Mitchison, the prolific novelist and left-wing journalist, some of whose works had been published by the Hogarth Press, wrote explicitly in the guise of "one [of] the 250 'daughters' who are in such an economic position that they can answer your appeal" to question Woolf's call for women to be "disinterested." After explaining in great detail her own private financial situation and why she writes what she does—that is, justifying her journalism—she turns to Woolf's passage on ridding oneself of various "motives" (TG 96) and replies:

> I think one can get rid of the power and advertisement motives and vanity motive, very largely, at any rate, and of the *direct* economic motive. But I can't see anyone but a saint getting rid of all motives, being as utterly disinterested, as you would have us be. . . . we are certain to have some persons we are fond of and want to protect or be biassed about. Especially if we are going to have an adequate amount of knowledge of public affairs, say, to write about them disinterestedly, we shall almost certainly, in the course of finding out, have been inveigled into action and bias. I think you demand an impossible ability to be and remain au-dessus de la melee, which only very long-term-minded people of either sex can achieve. If you are a short-termer, you get involved, as, indeed, I have done myself.
>
> Thus I am questioning the whole policy of "indifference." I think it postulates a very unusual kind of person, one who is not bound to the wheel of affection in any way. How can I, for instance, be indifferent to whether or not my sons get involved in the next war?

Mitchison continues by asking whether one should not become involved in revolutionary actions arising from "intolerable situations" that one shares with one's "fellow-beings," and whether "a writer does not lose something if he or she is remote from action, only a looker-on, dispassionate as a god?" She concludes with an apology: "Anyhow, forgive me for bothering you. Your book seemed like part of an eternal argument that is bound to go on in one's mind, on and off, the whole time" (MHL, 21 June 1938).[23]

I have emphasized Mitchison's response because it states clearly the "eternal argument" that women today still conduct in their daily lives—and in reading *Three Guineas*. Woolf answered Mitchison (as she did all her correspondents) and apparently answered her objections; for a second letter thanks Woolf for going far "to clear up what worried me. . . . Perhaps ['indifference'] is a word which has wrong connotations and should have something else substituted for it" (MHL, 4 July 1938). Unfortunately, Woolf's letter does not seem to have survived.

Other women raised different questions about Woolf's portrayal of women, past, present, and future. One, a Quaker and a pacifist, scolds Woolf for not going far enough in her analysis of the "infantile fixation" afflicting men—that is, for not recognizing women's role in perpetrating that fixation: "are not we mothers as well as fathers responsible in a very large measure for that fixation? Will you not now use the influence of your pen to expose and analyse the tendency in women to keep their sons fixed somewhere at the age of six, or is it two?" The writer also criticizes her fellow pacifists for failing to see that wars are fought for issues, rather than from a "fighting instinct," and ends by saying that women need to go ahead with their political education if they are to end war (MHP/Letters).

Meanwhile, Margaret Paul, a young married woman and family acquaintance of Woolf's who was then a student at Newnham, wrote to Woolf that she should have been harder on the Newnham treasurer. "I think," she says, "partly why my generation are such shocking slack feminists is because the forces are divided, our own dons side to some extent with the oppressors, and our energies are sidetracked into nagging at them, instead of both working to get more women's colleges etc." (MHP/Letters).[24]

And a woman office worker, writing of the tedium and "soul killing existence" of her nine-to-five job, exemplifies in her final comment why women might welcome war even after they have escaped from the private house: "Oh for a war to relieve the monotony. This isn't self-pity its just despair" (MHP/Letters).

Finally, a correspondent who describes herself as a "hermit by choice" wrote in December 1939 after the war had begun, to express her concern about "some kind of organisation among women for after the peace and of course toward it . . . [*sic*] as opposed to the absurd degrading and damaging regimentation of women on 'military' lines which has sapped our influence entirely. . . . It was not until the crisis of '38 that I realised that the mentality of most ordinary influential women was pre-war and pre-vote. . . [*sic*] so when emergency at last arose, the tentative enquirer, the doubtful and even the definitely antagonistic, were swept into the 'military' organisation." What, she wants to know, can she do, not to "retrieve lost opportunity" but "to create fresh opportunity" (MHP/Letters)?

It was this last letter that led Woolf to write Shena Simon on 16 December 1939 that she was "encouraged" in her attempt to write a projected essay on women and peace "by two letters today, one from a soldier in the trenches who says he's read Three Guineas and 'feels that its true'; . . . and another from a middle class provincial lady, who asks distractedly for help, and wants to start an outsiders Society among the women of Yeovil. She's shocked to find them all in uniform, greedy for honour and office" (L 6:375).

Woolf's comment here is a late example of her scattered references to the letters she received about her book and indicates the impact her correspondents had on her. "Thoughts on Peace in an Air Raid," published one year after this comment, offers a clear illustration of Woolf's responsiveness to the arguments raised by her critics and admirers alike. In her essay Woolf speaks directly to women and addresses their role in fostering the "subconscious Hitlerism"—"the desire for aggression; the desire to dominate and enslave" (174)—that encourages war: "If we [women] could free ourselves from slavery we should free men from tyranny. Hitlers are bred by slaves" (174). But there are other aspects of the *Three Guineas* letters that may well have struck Woolf, even as they strike the reader today, as making a "valuable contribution" to her continuing exploration of her culture's attitudes and psyche.

First, in contrast to the reviewers of the book, most of whom ignored Woolf's dissection of the Church and churchmen (or, like Graham Greene, found it old-fashioned),[25] several of her correspondents responded directly from a religious perspective. Quakers, not surprisingly, formed an appreciative audience, and several wrote to thank her. One letter in particular must have pleased her: a letter from Amelia Forbes Emerson, Concord, Massachusetts, who not only equated the Society of Outsiders with the Society of Friends, but traced Woolf's lineage and ideas to her aunt, Caroline Stephen, the Quaker theologian and mystic. Having discovered the family connection, Emerson wrote, "I held in my hand the key to 'Three Guineas' " (MHP/Letters).[26]

Two letters in the collection came from a woman who belonged to a lay group of practicing Catholics who "hate snobbery and love honest work" (she signed herself "Yrs. sincerely in Christ the Worker"). The writer loved the book, which she criticized only for its comments about physical chastity, adultery, and Saint Paul—comments she feared would prevent most of her co-religionists, who so sorely needed it, from reading the work. The first letter also explains why, although "From a natural point of view I would prefer sharing to enforced celibacy," the author chose to remain celibate—that is, her perception of "the natural male craving after polygamy." "I believe," she adds, "that bodily chastity is still one of the weapons for good" (MHP/Letters).

A third perspective is provided by a member of the Scottish Episcopal Church who had previously been active in the militant Women's Social and Political Union and had worked since in other movements for the equality of women. She wrote to thank Woolf for the book, particularly the last section on the Church: "the Church has always given me the old 'Votes for Women' feeling and now since reading your book it—the feeling—is upon me very strongly." Her conviction was that any change in women's position in the church would have to come from outside, "a non-sectarian movement of Christians." Did Woolf by any chance know of anything of the sort (MHP/Letters)?

Other correspondents were less enthusiastic and vented their often suppressed anger by criticizing her facts—a response I call criticism as correction. In several cases what were at issue were Woolf's facts about the Church. At least two people, for example, pointed out that the clergy of the Church of England were not paid by taxpayers' money, as she had implied (MHP/Letters).[27] (Implications that the Church was less than pure when it came to its worldly affairs particularly seemed to rankle.) More curiously, two writers, both apparently clergymen, questioned her statement that Jesus "chose his disciples from the working class from which he sprang himself" (TG 122), arguing that neither Jesus nor the disciples were "working class" (MHP/Letters). Others wrote to "correct" everything from single statements to the whole conception of the book. How, one exasperated woman asked, could the daughters of educated men avoid subscribing to newspapers that encourage intellectual slavery when it is necessary to subscribe to at least three different papers and compare them to arrive at any concrete conception of "the truth" (MHP/Letters)? Another woman wrote to criticize Woolf for ignoring those pioneer women who were earning money and struggling for an education in the mid-nineteenth century, and to whom, she feels, we owe more than to those who fought for the vote (MHP/Letters; this same woman had apparently written a similar criticism of *A Room of One's Own*). Several correspondents, as noted above, criticized Woolf for being impractical, not only because of her views on women, but based on the reality of what was happening in Germany in 1938 and on the rearmament of the rest of Europe. One woman, who raises an argument heard repeatedly during the thirties—as it is today—accused Woolf of confusing rearmament-for-defense with a desire for war. "Your suggestion," she concludes, "that educated women should stand aside indifferently from the whole question is a 'counsel of perfection' when bombs are killing their families and destroying their homes. I am afraid that advice would certainly leave you in a minority of one" (MHP/Letters).

One other letter in the category of criticism as correction is worth mentioning, in part for its glimpse of Woolf's "psychology" and her relation to

the political aspects of the women's movement: a letter from Helena Swanwick, an active member of the suffrage and peace movements, correcting
Woolf's misquotation from her autobiography, *I Have Been Young*.[28] In
describing the income of the suffrage societies in 1912 (TG 160), Woolf had
substituted the Women's Social and Political Union—the radical suffrage
organization—for what Swanwick had actually written: "Mrs. Fawcett's
great Union"—that is, the far less militant National Union of Women's Suffrage Societies. (An interesting slip on Woolf's part!) After providing more
facts about the income of these societies, Swanwick concludes her letter with
what many students of the suffrage movement might consider a rewriting of
history—her belief that Woolf gives a wrong impression when she says that
in 1912 the Women's Freedom League and the Women's Social and Political
Union were "opposed." Their object, Swanwick notes, was one; only their
methods of approach were opposed.

The post, however, brought more than criticism; there were many compensations, and that brings me to my third point. Numerous letters arrived
from women saying thank you: thank you as a mother of daughters, thank
you as a pacifist, thank you as an outsider, thank you as a woman who has
tried in various ways to fight for peace, for education, for liberty, for
tolerance. Many told her their life stories or anecdotes of their experiences
and their efforts to bring about change. Some of these are, to use Woolf's
word, "heartbreaking" (L 6:253); some read like black humor. Several
writers identify themselves as common readers or from the uneducated
classes, even while applauding her attitudes and stance. One unusual correspondent in this last group, Agnes Smith, a weaver from Yorkshire, expressed her agreement with the underlying sentiments of *Three Guineas* but
felt Woolf had ignored the fact that the daughter of the workingman not only faced the same problems of family dominance and subservience at work as
the daughter of the educated man but, being forced to work no matter what
the job, faced them in greater degree. Perhaps, Smith continues, the answer
would be for her [Smith] to write a similar book from the working woman's
point of view (MHL, 7 November 1938). Rather than antagonizing Woolf,
Smith's letter led to an extraordinary correspondence between the two
women that ended only with Woolf's death.[29]

Many of the letters thanking Woolf came from America, thereby belying
those American reviewers of *Three Guineas* who predicted that Americans
would not understand the book, or that it had no relevance for them, because
of their greater democracy, the fairer treatment of women in their country,
and, by omission, their distance from or indifference to the approaching war.

(Several American reviewers, that is, completely ignored the central question of the prevention of war, reading the book solely as a discussion of the position of women.)[30]

Ultimately one letter must suffice to express the response of the numerous readers who, whatever their disagreement with or hesitation about Woolf's arguments, found *Three Guineas* a source of inspiration and hope. The letter came from Gladys Rossiter of London, who before finishing the book had written, like others, to raise the issue of German aggression and to question how Woolf could ignore it. Now, however, she had "finished 'Three Guineas,' and am much moved by its magnificent idealism, and I marvel that you had enough faith to write such a stirring document whilst millions of tiny children (in Dictatorship countries) are being taught to Hate as their foremost creed. I am only sorry that some of the reviewers—mostly males —so deliberately ignored the real meaning and message of your very beautiful work" (MHP/Letters).[31]

One final aspect of the *Three Guineas* letters as a valuable contribution to cultural psychology deserves note: the age of her correspondents and how it affected their reading. One part of this equation, of course, reflects the nature of the reader's personal experience of World War I; another part, however, reflects changes in women's expectations since the Victorian period. Reviewing the book in the *Forum,* Mary Colum remarked that "Those women who now take a university training for granted, as a man does, would be astounded to know the efforts that had to be made to get it for them by the pioneers of women's education."[32] Next to this statement I would place the letters from two young women who were then students at Cambridge: Judith Stephen, Woolf's niece, and Toby Henderson, a family friend. Both, it seems to me, not only intimate that Aunt Virginia may be slightly out of touch, but reveal, unconsciously, how little reality or impact the actual arguments of the book had for them. Toby Henderson writes that she and Judith "took a boat up the river one after-noon & had a superb afternoon lazing in the sun reading Three Guineas & discussing it together & with other people as they passed by." After praising the style—"If only all our text books were written in such a style"—she concludes by describing the Oxford-Cambridge party she had just given that prevented her from writing earlier (MHL, 21 June 1938).[33] Judith writes to say that she enjoyed the book, although she found it rather diffuse and could not summarize the main argument at the end. Then, without a break, she adds: "By the way, did you know that Tom [T. S. Eliot] was being presented with an Honorary Degree here on Thursday? I am going to try to sneak my way in & see him,

& Anthony Eden receiving the purple or whatever one does receive'' (MHL, Monday [1938]).[34] Woolf reacted to Judith's letter in her diary with a combination of impatience and tolerance, noting the lack of gratitude and enthusiasm in the young, which she had expected, and reflecting that their self-confident attitude was perhaps the right one.[35]

Older women had a different response. Margaret Llewelyn Davies, Violet Dickenson, Nelly Cecil, Emphie Case, and Ethel Smyth all wrote of the pleasure her deadly aim had given them. Ruth Fry speaks for them all: ''I can't resist telling you that my dear Lady Gibb [the niece of Millicent Fawcett and Elizabeth Garrett Anderson] is reading aloud to me 'Three Guineas,' & we are chortling with delight & entertainment, on top of deep satisfaction at your effective telling! So thank you so much for writing it'' (MHP/Letters).[36]

It would be pleasant to be able to conclude with the image of the old women chortling, but for Woolf the publication of *Three Guineas* was not the end of her critical dialogue with the wider culture. Although she expressed in both her diary and her letters a feeling of relief at having finally gotten the book out of her system, she did not lose the sense of urgency that originally compelled her to gather her facts about public and private life and to offer an answer to the question, How can we prevent war? We know that she was asked to write an article for the *Forum* about women and peace at the end of 1939 and that she published ''Thoughts on Peace in an Air Raid'' in the *New Republic* one year later. How did she prepare for this? By continuing to discuss the issue with sympathetic correspondents such as Shena Simon (L 6:375, 379–80, 464); by continuing to read—and to take notes; by continuing to collect newspaper cuttings and to copy headlines from the daily press into her diary; and by continuing to create new words to replace the old words—and the old attitudes. One collection of notes bears the heading ''Supplement to the Dictionary of the English Language'' (MHP/B.4), thereby fulfilling (at least potentially) her call for such a work in *Three Guineas* (TG176). Another notebook, dated ''Friday, March 11th 1938''—that is, after *Three Guineas* was in print—opens with notes on Elizabeth Blackwell's autobiography and a set of notes on women and war that concludes, ''For Outsider: news. manufacture of toy soldiers for the buttonhole: to balance white feathers'' (MHP/B.2c).[37] Still another volume of notes, mysteriously labeled ''The Albatross Letters & Memoir Marriott 1839'' (MHP/B.2a), contains quotations about men, women, war, and politics similar to those found in *Three Guineas;* they derive both from contemporary works—for example, autobiographies by Jennie Lee and Franklin

Lushington (whose desire to fight is quoted in "Thoughts on Peace in an Air Raid," 175)—and from works by J. S. Mill and Edmund Burke.[38] A curious entry in Woolf's diary, dated 3 January 1940, records that she had just put down Mill's autobiography after copying passages from it into the volume that she called, deceptively, the Albatross.[39]

In December 1939 Woolf also began to read Freud's *Group Psychology and the Analysis of the Ego* (WD 309, 310, 314), almost as if she were responding to Mary Colum's comment in her review of *Three Guineas* that the Society of Outsiders would never work, for Woolf "does not take into account that overwhelming force, mass psychology, the epidemic-spreading power of passion-obsessed minds" (224). In her notes on Freud's study, Woolf continually expands his insights into the group mind and group prejudices by questioning what happens if they are extended to sex prejudice and applied to war. Her concern is the herdsman and the herd, and the role of gender in their relationship. One long speculative passage, probably written in January 1940 (see L 6:379–80), captures Woolf's continual probing into the role women must play to ensure that once Hitler is defeated—and she clearly felt that he must be—the subconscious Hitlerism that leads to war is also brought into the open and destroyed:

> That the herdsman has given the herd money when he opened the professions. Then gave them the chance to leave the herd. [*illegible*] say 1918. It also coincided with the 2 wars. Thus the woman on gaining her money power was also made forcibly to consider one aspect of the male—the fighting aspect.
>
> This was true of the 1914 war. The present war is very different. For now the male has also considered his attributes in Hitler, & is fighting against them. Is this the first time in history that a sex has turned against its own specific qualities? Compare with the woman movement.

"In the present war," she concludes, "we are fighting for liberty. But we can only get it if we destroy the male attributes. Thus the woman's part is to achieve the emancipation of the man. In that lies the only hope of permanent peace" (HRN, vol. 21).[40]

By this time the question might well be asked, Why is the history of *Three Guineas* so important—or so important to me? It is easy enough to respond, because I am a woman and a professional at a time when the world is increasing its nuclear arsenal and an Equal Rights Amendment has yet to be passed, and because I too feel the need to confess, to argue, to criticize, to cheer—to answer the book's challenge. But what impresses me as well is the courage and conviction that compelled Woolf first to write her book as a contribution to both individual and communal psychology and then to continue her search for answers in the hope that we, the next generation, would have the future that was being so rapidly destroyed for Woolf herself. Although increasingly recognized as a major document in the social history of the thirties and in the feminist/pacifist cause, *Three Guineas* has another tale to tell: it inscribes the central belief of a woman who, perceiving the destructiveness inherent in her culture, made the young intellectual Lily Everitt declare, "This civilization . . . depends upon me."[41]

Notes

1. A shorter version of this paper was presented at the Virginia Woolf Centennial Conference, West Virginia University, March 1982.

I am extremely grateful to Elizabeth M. Rodger, librarian, University of Sussex Library, for permission to reproduce the passages from the letters to Virginia Woolf that constitute the heart of this essay. Passages from Virginia Woolf's manuscript reading notes are quoted with the permission of Quentin Bell and Angelica Garnett, administrators of the author's literary estate; the University of Sussex Library; and the Henry W. and Albert A. Berg Collection, the New York Public Library, Astor, Lenox and Tilden Foundations. Both Quentin Bell and Anne Olivier Bell provided me with invaluable help in completing this essay, and I am pleased to be able to thank them here. I also wish to thank Elizabeth Inglis and Adrian Peasgood at the University of Sussex Library for their unfailing assistance; Nigel Nicolson for helping me trace several of Woolf's correspondents; and Kay Andrews, Jane Marcus, Susan M. Squier, and Charles T. Wood for their helpful comments.

2. Five of these volumes are in the Berg Collection, New York Public Library: Holograph reading notes (hereafter HRN), vols. 7, 10, 23, and 26; and [*Three Guineas*] Holograph reading notes. The other seven volumes are in the Monk's House Papers, University of Sussex Library: Monk's House Papers (hereafter MHP)/B.2f and B.16a, 16b, 16e, and 16f (3 vols.). See Brenda Silver, *Virginia Woolf's Reading Notebooks* (Princeton: Princeton University Press, 1981), for a description of the history and contents of these volumes.

3. For a description of some of these reviews and a reproduction of the account in "Time and Tide Diary" (25 June 1938, 887–88), see Jane Marcus, " 'No More Horses': Virginia Woolf on Art and Propaganda," *Women's Studies* 4, no. 2/3 (1977): 286–87. Leavis's article appeared in *Scrutiny* 7, no. 2 (September 1938):203–14. For the most part, Woolf seemed pleased with the reviews of the book, feeling at least that it was being treated as seriously as she had meant it to be: "The reviews . . . are better on the whole than I expected; more serious, less spiteful" (L 6:247).

4. These letters are found in two separate collections at Sussex: (1) Monk's House Papers/Letters. Virginia Stephen and Virginia Woolf. Various Persons (Books), which contains fifty-eight letters from forty-nine correspondents; and (2) Monk's House Letters (VW), which contains about seventeen letters from friends and relatives commenting on *Three Guineas,* filed under the writer's name. Subsequent references to the two collections appear as MHP/Letters and MHL.

5. "Thoughts on Peace in an Air Raid," in *Collected Essays* (New York: Harcourt Brace and World, 1967), 4:173, 174.

6. R. Barry O'Brien, *The Life of Charles Stewart Parnell* (London: Smith, Elder, 1898).

7. The notes on Elizabeth Mary Wright's *Life of Joseph Wright,* vol. 1 (London: Oxford University Press, 1932) appear in HRN, vol. 10. For Wright's influence on *The Pargiters,* see xi–xiv and Jane Marcus, "*The Years* as Greek Drama, Domestic Novel, and Götterdämmerung," *Bulletin of the New York Public Library* 80, no. 2 (Winter 1977): 280.

8. In dating the entries, I have relied upon the dates that appear within a cutting or were supplied by Woolf in the margins of a cutting, and on the dates of publication of the books she extracted.

9. The original "[Speech before the London/National Society for Women's Service, January 21, 1931]," is reproduced in *The Pargiters;* see xxx and xxxiv–xxxv for the quotations.

10. Charles Loch Mowat, *Britain between the Wars, 1918–1940* (London: Methuen, 1968), 551.

11. For other descriptions of this conference, see Mowat, *Britain between the Wars,* 550–53, and Leonard Woolf, *Downhill All the Way: An Autobiography of the Years 1919 to 1939* (London: Hogarth Press, 1967), 244–45.

12. See *Three Guineas,* 101, for Woolf's ritual burning of the word "feminist" and 176 for her discussion of the need for a "supplement to the *Oxford English Dictionary.*"

13. "It is to be hoped," Woolf wrote in *Three Guineas,* "that some

methodical person has made a collection of the various manifestoes and questionnaires issued broadcast during the years 1936–7'' (TG 172); in her scrapbooks she has done just that.

14. Portions of this and the next paragraph also appear in *Virginia Woolf's Reading Notebooks.*

15. Quoted courtesy of Professor Brian Simon.

16. Both of the attached cuttings document the Church's negative attitude toward female priesthood. Shena Simon's comment is the only direct reference to the collection of cuttings that I have found. Woolf did not show them, one gathers, even to Ethel Smyth. Before the book appeared, however, anticipating criticism, Woolf had written Smyth that it was ''hard work collecting the facts'' (L 6:232); later she remarked that the notes were ''the most meaty part of the book'' and that she ''had a mass more and still have. Yes—very hard work that was'' (L 6:235).

17. Quoted courtesy of Professor A. K. S. Lambton. Nelly ends her letter with a postscript: ''(not a pacifist yet!).''

18. The original of Vita's letter, dated 15 June 1938, is in the Berg Collection.

19. Woolf's lament to Vita about references to her '' 'lovely prose' and charm'' refers as much to the reviews of *Three Guineas* as to comments by friends. In the *Manchester Guardian,* for example, Mary Stocks ended her review: ''That [Mrs. Woolf] argues [her threefold case] in her own incomparably lucid and lovely prose is also undeniable. How therefore can the correspondent to whose questioning letter her argument is the reply complain that it is too long? Indeed we have no reason to suppose that he does'' (10 June 1938, 17).

20. Quoted courtesy of the Strachey Trust and Paul Levy, literary Executor.

21. Quoted courtesy of Nigel Nicolson.

22. The particular tone of respectful sarcasm employed in this letter (as well as its length!) is echoed in other letters from men.

23. Quoted courtesy of Naomi Mitchison.

24. Quoted courtesy of Margaret Paul, at present a fellow and tutor in economics at Lady Margaret Hall, Oxford. Mrs. Paul recalls that Woolf's reply, since stolen, was ''rather interesting'' and that she was impressed that Woolf had bothered to reply at all.

25. ''It is here we come on the one defect of this clear brilliant essay. When Mrs. Woolf's argument touches morality or religion we are aware of odd sounds in the shell. Can a shell be a little old-fashioned (quoting Renan),

a little provincial, even a little shrill? Can a shell be said to lead a too sheltered life?'' Greene's review appeared in the *Spectator* (17 June 1938, 111–12); journals such as the *Christian Century*, where one would expect a response, remained curiously silent about her treatment of religion and the Church.

26. Quoted courtesy of Lauran Emerson Dundee, Mrs. Emerson's granddaughter. Another Quaker, the senior resident master at a coeducational Quaker school, begins his letter, ''Dear Friend— In case you do not know, this is the Quaker method of address to a person whom one has not met'' (MHP/Letters). This letter is dated 12 July 1938; three days later Woolf wrote to Ehtel Smyth: ''Oh I've made some so furious: And then a Quaker or governess makes up by thanking'' (L 6:255).

27. The statement at issue occurs in *Three Guineas,* 54: ''The work of an archbishop is worth £15,000 a year to the State.'' Both writers, one should note, also express admiration for the book and hope it will reach a wide audience.

28. H. M. Swanwick, *I Have Been Young* (London: Gollancz, 1935).

29. Six letters from Smith are now at Sussex. Nigel Nicolson, while compiling and editing Woolf's letters, was unable to locate either Smith's remaining family or Woolf's side of the correspondence. For a further discussion of this correspondence, see Quentin Bell, *Virginia Woolf: A Biography* (New York: Harcourt Brace Jovanovich, 1977), 2:205. Agnes Smith did eventually publish a book—*A Worker's View of the Wool Textile Industry* (1944).

30. *Booklist,* for example, reviewed the book as follows: ''With the same ironic wit that characterized *A room of one's own* . . . the author considers the position of women in England in other fields than literature—in society, education, politics, and the church—and comments on their limitations of preparation and opportunity'' (15 September 1938, 19); I have quoted the entire review. Morton Dauwen Zabel, writing in the *Nation,* provides a classic example of American self-congratulation: ''In the pioneer society of the United States, the feminist reformer never labored under the disabilities of her English sisterhood. Here, where the matriarchal ideal was strong from the first, women passed on a tradition of culture, taste, and moral leadership. They had their colleges, seminaries, property, household keys, and citizenship'' (8 October 1938, 356).

31. Quoted courtesy of Gladys Rossiter.

32. ''Are Women Outsiders?'' *Forum and Century* 100.5 (November 1938): 225.

33. Quoted courtesy of Joan Cedar (Toby) Henderson.

34. Quoted courtesy of Nigel Henderson.

35. I am grateful to Olivier Bell and Andrew McNeillie for sharing this passage with me; it occurs in the diary entry for 11 June 1938.

36. Quoted courtesy of Pamela Diamand.

37. Elizabeth Blackwell, *Pioneer Work in Opening the Medical Profession to Women* (London: Longmans, Green, 1895). This entry also includes a reference to Swanwick's autobiography, *I Have Been Young,* which suggests that Woolf may have reread the book after receiving Swanwick's letter of correction.

38. Jennie Lee, *Tomorrow Is a New Day* (London: Cresset Press, 1939); Franklin Lushington, *Portrait of a Young Man* (London: Faber and Faber, 1940); John Stuart Mill, *Autobiography* (London: Longmans, Green, Reader and Dyer, 1873) and *On Liberty* (London: Parker, 1859); and Edmund Burke, *Reflections on the Revolution in France,* in *Works,* vol. 5 (London: Rivington, 1803). The quotation from Lushington begins, ''To fight against a real enemy.''

39. [*A Writer's Diary*] 3 January 1940–29 December 1940; Berg Collection.

40. Many of these ideas reappear in ''Thoughts on Peace in an Air Raid.''

41. ''The Introduction,'' in *Mrs. Dalloway's Party,* 43.

Index